This book makes an important contribution to the current re-evaluation of the origins of Stalinism. Although it is widely acknowledged by Western scholars that the Soviet grain crisis of 1927–8 and Stalin's Siberian tour of January 1928 were crucial factors in the decision to abandon the New Economic Policy (NEP) and return to a more ideologically rigid policy of collectivisation and rapid industrialisation, studies have hitherto concentrated on the role of leading personalities and 'high politics'. In this book, Dr James Hughes presents an in-depth examination of the crisis of the NEP from the regional perspective of Siberia and analyses the events and pressures 'from below', at the grassroots level of Soviet society.

Using publications of the Siberian party and statistical investigations of the countryside, Dr Hughes offers new insights into several largely uncharted features of the Soviet system in these years. These include party–peasant relations, the kulak question, Stalin's patron–client network in the provinces, the regional impact of the grain crisis and the use of emergency measures to overcome the crisis. The author concludes that Stalin's experience of conditions which were unique to Siberia accelerated his negative reappraisal of the NEP and initiated the descent into the cataclysm of his 'revolution from above' in late 1929.

Stalin, Siberia and the crisis of the New Economic Policy will be widely read by specialists and students of Soviet history, with special reference to the economic and social history of the 1920s, regional policy under the NEP, and the background to collectivisation.

STALIN, SIBERIA AND THE CRISIS OF THE NEW ECONOMIC POLICY

Soviet and East European Studies

To continue at back of book

STALIN, SIBERIA AND THE CRISIS OF THE NEW ECONOMIC POLICY

JAMES HUGHES
University of Keele

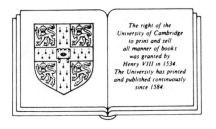

The right of the
University of Cambridge
to print and sell
all manner of books
was granted by
Henry VIII in 1534.
The University has printed
and published continuously
since 1584.

CAMBRIDGE UNIVERSITY PRESS

Cambridge
New York   Port Chester
Melbourne   Sydney

Published by the Press Syndicate of the University of Cambridge
The Pitt Building, Trumpington Street, Cambridge CB2 1RP
40 West 20th Street, New York, NY 10011, USA
10 Stamford Road, Oakleigh, Melbourne 3166, Australia

First published 1991

Printed in Great Britain by
Redwood Press, Melksham, Wiltshire

British Library cataloguing in publication data

Hughes, James
  Stalin, Siberia and the crisis of the New Economic Policy.
  – (Soviet and East European studies).
  1. Russia (RSFSR). Siberia. Economic conditions, history
  I. Title   II. Series
  330.957

Library of Congress cataloguing in publication data

Hughes, James (James Raymond)
  Stalin, Siberia, and the crisis of the New Economic Policy / James
  Hughes.
     p.   cm. – (Soviet and East European studies; 81)
  Includes bibliographical references and index.
  ISBN 0 521 38039 1
  1. Siberia (R.S.F.S.R.) – Economic conditions.   2. Soviet Union –
  Economic policy – 1928–1932.   3. Stalin, Joseph, 1879–1953.
  I. Title.   II. Series.
  HC337.R852S52435 1991
  338.957′5′009042 – dc20   90–41805   CIP

ISBN 0 521 38039 1 hardback

for my parents
John and May Hughes

Contents

Tables

Preface

Recently, a notable feature of Western studies of Soviet history of the 1920s and 1930s has been the controversy aroused by the work of a younger generation of social historians. Their conceptual approach eschewed the conventional wisdom of concentrating on leading personalities and 'high politics' and offered fresh insights and a more profound understanding of the events of this period by examining the interaction and influence of political pressures and movements 'from below', at the grassroots of Soviet society, on the determination and implementation of Stalin's 'revolution from above'. I considered that this methodological framework could be usefully applied to the era immediately preceding Stalin's revolution of the 1930s: the period of the New Economic Policy (NEP) in the 1920s. I have embarked upon a study of one region: Siberia. My goal is to stimulate further debate on the impact of NEP at the grassroots and to explain better why Stalin and the majority of the central party leadership decided to abandon it in early 1928 and return to a more ideologically rigid policy of collectivisation and rapid industrialisation.

The sources I have relied upon are primarily Siberian party publications (stenographic records of plenums, annual reports, journals) and statistical investigations of the countryside of the period, previously unused in the West. Although this inevitably raises the problem of bias, I believe that the Bolshevik party until 1928 was still one in which differing viewpoints and perspectives could be expressed openly and this is reflected in the sources. I have chosen to rely on details provided by modern Siberian historians, as, having had the opportunity of frequently crosschecking many of their references, I can testify to their general reliability in this respect, though clearly their interpretations suffer from the ideological constraints under which they operate.

The preparation of this book owes a debt of gratitude to numerous people and institutions. My special thanks go to Dr Dominic Lieven of the London School of Economics who, as my doctoral dissertation supervisor, was a constant source of invaluable critical assessment and advice on my work, and guided me to its successful completion. Professor R. W. Davies and Dr S. G. Wheatcroft of the University of Birmingham gave direction to my initial interest in the problems of NEP and Stalin's Siberian tour of January 1928 by suggesting that I undertake an in-depth regional study. Dr Robert Service of the London School of Slavonic and East European Studies, who together with Professor Davies examined my dissertation, offered generous and informed suggestions for revisions. Thanks are due also to Mr Frank Wright of Queen's University Belfast for his inspiring teaching skills that first sparked my interest in Soviet History. I am also indebted to Siberian colleagues of the Institute of History, Philology and Philosophy, at Akademgorodok, Novosibirsk; Professor N. Ia. Gushchin, V. A. Zhdanov and V. A. Il'inykh, who made my short working visit to Siberia in April 1986 so productive. The Department of Education of Northern Ireland provided a research award (1982–6) and the British Council a study scholarship to Moscow State University for the year 1985–6, and I would like to extend my thanks to these institutions and to the editorial board of *Soviet Studies* for permitting me to draw extensively from my previously published article on the 'Irkutsk affair' for use in chapter 7.

The book is a much revised version of my doctoral dissertation, and all opinions expressed here are my own, as is the responsibility for any errors. Finally a special thanks to my sister Collette Steele who typed numerous drafts of the manuscript, and to my wife Julia, without whose partnership and assistance this work would not have been accomplished.

Note on transliteration and dates; weights and measures

Library of Congress practice on the transliteration of Russian has been followed, except for names of persons and places in the text which have a widely accepted English form.

Soviet practice has been adhered to in the use of dates: 1927–8 refers to the calendar year; 1927/8 refers to the agricultural year 1 July–30 June, and the economic year 1 October–30 September.

Equivalent weights and measures

1 *desiatin* = 1.09 hectares = 2.70 acres
1 hectare = 2.47 acres
1 *pud* = 16.38 kilogrammes = 36.11 lb
1 ton = 61.05 *pud*s

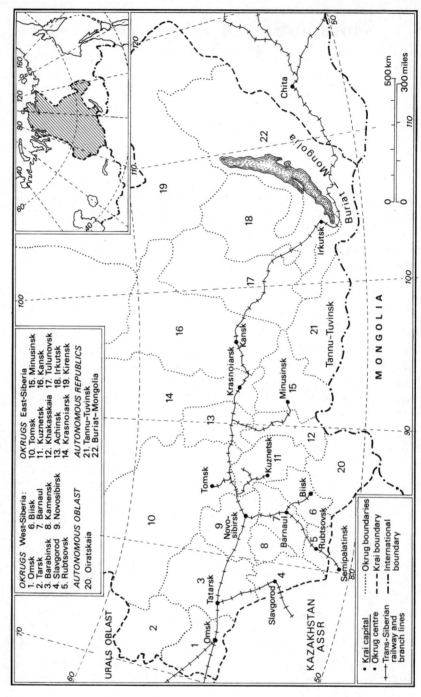

OKRUGS West-Siberia:
1. Omsk
2. Tarsk
3. Barabinsk
4. Slavgorod
5. Rubtsovsk
6. Biisk
7. Barnaul
8. Kamensk
9. Novosibirsk

AUTONOMOUS OBLAST
20. Oiratskaia

OKRUGS East-Siberia:
10. Tomsk
11. Kuznetsk
12. Khakasskaia
13. Achinsk
14. Krasnoiarsk
15. Minusinsk
16. Kansk
17. Tulunovsk
18. Irkutsk
19. Kirensk

AUTONOMOUS REPUBLICS
21. Tannu-Tuvinsk
22. Buriat–Mongolia

Krai capital
Okrug centre
Trans-Siberian railway and branch lines
Okrug boundaries
Krai boundary
International boundary

URALS OBLAST

KAZAKHSTAN ASSR

MONGOLIA

Buriat

Mongolia

Tannu-Tuvinsk

Omsk
Tatarsk
Slavgorod
Semipalatinsk
Novo-sibirsk
Barnaul
Rubtsovsk
Biisk
Tomsk
Kuznetsk
Krasnoiarsk
Kansk
Minusinsk
Achinsk
Irkutsk
Chita

Location of the Sibkrai in the USSR. Source: Atlas SSSR 1928 (Moscow, 1928)

Introduction

Western approaches to the study of Soviet history in the era of NEP and Stalin's 'revolution from above' generally suffer from an over-preoccupation with 'high politics' and a tendency to consign provincial areas of the country to the historical margins. Consequently, local influence on policy-making at the centre and local considerations in the implementation of orders 'from above' are downplayed and glossed over. This fundamental gap in our understanding of events in this period has been partially overcome by the substantial body of Western scholarly works that have focussed on the Smolensk Archives in the USA, a unique and rich source of local material, while studies of the 'big city' party organisations of Moscow and Leningrad remain access-ible and popular. Outside of these areas our knowledge of events across most of the country is patchy. In the 1980s the conceptual approach of local studies, assessing the dynamic of history in oper-ation at the grassroots where party and government most impinged upon the vast majority of Soviet citizens, has been applied by some social and economic historians to the years of Stalin's revolution, but so far the NEP era has escaped investigation from this angle.[1]

The deficiency in our knowledge of NEP – the strategic retreat to a gradual transition to socialism imposed by Lenin in 1921, whereby the 'commanding heights' of the economy (large-scale industry, banking, transport, foreign trade) remained under state ownership and management, while a regulated market mechanism was established in the economic relationship between the state and the peasantry – is highly unsatisfactory given that it is part of the Western academic conventional wisdom that local factors were of crucial importance in Stalin's decision to abandon NEP in favour of a 'great turn' to rapid collectivisation and industrialisation. It is generally recognised in the classical works on this period that the grain procurement crisis of 1927/8 was a watershed in Soviet history, and that Stalin's experiences during his tour of the Siberian Krai in January 1928 in search of a quick breakthrough in the crisis had a critical, negative effect on his outlook towards the programme of socialism 'at a snail's pace' entailed in NEP. There is agreement that Stalin's enthusiastic advocacy of the use of emergency coercive measures against peasants delivered a death blow to NEP, and initiated a new radicalism which led to the second revolution of late 1929. It also brought to a close the years of oligarchic rule by a party elite, as on his return from Siberia Stalin inaugurated the power struggle with his former political allies on the Right of the party that ended with the consolidation of his personal dictatorship.[2]

This book seeks to contribute to a more complete understanding of the processes at work during NEP and the reasons for its disintegration by means of an interpretive structure that analyses the events of these years from the regional perspective and Siberia, given its significance in 1928, seemed an interesting candidate. I begin with a survey of Siberian rural society and agriculture in the 1920s which brings out how peculiar Siberia was in comparison with other areas of the country, in terms of the wealth of its peasantry and their use of advanced, mechanised farming methods. This aims to explain how the region developed so dramatically into one of the most important agricultural bases of the country in the mid-1920s, particularly for state wheat procurement, and assesses the claims that there was a prolific growth of petty-capitalist kulak peasants in the territory during the years of NEP. It examines the nature, organisation, recruitment and social composition of the regional party and reveals the extent to which the exceptionally large component of peasant communists in Siberia were linked with the well-off stratum in the countryside, and how unreliable they proved once NEP was reversed. In this respect, it should be noted that the population and party membership of Siberia were overwhelmingly Russian and therefore relations between the party and the peasantry were not complicated by nationalist or ethnic tensions as in the Ukraine and North Caucasus.

The theme of centre–periphery relations is pursued mainly in relation to the operation of Stalin's patrimonial system of client provincial party chiefs, a much emphasised but relatively uncharted aspect of political life in the 1920s. The activities of senior regional officials are shrouded in obscurity and it is surprising just how little we know about them considering their importance in deciding the outcome of the factional disputes in the central party leadership through their membership of the Central Committee and control of the voting power of the constituent party organisations at congresses and conferences. In tracing the career and opinions of the Siberian Kraikom Secretary, S. I. Syrtsov, a Stalin loyalist, a new insight into Stalin's relationship with his network of party clients is provided. Given that Syrtsov's views on NEP and the peasant question were consistently closer to Bukharin's than to Stalin's at this time, it would suggest that Stalin's ability to maintain the support of his party political machine owed less to policy issues and choices, and more to his power of patronage as General Secretary. The regional dimension of intra-party factionalism is also reviewed: specifically, the degree to which political differences in the Siberian party elite mirrored the contours of the schism in the Politburo in the aftermath of the grain crisis or were determined by and reflected purely local matters.

At another level this book may be viewed as a study of the origins of Stalin's 'revolution from above' in the crisis of 1927/8. The causes of the grain crisis are well established but we know less about its development and impact at the regional level. Thus, the extent to which price imbalances, goods shortages, high peasant incomes and other factors were involved in the drastic fall-off in Siberian grain procurement is detailed. Stalin's decision to go to Siberia in early 1928 was clearly a momentous event, for it was the first time since the civil war and, as far as is known, the last time that he visited the countryside. An account of the tour and its significance for local and Soviet politics concludes that the date of Stalin's decision to implement all-out, forced collectivisation and the 'liquidation of the kulaks as a class' should be projected backwards from late 1929 to the time of his stay in Siberia.

The emergency measures taken at Stalin's insistence were a decisive factor in the successful resolution of the grain crisis, and he was now convinced that coercion was the best method of dealing with the peasantry and bringing them to heel. However, his frame of mind was rattled and his confidence in the efficacy of NEP shaken by his Siberian experiences. His actions and speeches in the region bear witness to the outrage he felt not just at the obstructionism and recalcitrance of regional officials in the application of the emergency measures, which he interpreted as connivance with 'kulak sabotage', but also at what he considered to be their outright siding with the kulak against the party. Thereafter, he had an abiding mistrust of lower-level officialdom. At the same time, there were positive results in the performance of the party from Stalin's viewpoint because he regarded those few officials in Siberia who enthusiastically embraced the emergency measures as evidence of a dynamic 'from below' in support of a new militant line. Moreover, he left Siberia confirmed in the belief that he had hitherto underestimated the growth in the economic power of the kulaks, as the disturbing stranglehold which Siberian kulaks held on agriculture in the region indicated that they did indeed pose the kind of threat of which the Left Opposition had been repeatedly warning.

Stalin extrapolated from these distinct Siberian conditions and concluded that the degeneracy of the party and the existence of a powerful kulak stratum were endemic in the country as a whole. The only solution, he determined, was immediate large-scale purging of the party and a rapid advance to collectivisation, otherwise the party's continued monopoly of power was threatened. Although a shift in the mood of the Stalinist section of the party leadership against NEP and in favour of an acceleration of industrialisation and collectivisation was evident from the late autumn of 1927, the Siberian expedition saw a significant radicalisation of Stalin's views against the policy of conciliation of the peasantry enshrined in NEP. This point marked the juncture where the Soviet Union began the descent into the cataclysm of the 'second revolution'.

Finally, the evidence presented in this work facilitates the drawing of more sophisticated comparisons and contrasts between Soviet politics in the 1920s and 1930s: periods currently under reassessment in the Soviet Union and the West in the light of *glasnost*. In particular, a recent Western reevaluation of the Great Purges of the mid-1930s from the regional perspective concluded that Stalin's role as political prime mover in this instance has been exaggerated and that his function was secondary to the 'existence of high-level personal rivalries, disputes over development or modernization plans, powerful and conflicting centrifugal and centripetal forces, and local conflicts', all of which 'made large-scale political violence possible and even likely'.[3] What is striking about the study of Siberia in the 1920s is the extent to which regional politics were determined by local antagonisms and the competition of a plurality of local interests and forces, and centre-periphery relations were played out against this background. In the late 1920s prior to Stalin's consolidation of absolute power, regional conflicts, no matter how bitter, did not lead to the mass fratricidal destruction of intra-party political opposition.

1   The Siberian peasant utopia

The pre-revolutionary heritage

Siberian society and economy under NEP were unique by Soviet standards as they were distinguished from other areas of the country in several significant respects, some of which were a legacy of the pre-revolutionary settlement of the region. The development of Siberia followed the common pattern of colonisation of new territories in the latter part of the nineteenth century and was largely determined by its rich economic potential, climate, means of communication with other developed areas and the character of its settlers. The 'endless steppes' of Russia are a mere prelude to the unchecked expanses lying east of the Urals, for the west Siberian lowland steppe encompasses one of the most vast plains of arable and pasture land on earth. From the Ishim river over 1,000 kilometres east and south-eastward to the Altai mountains stretches an unbroken tract of practically level steppe 300–500 kilometres wide intersected by two great rivers, the Irtysh and the Ob, and their tributaries. The soils of much of this area are of the highly fertile black-earth and chestnut-brown kind but unstable continental climatic conditions create difficulties in agricultural production and the wide divergences in winter and summer temperatures make the area highly susceptible to droughts and winter killing of crops and animals. The most suitable area for agricultural production in the region is the Altai steppe in south-west Siberia where the climate is milder and the chestnut-brown soils receive adequate rainfall.[1]

Grain cultivation in Siberia is crucially affected by climatic conditions in two main respects. Firstly, seasonal changes are sudden as winter sets in very quickly in late October and ends just as suddenly in early April. The effect of this is to shorten the spring sowing and autumn harvesting to a matter of three weeks and thus to greatly enhance the time-saving benefits and profitability gained by the use of agricultural

5

machines. Secondly, as a consequence of the short sowing season the grain harvest critically depends not only on the level of precipitation but also on its timing. A good grain harvest in south-west Siberia is determined by soil humidity and this depends on the scale of snowfalls in winter followed by sufficient rainfall in the first stages of growth during late June and early July. Grain farmers in this region faced a precarious situation of drought once in every three years on average, and a severe drought once in every decade. However, after the drought of 1920–1 Siberian grain producers entered a trouble-free boom period and within the Altai the area enclosed by the Biisk–Barnaul–Rubtsovsk triangle became a major source of high quality wheat for the country.[2]

Siberia was Russia's contemporaneous frontier equivalent to the American and Canadian 'Wild West', and the settlement of its steppe regions in the late nineteenth and early twentieth centuries is comparable both in scale and endeavour. Pre-1870 settlers and their descendants in Siberia were the kind of hetereogeneous mixture common to all societies at the margin and may be divided into five main groups: religious fundamentalists (Old Believers or non-Orthodox sectarians), political exiles and convicts, voluntary migrants (mainly runaway serfs, small-time entrepreneurs and freebooting adventurers), Cossack and military personnel, and government officials. Siberia was also sparsely populated by indigenous nomadic peoples (though in colonial jargon it was an 'empty' land) and consequently became an obvious resettlement area for the impoverished land hungry peasants of the European Russian empire. From 1885 to 1914, with the construction of the Trans-Siberian railway and its branch lines, a flood of over 5 million immigrants poured into Siberia, most of whom settled in the Altai. The bulk of these (over 4 million) were peasants from the overcrowded agricultural regions of European Russia and the Ukraine. The tsarist government actively encouraged voluntary migration to Siberia primarily by keeping railway charges low and through the promise of generous land grants to new settlers. From this time forward, as G. T. Robinson observed: 'Among the peasants west of the Urals, Siberia was regarded as a kind of Utopia.'[3]

As immigration reached a peak in the first decade of the twentieth century, there was a considerable counter-movement of peasant 'returners' to European areas as the best Siberian lands had already been claimed by earlier settlers. The formidable experience of migration and settlement led to the emergence of a society and subculture which was different in character from that which existed in

European Russia. Although the dividing line of the Ural mountains was not a major geographical obstacle in terms of size, it constituted a significant psychological barrier as illustrated by the Siberian description of the return journey across the Urals as 'going to Russia'. The huge distances and poor communications insulated Siberians from Russian society and caused them to develop a consciousness as a people and place apart. On the eve of the First World War one traveller in the region noted that 'just as the English settler in Canada has become Canadian, so the Russian settler in Siberia has become a Siberian'.[4] Unlike Russia, Siberian society was a melting-pot, with the inter-mingling of Russians, Belorussians, Ukrainians and indigenous peoples, and there was even a linguistic dimension to its development as it has been asserted that Siberian Russian is 'almost as distinctive as ... American English'.[5] The 'frontier spirit' of Siberia fostered amongst its people a temperament of fierce resentment of established authority and a great willingness for self-help and cooperation. The Russian Prime Minister, P. A. Stolypin, returned from a fact-finding tour of the region in 1910 disturbed by the ethos of independence in this 'enormous, rudely democratic country', and other writers have mentioned the tendency of Siberians to address 'highly placed officials as equals, not superiors'.[6] Hugh Seton-Watson described Siberian society as one where: 'There were no noble landowners. The leading people were largely self-made men, farmers or merchants who were proud of their success, and judged others by their merits and not by their social status. It was an individualist, self-reliant society, the only part of the empire in which anything like a bourgeois ethos prevailed.'[7]

Given the poor communications and the absence of landlords, Siberian peasants were not subject to the kind of outside pressures that weighed heavily on the peasantry of European Russia. In keeping with the 'Siberian spirit' the peasants of the region eschewed the *pokornost'* (resigned submissiveness) of their counterparts west of the Urals. Most striking of all was the superior economic condition of the Siberian peasantry and it has been estimated that the average settler family more than tripled its possessions in eleven years. This comparative prosperity was accurately encapsulated by the peasant saying: 'the Siberian bedniak is your Russian seredniak'.[8] The main reason for such prosperity lay in the large size of farms and the method of land tenure in the territory. The most distinctive feature of the Siberian countryside under the *ancien régime* was that land was held in what amounted to a state of nationalisation and the latifundia of European Russia were almost non-existent. In 1917 the ownership of agricultural land was as follows: state (35.5%), Cossack military colonies (8.1%), Tsar's personal demesne (7.2%), private (0.5%) and peasant (48.9%). Of the land held by peasants some was occupied at small quit rents on long leases from the state (8%) and Tsar (12.2%), but a substantial part was in tenure by unregulated means (28.7%) i.e., by right of permanent usufruct (*zemlepolzovanie*) or squatting (*vol'nozakhvatnyi*). During the great migration period the government attempted to restrict peasant holdings to a norm of 15 desiatina (16.35 hectares) per household (*dvor*) but, given the abundance of open virgin steppe, squatting or freeholding was widespread and settlers often held 40–50 desiatina (45–55 hectares) of arable land alone.[9]

The harsh experiences of settlement, the shortage of open water sources on the steppes and, specifically, the opportunities for establishing extensive landholaings gave rise to the development of a peculiar Siberian form of the peasant commune (*obshchina*) A distinctive feature of villages, particularly in the Altai, was their large size, containing 200 or more households on average, often 500–600 and sometimes even 1,000. Contemporary observers of village life in Siberia noted that whilst nominally the commune regulated land tenure, in reality many did not engage in general or even partial redistributions of land and even fewer established equal divisions of land as was the tradition in European Russia. This brought one commentator to declare that the Siberian commune was 'at present being shattered at its foundations'. In fact, the fundamental principle of the redivisions which did occur in Siberia was 'the right of each householder to remain on his own place', and the transfer of land among households was rare.[10] The incentive to improve productivity arising from the stability of land tenure was another factor contributing to the prosperity of many Siberian peasants.

Revolution, civil war and NEP

One of the principal causes of the revolutionary upheavals of 1917 to 1921 was the land hunger of the peasantry and its disgruntlement with the great landed estates of the nobility. During these years land was not an issue in Siberia as there were huge state reserves and only an insignificant number of landed estates. Consequently, the peasant revolution which transformed the Russian countryside in 1917–18 had no counterpart in Siberia and therefore it escaped the sudden, mass forcible seizure of estates and general redistribution of

land characterised by the 'black transfers' (*chernye peredely*) in European Russia. Rather, there was a relatively peaceful process involving
the 'nipping off' and redistribution of small plots of land from large
holdings which were close to settlements whilst distant holdings were
left intact. Large peasant farms emerged virtually untouched by the
redistributive process because the extensive reserves of unsettled state
land (substantially increased by the incorporation of the Tsar's demesne into the Treasury by the Provisional Government in March
1917) were available. Landless and small-scale peasant farmers received grants of land, the norms and distribution of which were administered by local soviets and varied by district, for example, in the
Altai grants were per family member, in Enisei Guberniia by farm
worker, but both procedures favoured the larger, well-off peasant
families.[11]

As with the rest of the country the redistribution of land in Siberia
was conducted in an anarchic manner during 1917–18, when state
lands were seized wholescale by the peasantry, and was only regularised after the Bolsheviks defeated Kolchak and established their
authority in the region at the end of 1919. In March 1920 a decree of the
Bolshevik dominated Siberian Revolutionary Committee (Sibrevkom)
established labour norms for land redistribution, forbade the use of
hired labour in agriculture, and established collective farms as 'schools
for working farms'. This was followed by a decree in August 1920
which transferred 'unused' lands for redistribution among the 'unreg-
istered' peasant population and further restricted the hiring of labour,
the leasing of land and decreasing of sowings. These acts were framed
as 'anti-kulak' measures and were intended to curb the large holding
farms which had escaped the revolutionary 'levelling' process which
had occurred in other parts of the country. The main instruments for
the general 'levelling' amongst the peasants of European Russia were
the poor peasant committees (*Kombedy*). Yet the Siberian countryside
was left unscathed by the attentions of these committees as they were
dissolved by the Bolshevik government at the end of 1919, just before
the establishment of Soviet control of Siberia. In fact, the Siberian
peasantry escaped the kind of havoc and massive destruction which
the civil war brought to other major agricultural regions such as the
Ukraine and North Caucasus because the struggle between the Bolsheviks and Kolchak had been concentrated along the Trans-Siberian
railway network whilst foreign intervention was largely confined to
the Far East. As in European Russia the loyalties of the Siberian
peasantry fluctuated during the civil war and it would be more accurate

to say that they fought to preserve their land rights against Kolchak's reactionism rather than for the Bolsheviks.[12]

During 1920–2 the Bolsheviks attempted to organise a more systematic policy of 'levelling' in the Siberian countryside. These campaigns had two important consequences for the future of agriculture in the region. Firstly, there was a significant equalisation in peasant livestock holding, especially of cattle, which as we shall discuss below had a disastrous effect on the Siberian butter industry. Secondly, the greater part of 'dead' farming equipment (agricultural machines and implements) remained untouched and in the hands of their owners, despite the fact that the short sowing and harvesting seasons in the region meant that mechanised agricultural equipment (particularly mowers and threshers) made a significant contribution to peasant prosperity. Further, although most poor peasants had received land it was impossible to work this efficiently without implements. In chapter 3 I shall discuss how after the introduction of NEP these machines and implements played a crucial role in the development of peasant differentiation and the emergence of a petty-capitalist kulak stratum in the Siberian countryside.[13]

In the mid-1920s the predominant features of Siberian society and economy were small-scale peasant family farms and agriculture. According to the census of 1926 there were over 8.6 million inhabitants of the Siberian krai, of whom almost 7 million (80.6%) were classified as peasants by employment (about 1.4 million farms in all), while over 7.5 million (87.2%) actually lived in the countryside. Only 12.8% of the population of Siberia were defined as town dwellers (against just under 18% for the USSR) and as many as 10% of these were actually peasants (typically semi-settled peasant migrants en route to rural settlements). Before the rapid industrialisation of the early 1930s Siberian towns were mainly small rural market centres, with a handful of medium sized industrial and commercial cities that had developed along the Trans-Siberian railway. Business and industrial enterprises were predominantly small scale and privately owned and in late 1925 state-owned industry employed just 27,000 workers. As late as 1927 the industrial output of the region was a meagre 1.9% of the USSR total and much of that was accounted for by agriculture related industries.[14]

Immigration to Siberia fell to a trickle during the turmoil of 1914–21, but with the establishment of the Soviet regime and the introduction of NEP it was revived with official encouragement and in the years 1920–4 over 330,000 migrants arrived. The Bolsheviks initiated a planned settlement policy and an All Union Migration Committee was established in March 1925 to implement targets set by Gosplan. Accordingly, in August 1925 a regional migration administration was established in the Siberian capital Novonikolaevsk (Novosibirsk) and preliminary targets were set at 50,000 new migrants per year. The Fifteenth Party Conference at the end of 1926 opened sixty-one districts of West Siberia for peasant settlement, initiating a new wave of migration from European parts of the country, and in 1924–9 over 550,000 migrants arrived (only 34.6% of whom were 'planned'), the majority of these were poor peasants (*bednota*). The Soviet authorities attempted to channel new migrants to the under-populated and less hospitable north-eastern areas of the territory and closed the fertile pastures of the Altai steppe to new settlement in 1924. Nevertheless, it is estimated that over 60% of new migrants settled in the Altai area, illustrating the ineffectiveness of government authority in the countryside at this time. There was a demographic explosion in Siberia in the 1920s as immigration resumed and the local birth rate increased. By 1927 the rural population numbered 7.6 million against 5.9 million in 1923 (a massive increase of 29.7%), while the number of peasant farms rose to just under 1.4 million compared with just over 1 million in 1913 (a 41% increase). With an estimated extra 1.7 million peasant family members to feed, rural consumption of agricultural surpluses became a major problem for the state and we shall return to this later.[15]

Generally, although immigration continued to be a feature of Siberian life under NEP the new settlers found it much more difficult than their precursors to establish viable farms, given that the best and most accessible lands had already been claimed by the majority of the rural population who by now had been settled for at least a generation. Of the three forms of land tenure recognised by the Soviet Land Code of 1922 – collective, communal, household – the communal predominated in Siberia as in the rest of the country. In 1924 93.6% of Siberian peasant holdings was regulated by communes, 0.6% by collectives, and the rest was accounted for by independent farms of the *otrub* (4.8%) or *khutor* (0.4%) type or by mixed forms (0.6%). Land tenure by *otruba* was significant only in the guberniias of Omsk (13% of the total) and Tomsk (8.9%). At the same time, collective farms played a minuscule role in Siberian agriculture until collectivisation and in early 1928 less than 1% of peasant farms were members of collectives, accounting for less than 1% of sowings and gross and marketable production of both crops and livestock. However, as noted earlier, Siberian conditions moulded the commune into a peculiar institution often containing several hundred households (compared with an RSFSR average of fifty in the mid-1920s) and generally not engaging in redivision and transference of nominally communal lands amongst members. According to the Land Code of 1922 a 'general redistribution' of farmland was to take place once every nine years but in many areas of the country a redistribution of some kind took place more regularly. By contrast, in Siberia a Krai Land Administration report on the commune published in 1926 stated that 'a fully developing commune, with a systematic levelling redivision, with a full reshuffling of land, is rarely encountered'.[16]

This was confirmed by a sample survey of farms conducted throughout Siberia in the spring of 1927, which revealed that only 37.8% were of the redivisional commune type, 36.6% were freehold, 8.6% *otruba* and *khutora* and 16% did not own their own land. According to the survey the redivisional commune was most prevalent in the south west (Altai) but even here it largely existed in name only. This situation was confirmed by research in the Barnaul Okrug in 1928 which showed that 30% of communes studied had not held a redivision for 9–12 years, 41% for 15–18 years and 24% for 21–45 years. In such circumstances, the reality of the Siberian peasant commune was that many farms were *otruba* and *khutora* in practice.[17]

Another distinctive feature of Siberian peasant farms under NEP was that they were much better supplied not only with land but also with equipment than those in the rest of the country. In the late 1920s the average holding per farm was 47.3 hectares, of which 37.5 hectares were prime land (an average of 8.7 and 6.7 hectares per family member). According to the selective census of 1927 the allotment (*nadel*) of Siberian farms was over twice the USSR average at 12.2 hectares of arable land and 3.1 of pasture compared with a USSR average of 6.1 and 1.2, 5.2 and 0.3 hectares in the Ukraine, and 10.2 and 0.7 in the North Caucasus. Given the huge land surplus in the region, the predominant system of land use was long-term fallow (*perelog* or *zalesh*). By this method arable land was cultivated (mainly with grains) until its fertility was exhausted. It was then left idle for natural recovery and over a period of many years (6–15) would be used for grazing cattle. It was possible for this system to persist successfully as long as less than half the arable land was cultivated for crops. By comparison, the simple three-field system which prevailed in European parts of the country was actually progressive since this made it possible to cultivate two-thirds of arable land at any one time. The inefficiency of the zalesh system was not of great consequence while Siberian agriculture was focussed on dairy farming, as it was in the pre-NEP period. However, by the late 1920s problems of declining soil fertility became increasingly apparent as the land surplus diminished, grain production expanded and dairy farming contracted under NEP.[18]

A major hindrance to efficient land use in peasant communities was the strip farming system. As we have already observed, communal settlements in the prime arable area of Siberia, the Altai steppe, were normally several hundred strong. Consequently, the strips of these villages were spread over a considerable distance, often 20 or 30 kilometres or more, with concomitant sharp increases in the costs of fieldwork. Such long distances made a means of transport essential and considering the shortness of seasonal work in Siberia compared with other major agricultural areas, gave agricultural machines and implements an importance which far outweighed their value. Under NEP the Krai Land Administration, following the lead of Narkomzem pursued a policy of increasing the efficiency and productivity of farms whilst preserving the existing communal form of land tenure. The economic and social changes engendered by these improvements were a source of much political controversy, particularly on the question of peasant differentiation, which reached a peak in 1927–8. They were also accompanied by tremendous changes in agricultural production in Siberia which will be discussed below (pp. 19–25). The paradox of land tenure stability in Siberia was that it raised peasant incentives for self-improvement while complicating the tasks of the local authorities regarding land improvements and consolidation of strips.[19]

While a major obstacle to the modernisation of peasant production was the lack of draught animals, agricultural implements and machines, of the main grain producing areas of the country Siberia was the best provided in all these respects. Over the country as a whole just over 31% of peasant farms had no draught animals, over 34% had no ploughing equipment and only 18.4% possessed agricultural machines. In Siberia, the figures were 12%, 25.9% and 35.8% respectively (compared with 36.7%, 40.5%, 23.5% in the Ukraine and 40.1%, 50.6% amd 26.8% in the North Caucasus, the two most important agricultural regions). The Krai Land Administration noted in 1927 that, by comparison with other areas, the Siberian countryside had a surplus of horses, large numbers of which were annually exported (73,000 head in 1926) to other parts of the country and they were well under-used on Siberian peasant farms.[20]

The condensed period of fieldwork, the large size of farms and the open nature of farming on the Siberian steppes created a particularly high profit return from modern mechanised farming, and indeed the Siberian peasantry accounted for a high proportion of purchases of agricultural implements and machines in the 1920s. Between 1925 and 1928 they bought an average of 25% to 30% of all agricultural equipment sold in the RSFSR while farming just under 10% of its sown area, and they took 18% of sales in the whole country, with only 6.8% of the total USSR sown area. Sales in Siberia rose sharply under NEP, amounting to 6.4 million (100%) roubles in 1923–4, 18.3 million (286%) in 1924–5, 24.5 million (383%) in 1925–6, 27.6 million (431%) in 1926–7, and just under 30 million (453%) in 1927–8. The rising technological level of Siberian farms was signified by the increasing number of 'complicated' or 'advanced' agricultural machines in operation, such as mechanised harvesters, mowers, threshers, seeding machines and, on a smaller scale, even tractors. For example, between 1923/4 and 1926/7 the number of advanced machines in operation rose as follows: mowers from 2,058 to almost 26,000, various types of harvesters from just over 1,000 to almost 19,000, and threshers from 1,868 to over 10,000. There was also a sharp increase in the number of machines for cleaning and grading seed, from 733 in 1923/4 to over 5,000 in 1928, processing over 171,990 tons. This significantly improved crop yields and by 1927 this type of seed was used on 22.6% of the area sown to wheat. One of the earliest known tractor detachments to work in the Soviet countryside operated in Siberia in 1922, and from 1925 to the end of 1927 the number of tractors in use rose from 148 to almost 1,000. Private purchases of tractors were restricted by a government decree of October 1926 which limited sales to sovkhozes, kolkhozes and peasant producer cooperative societies. Consequently, by 1927 only 2% of tractors in Siberia were held by individual peasants, 23% by kolkhozes, 15% by sovkhozes and other state enterprises, while most (55%) were held by peasant machine cooperatives. In Siberia in the mid-1920s machine cooperatives were the most important means of purchasing and distributing agricultural machines and implements amongst the peasantry.[21]

The cooperative movement was deeply rooted in the Siberian countryside and had a tradition stretching back to the great settlement period of the late nineteenth and early twentieth centuries. Under NEP several types of cooperatives proliferated in the countryside, with generous state encouragement in the form of credit and priority services. In his last writings Lenin outlined his 'cooperative plan' for the transformation of the backward peasant masses into 'civilised cooperators' by means of a 'cultural revolution' in the countryside.[22] The hope was that the peasantry would accommodate itself to the Soviet regime through engaging in socialist forms of organisation and production, by progressive stages of cooperation: firstly, in farm improvements, then marketing and selling and, ultimately, production. The general consensus in the party during the NEP period was that the state could determine the pace and scale of development of cooperation through its control of the dispersion of credit. Bukharin at one stage suggested that even the kulaks could peacefully 'grow into' socialism via the cooperatives.[23] However, the evidence of cooperation on the ground in this period clearly demonstrates that Lenin's goals were unrealistic.

There was an inherent contradiction between the Bolshevik view of the cooperatives as an intermediary stage to socialist collective farming and the attitude of peasants who joined the cooperatives for mutual gain and private profit. To make matters worse, the cooperatives attracted the well-off peasants and the kulaks in large numbers because they operated the most advanced farms in the countryside and were more aware of the economic advantages of cooperation. As the most respected and influential peasants, the well-off dominated the elected administrative boards of cooperative societies and were in a position to control their operations in accordance with their interests. Faced with a situation where the cooperatives were actually assisting the more prosperous peasants to expand, the party attempted to exercise more strict political and economic control of the cooperative network. Cooperatives were fundamentally self-help organisations where groups of peasants contributed regular share payments and pooled resources for a particular economic purpose. The three main branches of the system were consumer, agricultural and credit cooperatives. Consumer cooperatives, under the central direction of Tsentrosoiuz, played a key role in sustaining peasant incentives to increase output by providing them with a regular supply of cheap goods and services and priority sales of scarce (*defitsitnyi*) products. Agricultural cooperatives were intended to be the driving force for raising and improving the quality of peasant production and were under the central direction of Sel'skosoiuz. From August 1924 this body worked closely with the financial organs of the state to provide extensive credit facilities for the cooperative system.[24]

Consumer cooperatives had the longest tradition and strongest base in the region, given the difficulties of securing supplies in such a remote area of the country. By 1913 there were over 1,900 cooperative stores in Siberia, which accounted for 46.8% of the retail trade. Similarly, agricultural cooperatives such as those in the dairy industry had their organisational roots in the milk and butter artels established by peasants in the early 1900s to protect their interests against the multinational companies then moving into the region. Credit cooperatives had been established by Siberian local government officials as early as the 1870s, and, as the region was settled and developed, the number of these expanded rapidly and by January 1915 there were over 1,300 with around 1 million members. Under NEP the existing cooperative network in Siberia was incorporated into the Bolshevik system and it expanded to become one of the most developed in the USSR.[25]

The Siberian Krai Union of Cooperatives (Sibkraisoiuz) was established in January 1924. Its hierarchical structure extended down through okrug and raion networks to the basic unit, the village store (*lavka*). During the mid-1920s the number of stores multiplied rapidly, rising from 2,061 in 1925 to 2,555 in 1928. In the same period the number of shareholders in consumer cooperatives surged from about 555,000 to over 1.2 million, amounting to almost 75% of the peasant households in the krai. By 1927–8, the peak year of NEP, the cooperative stores cornered 88.7% of all retail trade in Siberian villages. Agricultural cooperatives in the region were organised by Sibsel'skosoiuz, which grouped its units into three broad categories according to their functions: marketing cooperatives, simple producer unions and credit unions. Siberian marketing cooperatives were overwhelmingly concentrated in the dairy industry of the Barabinsk steppe in the west of the krai. On 1 January 1928 there were 2,346 dairy cooperatives (about half the total number in the USSR), 2,119 of which were located in West Siberia, where almost half a million farms (over 55% of the total) participated. In addition many non-members sold their milk to the cooperatives as they owned most of the dairy factories. In all, over 67% of the Siberian dairy herd was held by farms belonging to cooperatives. In this network there was a progressive assessment of share payments as members paid a basic entry payment plus dues and then increments for each cow held.[26]

By the end of 1928, over 40% of Siberian peasant households were involved in some sort of agricultural cooperative, and peasant produce was overwhelmingly marketed through the cooperative system, for example in 1927/8 it accounted for 77.8% of grain and 66.4% of meat procurements. As simple producer unions within this system were designed to generate improvements in the quality and scale of agricultural production they were involved in a gamut of activities, from supplying modern machines and graded seed, to assisting with land improvements, agronomical advice, livestock breeding and others. Machine cooperative societies dominated this network in Siberia, accounting for 69% of the total number of participating units. Between 1926 and 1928 the number of machine societies more than doubled, sharply increasing from around 2,000 to 4,877, about one-third of the USSR total, with about 80,000 peasant households registered as members, and purchasing upwards of 80% of the sales of agricultural machines in the region in 1928. The number of peasants involved in machine societies, compared with other types of cooperatives, is surprisingly low given that advanced agricultural machines were highly advantageous in Siberian conditions. One reason for the low membership was that this type of equipment was in great demand for purchase by the well-off peasantry and there is evidence to suggest that cooperative machine societies were dominated by this group to the exclusion of other peasants, as a means of circumventing state regulations restricting credit and sales of advanced equipment to individual peasants.[27]

Perhaps the greatest obstacle to attempts to raise the technical level of agriculture in Siberia was the severe shortage of agricultural specialists and technicians and the general cultural backwardness of the peasantry. For example, in 1925 there were only 1,250 specialists in land consolidation for the whole of the krai and in 1928 just 699 agronomists, of whom only one-fifth had higher education. Peasant literacy, as in the rest of the country, was scandalously low at just under 40% for peasant men and a pitiful 14% for women. It was not just a question of low literacy but a lack of cultural awareness of the application of modern technology in farming as peasants often did not know how to operate and care for machines properly. It was also a question of an inadequate technical infrastructure as there were shortages of spare parts and a general absence of storage facilities on farms for machines, implements and produce. The weak technical infrastructure of the regional economy was most apparent in the complete inadequacy of grain storage facilities. Due to the fact that it was usually harvested in wet conditions Siberian grain had a high humidity level. Considering this and the vast distance to internal markets and ports, Siberian grain required good storage and speedy transport facilities to preserve its quality. In 1905 four grain elevators were built along the Trans-Siberian railway but, given the stress on butter at that time, no further construction took place. When Siberian grain production expanded in 1912–14 plans were made for further investment in elevator construction but these were suspended during the traumatic years between 1914 and 1921. When grain output expanded rapidly in the 1920s a series of good harvests revealed appalling deficiencies in

storage facilities. In 1926/7 and 1927/8 huge quantities of grain, as much
as 13,000 wagon loads according to one estimate, were left in piles to
rot at procurement points, railway stations and wharves for lack of
storage and transport. It was only in 1926/7 that the state began to
construct eleven new elevators and four mechanised granaries in the
region with a total capacity of about 39,312 tons. During the grain crisis
of 1927/8 there were still only four elevators operational for the whole
of Siberia, with a capacity of just 7,800 tons (less than 1% of state grain
procurement in the region).[28]

As in the rest of the country, the introduction of NEP ushered in a
period of tremendous expansion in Siberian agricultural output. The
region had largely escaped major destruction in the course of the
revolution and civil war and by 1920 the pre-war sown area levels were
exceeded; however, Bolshevik food requisitioning (*prodrazverstka*)
campaigns in 1920–2 (discussed below, p. 22), coupled with harvest
failures, brought about an agricultural collapse. The years 1924–8,
however, saw an agricultural recovery in the region that outpaced the
rest of the country in reaching and exceeding pre-war levels of production, as well as the peak levels of Siberian agriculture reached in 1920.
By the main agricultural indices of sown area and livestock numbers
Siberia had reached or overtaken 1920 levels by 1927. The sown area, at
just under 7.8 million hectares, registered more than an 11% increase
compared with 1926, 6.5% higher than that of 1920 and over 20% up on
the 1913 level. The number of cattle stood at over 6.3 million head
compared with about 4.4 million in 1913 and 1920, while the number of
horses had stabilised at just over 3.8 million against 3.6 million in 1913
and 3.9 million in 1920. There was an enormous increase of about 33%
in gross agricultural output in 1925–8, with gross field-crop output
rising by 24.7% and gross livestock production a staggering 46.5%.
Despite this rapid recovery and growth in agriculture peasant production continued to present the Bolshevik regime with a series of dilem-
mas. The most serious problem for the government in this period was
the falling scale of peasant marketings of agricultural production.[29]

In Siberia, where production levels were expanding well beyond
pre-war limits, the decline in marketings was particularly striking. In
1913 the marketed share of agricultural produce amounted to about
30% of gross output but in 1925–6 the proportion was 26.9%, falling to
22.7% in 1927–8. The decline was produced by several factors, including the rural demographic explosion and increase in consumption
discussed above (p. 11) and state procurement price policy which I
shall deal with later. The question of falling marketings and increased

consumption was related to a major transformation in the nature of agricultural production in the krai, for the NEP years witnessed the displacement of the Siberian dairy industry and the rise of the region as a major grain producer in the Soviet Union.[30]

From butter to grain production

Pre-revolutionary Siberia was world renowned for its fat-rich butter which was an important export commodity for the tsarist state. It was so valued by the government that P. A. Stolypin once remarked that 'Siberian butter production yields twice as much gold as the whole of the Siberian gold industry.'[31] The original impetus for the development of dairy farming was the imposition of the 'Cheliabinsk grain tariff' in 1891. Then, the entrenched vested interests of the great grain barons of European Russia, fearing competition from the nascent Siberian grain industry, had pressurised the tsarist government into a policy of internal protectionism. The Urals rail junction of Cheliabinsk, 'the gateway to Siberia', became a 'break' beyond which point a rail tariff surcharge was imposed on the transport of goods. This made the shipment of grain by railway expensive and forced the Siberian peasantry to concentrate on dairy and livestock production which yielded higher profit returns per weight shipped by rail.[32]

The first Siberian butter factory was founded by the St Petersburg merchant Valkov in the Kurgan steppe in 1894, and production surged after the opening of the Cheliabinsk–Novonikolaevsk section of the Trans-Siberian railway in 1896. In 1894 only two butter factories were operating in all Siberia shipping 6.5 tons annually with a value of just 4,000 roubles. By 1900 there were more than 1,000 enterprises and by 1913 over 2,000 shipping out around 70,000 tons annually with a value of about 70 million roubles that ranked Russia as the second largest butter exporter in the world after Denmark. In fact, most Siberian butter 'factories' were nothing more than small-scale family businesses using primitive hand operated machines and marketing their produce via Danish companies. The high point was reached in 1915 when over 75,600 tons were shipped, nearly all of which (about 98%) were exported. Normally, the bulk of these exports (over 90%) went to England and Germany where Siberian butter was blended with the inferior local products. The years of the First World War caused no major dislocation to the butter industry although there was a fall off in exports as the German market was closed and supplies were directed to the armed forces. A serious decline only set in from 1918 with the outbreak of civil war and military engagements and chaos along the Trans-Siberian railway, Siberia's lifeline to the outside world, but the major collapse ensued from the severe ravaging of the Siberian countryside by Bolshevik food detachments in 1920–2, after the civil war had ended in Siberia. The shortages brought about by Bolshevik food seizures were compounded by two years of bad harvests and the result was rural distress and famine.

During these years state procurement of butter fell drastically to around 6–7,000 tons, a mere 10%–12% of pre-revolutionary deliveries. Fodder shortages and slaughterings for food took a massive toll and between 1920 and 1922 the cattle herds had fallen by 600,000 head (25%) to 1.8 million head. However, by far the most damaging blow to the Siberian butter industry in the longer term was the levelling process in livestock ownership which occurred in the countryside as a consequence of the revolution.[33]

The redistribution of livestock on a more equitable basis among the peasantry effectively broke up the largest and most productive dairy herds which had a high factor of marketability. Studies conducted in the krai in the mid-1920s revealed the full extent of this process. An analysis of the network of cooperatives (which held most cows) revealed that whereas in 1907 over 42% of members held up to 3 cows (18.5% of all cows), 46.5% had from 4 to 9 (over 51%) and just over 11% held 10 or more (over 30%). By 1928 these figures had radically altered as almost 85% of members held up to 3 cows each (over 65% of the total cowherd), 14.7% had from 4 to 9 (32.2%) and less than 1% held 10 or more (only 2.6% of all cows). This dispersal of cows amongst the peasantry had an immediate impact on the marketing of dairy and livestock produce since peasant consumption of these products rose sharply. For example, annual individual milk consumption norms rose from 90 kilogrammes in 1923/4 to 220 by 1926/7 and 236 in 1927/8. The impact of this may be demonstrated by the fact that the increase of 16 kilogrammes per person in 1927/8 meant a decrease in marketed milk of 130,000 tons or in butter of 6,560 tons (about 18% of procurements that year).[34]

The local problems for the butter industry were compounded by the loss of traditional export markets. In 1923 only about 2,800 tons of Siberian butter were exported, a little over 4% of average levels in 1909–13. The dislocations and interruptions of supply caused by the war, revolution and civil war and the tarnished international image of the new Bolshevik government in the 1920s brought about a sharp fall in the Soviet share of foreign markets, especially in England (from over

15% pre-war to 5.5%) and Germany (from 55% to 7%). Although herd numbers and dairy output were restored in excess of their pre-war levels by 1927/8, state procurement of butter at around 36,000 tons was only about 60% of 1913 deliveries. Nevertheless, Siberian shipments still accounted for around 75% of the butter exports of the USSR, the vast bulk of which came from south-west Siberia. In essence the Siberian butter industry had died by default before collectivisation was enforced. With proper state encouragement and investment it might well have survived the difficulties of the late 1920s, but the attention of the state was consumed by the struggle for grain. The decline of the Siberian butter industry under NEP was concurrent with the re-emergence of the grain industry which the *pomeshchiki* of European Russia had effectively destroyed in the 1890s.[35]

The grain-growing areas of south-west and eastern Siberia were particularly suitable for the production of high quality durum wheat which was a potentially valuable source of export revenue. Traditionally Siberian wheat was exported to Italy for pasta and was highly prized on the domestic and foreign markets for breadmaking. The development of the grain industry in the region (as with butter) was inextricably linked to the improvement of rail communications with the industrial heartlands of European Russia and with export markets. After the imposition of punitive rail tariffs in 1891 the cost of transporting Siberian grain to European Russia was prohibitively expensive and shipment down the Ob, Irtysh and Enisei rivers to ports on the North Polar Sea (a distance of several thousand kilometres) was time-consuming, costly and restricted to the ice-free periods in mid-summer. As a result grain prices within Siberia were consistently so low that grain was used as a feed in the dairy and livestock industry, on which agricultural production then concentrated.[36]

The opening of the Tiumen–Omsk railway branch-line in 1913 was a turning point for grain production in Siberia. The route to Moscow, Leningrad and the Baltic ports was shortened by several hundred kilometres, reducing rail charges for the transport of commodities and thus undercutting the Cheliabinsk tariff. With the active encouragement of the tsarist government grain production in Siberia expanded rapidly and its export earning potential began to be realised. In 1913 over 330,000 tons were transported from Siberia (by rail and river) of which about 285,000 tons (mostly wheat) were exported. Between 1914 and 1922, exports of Siberian grain were curtailed and production was directed to satisfy domestic market and war needs. The potential of the industry remained strong and further possibilities for development opened up with the completion of a network of branch-lines to the Trans-Siberian railway between 1912 and 1926, particularly those to the main grain areas of the Altai, Achinsk and Minusinsk.[37]

The most destructive episode for Siberian agriculture was the Bolshevik prodrazverstka campaign of 1920–2, indeed this was belatedly recognised by the regional party secretary at the time, S. V. Kosior, who admitted that 'during the *razverstka* period, the Siberian peasantry carried on their shoulders, like no other, an extraordinary burden. The population was terribly ravaged.'[38] Siberia suffered the brunt of requisitions in these years because of the more severe collapse of agricultural production in European parts of the country in the wake of the civil war, and the widespread famine which ensued in those regions. In July 1920 a Sovnarkom decree fixed the prodrazverstka plan for Siberia at a massive 163,800 tons of grain (24% of the total state plan), amounting to about 45% of the estimated harvest. To ensure a rigorous campaign, 26,000 activists were mobilised from the famine-stricken areas of Russia and the introduction of NEP in March 1921 was deliberately delayed in Siberia. Yet only 61% of the plan was successfully collected by June 1921. Requisitioning was only replaced by the food tax in most districts from August and even then it was fixed at a much higher level than in the rest of the country (20%–30% of gross harvest compared with a USSR average of 12%–13%). Another harsh procurement campaign followed in 1922 when over 27% of total grain procurements in the RSFSR came from Siberia.[39]

As these campaigns were conducted during two consecutive harvest failures which saw yields drop to over half normal levels, the result was famine and widespread rural unrest. With neither the incentive nor the seed to cultivate their land peasants went over to subsistence farming and their rage at Bolshevik pillaging exploded in a spontaneous revolt. Soviet historians euphemistically refer to a widespread 'SR–kulak' uprising in West Siberia in this period, organised under the banner of the 'Siberian Peasant Union'. In fact, there was a widespread peasant revolt across western Siberia in the second half of 1920 and early 1921, culminating in the capture of Tobolsk in February by an army of 30,000 peasant insurgents. It was only in April that the Red Army restored order but at a cost of countless thousands killed and wounded on both sides, including an estimated 5,000 Siberian communists and local soviet officials.[40]

The introduction of NEP resulted in a rapid agricultural recovery and the period from 1923/4 to 1926/7 was one of resurgent growth and renewed prosperity. A fundamental principle underpinning NEP was the restoration of market relations in the countryside, which the Bolsheviks hoped would engender a new cooperative 'link' (*smychka*) relationship with the peasantry that would lead to a recovery in peasant marketings of agricultural produce. Given its importance as the basic food staple and its value as an export earner the expansion of grain output became a prime policy goal for the government. The incentive of free market conditions boosted the sown area of Siberia from just under 5.56 million hectares in 1924 to over 7.73 million in 1927, a huge 37.8% increase. This compared with an average USSR increase in sown area of just 13% in the same period. During the peak years of NEP, 1923–7, the share of wheat in the sown area of Siberia rose by 19% (to 54.3% of the total), oats by 7.4% (to 25.6%), the proportion of rye fell by 16.8% (1.5%) while industrial crops increased to only about 2.6% of all sowings. The Siberian peasantry may have been ravaged by the Bolsheviks in 1920–2 but they were quick to take advantage of the more propitious circumstances of NEP. As the sown area expanded so the grain harvest increased, exceeding 5.5 million tons in 1925 and 6.5 million in 1926, a rise of almost 28% on the 5 million tons produced in 1913. This rapid rate of growth was assisted by a favourable period of climatic conditions and high yields.[41]

Siberia became a grain surplus region of national importance, accounting for 6% of the USSR area sown to grains and 11.2% of wheat sowings in 1925, rising to 8.8% and 17.1% by 1928. By the mid-1920s it had become a major source of wheat for the industrial regions of the central and north-eastern European parts of the country and for export to the international markets. In the record post-revolutionary harvest year of 1926/7 state grain procurement in the region totalled over 1.3 million tons which was 11.6% of the USSR total. Significantly, over 76% of this was wheat, constituting 15.7% of USSR wheat procurements and 21.3% of those in the RSFSR. An important feature of this surge in grain production was the dominating role played by south-western okrugs, which accounted for about 80% (overwhelmingly wheat) of the total. Shipments of wheat far exceeded pre-war levels and peaked at over 890,000 tons in 1926/7. By far the most significant increase was in the amount of Siberian wheat exported. This rose from 22,000 tons in 1925/6 to 345,000 in 1926/7, about 35% of all Soviet wheat exports that year and 23% of the value of all grain exports (the increase in value of which accounted for 50% of the total increase in export earnings). When one adds butter shipments, it is clear that Siberia had once again become an important source of food and hard currency earnings for the state at the crucial juncture when Bolshevik

industrialisation plans were becoming more ambitious and their successful realisation increasingly dependent on guaranteed deliveries of
cheap agricultural produce.[42]

Still the low ratio of peasant marketings to gross production
remained a serious problem for the state. In the country as a whole,
marketings of all types of agricultural produce in the mid-1920s were
substantially lower than peak pre-war levels. Several factors have been
advanced as contributing to this depressed market, notably: disin-
centives for peasants to sell their produce, including the 'scissors' gap
between high industrial retail prices and low agricultural prices, and
shortages in manufactured goods. Also, it is argued that a rising rural
population led to increased subdivision of peasant farms, resulting in
lower productivity and higher peasant consumption. At the same time
restoration of livestock herds to pre-war levels absorbed a rising proportion of grain as fodder. Finally, since agricultural tax and rent
burdens were substantially lower than before the revolution there was
less financial pressure on the peasantry to market their produce. The
decline of grain marketings was particularly serious with an estimated
8.8 million ton shortfall in supplies for the towns, army, industry and
export in 1926/7 compared with average levels in 1909–13.[43]

In Siberia, the problem of marketing of grain was very different from
that in the country at large. As we have already noted, there was a
huge expansion in Siberian grain production under NEP and state
procurements had surged in 1926/7. In the mid-1920s both marketings
and state procurement of grain in the region were increasing not only
in volume but also as a percentage of gross production. The main
problem was that the rate of growth in marketings and state procurement as a percentage of gross production was lagging behind that in
other areas of the country and in grain surplus regions in particular. In
1925/6 and 1926/7 the ratio of marketed grain to gross production in
Siberia, at 19.1% and 21.9%, was the second lowest of the main grain
regions and while the ratio of state procurement to gross production
was slightly higher than most in 1925/6 (14.6%), it hovered around the
average in 1926/7 (18.8%), and this was a boom harvest year. In 1927/8
both these indices exceeded the 1926/7 levels and, although the gross
harvest and procurement were lower, there was a good increase in the
ratio of marketings. This was largely explained by increased state
pressure on the Siberian peasantry during the grain crisis of that year.[44]

A French traveller to Siberia in the early 1930s was told over and over
again by peasants that 'in 1926, 1927 and 1928 we had so much grain, so
much bread, that we did not know what to do with them'.[45] Certainly

the Siberian peasants' consumption of grains and especially wheat
rose sharply under NEP. Krai Statistical Department investigations
revealed that whereas between 1923/4 and 1926/7 there was a 9.5%
increase in annual grain consumption by the peasantry, during the
same period wheat consumption rose by over 70%, from 106.5 kilogrammes per person (43% of all grains consumed) to over 180 (66%).
These figures, together with those mentioned earlier in relation to
butter, indicate a general rise in peasant living standards as they
consumed more of all types of agricultural produce and reduced significantly the surplus made available for the state. We remarked previously on the large increase in peasant population and farms in Siberia
during these years, but such demographic changes were more easily
absorbed and subdivision had less of an impact here than in other
regions for several reasons. Firstly, there were extensive reserves of
land in the krai which were brought under new cultivation. Secondly,
because of the shift in the nature of agricultural production under NEP,
as Siberian peasants moved away from livestock and dairy farming,
large areas of pasture were ploughed up and turned over to grain
production. Thus, as the sown area and agricultural population grew
simultaneously problems arising from overcrowding of land were
minimised. The extent to which price differentials, goods shortages
and increased peasant income affected marketings of agricultural produce are areas in which state policy had the overriding influence and
therefore they will be discussed in chapters 4 and 5 when we shall
examine state procurement activities in the region. We shall see that all
of these factors coalesced to bring about the grain crisis of the winter of
1927/8.[46]

2 The party and the peasantry

Centre–periphery relations

Between 1919 and 1922 the central party organisation was modified and reconstructed to transform the Bolsheviks from an underground movement of revolutionary activists into a party of government. In the process of this revamping, a hierarchical bureaucratic apparat was created in the party and changes were made to ensure that power at all levels was transferred from the soviets and resided with party committees so that the senior administrative figure was the party secretary. The tightening of central party control in this period may also be explained by the desire of the top leadership to maintain political conformity within party ranks and to combat and curb 'local separatism' which had surfaced in all areas of the country in the wake of the collapse of the *ancien régime*. Given the enormity and ethnic diversity of the territory, its poor communications, the administrative chaos and the small number of Bolsheviks scattered across the country, a policy of strict overlordship was essential to sustain the party's monopoly of power.[1] To this end the Central Committee was empowered by the party leadership with two principal measures: firstly, it had the final say in the assignment of all party personnel to posts in the provinces, and secondly, it regularly assigned special instructors to tour provincial areas, investigate and verify the work of local party organisations and report back on intra-party political loyalties.[2]

The party bodies concerned with the implementation of these new procedures were the Orgbiuro, which vetted most provincial appointments, and two of the departments of the Central Committee Secretariat, the Orgotdel, which supervised the sending of instructors, and Uchraspred, which compiled and administered the party personnel records that were to become the foundation of the party's appointment system (nomenklatura). The latter two bodies (merged to form Orgraspred in 1924) became particularly important as the party normalised its operations and moved away from war-time mass mobilisations of cadres to a policy of individual selection based on personnel records. As General Secretary, Stalin dominated these organs and this gave him a tremendous advantage over his party rivals in the internecine strife for the succession to Lenin, as he manipulated his power over party appointments to build a patrimonial system by promoting clients and marginalising opponents, particularly in the provinces, and thereby ultimately determining the composition and voting of provincial delegations at party congresses. This 'circular flow of power' was the key to Stalin's successful outmanoeuvring of political rivals and rise to power in the leadership battles of the 1920s.[3]

The geopolitical and economic significance of Siberia made for an intensive interest in its affairs on the part of the central authorities. Given the leadership's aims of building up the party in the provinces and eliminating political differences and 'local separatism' from within its ranks, their intervention in the activities of the Siberian party organisation was all the more rigorous as this was a region where all these elements featured prominently. During the revolution and civil war popular support for the Bolsheviks among Siberians was minimal. In 1917 there were just 2,500 party members and it was only after the civil war ended in victory for the Bolsheviks that party membership began to rise sharply, from about 8,000 to over 80,000 in 1920. The lack of mass popular appeal of the Bolsheviks, a proletarian based party, may be explained by the rural and provincial nature of Siberian society and was evident from the returns of the free elections to the Constituent Assembly in November 1917. Siberia proved to be a bastion of SR support as they swept the field polling over 78% of the vote, while the Bolsheviks took second place with just 11.6%. No other region in the country gave the SRs such a large percentage share of the vote. The Siberian SRs were so persistent in asserting demands for regional autonomy (oblastnichestvo) that they brought the SR's leader, V. M. Chernov, to characterise separatist sentiments in his party as a whole as 'the Siberian orientation'. Indeed, during the civil war Siberia was the scene of several anti-Bolshevik governments, including those of the Directory and Kolchak, but they had difficulty in sustaining the interest of Siberians in military campaigns against the Bolsheviks west of the Urals.[4]

A worrying factor from the viewpoint of the central Bolshevik leadership was the fiercely independent and conciliatory line taken by many Siberian Bolsheviks throughout 1917 in their relations with other socialist parties and their rejection of central control through the imposition of democratic centralism. To reassert central control during the civil war the Central Committee established a Siberian Bureau (Sibbiuro) in Moscow at the end of 1918 to administer the affairs of the region for the centre.[5] Siberia was of key importance because its reserves of grain and other agricultural produce supplied the central industrial regions of the country, and the Central Committee retained direct control through the Sibbiuro until 1924. However, as part of the normalisation of administration in the aftermath of the Bolshevik victory in the civil war the tight rein of the centre had to be eased. The process of regionalisation undertaken in the country in 1921–4 also necessitated the reorganisation of the Siberian party and the reintegration of its leading organ with the territory.

A perennial complicating factor in Siberian local politics was the long-standing intra-regional rivalry between West and East Siberia which had grown out of the decision by the tsarist state in the early nineteenth century to govern the territory by dividing it into two provinces: Western (capital: Tobolsk) and Eastern (capital: Irkutsk). In 1920–3 a series of proposals were made to reform the old tsarist boundaries, the most radical of which were Gosplan schemes to carve the country into economic regions. Under one of these schemes Siberia was to be dismembered into six economic regions, with three west and east of Lake Baikal. This ran counter to a strong current in the regional party leadership that favoured a unified Siberian administration, and indeed this was tapping a popular aspiration for unity only recently expressed during the civil war by an armed struggle for Siberian autonomy. Such sentiments cross-cut party allegiances and the local Bolsheviks themselves, as we have seen, were by no means immune from identifying with regional ties against central interference. Consequently, the Sibrevkom successfully frustrated all the Gosplan proposals and later the whole scheme of regionalisation of the country on an economic basis fell by the wayside at the Twelfth Congress in April 1923, due mainly to the opposition of entrenched local vested interests.[6]

The scare over the Gosplan proposals and the loss of three provinces of West Siberia (Ekaterinburg, Tiumen and Cheliabinsk) to the new Urals Oblast, in November 1923, spurred the Siberian authorities to cooperate with the centre in the process of redrawing regional boundaries. The ground for the formation of the region into a single administrative krai was prepared by the reorganisation of Siberian local government in late 1924, which rationalised volost boundaries and reduced the number of these from 871 to 257. The centre and the Siberian party leadership began to restructure their organisations on the basis of a unified jurisdiction centred on Novonikolaevsk and in the autumn of 1923 the Central Committee convoked a regional party conference in order that the Sibbiuro be transformed into a Kraikom with the formal stamp of approval by district party organisations. The First Krai Party Conference duly convened in Novonikolaevsk in May 1924 and elected a Kraikom of thirty-seven members, which formed a bureau (Kraikombiuro) of nine members and two candidates, and established several departments (organisational, agitational-propaganda, women). This provoked intra-regional antagonisms to flare up as the Irkutsk authorities were reluctant to see the traditional bicentral concept of administration in Siberia abandoned, with the diminution of their local authority and status. There was vigorous opposition from the Irkutsk Gubkom, which demanded not only complete local autonomy for itself based on the Gosplan proposals but also the inclusion of parts of the territory of Enisei, Buriat-Mongolia and Chita. Circumventing the Kraikom, the Irkutsk party leadership appealed directly to the Central Executive Committee of the RSFSR (VTsIK).[7]

In September 1924 VTsIK ratified the plan for a single krai in Siberia and rejected the Irkutsk appeal for autonomy on the grounds that the creation of several separate regional authorities in Siberia would cause administrative chaos and complicate the distribution of experienced party personnel (who were at a premium). Meanwhile a decision on the territorial claims made by Irkutsk was postponed. In May 1925 a VTsIK decree, based on the recommendations of a boundary commission headed by R. I. Eikhe, formed all of Siberia west of Lake Baikal to the Urals Oblast into a krai (capital: Novonikolaevsk), composed of sixteen okrugs and one autonomous national area. Eventually, in June 1926 the Irkutsk Guberniia was formally included within the jurisdiction of the krai and subdivided into three okrugs. This bitter dispute had a significant impact on local politics for it spoiled relations between the Irkutsk party organisation and the Kraikom throughout the remainder of the decade. We shall see later how these differences re-emerged in the aftermath of the grain crisis of 1927/8.[8]

The Central Committee continued to exercise control of the Siberian party through its power to appoint and remove senior local officials, and the prerogative to despatch special instructors to check local party organisations for political conformity and guard against abuses. From the early 1920s both these instruments of control were employed extensively. At the same time it would be wrong to assume that the assignment of leading officials from the centre was merely a question of the extension of central power, for the civil war had devastated the Bolshevik party in Siberia and left it short of experienced leaders. Kolchak had executed about one-half of the local party leadership, including the Obkom Chairman, Rabinovich, and six of its members, in addition to local underground leaders in Omsk, Irkutsk and other important towns, while the peasant uprising of 1920–1 had also taken a heavy toll. Consequently, during the NEP period the leading party and state posts in Siberia were held by experienced Bolsheviks of non-Siberian origin assigned by the Central Committee: S. V. Kosior (Polish) was Secretary of the Sibbiuro (1922–4) and then Secretary of the Kraikom (1924–5), and M. M. Lashevich (Ukrainian) was Chairman of the Sibrevkom (1922–5) and then, briefly, Chairman of the Kraiispolkom (1925). In fact, of the nine members and two candidates in the first Kraikombiuro selected in May 1924 only one-third were Siberians. At the First Krai Congress of Soviets in December 1925 half the delegates had lived in Siberia for less than five years and as only 49% of delegates were party members it would be tempting to suggest that there was a considerable overlap between these two figures. This could be a further indication that non-Siberian Bolshevik activists had been imposed from the centre to bolster the depleted local party organisation.[9]

The post-civil war process of normalisation of party control of the administration of the region was promoted by a series of party and soviet congresses and conferences held in the krai in late 1925. The Second Krai Party Conference in late November to early December expanded the membership of the Kraikom to forty-four members and sixteen candidates, established a Secretariat and Control Commission, and reorganised the publication of local party newspapers and journals was reorganised. The veteran Latvian Bolshevik, Eikhe, who had been working in Siberia for several years, was nominated by the Kraikom and duly selected as the Chairman of the Kraiispolkom at the First Krai Congress of Soviets in early December. The Krai Congress of Soviets finally brought to a close the Sibrevkom period and in a symbolic gesture to the new Soviet dawn, one of the vestiges of tsarist rule was eliminated when the name of the krai capital was changed from Novonikolaevsk to Novosibirsk.[10]

The selection of Eikhe as the senior state official in Siberia followed the appointment of Lashevich as Deputy People's Commissar for War in early November. Lashevich was a popular civil war hero and a prominent supporter of Zinoviev and the 'Leningrad Opposition', and in the months leading up to and after the Fourteenth Congress in December 1925 he played an active role in oppositional activities against the Stalin–Bukharin majority on the Central Committee. Although the considerations which motivated these personnel changes are impossible to verify, clearly Lashevich's promotion to a key military post, located in the political centre of the country meant he was better positioned to assist Zinoviev. On the other hand, this appointment divorced him from his regional party base and, as we shall see later when we discuss the Opposition in Siberia (pp. 34–8), greatly reduced his effective power where it mattered, namely, in influencing provincial party cadres. Signs of Stalinist intrigue were also evident in the promotion and replacement of Kosior as Secretary of the Kraikom. At the Fourteenth Congress Kosior revealed himself as a fervent supporter of Stalin against the Opposition and subsequently was promoted as one of the new Central Committee Secretaries. He was succeeded as Siberian party boss by the Ukrainian S. I. Syrtsov, one of Stalin's bright young apparatchiki in the Central Committee.[11]

Since the intra-party struggles of this period were mainly decided at party congresses and in the Central Committee chosen by the congresses, the leadership faction which secured the support of provincial delegations was guaranteed victory. Stalin's triumph over his political opponents in the 1920s was largely due to his realisation of this fact and his successful machinations in placing his clients and supporters in key provincial posts. The turnover of personnel in Siberia was part of a series of changes in the leading echelons of the party carried out in late 1925 and early 1926 which brought to the fore a new generation and type of leader in the small ruling elite of the nomenklatura, who were marked out by their consistent loyalty to Stalin's leadership and a tough anti-Trotskyite stance. Syrtsov and Eikhe were prototypical examples of the new emerging breed of hardened 'Old Bolshevik' officials. As these two figures remained the senior party and soviet leaders in Siberia in the period leading up to and beyond the grain crisis of 1927–8, and were representative of the kind of high-ranking officials whose support determined the outcome of the leadership disputes of the 1920s, it is worth looking at their political careers in more detail. Later, we shall look at their standpoints and actions in 1927–8 in order to understand and explain how Stalin secured their support and triumphed (chapter 7).[12]

Sergei Ivanovich Syrtsov (1893–1937) was one of Stalin's young rising stars in the party during the 1920s but fell out of favour in late 1930 and perished in the great purges. He was born in the small rural backwater of Slavgorod, Ekaterinoslav Guberniia, in the Ukraine. The son of a white-collar worker, he attended St Petersburg Polytechnic Institute from 1912 to 1916, and there joined the Bolshevik party in 1913, at the age of 20. After several periods of political detention by the tsarist authorities, he was sentenced to administrative exile in the remote Verkolensk district of Irkutsk, Siberia. Following the amnesty, in February 1917, he returned to Petrograd and then (probably on Bolshevik orders) to Rostov, his native area. He was a delegate to the Sixth Congress, Chairman of the Rostov-Nakhichevan Soviet during the October Revolution and, as head of the local Military-Revolutionary Committee, led an uprising in Rostov in November 1917. Syrtsov had a 'good' civil war and, while serving as a political commissar with a front-line Red Army division on the Southern Front in 1918–20, was wounded and decorated with the Order of the Red Banner. Subsequently, he was appointed to a number of leading party and soviet posts in the Don region until in 1921 he was made Secretary of Odessa Gubkom. While attending the Tenth Congress in March 1921 he participated in the bloody suppression of the Kronstadt revolt. During the intra-party disputes of this period he frequently opposed Lenin from the left, joining the Left Communists in opposition to the Treaty of Brest-Litovsk in March 1918, and siding with Trotsky in the 'trade union controversy' of 1920–1. Like many other Leftists, Syrtsov only supported Lenin's platform of NEP and authoritarian restrictions on intra-party democracy after the shock of Kronstadt. Thereafter, he rose quickly in the party hierarchy and, at the relatively young age of thirty, was appointed to senior posts in the heart of the Central Committee apparat, first as head of Uchraspred (1921–3), and then of the Agitprop Department (1924–6). It was while serving in the latter capacity that he became a member of the Presidium of the Communist Academy and edited the journal *Kommunisticheskaia Revoliutsiia*. After the Thirteenth Congress in May 1924 he was elected a candidate member of the Central Committee and became a voting member after the Fifteenth Congress in December 1927.[13]

Syrtsov may have struck up a relationship with Stalin earlier in his political career that might explain his rather sudden promotion to Moscow in 1921. On the other hand, in the space of a year between March 1920 and 1921 the staff of the Central Committee increased fourfold, from 150 to 602, and there was a dearth of experienced organisers (like Syrtsov) in the appointment of senior apparatchiki given the manpower losses incurred as a result of the civil war. As head of Uchraspred Syrtsov was responsible for the detailed party

personnel records which were central to the functioning of the nomenklatura system of the Central Committee and evidently he must have
had a close working relationship with his immediate superior, Stalin.
According to a Soviet historian, Syrtsov, together with L. M. Kaganov-
ich (head of Orgotdel) and A. S. Bubnov (member of the Orgbiuro),
formed Stalin's 'first "general staff" in the party apparatus'.[14] From this
time onward his career prospects became inextricably linked with
Stalin's patronage. Syrtsov was somebody of whom Stalin, as one
biographer put it, 'could be sure, right or wrong'.[15] The appointment of
Syrtsov as Secretary of the Siberian Kraikom to replace Kosior, indicates that Stalin regarded him as sufficiently reliable and competent
to deliver the support of an important regional party organisation
during a period of tense intra-party strife. There may also have been
the promise of greater advancement after a tour of duty in the
provinces.

Like Syrtsov, Robert Indrikovich Eikhe (1890–1940) was murdered in
the Stalin purges of the 1930s despite his impeccable revolutionary
credentials. He was born near Doblen, Latvia, the son of a farm
labourer (batrak) on a pomeshchik estate. As was typical of his class, he
was compelled by poverty to work from an early age, first as a shep-
herd, then as a blacksmith's apprentice. While still but a boy, at the age
of fifteen, he joined the Latvian Bolshevik party (SDPLR) in 1905. In
1908, to escape arrest, he fled abroad to Britain and worked first as a
stoker, then as a coalminer near Glasgow, where he was secretary of a
socialist club. He returned to Riga in 1911, resumed his party activities
and, in the following year, was appointed to the local Bolshevik committee. At the Fourth Congress of the SDPLR, held in Brussels in 1914,
he advocated closer cooperation with Lenin and the Russian Bolsheviks and was elected to the SDPLR Central Committee. However, on
returning to Latvia he was arrested, brought to St Petersburg and
sentenced to life-long exile in Siberia with deprivation of all civil rights,
an extraordinary punishment for the time. In keeping with his character, Eikhe soon escaped and lived freely in Siberia under a pseudonym
until the February Revolution. He returned to Riga and was elected to
the local soviet executive committee, where he worked assiduously for
a Bolshevik seizure of power. In January 1918 he was arrested and
interned by the Germans, but he escaped to Soviet Russia in July and
thereafter was assigned to the People's Commissariat of Food Supplies
(Narkomprod), until his appointment as Food Commissar to Siberia in
May 1922. Under Eikhe's direction food procurement campaigns were
conducted in the more propitious conditions of NEP and therefore his

local reputation was untarnished by the prodrazverstka of 1920–1. In 1924 he became Deputy Chairman of the Sibrevkom, from which post he was selected Chairman of the Kraiispolkom in late 1925 and he served continuously in senior krai party and soviet positions until the late 1930s. Eikhe's international background made him an ideal choice to combat separatist tendencies in the region, for as he once declared: 'For us Bolsheviks, there is no such thing as Siberian, Caucasian, or Ukrainian interests. For us, the interests of the revolution as a whole are paramount.'[16]

Throughout his revolutionary career Eikhe had displayed qualities of personal bravery, resilience and leadership, but these were not sufficient to secure promotion in the nomenklatura of the faction-ridden party of the 1920s. A disciplined loyalty to the party leadership was the overriding criterion in promotions and Eikhe had proved himself to be a consistently loyal supporter of Lenin in the past and presumably, had transferred that allegiance to Stalin's 'general line'. His promotion may be seen in this context for two reasons: firstly, his career record throughout the 1920s and 1930s proved him to be a Stalin loyalist; and secondly, the fact that he was nominated by the Kraikom led by Kosior strongly suggests that he was deemed suitably reliable.

The defeat of the Left Opposition

The main difficulty in accurately gauging the extent of support for the Left Opposition in the Siberian party organisation in the years before the grain crisis of 1927–8 is that the main sources for these events made available to the author were party publications supervised by the Kraikom leadership which had a vested political interest in downplaying local divisions. Nevertheless, it seems that the Left did not pose a serious threat to the Kraikom leadership and the reason for this largely lay in the social composition of the Siberian party membership in this period. The question of the social content of the Siberian party will be discussed in the next section. Here, we shall be concerned with the activities of the Left Opposition in Siberia prior to the grain crisis of 1927–8.

After the end of the civil war, factional squabbles in the Siberian party organisation resumed and, reflecting divisions at the centre, coalesced around the Democratic Centralists and the Workers' Opposition. Both groups opposed the continuation of authoritarian hierarchical administration by the central party apparat now that the civil war was over, and, initially, attracted some support in the Siberian party elite as they were associated with popular aspirations for greater local autonomy. For example, in late 1920 and early 1921 the Democratic Centralists dominated the Enisei Gubkom, responsible for the key Bolshevik centres of Krasnoiarsk and Kansk, and in late 1921 and early 1922 the Workers' Opposition controlled the Omsk Gubkom, and both refused to recognise the authority of the Sibbiuro. These crises echoed the disputes of 1917–18 and foreshadowed the events of the 'Irkutsk affair' in the spring of 1928.[17] By the time the Left Opposition emerged around Trotsky in October 1923, the Central Committee had an established pattern of strong-arm tactics in dealing with the problem of factions, involving the dissolution of recalcitrant party committees, the purging and re-registration of dissident party organisations (supervised by Central Committee instructors) and the cross-posting of opponents. The signatories of the Leftist 'Platform of the 46' concentrated their fire on two areas of party policy: firstly, they accused the triumvirate leadership of Stalin, Zinoviev and Kamenev of bringing the country to the verge of economic collapse in the 'scissors crisis', and secondly, claimed that intra-party democracy was being threatened by the increasing bureaucratisation of the party's organisational structure and the erosion of the leadership's links with the rank and file by the dictatorship of a 'secretarial hierarchy'. In the economic sphere the Left called for a rationalisation of state planning and a rapid increase in industrial investment, but they reserved the main thrust of their attack for a demand for a return to greater internal party democracy. In particular, they were concerned by the accumulation of power by the Orgbiuro (and Stalin) and the erosion of proper elections to party offices. In addition, after Stalin developed the concept of 'socialism in one country' in 1924, the Left were highly critical of what they saw as the party leadership's betrayal of the internationalist ideals of the October Revolution. There was also a large element of personal animosity and rivalry between the key players in this dispute.[18]

In Siberia, support for Trotsky was strongest in the party cells of institutes of higher education and in the military (a reflection of his appeal to the army and to the young) but some local party organisations also showed sympathy with his demands. For example, at the time of the Thirteenth Conference in January 1924, party officials in Irkutsk and Tomsk expressed solidarity with Trotsky's demands, and support for the party leadership was only restored when the Gubkom Secretaries returned from the conference. In the Omsk and Krasnoiarsk party organisations support for Trotsky persisted until well after the Thirteenth Congress in May 1924, with many local leaders opposing the Central Committee. In January, M. Trifonov, the head of the Agitprop Department of Krasnoiarsk Raikom, spoke of a 'conservative opportunist tendency' in the party leadership and pledged himself to fight for 'the idea of a Left communist course'.[19] The Sibbiuro, headed by Kosior, moved to restore order and in April a special joint plenum of the Enisei Gubkom and Control Commission expelled several prominent Leftists in Krasnoiarsk. The results of this plenum were forwarded to the Central Committee which responded by sending a special investigator, N. P. Rastopchin, to the area and Stalin personally reprimanded Kosior for allowing factionalism in the local party to get out of hand. Although discontent simmered in Krasnoiarsk throughout the rest of 1924, the Siberian leadership ensured that the Left did not gain a foothold in any other local party organisation.[20]

The unity of the regional party leadership was finally undermined by the 'New Opposition' of late 1925. Lashevich, Chairman of the Sibrevkom and a senior member of the Kraikom was a staunch supporter of Zinoviev but his promotion to Leningrad as Deputy Commissar for War in November removed his influence over the selection of Siberian delegates for the Fourteenth Congress. He was also powerless to prevent Kosior from convening a pre-congress meeting of Siberian delegates to work out in advance a united platform against Zinoviev's 'Leningrad Opposition' and, consequently, the vote of the Siberian delegation was secured for the Stalin–Bukharin line. The formation of the 'United Opposition' of Trotsky and Zinoviev in July 1926 and their renewed charges of bureaucratisation and a 'kulak danger' brought little immediate response from party organisations in Siberia. Organised factional activity only resumed in the region in late 1926, when several party groups were established following the visits of Opposition activists from Moscow and Leningrad. Once again it was an Opposition group in Omsk which proved the most intractable for the regional leadership, though other groups were formed in the Irkutsk, Novosibirsk and Tomsk party organisations. The Omsk group posed a serious danger for the Kraikom because it succeeded in winning significant support among the local party rank and file. In the elections of delegates to the Third Omsk Okrug Party Conference in January 1927, the Opposition distributed propaganda and electoral lists of its own candidates in working-class areas and the railroad workshops. Subsequently many of its candidates were elected and the debates at the conference were particularly heated. An important reason for its success was that it won over remnants of the Workers' Opposition which had a strong following in Omsk in the early 1920s. Once again the

Central Committee was compelled to despatch a special investigator–instructor, S. A. Bergavinov, to supervise the purge of Oppositionists and secure compliance to the policies of the central party leadership.[21]

In Irkutsk a group of Left Oppositionists was formed by several lecturers at the university (Ia. A. Furtichev, I. A. Bialyi, G. M. Kartashov) and it attracted support from the Central Workers' Cooperative, railroad workers and some officials in the Land Department of the local soviet. Most significantly, it was led by G. Ia. Belenky, a former member of the Presidium of the Irkutsk Okrispolkom who had previously worked in the Executive Committee of the Comintern, and was a close associate of Zinoviev. As in the rest of the country, the activities of these and other smaller groups in Siberia escalated in October–November 1927, in the build up to the Fifteenth Congress, though whether they were spontaneous local actions or coordinated by Opposition leaders at the centre is not certain. In Irkutsk, pre-congress official party meetings were disrupted and demonstrations held in support of the Left. In Novosibirsk, Syrtsov and the Okruzhkom Secretary, P. V. Klokov, were shouted down at party gatherings, and in Omsk the Left called for a general strike.[22]

The evidence available suggests that rank and file party or popular support for the Opposition in Siberia was localised and, given the enormous power of the party apparat, easily marginalised. At the same time, local leaders had a material interest in playing down the scale of oppositional activity within their fiefs in order to demonstrate their competence and efficiency at maintaining organisational discipline to the party line. The statement by V. S. Kalashnikov, the Head of the Krai Control Commission, to the Fifteenth Congress in December 1927 that the Siberian Opposition was 'so small that it was hardly worth mentioning', is a case in point.[23] In late 1927 an article in the main krai party journal, *Na Leninskom puti*, claimed that there were no more than thirty to forty Oppositionists in the whole of Siberia (though significantly this excluded Omsk) and offered the comprehensive statistics that, in the pre-congress party discussions, in 941 local cells, 27,972 members supported the Central Committee, 128 voted against and 134 abstained. Nevertheless, in Irkutsk in November, at the height of the struggle, Lashevich returned from Moscow (a move which suggests central coordination) to galvanise local support for the Left. He was greeted by a demonstration of supporters at the railway station and was told by Belenky that of the local party organisation, 'One-third are with the Opposition, one-third are vacillating and one-third are *chinovniki*.'[24] Following the rout of the Left at the Fifteenth Congress

leading Oppositionists were expelled from the Siberian party organisation. The scale of the purge carried out in Irkutsk suggests that
support for the Opposition in this area was considerable: 79 party
officials were sacked, 50 of whom were expelled from the party (13
were subsequently reinstated after suitably renouncing their former
opinions). As we shall see later, the question of the 'Leftism' of the
Irkutsk party organisation was to be a central feature of the 'Irkutsk
Affair' which erupted in the spring of 1928. Similar purges conducted
in Omsk, Novosibirsk, Tomsk and other areas of Opposition support,
testified to the complete domination of local party organisations by the
Kraikom and, above it, by the Central Committee in Moscow.[25]

The success of the Kraikom in containing factionalism was not due
only to its hierarchical control over party organisations, but also because the social composition of the membership of the Siberian party
organisation made it generally unreceptive to the policies of the Left
Opposition. The 'Platform of the Left' aimed to reduce bureaucratisation in the party and increase the proletarian content of its membership, to curb NEP by placing greater restrictions on the development of
private peasant agriculture and to quicken the pace of industrialisation. This programme represented an attack on the interests of the
two social strata which made up the bulk of the Siberian party membership, white-collar employees and peasants.[26]

Party structure and social composition

During the NEP period, the party launched a series of recruitment drives with the aims of replacing civil war losses and reju-
venating and expanding its membership throughout the country.
Accordingly, between 1 January 1924 and 1 January 1928, party
membership in the country at large increased almost threefold, from a
total of 472,000 to 1,304,471 members and candidates. The rate of
increase of the Siberian party membership was substantially lower
than this, almost doubling in size over the same period, rising from
38,697 to 74,484 members and candidates. The main goal of the party
leadership in these years was to raise the proletarian content of its
membership by increasing the recruitment of 'workers from the factory
floor'. In this respect there were two main recruitment drives during
this period: the 'Lenin' enrolments of early 1924 and 1925, and the
'October' enrolment of 1927. During 1924 to 1926, at the height of
NEP and the 'Face to the Countryside' policy, this goal was broadened

to include a major drive to extend party membership among the peasantry. One consequence of this massive influx of new recruits was that it altered the social profile of the party membership, which became increasingly characterised by youth, masculinity and low educational standards. This had significant political ramifications since, by comparison with the 'Old Bolshevik' cadres, such members were more likely to be deferential to the new authoritarianism which was emerging in the party under Stalin's leadership. However, by the end of 1926, Opposition charges that the recruitment effort had resulted in 'party degeneration' put the question of the social profile of the party at the head of the political agenda and the party leadership increasingly voiced concern at the high membership levels of employees and peasants and correspondingly low proletarian content.[27]

Given the nature of the Siberian economy and society, the industrial proletariat of the region was comparatively small and party recruitment here inevitably entailed the drawing in of large numbers of employees and peasants. The Siberian party organisation was overwhelmingly rural based in terms of the location of its cells. According to the party census of the spring of 1927 there were 3,112 cells containing 61,645 communists. Of these, only 519 (16.7%), holding 20,329 (33%) communists, were classified as worker cells; 459 (14.8%) with 15,339 (24.9%) members and candidates were institutional, educational, military and other; 439 candidate groups held 1,941 (3.1%) members and there were just over 100 individual communists. The mass of party cells, 2,134 (68.5%), were situated in the countryside and incorporated 23,933 (38.9%) members and candidates. Similarly, on 1 January 1928, of a total of 293 raikoms only 32 were urban-industrial (*gorpromraikomi*), the other 261 being rural (*sel'raikomi*).[28]

Research into the social composition of the local party was conducted by the Statistical Department of the Kraikom throughout the years 1927 to 1929. These studies categorised members by both 'social status' and 'type of occupation', reflecting the ambiguity of party policy as to which of these had the greater influence on the class consciousness of members. On 1 January 1928, the composition of the Siberian party by 'social status' was estimated at 39.2% workers, 43.5% peasant, 17.3% employees and others. However, the categorisation by 'type of employment' revealed a strikingly different profile, with 23.1% of party members classed as workers, 23.3% as peasants engaged exclusively in agriculture, 2.3% as agricultural labourers, while officials, employees and others accounted for 43.6% (and 7.7% who worked in rural areas). Thus, while rural cells represented over two-thirds of all types of party cell in the region, peasant farmers accounted for about one-quarter of party membership strength. The latter figure was one of the highest in the country and compared with a USSR average of just 9.8%. Furthermore, there were significant intra-regional variations in party membership. A study of the social composition of okrug party organisations in early 1928 disclosed that there was a wide disparity between different areas which reflected the nature of their social make up. The okrugs of the main agricultural area of south-west Siberia had the largest contingent of members classified as peasants by occupation (on average about one-third of the total), with the highest levels in Slavgorod (35.5%), Kamensk (35.4%), Biisk (34.3%), Rubtsovsk (33.8%) and Barabinsk (30.8%).[29]

According to the official data it was clear that party officials formed the core of members who were classified as 'employees and others', both by social origin and current occupation. The further up the party hierarchy one looks, the more obvious this becomes. For example, in 1927 at the pinnacle of the krai party organisation, of 69 members and candidates of the Kraikom, 56.5% were classed as workers by 'social status', 39% as employees and only 4.5% as peasants. Considering that categorisation by occupation is a more accurate reflection of social composition, the above figures for workers and peasants on the Kraikom are undoubtedly exaggerated as, obviously, full-time party officials were employees by occupation. A detailed statistical breakdown of the social profile of plenums, bureaus and secretaries of Siberian party committees published in early 1928 classified office holders by both social status *and* occupation, and illustrates the increasing bureaucratisation of the party apparat in the provinces in this period. The study revealed that of a total of 282 secretaries in 1927, all were full-time employees by occupation with the exception of just 6 (2.6%) out of 233 secretaries of sel'raikoms, who were peasants. The representation of workers and peasants by occupation increased at the bureau and, in particular, at the infrequently called and less powerful plenum levels. In sel'raikoms peasants constituted only 18% of members of bureaus but 36.8% of members of plenums, while on gorpromraikoms workers accounted for just over 22% of bureau members and almost 38% of plenum members. However, an overwhelming 77% of members of bureaus of sel'raikoms and almost 55% of members of plenums, and 77.8% of members of bureaus of gorpromraikoms and almost 60% of plenums were categorised as 'others' (mostly employees). A very different picture is drawn by the categorisation of officials by social origins which presents a vastly increased proportion of workers and peasants and greatly diminishes the representation of employees and others.[30]

That the Siberian party organisation was led by a predominantly younger breed of official is demonstrated by the fact that in 1927 over 95% of party secretaries in the region were aged under 40, as were 82%–83.5% of members and candidates of all committees to raikom level. Since important office-bearers were mainly those members with a party status dating from before 1920, this included 97% of the Kraikom elected by the Third Krai Party Conference in March 1927 and, in the same period, over 75% of the membership of okruzhkoms, almost 57% of those on gorpromraikoms and about 54% of sel'raikom members. As with other areas, the Siberian party was predominantly masculine, and poorly educated. There were only 8,330 (10.8%) female members and candidates on 1 January 1928, and although there was a Women's Department in the Secretariat of the Kraikom, only about 2% of party secretaries of all types were women. The level of education of party members was atrociously low and given the increasing bureaucratic complexity of the apparat in the NEP period, this presented a major problem. In 1927, less than 1% of all communists in the country had completed higher education, and the lowest standard of all was in village cells and committees. In Siberia even senior level officials were barely literate, as, for example, of 21 okruzhkom secretaries only 6 had middle level education while 15 had only attained primary level education. This raises serious questions as to their competence in dealing with administrative tasks. Even here it is quite possible that these figures may have been distorted, intentionally or not, in order to present a better picture of the state of the party. Syrtsov told a story of one party official who, when asked to state his level of education at a krai party conference, wrote 'middle' and when asked to say why, declared that he was not illiterate but had no formal education either. The Kraikom attempted to raise the political literacy of members by organising special courses and party schools but by early 1928 less than half the communists in the region had attended. The situation was exacerbated by the fact that Kraikom instructors, who were supposedly in charge of party education, found themselves increasingly tied down by bureaucratic chores, preparing about 40,000 Kraikom documents of various kinds in 1927.[31]

In conclusion, the political preferences of the Siberian party were to a large extent determined by two facts; firstly, a substantial minority of its membership and the great mass of its cells were concentrated in the countryside, and secondly, the business of the region was overwhelmingly agriculture. Furthermore, many recruits were relative new-comers as, by 1 January 1927, over 46% of Siberian party members and over 38% of members of sel'raikoms had joined since 1924. As one scholar noted, the practical effect of the party recruitment drives in the peak years of NEP was that rural organisations 'were composed largely of peasants for whom the CPSU was the party of encouragement for private peasant enterprise'.[32] The statistical evidence from Siberia supports the Left Opposition charge that the proletarian base of the party had been undermined by a flood of recruits from white-collar workers and peasants under the auspices of NEP. However, their claim that rural party organisations suffered from 'kulak' infiltration and their propositions on peasant differentiation and the nature of the 'kulak' danger in general, are much harder to substantiate due to difficulties in defining class categories in the countryside. The thorny question of the scale of peasant differentiation will be examined in chapter 3. It is to the equally problematic issue of the extent to which rural party organisations were 'infiltrated' by kulaks that we now turn.[33]

Party control of the rural soviets

Although a declared aim of the Bolshevik regime during NEP was the establishment of elected but party dominated rural soviets (*sel'soveti*) as the pivot of local institutional authority in the country-side, the adherence of the peasantry to traditional forms of self-organisation in the village commune proved difficult to surmount. The continuity of the authority of the communal gathering (*zemel'nye skhodi*), the regular meeting of male heads of peasant households, and its predominance over the rural soviet brought leading Siberian party officials to express fears of a situation of 'dual power' developing in the region. Indeed, Western studies have shown that, contrary to the aims of party policy and legislation, the functions of the rural soviet as regards the everyday administration of peasant life were usurped by the gathering.[34]

The VTsIK RSFSR decree of 1925 which reorganised the administration of Siberia ordered a norm of one rural soviet per 600 inhabitants, but by late 1926, when 5,871 had been established, each was responsible for an average population of 1,300 persons. Considering that village communes on the steppes of south-west Siberia were exceptionally large, often composed of several hundred households, a rural soviet in this region encompassed a much smaller number of villages (approximately three to five) within its territorial jurisdiction than the average of nine for the RSFSR. Whether this facilitated better control of the countryside by the rural soviets is debatable. It could be argued that the greater the symbiotic relationship between the two, the greater the possibility that the communal gathering would subvert the rural soviet and transform it into a veneer of party–state control. The legal division of powers between both institutions was suitably ambiguous. The Land Code of 1922 charged the communal gathering with the administration of all land and agricultural matters within its area. However, the decree on the rural soviets passed in 1924 imposed upon them similar duties of rural administration and the provision of services. The successful implementation of these responsibilities had two essential requirements which, in general, rural soviets lacked: adequate finances and efficient personnel.[35]

Only a fraction of rural soviets (4% in Siberia) had their own budget. Their officers were characterised by low education and cultural standards, endemic corrupt practices and drunkenness. Further, the bad pay and low prestige of rural soviet posts were a major disincentive and greatly impeded efforts to attract a better quality of administrator. Maynard shrewdly observed that sometimes a man was elected to a rural soviet simply 'to spite him'. It was generally recognised that the low pay of rural officials made them highly susceptible to bribes from the well-off peasantry. According to official figures, in 1926 the average monthly salaries of chairmen and secretaries of rural soviets in the USSR varied from 6 to 15 roubles per month. By comparison, Siberian rural soviet officials received a pittance due to under funding from central government, for in early 1928 the annual average pay of a Siberian raiispolkom chairman was only 70 roubles and the chairman of a rural soviet could expect the paltry sum of just 12–18 roubles per annum. Low pay must have been a significant contributory factor in the high turnover of rural soviet officials which persisted throughout these years, with annual rates of 50%–60% common in south-west Siberia in the mid-1920s. This further undermined the credibility of such officials in the eyes of the peasantry.[36]

Not surprisingly, in order to simply subsist most officials had to supplement their pay from other sources, and this opened the door to all kinds of corrupt activities. The corruption of local officials was usually directed towards the circumvention of laws penalising kulak farms, such as restrictions on the leasing of land, hiring of labour and purchase of machinery. Thus, in 1927 only about half of Siberian batraks worked under written agreements registered with the rural soviets as required by law. A common ruse for avoiding the labour laws which the rural soviets generally turned a blind eye to was the faked 'adoption' of young batraks who were condemned to a life of indentured servitude on well-off peasant farms. In Kuznetsk Okrug there were instances when even the buying and selling of batraks was formalised by rural soviet documentation.[37]

In contrast to the rural soviet, the communal gathering, the regular assembly of the male heads of farming households in a given area, attracted the best, most respected and well-off local peasants for its elected offices. It had its own source of funding in self-taxation (*samooblozhenie*), which involved all peasants voluntarily contributing to the administrative costs of the village commune. There was certainly a large degree of social pressure in the financing and functioning of the communal gathering but attempts at state control under NEP failed ignominiously. From late 1926 the party stepped up its attempts to undermine the influence of the communal gathering and strengthen its power in the countryside. At the political level this entailed eliminating kulak influence in the rural soviets by disenfranchising them, and replacing the authority of the communal gathering by that of a village gathering (*sel'skii skhod*) where kulaks were excluded because only those with the franchise could participate. In practice, the authorities were still unable to draw peasants away from their traditional structures as the village gathering often became subjugated to and synonymous with the communal gathering and kulaks continued to dominate its proceedings. Another important factor in the failure of the party to control rural affairs in this period was the sheer isolation of most rural communities in Siberia, and their inaccessibility and remoteness facilitated a culture of inertia to permeate rural soviet and party officialdom.[38]

One reason for the unwillingness of the peasantry to accord the rural soviet the sort of reverence they attached to the communal gathering was the fact that they saw the soviet as part of the state governmental structure and an 'outside' imposition on their way of life. The duties of the rural soviet in regard to tax assessment, establishing lists of kulaks, disenfranchisement and general law and order in the countryside reinforced peasant resentment. Shanin has distinguished rural soviet office-holders as part of the 'rural salariat' group of 'outsiders' who were seen as suspect by the peasantry. Yet we must be careful not to draw too sharp a distinction between these groups and the peasantry as in many cases there would have been a considerable overlap between the two. A particular hostility was felt towards urban party plenipotentiaries sent to the countryside to act as 'shock workers' in the implementation of party campaigns.[39]

The presence of an influential and economically powerful kulak stratum in the Siberian countryside was regarded by the party as a major threat to its political control of the peasantry. The kulaks were the natural leaders in the countryside, the most well-off and best educated farmers, held in high esteem by some but certainly in jealous regard by most peasants. To protect their economic hegemony in the countryside inevitably involved them in political activity, dominating the communal gathering, undermining the authority of the rural soviet and taking advantage of state benefits under NEP while encouraging non-cooperation with measures aimed at consolidating state control in the countryside. The actions of the kulak farmers, whether economic or political, must be seen as mutual protection of their interests against an assault by the Bolshevik regime, particularly as this gathered pace in 1927. Carr proposed that Siberia 'seems to have been the paradise of the politically minded kulak'.[40] In 1924–5, at the height of the pro-peasant economic and political programme, a major goal of the party was to widen the process of peasant voting and participation as non-party representatives in local soviets. The evidence from Siberia suggests that the party campaigns were self-defeating, since, coupled with the relative political liberalisation of these years, they served merely to heighten the political activity of the well-off and most anti-communist section of the peasantry. In 1925–6 peasant political activity in the region reassumed the hostile posture of 1921 and there was an attempt to revive the SR inclined 'Siberian Peasant Union'. This was received with substantial sympathy in south-west Siberia where thousands of peasants signed petitions demanding a return to the multi-party system so that the 'Peasant Union' could be given legal status as a political party.[41]

The wave of anti-Bolshevik opinion seems to have reached a peak during the election campaign for the rural soviets in 1925, when the party denounced 'kulaks' for stirring up peasant unrest under the slogan 'soviets without communists'. The raised political awareness of the Siberian peasantry was reflected in the sharp increase in voter turnout at the elections, rising from 31.4% in 1924 to just over 50% in 1925, with peasant participation almost trebling. The results of the elections were a considerable success for the Siberian kulaks as, according to official reports, they won about 10% of the seats in the Altai. One Siberian party official described the post-election climate of demoralisation and anxiety among some local communists in stark terms:

'their state of mind was distracted, even panic-stricken. The turn of the party's "Face to the Countryside" shocked them. It seemed a dangerous retreat before the kulak element, a step far more important and hazardous than NEP.'[42] Although the party intended to reduce its own membership content of rural soviets, the final outcome in Siberia was particularly disastrous given that the party leavening in the soviets there was already much lower than the average for the whole country. Therefore, while party representation was cut by almost one-half (12% to 7%) over the whole country, in Siberia it fell from 9.5% of members in 1924 to 4.8% in 1925.[43]

In the wake of these poor results, repeated across the country, the party took action to limit the influence of the well-off peasantry in the elections of 1926–7 by stringently enforcing the disenfranchisement of kulaks. The central authorities decided against allowing local control of this and arbitrarily instructed that a quota of approximately 3% to 4% of the better-off peasants be disenfranchised, as opposed to the level of around 1% imposed in 1925–6. In Siberia the level of disenfranchisement rose accordingly, from just under 1% to about 3%, but in rural areas of the krai the number denied the vote surged by over five times, from 15,341 to over 86,000. This campaign led to bitter clashes in the krai party leadership over how kulaks were to be assessed and gave added impetus to the series of studies on peasant differentiation being undertaken by the Kraikom at this time.[44]

The Kraikom plenum of December 1926 prepared the ground for the soviet elections of spring 1927 and Eikhe exhorted local officials to ensure that not a single kulak be elected to the rural soviets. Syrtsov, on the other hand, in a pamphlet published in early 1927 and intended for party officials, took a different stance and condemned electoral abuses and excesses in disenfranchisement. He revealed that some local electoral committees had disqualified as many as 15%–20% and, in one case, 36% of village inhabitants eligible to vote. Syrtsov discussed his experiences of the disenfranchisement campaign encountered during a tour of some villages in the company of an okruzhkom secretary. They told local officials that 2% or 3% of households in the raion were likely to be kulaks, only to discover later that after their departure 2% to 3% of the well-off seredniaks in these villages had been automatically denounced as kulaks. The pressure on local officials to expose kulaks was such that in one village seredniaks, including the chairman of the rural soviet, temporarily assumed the title of kulaks in order to fulfil their quotas. The party attempted to conduct the election campaign under the political slogan of organising

the 'bedniak–seredniak bloc'; however, at the grassroots soviet and
party officials generally misunderstood or were ignorant of what this
meant.[45]

The party not only had to deal with the ignorance of local officials but
also with active resistance by the well-off peasants who were threatened with disenfranchisement as kulaks. Local electoral committee
members were frequently assaulted and terrorised. In Krasnoiarsk
Okrug kulaks used their economic muscle to retain voting rights by
threatening to leave the cooperatives. Perhaps the greatest difficulty
facing the party was its failure to stir up class antagonisms among the
peasantry, for the poor were reluctant to quarrel with their well-off
neighbours for whom they worked or from whom they rented implements, animals, machines, seed and so on. In parts of Barnaul Okrug,
the well-off peasants supported only bedniak candidates in the soviet
elections because they were easily manipulated and allowed the well-
off to maximise their influence over the soviets.[46]

The exertions of the Siberian party in the election campaign of 1927
successfully restored its representation on rural soviets to the level of
1924. Of the 76,584 deputies elected to 5,835 rural soviets in the krai,
6,958 (9.1%) were party members, 3,391 (4.4%) Komsomol members
and 17,690 (23.1%) ex-Red Army personnel. More importantly, the
party stranglehold on positions of authority in the soviets progress-
ively increased up the hierarchy of control. Whereas only 29% of
chairmen of rural soviets were party members, 99% of raiispolkom
chairmen were in the party. Nevertheless, the fact that over 45% of
members of raiispolkoms, 30% of okriispolkoms and 28% of the Kraiispolkom were non-party meant that there was a potential for opposition
and inertia in the implementation of party directives on the countryside even at senior levels. The most glaring organisational deficiency of
all was that more than half the rural soviets in the region had no party
cell, and in West Siberia about two-thirds had none, and therefore
were effectively outside party control. A German academic specialist
on Siberia, travelling in the Altai in early 1928, claimed that the rural
soviets were 'thought to be too dependent on the village psychology
[dorfpsyche], and thus on the strong peasants, to be fully accepted by
the party'.[47]

One sector where the rural soviets played a key role in the party's
attempts to exercise control of the countryside was in the nurturing of
cooperatives and the dispersion of credit. By the mid-1920s the appre-
hensions as regards the problem of kulak domination were being felt in
these areas also, in addition to increasing concern at the growth of the

cooperative bureaucratic apparat. An illustration of how this burgeon-
ing bureaucracy directly affected the peasantry was revealed by
Syrtsov to the Third Krai Party Conference, when he told of how a local
credit union in Barnaul had to fill in three pounds of forms to apply for
a simple land improvement grant. In late 1926 Syrtsov published a
pamphlet titled 'Bureaucracy and Bureaucrats', outlining his frus-
tration at the 'colossal hypertrophy' of the cooperative bureaucracy
and disquiet at its political conservatism and failure to implement party
directives. He vilified its lower level apparat for the regular cases of
misdemeanours, such as embezzlement and drunkenness. The shortage of qualified staff was a major weakness here, as in other areas of
government, since over one-third of cooperative officials had less than
one year's experience and many areas had a 100% turnover in staff
each year. Following central directives the Kraikom attempted to
reduce cooperative staffing levels by 20%–25%, and the excess were
dismissed by Syrtsov as 'locusts, ballast, useless officials'. He stated
that the aim was to clean out the 'rump of old *chinovniki*' and other
'socially alien' officials and to ensure that 'politically conscious peasants' were elected to the boards of cooperatives in the villages. It is
worth noting that the central cooperative bureaucracy was mostly
staffed by non-communist intellectuals, many of whom were former
SRs and reluctant to support Bolshevik policy, and the same was
probably true at the regional level. Nonetheless, the cutbacks and
political cleansing of the cooperatives failed to materialise and, as
Syrtsov himself admitted a year later, the policy remained
unimplemented.[48]

As for the main worry exercising the minds of the party leadership
that the cooperatives were being controlled and exploited by kulaks, a
Siberian delegate struck a common chord of resentment when he
warned the session of VTsIK in October 1925 that 'old speculators and
traders quickly worm their way into the cooperatives'.[49] The Kraikom,
at the behest of the central party leadership, repeatedly issued directives demanding the ejection of kulaks from the boards of cooperatives, only to find that they went unheeded or were obstructed by the
lower cooperative apparat. This inertia was contributed to by the
Siberian party leadership itself, for while it issued directives to improve the social profile of the boards of cooperatives by increasing the
representation of bedniaks and communists, ambiguity prevailed
when it came to whether the well-off most productive sections of the
peasantry should be excluded from the cooperatives altogether. Syrtsov told the Third Krai Party Conference, 'even though they are kulaks

we must bring them into the cooperatives'.[50] In contrast, Eikhe made clear his resolute opposition to any kulak participation in the cooperatives in his main report on agriculture at the conference. He quoted Sibsel'kredit figures which showed that the 8.6% of well-off peasants (those sowing 8 or more desiatinas) received 10% of all credit and accounted for 22% of total purchases of equipment. In the case of the most useful and expensive item of agricultural machinery, the tractor, Eikhe claimed that although only 2% of the 612 in the krai were owned by individual peasants, many more were held by machine societies acting as a cover for individual kulak purchases.[51]

The entrenched position of the kulaks in the Siberian cooperative and credit system was brought to the attention of the central party leadership in early 1927 when the Central Committee instructor, S. Bergavinov, reported on the flagrant abuses of the Omsk party organisation in this respect. This was followed by a Rabkrin investigation of ten raions in Omsk Okrug in late 1927 which found that of 18 machine-tractor societies, with a membership of 180 peasants, 9 (5%) were batraks, 50 (27.7%) bedniaks, 56 (31.1%) seredniaks, and 65 (36.2%) kulaks. Around the same time a Kraikom report into 300 machine societies in Omsk revealed that 76% of the membership were kulaks or well-off peasants. One of the allegations frequently levied in these investigations was that the kulaks operated 'pseudo-cooperatives' or 'bogus cooperatives' in order to claim credit and purchase machines but which in reality were a front for private enterprise activities.[52]

The mid-1920s were paradisaical years of access to easy money for the peasantry as the State Bank (Gosbank), the All-Russian Agricultural Bank (Vsekobank) and the Agricultural Bank (Sibsel'kredit) offered long lines of credit. In addition, by 1 October 1927, 633 credit unions had been established in the krai, with over 440,000 peasant members in debt to the state to the tune of 36.7 million roubles. In 1927–8 the countryside was literally awash with money as the total sum of agricultural credit dispensed increased from 11.3 million to 29.6 million roubles, of which 60% went to collectives and cooperatives and 40% to individual borrowers. Defaulting on loans was a widespread problem and in early 1928 the state had a deficit of 1.3 million roubles of repayments. Rather than tighten procedures, the party decided to raise the proportion of long-term credit granted from 21.8% of the total in 1926–7 to over 54% in 1927–8. Arrears were bound to mount given that poor peasants, that is to say those least likely to manage repayments, were supposed to receive 50% of all credit issued, mainly for consumer purchases. Gradually, the faith of the party in this type of munificence dissolved as it dawned on them that they were pouring scarce resources into a bottomless pit of peasant demand and corruption, and it became apparent that the main beneficiaries of credit and the cooperatives were the well-off and kulak peasants.[53] It seems likely that kulaks resorted to underhand methods not only as a means of manipulating state credit for their own ends but also because as individuals they were denied access to the kind of expensive advanced machinery that they needed to farm profitably. Furthermore, considering the huge sums of money slushing around the system it is not surprising that there were financial irregularities. In Barnaul Okrug alone in 1927–8, 4 to 5 million roubles was available on credit. Gradually, the party tightened up procedures and from late 1927 a plethora of exemplary corruption scandals, often involving ties between rural soviet and communist officials and the kulaks, were brought to light and given wide publicity. In this process the Irkutsk Okruzhkom seems to have taken the lead as two of the most notorious prosecutions occurred there.[54]

The winter of 1927–8 brought the grain procurements crisis and with that a sharpening in the hostility of the party towards the kulaks. Whereas previously credit had often been distributed under the sensible business slogan of, 'to the most creditworthy, the most credit', in January 1928 the party line confirmed the more politically orientated slogan, 'the kulak must not receive a single kopeck'.[55] To comply with a VTsIK RSFSR decree of October 1927, the Kraikom ordered a general review of the workings of the cooperative system and the reregistration of all its associations by 1 July 1928. This was intended to purge the system of pseudo-cooperatives, and was particularly aimed at southwest Siberia, but as late as 1929 kulaks in Omsk were still receiving credit and supplies of machines.[56]

The rural communists

Rural communists in Siberia deserve particular attention considering that the regional party organisation was predominantly rural based in terms of its cells, and had a high peasant membership profile in comparison with other areas of the country. They also had a crucial impact on the implementation of policy in the countryside as they were supposedly the front line troops of the party. The greatest concentration of rural cells in Siberia was in the main grain okrugs of the south west where the ratio to total cells was 221 of 287 in Barnaul, 235 of 283 in Biisk, 116 of 151 in Rubtsovsk and 122 of 137 in Slavgorod. In the mid-1920s a typical party cell in the Soviet countryside had 4 to 6 members, distributed over several villages, perhaps 10 or 15 kilometres apart. The huge distances in Siberia meant that rural cells were larger and more isolated, averaging 9 members responsible for a dozen or more villages, often dispersed over tens of kilometres and in some cases hundreds. Generally, rural committees were composed of 9 to 11 members and a bureau of about five but daily administrative duties were normally undertaken by a working 'committees of three' (*troiki*) of the secretary and two assistants. A raikom incorporated an average of 11 party cells with around 150 communists from approximately 1,000 settlements, but there were wide intra-regional disparities. Syrtsov told the Third Krai Party Conference in March 1927 that rural cells in many areas were so small that they were formed by single families or a clique of relatives and were known by family names.[57]

As a tier of party control in the countryside rural communists suffered from weaknesses similar to those exhibited by rural soviet officials: isolation, low literacy, a lack of understanding of their responsibilities, low morale, inertia, drunkenness, and subjection to domination and infiltration by the well-off peasant stratum. A survey of Siberian sel'raikom officials conducted in October 1927 revealed that 86.2% had only primary education, 7.6% middle, 5.8% were educated 'at home' and a negligible 0.4% had received higher education. This unsatisfactory state of affairs was confirmed by a Central Control Commission investigation of 120 party cells in West Siberia carried out in 1927, which found an extremely low level of political and educational literacy, particularly in rural areas, with many communists unable to understand party rules, programmes, instructions, newspapers or journals. However, the Siberian Control Commission report to the Third Krai Party Conference noted that while the rural organisations suffered from poor educational standards the main 'sickness' at this level was drunkenness.[58]

The massive recruitment campaigns in the countryside in the mid-1920s meant that by 1 January 1927 around 38% of sel'raikom members had joined the party since 1924. Given the official encouragement for private enterprise in the countryside at this time, it was natural that the party attracted the best and better-off peasant farmers into its ranks. The Central Control Commission ordered a series of studies into Siberian rural party organisations in this period and arrived at the conclusion that the role of the well-off peasantry was dangerously excessive. One of these studies, conducted in 1926, disclosed that 49% of rural communists in the cells investigated were 'economically secure' and distinguished by their use of modern farming techniques, advanced equipment and hired labour, compared with estimates of 17% of rural communists in the country as a whole and 21% in the North Caucasus, a similar major agricultural area. The party leadership was sensitive to the charge of 'kulak infiltration' of rural cells made by the Left Opposition and, although the scale of this was downplayed, campaigns were launched to ensure a proper social content of rural organisations through increased recruitment of the rural poor, and the purging of 'class alien' or 'socially degenerate' (i.e. kulak) communists. However, not much progress was made in this respect since the practical implementation of this policy on the ground was left to rural cells that were often dominated by the very communists from the well-off stratum that were targeted for expulsion.[59]

The exasperation felt by party leaders at the independence of rural communists from regional control, let alone central, was vented by Syrtsov in early 1927 when he complained that 'party organisations in the countryside still do not live a full life in the party' and condemned a 'significant part' of rural cells for their stagnation, freezing of membership recruitment and political inertia.[60] Notwithstanding this sort of criticism, Syrtsov remained anxious to ensure that the Siberian party's reputation for 'kulak' influence was not tarnished any further than official reports and the Left had already achieved. The Kraikom Conference on Rural Affairs held in March 1927 rather tentatively decided that many peasant communists were beginning 'to exceed the limits of seredniak labouring farms' by hiring permanent labour, renting out machines and money-lending.[61] Shortly afterwards, at the Third Krai Party Conference, Syrtsov sent out mixed signals in his keynote address. He attempted to neutralise claims made by Siberian elements of the Left Opposition about 'kulak growth' by asserting that they had exaggerated the political and economic power of the kulak stratum, yet he himself talked of a 'commonwealth of cooperation' between the kulaks and the party in the countryside.[62] R. Ia. Kisis, the Latvian Second-Secretary of the Kraikom, responded to criticisms of the Kraikom leadership by apportioning blame for campaign failures on the lower levels of the party hierarchy and admitted that the rural cell 'in essence, does not control our economic work in the countryside'.[63] The conference passed several resolutions on the need to reactivate rural cells and fully integrate them into the party machinery but that these resolutions remained on paper only was recognised by Syrtsov several months later, in July 1927, when he appealed to the Siberian organisation to 'act with more fervour' (oginaias'), fearing that negligent and slipshod work over the summer period would imperil party operations in the countryside during the coming autumn and winter.[64]

In the course of 1927 the party outlined two main functions for rural communists. Firstly, rural cells were instructed to draw up lists of the different economic categories of peasants within their jurisdiction, note yearly changes in status and rigorously enforce party directives and Soviet laws to protect the poor peasants and penalise the kulaks. Secondly, they were the key actors in the implementation of the campaigns to enliven class antagonisms and rejuvenate the party in the countryside by expelling 'kulak-communists' and expanding the recruitment of bedniaks and batraks. Until the height of the grain crisis, and Stalin's tour of Siberia in January–February 1928, these functions were fulfilled in a passive manner not only by the rank and file peasant communists but also by many officials. Although formally rural party organisations were required to keep lists of kulaks and purge 'socially alien' elements from their ranks, it is clear from the frequency of Kraikom directives on this policy that it was widely ignored. From the autumn of 1927 the krai party leadership adopted a harsher posture and inactive, negligent or otherwise obstructionist rural communists were regularly branded 'kulak accomplices'. Party pronouncements generally characterised the situation as one where rural cells were 'falling for kulak bait', with rampant bribery of village communists to ensure their collaboration with the kulaks.[65] The evidence suggests that many of the communists so accused were peasants who had built up their farms under NEP, in the years of party encouragement for individual peasant enterprise, and who became a political embarrassment for the party as it turned its back on this policy.

The fact that about one-third of Siberian party strength was made up of peasants exclusively engaged in agriculture or combining farming with an official post or other employment, and that the krai party leadership constantly droned on about the degeneration of rural cells at this time, suggests that a large number of rural communists fell into the well-off or kulak stratum. Several types of 'kulak-communist' from different areas of Siberia, who were expelled from the party and disenfranchised during the soviet election campaign of 1926–7, were described in an article by an outspoken Right-wing party critic of the anti-kulak policy, Parfenov, in *Na Leninskom puti* in November 1927. His selective and prejudicial account of kulak expulsions drew on examples from local party organisations that were uncompromising in their implementation of party directives on this matter. In so doing, he unintentionally underscored the extent to which rural communists were intertwined with the well-off stratum of the peasantry.[66]

Parfenov concentrated on the high levels of activism of those denounced and their past services to the party but was vague or ignored the scale of their economic activities which had brought the wrath of the party down on them in the first place. For example, in the village of Zykovo, Pankrushikhinsk Raion, Kamensk Okrug, which had been one of the most committed to the Red partisan movement in 1919, 67 out of 311 households (just under one quarter of the total) were branded as kulaks. Similarly, in the village of Len'ki, Blagoveshchensk Raion, Slavgorod Okrug, 82 of 600 households were disenfranchised, including the communists Gritsek and Babinov. They had been elected to soviet and cooperative posts several times and were active officials. Another communist, Tikhon Krivosheev was disenfranchised even though two of his sons held commands in the Red Army (the eldest was a decorated party member). His family was known throughout the district for its party activism, his sons were prominent members of the Komsomol and his wife was a member of the rural soviet. Krivosheev was a blacksmith by trade but he had been listed as a kulak for operating a small mill. He had subsequently sold the mill but his rights were still not restored. In another case, the secretary of the party cell in the village of Elban', Ordinsk Raion, Novosibirsk Okrug, was disenfranchised and refused entry to the collective farm by the raikom, because his farm was 'economically overgrown'.[67]

Frequently, the response of peasant communists denounced as kulaks was to change the nature and scale of their farming activities, albeit unwillingly, to conform with party strictures and in the hope of regaining their political rights (and perhaps also from a fear of future penalties). For example, the communist Kononov, from the village of Sidorovka, Kamensk Okrug, was the first in the area to apply fodder grass cultivation and was literate and well-read. His son was active in the Komsomol, and eight years previously had been sent by the *volost-kom* to study in Barnaul and he was now a Red Professor at the Communist University in Sverdlovsk. In the hope that his rights would be restored Kononov had reduced his sowings to ten desiatinas, sold his 'surplus' horse and two 'surplus' cows. Similarly, the farm of the Pushko brothers in the village of Zlatopol', Slavgorod Okrug, had twenty-three family members and was considered an exemplary communist household. The eldest brother was regarded as the best chairman of a rural soviet in the okrug and two of the young boys in the family were Komosomol leaders in the village. The brothers were disenfranchised because they had hired labour for three years, and in response they stopped their party and soviet work and subdivided their farm into four. Whereas formerly they had paid annual state taxes of 200 roubles, now they paid none at all. The peasant communist Glushko, in the settlement of Novogolubchinskii, Kamensk Okrug, had migrated to Siberia from Chernigov Guberniia in the Ukraine in 1909. He had arrived penniless but after fifteen years hard work had built up a reasonable farm of the strong seredniak type: two horses, two cows and some agricultural equipment, berry trees and a small orchard. Glushko applied modern agricultural techniques on his farm and produced seed which was distributed by the Raion Agronomical Station. Peasants from other areas even came to him for advice. He had never used hired labour until 1926, when he employed a young batrak girl for the season and consequently was listed as a kulak. Thereafter, he reduced his sowings to 8 desiatinas, uprooted his orchard and berry trees and broke up his covered farmyard. Now disenchanted with the regime, he wanted to move further east to the Amur region or Sakhalin.[68]

Such rural communists must have felt a deep sense of betrayal by the party as they saw themselves derided by a state for which they had worked and often fought. The inability to comprehend the rationale for the party campaign against the well-off peasantry was plainly stated by the peasant communist Kostrichenko in the village of Konyrai, Irkutsk Okrug: 'Why have I been put on the same level as the kulaks? Kolchak ravaged my farm, Kolchak shot my father, I shed my blood for Soviet power. For four years I was in the Red Army. Like a worm I dug the earth, day and night, with my own labour I expanded my farm.' Kostrichenko sowed 16 to 18 desiatinas, owned 4 horses, 4 cows, 20 sheep, 3 pigs, had an iron roof on his house and good outbuildings. He also owned a harvester personally and a thresher jointly with a fellow villager. Not surprisingly, for this wealth he had been listed as a kulak and disenfranchised.[69]

The anti-kulak policy was a two-edged sword for the party as, on the one hand, it may have restricted somewhat the productive capacity of the well-off communist peasant households and made some inroads into party-kulak ties, but it also created a core of disaffected and politically aware peasants. Furthermore, in the short term, it often served to considerably worsen the plight of the poor peasantry who, given their dependence on the well-off, were the first victims of a contraction in kulak economic activities. When one secretary of a rural cell in the village of Krutinsk, Omsk Okrug, was taken to task by a trade union plenipotentiary for hiring a batrak girl without a labour agreement, he harshly replied, 'in that case you can take her and feed her, because I don't need her'.[70]

In the Soviet countryside there was an instinctive prejudice among the well-off peasants to look upon the rural poor as indolent good-for-nothings, a feeling sometimes shared by party leaders. Kosior's statement at the Fourteenth Congress exemplified this attitude when, rejecting Lashevich's allegations of kulak exploitation in Siberia, he remarked: 'Surely you know that among the rural poor there is a definite per cent who, in general, do not work at anything, who can simply be called loafers.'[71] Under NEP, party policy increasingly focussed on the need to raise the productive level of poor peasant farms through cooperation and state credit, as well as protecting them from exploitation by the well-off through stringent enforcement of legal restrictions on the hiring of labour. Essential to the realisation of these goals was the strengthening of the political and social cohesion of the rural poor under the direction of rural communists. In 1924–6 the party adopted measures designed to strengthen Peasant Committees of Mutual Aid (Krestkomy) which provided a welfare safety net in the countryside by a range of activities; dispensing seed and loaning implements at preferential rates, creating work and developing co-operation. Whereas the Krestkomy remained a generally dormant instrument of party policy in the mid-1920s, as we shall see later, they were stirred into action by Stalin in January–February 1928 for the purpose of seizing grain during the procurements crisis.[72]

The pivot of the political organisation of the poor lay in the bednota groups formed in October 1925 at the direction of the Central Committee. They were intended to be the political lever by which rural soviets would be delivered from the influence of the well-off peasantry. Later, from late 1926, the party attempted to increase its recruitment of members from the batraks and bedniaks. The repetitive pattern of directives from the Siberian Kraikom on these issues in 1926–8 demonstrates the singular lack of success in the implementation of this policy at the local level. Party work in this field was hampered by the fact that the bednota were the most illiterate and downtrodden peasants, and rural cells dominated in the main by the well-off peasantry were unwilling to work with those they considered 'idlers', never mind recruit them as party members. As a result, on 1 January 1928 of over 79,000 communists in Siberia only about 2% were batraks.[73]

The lack of political will to organise the bednota in Siberia seems to have extended right up to the krai party leadership. At the Kraikom plenum in October 1927 a directive from the central party leadership to hold raion and okrug conferences of bednota was discussed. Syrtsov acknowledged that the countryside was becoming 'more and more difficult to lead' and paid lip-service to the idea that the bednota groups could become 'an immediate reserve from which we can draw strength for replenishing our party ranks in the countryside'.[74] However, the majority of those present felt that these conferences were a waste of time and opposed the very principle of engaging in political work among the poor peasantry. At the Fifteenth Congress in December Molotov was highly critical of the Siberian party leadership on this account, particularly since the region had been singled out as one of high peasant differentiation and thus had a greater political need for such measures. N. N. Zimin, the Irkutsk party leader, must have embarrassed some of his Kraikom colleagues by revealing to the congress that some of them also wanted to liquidate the Krestkomy altogether. Whatever the extent of intra-party political differences on the organisation of the rural poor, perhaps a more straightforward explanation for the lack of attention to this question was suggested in the annual report of the Barnaul Okruzhkom. This complained that the party was over-burdened by other issues and campaigns – the struggle with the Opposition, the kulak question, economic campaigns and so on – and as a result party work with the bednota was rarely consistent and usually only increased at elections or under specific pressure from higher authorities.[75]

The pro-NEPism of the Siberian party

The period between the Thirteenth and Fourteenth Congresses (May 1924 to December 1925) was the apogee of NEP where party policy offered a range of economic and political concessions to the peasantry as a whole and to the well-off peasant farms in particular (the so-called 'wager on the strong'). In the economic sphere agricultural taxes were reduced, the 'Temporary Rules' gave official permission for the hiring of rural labour, restrictions on the leasing of land were eased and unfavourable state procurement prices were improved. In the political arena, the 'Face to the Countryside' and the 'Revitalisation of the Soviets' campaigns aimed to expand party recruitment among the peasantry and increase peasant political

participation. After the Fourteenth Congress this approach was modified as increasingly concern was expressed at a perceived growth of the
kulak stratum and its negative political and economic influence on the
rest of the peasantry. As we have seen, at the political level the party
attempted to strengthen and mobilise its instruments of control of the
countryside: the rural soviets, cooperatives and credit, rural communists and the rural poor. The economic counterpart of this toughened
approach was the imposition of a series of restrictions on the growth of
the well-off peasants: more progressive and increased taxation was
introduced, and laws limiting the hiring of labour and leasing of land
were more stringently enforced. These were the goals of party policy in
the course of 1926–7 but the reality of their implementation in Siberia
was beset by distortions, obstructions and frequently simply inertia.
As the party's commitment to the development of small-scale private
peasant agriculture waned, factional squabbles erupted in the central
leadership over the economic direction of the country, and as a result
of personality clashes and political intrigues. Here we shall be concerned with the regional implications of the shift in the direction of
agrarian policy at the centre.

The most intractable problem for party policy in the countryside in
the mid-1920s was the scale of peasant marketings of agricultural
produce. Grain marketings were of particular concern for the authorities because this crop was the main food staple and potentially the
most lucrative export earner at a time when hard currency was needed
to realise the party's industrialisation plans. What is striking about
Siberian politics in this period is that the predominant outlook of the
krai party leadership under Syrtsov was one which favoured a concentration on raising the productivity and marketings of small-scale private peasant farms. There was a general consensus in the ranks of the
Siberian party that the industrialisation of the region should be geared
towards the primacy of satisfying the requirements of agriculture;
supplying agricultural machines, implements, improving transport
and storage facilities, and the development of processing industries for
agricultural products. The actions of the Siberian party throughout this
period must be viewed against the light of these preferences.

Following Syrtsov's political disgrace in the wake of the 'Syrtsov–
Lominadze Affair' in December 1930, a hostile account of his opinions
was published and drew from his speeches in Siberia in the mid-1920s
to demonstrate that his 'Rightism' could be traced back to his time as
Secretary of the Kraikom. One of the political charges to which Syrtsov
was exposed was his view that the industrialisation of Siberia would be

a 'by-product' of the development of Siberian agriculture under NEP and, in particular, of its dairy industry. Apparently, in one of his speeches Syrtsov had drawn a direct link between the Siberian cow and the construction of the Tel'bes iron and steel works, with the latter being built as 'a secondary result of the reconstruction of agriculture'. At the time these comments brought some of his regional party colleagues to jeer that he was 'going to industrialisation on a cow'.[76] On the question of the extent of support for the Bukharinist Right, Cohen assumed that with the exception of Moscow 'no major party organization can be specifically identified with its policies or leaders'.[77] In fact, Syrtsov and most of the Siberian Kraikom identified closely with the pro-peasant policy. The difficulty arises in explaining Syrtsov's apparently contradictory actions of lending his political support to Stalin in the leadership struggle against the Right while his political beliefs put him firmly on the pro-NEP wing of the party. This issue will be dealt with in chapter 7.[78]

In Siberia, the policy of subordinating industrial development to the requirements of agriculture may be traced to the First Krai Congress of Soviets in December 1925. It recognised the need to develop metal industries in the region to provide machines and implements for agriculture and laid plans to expand the industrial processing of agricultural produce which hitherto was shipped from Siberia largely in an unprocessed form. A major factor impelling industrialisation was the cost of transport. The region imported around 50% of its manufactured goods from the Urals and beyond, which was not only costly in freight charges but also in terms of lost revenue due to discount tariffs for specified items (for example, ploughs) and the overburdening of the inadequate transport network. The Control Figures for the Siberian economy in the mid-1920s reveal the extent to which agriculture dominated the industrial sector. In the three-year period 1925/8, agriculture accounted for an average of about 81% of the total value of the gross production in the krai, while industry averaged just over 19%, and well over one-third of this figure came from the processing of agricultural produce. In the autumn of 1926 the government decided to finance two of the most important industrial projects of the decade in Siberia. The first of these was the Tel'bes metal works which was located in the Kuznetsk basin to exploit the huge coal reserves of that area. The second was the Turkestan–Siberian (Turk.-Sib.) railway, which was to link the grain surplus regions of south-west Siberia with the cotton growing republics of Central Asia. Notwithstanding the official pronouncements, central government funding for these projects was slow to materialise given the budgetary constraints of the mid-1920s. At the plenum of the Kraiispolkom in December 1926 and again at the Second Krai Congress of Soviets in April 1927, the Siberian authorities complained at the delays in construction due to under-funding from the centre.[79]

Apart from these two capital construction projects, the broad plan of industrialisation of Siberia was mainly directed towards branches of the economy related to agricultural infrastructure and processing. The goal was to raise the output, marketability and quality of Siberian agriculture and expand its export earning potential, particularly in grain and butter production. This policy was reflected by the fact that investment in agriculture grew faster than in any other sector in 1926/7 and 1927/8, with almost 45 million roubles planned in 1927/8 as opposed to 36.7 million for industry and 32.6 million for transport.[80] The question of raising the productivity and marketability of agriculture was not only an economic but also a political issue. A typical example of the more indulgent Bukharinist attitude of the Siberian party leadership towards the kulak in 1925, was the comment of A. Povolotsky, the Deputy Chairman of the Siberian Food Commission (Sibprodkom): 'to keep a course of speedy development of marketability of peasant farming, requires an immediate cessation of the persecution not only of the diligent well-off farms but of the kulaks also'.[81]

In the years 1925–6 the so-called 'Siberian Kondratievtsy' were at the height of their influence in economic thinking and politics in the region. This ultra-NEPist group lobbied for a policy of financial incentives to be directed at the well-off farms, and argued that the future lay in expanding the size of the well-off most efficient farms and squeezing the poor and inefficient out of existence. As one of their leading spokesmen, the economist V. E. Maksimov, explained in mid-1926: 'the Siberian countryside suffers from a multiplicity of farms, killing the initiative of the minority as regards the improvement of agriculture'. Another Siberian economist, I. Shildaev, observed in early 1927 that the peasants needed more freedom to develop private enterprise: 'We have no guarantee that we can use the results of labour, yet that is where the incentive to work comes from.'[82] This group focussed their demands on extending the multi-field system and expanding the process of land consolidation, whereby the dispersed narrow strips of peasant landholdings were reallocated to form large-scale, and more efficient, integrated private farms. However, not much success was registered on any of these points, even among the wealthier and more forward looking farms in the grain-producing areas of south-west Siberia.[83]

The other main component of the policy to raise productivity and marketings among the peasantry was the readjustment of the price 'scissors' in favour of agriculture. The aim was to give the peasant a greater incentive to produce and sell by making manufactured articles cheaper and the sale of agricultural produce more profitable. P. A. Mesiatsev, the plenipotentiary of Narkomzem, reporting to the Krai-kombiuro on 30 March 1926 on the results of the All-Union Conference on Rural Affairs and its conclusions for Siberia, expressed full support for the Bukharin–Rykov line which held sway at this time, that the tempo of industrialisation should be determined by growth in the agricultural sector and that prices had to be 'rationalised' in favour of the peasantry. In particular, Mesiatsev lobbied for an increase in grain procurement prices but this was resisted by the Kraikom.[84]

Although from late 1926 the party took a harsher attitude to kulak growth in the countryside and the 'Siberian Kondratievtsy' lost political favour, their views of rural development remained central to Syrt-sov's understanding of agrarian policy, as was clearly demonstrated by his speeches in early 1927. At a Krai Conference on Rural Affairs in late February Syrtsov uttered the exhortation: 'To the seredniak peasant, the strong farm and the well-off, we say: Accumulate and good luck to you.' Although he hedged this declaration with several qualifications (for example, the hiring of labour was to be avoided) its emphasis on accumulation by the well-off peasant established Syrtsov's Rightist credentials. It was blatantly reminiscent of Bukharin's 'get rich' call to the peasantry of April 1925, which had been disowned by the party leadership and subsequently retracted by its author in embarrassing circumstances.[85] A few days later, at the Third Krai Party Conference in March, in delivering the main political report of the Kraikom, Syrtsov spoke of the 'inseparable link' between the party's goal of industrialis-ation and the need to raise peasant marketings of agricultural produce. He attributed the decline of peasant marketings to demographic growth and the imbalance in prices for different agricultural products but, extraordinarily, he was also critical of the post-revolutionary lev-elling in the countryside for radically altering the social ownership of the cattle herds and destroying the large cattle-owning farms, which were the most productive and had the highest factor of marketability. More importantly from the political viewpoint, he advocated state cooperation on a massive scale with the well-off peasants and stressed the need for the large farms, the most productive, those with proved high levels of marketings, to join the cooperatives.[86] For the bedniaks he advocated collectivisation, not because it was socialised agriculture but on the contrary because it would 'put them on their feet and turn them into farmers no longer needing support in the future'.[87] The whole tenor of such an approach of favouring the well-off peasants lagged two years behind the general mood of the majority of the central party leadership on this issue.

As for the kulak, Syrtsov denied that they existed on a meaningful scale in Siberia and demanded a change in the way the party viewed the top 5%–6% of peasant farms which were 'by no means kulak' and 'should not be termed kulak' and who should be protected from 'methods of administrative pressure'. He invoked the experience of War Communism and the turn to NEP, declaring that 'it would be wrong to think that only by increasing pressure on the kulak can we help the bedniak and seredniak farms'. Some local party organisations, he revealed, wanted 'to seize the kulak by the gills' and take up arms against him in a return to civil war methods. The task of the party was 'not to dekulakise him but to remove his monopoly by creating conditions where the cooperatives could compete'.[88] Eikhe joined in the chorus of reproof of the policy of the Left and warned that 'those comrades who in their fear of the kulak think that by ravaging strong farms we will speed up socialist construction ... are deeply mistaken'.[89]

This picture of tolerance towards the well-off and indulgence of accumulation was not unanimous. Kisis, the Second Secretary of the Kraikom, forcefully asserted that 'there is no political wager [stavka] on the well-off peasant as some comrades think', implicitly reminding the delegates that Syrtsov's Bukharinist approach had been rejected by the party leadership in mid-1925.[90] He also voiced the concerns of urban workers and communists who had openly expressed disillusionment with the manner in which the Siberian party leadership accorded priority to agricultural questions and felt their problems were being ignored. Two okruzhkom secretaries from important industrial areas of the krai, Zimin for Irkutsk and Z. Ia. Novikov for Kuznetsk, argued for a greater tempo of industrialisation than that currently envisaged by the Kraikom, fearing that otherwise an unbridgeable gap would develop with the advancing agricultural sector. However, the resolutions of the conference reflected the Syrtsov approach, concentrating on the need to raise productivity and marketings of individual peasant farms. This was declared the 'main task' of the party in the countryside. The conference also decided to reduce the price of manufactured goods by 10%, in accordance with central government directives, as an incentive for increasing peasant marketings.[91]

At this stage collectivisation was a minor issue. In 1927, there were 670 kolkhozes in Siberia containing about 9,200 peasant households (0.7% of the total), occupying about 1% of the sown area and producing a marginal 1% of marketed crop output. Compared with the millions of roubles of credit poured into the private sector only a paltry 150,000 roubles was expended in kolkhoz construction in Siberia in 1927–8. At the Third Krai Party Conference Syrtsov exhorted rural communists to act as role models in forming collectives but with little success as, some months later, he drily observed that 'in this area we have had plenty of good resolutions rather than positive, concrete results'.[92] The turning point in party policy towards the collectives came at the Fifteenth Congress in December 1927, when their construction was declared the 'main task' of the party in the countryside. In early January complaints were made at a meeting of the Presidium of the Kraiispolkom that no concrete directives had been given by Moscow on how this task was to be carried out. As we shall see later, Stalin's arrival in Siberia in mid-January 1928 abruptly changed the whole mood towards the acceleration of collectivisation.[93]

With regard to economic developments it is clear that similar divisions existed in the Siberian party elite as prevailed in the central party leadership and no doubt in the party across the country. The views expressed at Siberian party conferences and plenums, and in journals and other publications were overwhelmingly supportive of the full economic development of private peasant agriculture under NEP and firmly rejected the 'ultra-bedniak' proposals of the Left for repression of the well-off peasants.[94] It is also evident that Syrtsov was an ardent advocate of the type of pro-peasant policy favoured by Bukharin, even after the commitment of the Stalin wing of the party leadership to NEP began to wane in the autumn of 1927. The ambivalent response of the Siberian party organisation to the demands of the centre for a programme of action to clearly delineate, and then politically and economically contain the kulak stratum in the countryside, the subject of the next chapter, must be viewed in the light of this widespread support for the development of private peasant enterprise through NEP.

3   Who was the Siberian kulak?

Problems of definition

The attempt to rigidly define peasant economic or class differentiation in the Soviet countryside was a will-o'-the-wisp, which consumed much effort on the part of the party in the course of the 1920s. It is fair to say that no successful resolution to this question was ever reached by the Bolsheviks due to the fateful dichotomy inherent in the Marxist analysis of the peasantry as a class. This was conceptually ambivalent and emphasised, in contradiction, the revolutionary potential and conservative nature of the peasantry, its group solidarity and class divisions based on the exploitation of poor peasant labour by the petty-capitalist farmer. During War Communism (1918–21) the party attempted to stir up class antagonisms among the peasants and turn the poor and middle peasants against 'kulak exploiters'. The failure of this policy and the introduction of NEP revealed Lenin's pragmatism with regard to ideological questions, as he stressed the need to conciliate the peasantry. This circumstance was accurately encapsulated by E. H. Carr's dictum that: 'It was no longer true that the class analysis determined policy. Policy determined what form of class analysis was appropriate in the given situation.'[1] A fundamental weakness in the investigations of peasant differentiation undertaken in the NEP era, and one which has been repeated in modern studies by Western scholars, was the conspicuous neglect of the regional dimension. In Siberia a combination of specifically regional factors contributing to acute peasant differentiation were revealed in all analyses of data gathered by the Kraistatotdel in the mid-1920s. The aim of this chapter is to analyse this body of work with a view to providing a new understanding and perspective to this question.[2]

In considering the data of this period a number of important qualifications must be taken into account. Firstly the extent of peasant

64

differentiation was the subject of a bitter intra-party political controversy in which the Left Opposition sought to exaggerate the class polarisation of the peasantry and the growth of the kulak and poor peasant strata in particular, while the Stalin–Bukharin leadership attempted to highlight the increasing prosperity of all peasants and the expansion of the middle peasant stratum at the expense of the kulak and the poor. Consequently, political manipulation of data was evident in two main areas: firstly in the differing methodologies adopted in the compilation of data, as indices of peasant class divisions were selected to reflect conflicting political concerns; secondly, in the outright distortion of data to meet political requirements. The apparent cases of political juggling of data, coupled with the intricate complexity of the task of categorising the peasantry by class factors, has led many Western historians to confidently, but often rather enigmatically, dismiss out of hand the conclusions reached by party statisticians in the mid-1920s. Carr spoke of the 'largely imaginary line between the kulak and the middle peasant' which the party drew in this period, while Lewin declared that the class divisions established by the party were terms 'used as political means, irrespective of possible Marxist sociological analysis'. In the recent study of party policy in the Ukrainian countryside Conquest claimed that, 'however defined, the kulak was, as an economic class, no more than a party construct'.[3]

A more incisive and innovative critique of the empirical studies conducted on the peasantry under NEP has been presented by Shanin, based on the work of the 'Organisation and Production School' led by the Soviet economist A. V. Chayanov. Shanin argued that the centripetal socio-economic dynamics of land-redivision by the commune, 'substantive changes' in peasant farms (sub-division, merger, liquidation, emigration) and the 'random oscillation' of events over which the peasant household had little or no power (the vagaries of state policy, market conditions, climate, births and deaths, natural disasters and so on) resulted in a pattern of 'multi-directional and cyclical mobility' among peasant groups which, he assumed, made a nonsense of the division of the peasantry into antagonistic classes in the Marxist sense of self-perpetuating economic groups with a collective political consciousness.[4] He characterised this mobility in the statement that, 'the higher the relative socio-economic position of the peasant household, the greater, on the whole, is the likelihood that it will begin to deteriorate, and vice versa, the lower its position the better its chance of showing an improvement'.[5]

Notwithstanding the complications in gathering accurate data in the

Soviet countryside of the 1920s and whatever the political use or misuse made of this, there is no question but that real economic divisions existed among the peasantry. The fundamental question is whether these divisions were a product of perpetuating class distinctions within the peasantry. It should be noted that the first of Shanin's centripetal forces acting on the peasantry, land-redivision, was a rare occurrence in Siberia and, as regards the impact of substantive changes and random events, it is self-evident that the most economically secure peasant households were best positioned to cope with these. Arguably, Shanin's 'multi-directional and cyclical mobility' is a euphemism for interchange, on the whole, between the upper and upper-middle strata of the peasantry. In addition, the most important 'substantive change', farm subdivision usually between adult sons, would have a significant impact only over a long period of years, perhaps as much as a full generation, as peasant children matured into adults. Thus, real economic divisions persisted for long periods and it may have taken many years before a peasant's economic fortunes changed radically. This suggests that sub-groups of peasant households consolidated their positions on the socio-economic ladder for a sufficient length of time to develop distinct, mutually exclusive economic and political interests. Unfortunately, this is one area for which evidence from Siberian peasant households is sparse as the only study carried out covers a two-year period and is inadequate for a proper analysis of this aspect of differentiation. Probably the greatest destructive impact on the fortunes of a peasant household was that made by natural disasters, such as deaths of family members and animals and, in particular, harvest failures. Once again material on these aspects of peasant life is lacking but we should remember that harvest failures were a recurrent feature of Soviet, and especially Siberian, agriculture.[6]

In general, the studies of the peasantry in the NEP period distinguished four generic groups: the kulak (well-off or rich peasant), the seredniak (middle-peasant), bedniak (poor peasant), and batrak (agricultural labourer). In the more sophisticated investigations organised by the Central Statistical Administration of the RSFSR (TsSU), in particular the 'dynamic studies', a seven-fold categorisation was employed with the batrak group divided into 'proletarians' and 'semi-proletarians' and the kulaks split into 'peasant entrepreneurs, traders and commercial entrepreneurs'. Frequently, much more vague definitions were employed by political leaders, such as 'the weak' (*malomoshchnyi*), 'the well-off' (*zazhitochnyi*), 'the strong' (*krepkii*) and 'the upper stratum' (*verkhushka*). The latter terms broadly correspond with the classification of the peasantry into 'privileged, less privileged and under-privileged strata'.[7]

The most politically charged and emotive label applied to a peasant category was that of 'kulak' (meaning literally 'a fist'), which was a traditional term of abuse applied to rural usurers, middle-men and spiv-like characters and was in no way associated with strong peasant farmers. In 1898 Lenin had distinguished between the 'kulaks', extortionist usurers and traders, who did not make their living directly from agriculture and the prosperous 'peasant entrepreneurs' who did.[8] By the mid-1920s the term generally covered the petty-capitalist peasant farmer who engaged extensively in exploitation of other peasants, for example, by hiring labour, renting out the 'means of production' (animals, implements, machines and buildings), and who was particularly wealthy, usually measured by the size of sown area, ownership of means of production, scale of commercial enterprise activity and income. During the grain crisis of 1927/8 the labels of 'kulak' and '*podkulachnik*' (kulak lackey) were adopted by Stalin as a byword for any peasant who refused to collaborate with the policies of the party or refused to sell his agricultural surpluses at state prices. As Stalin secured his dictatorship over the party, this politicisation of the definition of 'kulak' became dogma and, by disassociating the term from the realities of economic differences among peasant households, made meaningless any further studies into the question of peasant differentiation.

As stated above, the choice of indicators of peasant class differences, exploitation and wealth was largely an arbitrary process and results varied according to the indices selected. Given the political significance of the surveys it would be reasonable to assume that pressure was exerted on those collecting and analysing the data to produce the desired outcome. Another factor to be considered is the extent to which data underestimated peasant economic strength, especially that of the well-off, due to the concealment of indicators of wealth from the authorities. Certainly peasant memories of the prodrazverstka campaigns of 1918–20 in European Russia and 1921–2 in Siberia would have been a good reason for circumspection in their cooperation with surveys, especially considering that the data was used by the authorities for tax assessment purposes. No doubt, such obfuscation in responding to surveys was reinforced by the increasingly hostile posture of the party towards the well-off peasants from the end of 1927. One must also place a question-mark over the qualifications of those who collected the data on the ground in rural areas. Frequently a leavening of qualified statisticians were responsible for supervising barely literate soviet and party officials over a huge area in the collation of detailed information and filling out of complex questionnaires. This left ample scope not only for error but also for the falsification of data records according to the political prejudices of the compilers.

Perhaps the most detailed study into peasant class differentiation on a country-wide basis conducted in the 1920s was the sample census of peasant households carried out in the spring of 1927 under the central supervision of V. S. Nemchinov. His methodology was to group peasant households into seven categories by the value of the means of production owned. A petty-capitalist stratum was then sieved out from the top category of households according to whether they engaged substantially in exploitative activities such as hiring labour and 'entrepreneurial non-agricultural occupations' (hiring or renting out goods and services, trade, money-lending, substantial industrial production and so on). A similar methodology was used in the sample cluster (gnezdo) surveys conducted in south-west Siberia in the spring of 1927 and 1928, which were the basis for joint publications on the question of peasant differentiation by the krai statisticians, V. A. Kavraisky, head of the Kraistatotdel, and I. I. Nusinov, a Kraikom instructor.[9]

The Siberian studies gave pre-eminence in their analysis to indices of exploitation and wealth which were of peculiarly regional significance. In Siberian farming conditions of extensive land holding and relatively short sowing and harvesting periods, these indices were: size of sown area, ownership of animals and implements and, particularly, possession of advanced agricultural machines and the hiring of labour. In effect, these studies were the official Siberian party publications on this question and both had glowing forewords written by Syrtsov. Consequently, there is a prima-facie case that the results presented by these statisticians were tailored to the political requirements of the regional party leadership. In their 1927 study Kavraisky and Nusinov produced an analysis of rural developments in Siberia which confirmed the correctness of the party policy that the seredniak was 'the central figure in the countryside'. By the time of their second study in late 1928 the tone and direction of the party leadership had become vehemently anti-kulak and the authors followed suit by amending their previous conclusions to confirm that the main trend in peasant differentiation was the increasing polarisation of peasant strata which was reflected in the 'proletarianisation of the seredniak stratum'.[10] Nevertheless, that such fluctuations in the interpretation of data were determined by political factors does not necessarily invalidate the data itself, and we shall see later that a significant degree of economic differentiation among the Siberian peasantry was revealed by the studies of this period.

Politics, statistics and the kulak question

The first studies of socio-economic divisions among the Siberian peasantry were undertaken by the tsarist authorities in the mid-1890s, at a time when the Siberian countryside was undergoing a process of radical change as the great peasant migration to the region was just getting under way. Some of the data from Enisei Guberniia was incorporated by Lenin into his landmark work, *The Development of Capitalism in Russia*, which he wrote during his Siberian exile in 1897–9. In this instance differentiation between peasant groups was measured by the extent of ownership of working animals, particularly horses. Accordingly, Lenin distinguished a higher group of peasants who accounted for just over 24% of households (owning five to nine and ten or more horses), engaged in large-scale hiring of labour and cultivating extensive plots (up to 36 desiatinas). The only other Siberian data available from the pre-revolutionary period is material from comparative studies of peasant households in Barnaul Volost conducted in 1897 and 1905. This further demonstrated the sharply increasing trend of differentiation and revealed wide disparities in sown area and ownership of animals, implements and machines among peasants. For example, the 1897 study, based on a sample of 3,992 peasant households, revealed an upper stratum of 22.5% of well-off households sowing 10 or more desiatinas, accounting for 53.5% of the total sown area and owning over 45% of horses and 46% of cows. By the time of the 1905 study, based on a sample of 6,033 peasant households, the proportion of well-off farms fell to 16.3% but they owned over 33% of all ploughs (1,082), 85% of mowers and harvesters (446) and over 75% of threshers (265). This data constitutes early evidence for the emergence of a kulak stratum in Siberia and referring to it, Lenin spoke of a process of 'depeasantification' in the Siberian countryside as many peasants were increasingly squeezed into the position of impoverished wage labourers being exploited by the better equipped well-off stratum.[11]

The development of a stratum of 'petty-capitalist' farmers in Siberia was a recurrent theme of Lenin's analyses of rural affairs. At the height of War Communism in 1919–20, he disparagingly characterised them as the 'fattest peasants' and 'the powerful and strong peasants' of the country, and saw them as 'corrupted by capitalism'.[12] Indeed, in February 1920 Trotsky made a tour of the Urals region and, with some foresight and in advance of the introduction of NEP, proposed that the Central Committee weaken the pressure on the kulak and introduce a policy of selective conciliation of the peasantry in the richest agricultural regions: Siberia, the Don and the Ukraine, where prodrazverstka should be replaced by a progressive agricultural income tax and an increase in the delivery of manufactured goods to the countryside in order to stimulate production. However, as the Left of the party turned against NEP, in part because it was felt to be resuscitating a petty-capitalist class of peasants in the countryside, the Siberian kulak came in for renewed attack. The earliest comprehensive critique of NEP came in March 1922 when the Leftist economist, E. A. Preobrazhensky, submitted a set of theses to the Central Committee in advance of the Eleventh Congress, warning of the 'emergence of an agricultural bourgeoisie' and citing in support evidence of 'a strengthening of large-scale general farming in Siberia' which involved the regular exploitation of hired labour.[13] Over the next several years developments in the Siberian countryside were frequently cast up to illustrate the attacks of the Left on NEP. The debate in the party over differentiation and the need for accurate data on this issue brought the leadership to order a series of detailed studies to be made on the peasantry.

The implementation of the party's whole economic strategy, never mind the completion of such a widespread programme of rural surveys, depended on the cooperation of a large number of professional and skilled persons, known in party jargon as 'specialists', whose political allegiances often did not lie with the Bolsheviks. At the Eleventh Congress in April 1922 Lenin addressed this problem and stressed the need 'to build communism with non-communist hands', by recruiting those specialists who were prepared to collaborate with the new regime in running the country.[14] The participation of non-party specialists was particularly evident in the economic institutions of government. A high percentage of personnel employed by Narkomzem and Narkomfin were former tsarist officials who continued to work under the new administration and many were ex-SRs and Mensheviks. An illustrative example of Bolshevik tolerance and pragmatism in the deployment of 'specialists' at the local level was the appointment in December 1926 of V. G. Boldyrev as a member of the Siberian Planning Commission (Sibplan) and Head of its Scientific

Research Bureau. Boldyrev, a former professor at the Academy of the Imperial General Staff, had been a prominent Siberian SR in the civil war, a member of the 'Ufa Directory' in 1918 and, for a time before Kolchak's arrival, Supreme Commander-in-Chief of anti-Bolshevik forces in Siberia. He had been arrested by the Bolsheviks in 1922 but was subsequently released and recruited to work for the new government.[15]

At the same time, not all Bolsheviks were disposed to the employment of specialists, particularly if they had been former enemies. At the Third Krai Party Conference in March 1927 one delegate complained that the specialists in his okrug (Kamensk) were mostly 'ex-Kolchak men and *chinovniki*'.[16] On the whole, details on non-party officials in Siberia are sparse and they remain an unknown quantity. Frequently, Soviet historians only serve to further obscure the issue since they concentrate on heaping slurs on these officials for their political unreliability. For example, one scholar stated that in the 1929 purge of 215 officials from the Krai Land Administration 78 were revealed to be: 'former nobles and *pomeshchiki*, who had fled from western areas of the country, merchants, priests and other anti-soviet elements', and 48 of these were 'out and out counter-revolutionaries'.[17] Nevertheless, the specific political labelling of purged officials does give a broad indication of political stances taken by Siberian economists and statisticians in the mid-1920s and three main groups can be distinguished amongst the specialists in agricultural economics.

The first of these has been dubbed by Soviet historians alternatively 'kulak theorists' or the 'Siberian Kondratievtsy', after their mentor the influential economist N. D. Kondratiev, because of their active support for the promotion of unhindered private peasant farming and their acceptance of increasing differentiation in the countryside as a necessary concomitant of the development of strong peasant farms. The most prominent members of this group were P. A. Mesiatsev, the plenipotentiary of Narkomzem for Siberia, Head of the Krai Land Administration, member of the Kraikom and Presidium of the Kraiispolkom and Chairman of the Kraikom Rural Commission; Professor I. I. Osipov, a leading krai agronomist; V. E. Maksimov, Head of the Department of Land Improvement; and P. Ia. Gurov, Head of the Agricultural Section of Sibplan. This group was most influential in the peak years of NEP, from 1924 to mid-1926, and was centred around the journal *Zemel'nyi rabotnik sibiri*. It lost most of its political clout in the latter half of 1926 when the party began to tighten up NEP and abandoned the policy of encouraging accumulation by the well-off peasantry. Mesiatsev and others were removed from their posts, although their ideas continued to be propagated until mid-1928 through Gurov's position as editor-in-chief and Osipov's membership of the editorial board of the main krai economic and political journal *Zhizn' sibiri*.[18]

In 1926–7 as the tempo of the struggle between the Left Opposition and the pro-NEP party majority intensified, Siberian economic officials polarised along these lines with a Left group led by S. K. Brike, a member of the Krai Rural Commission, and a pro-NEPist one under Kavraisky which reflected the views of the krai party leadership, both of whom were party members. Indeed, at the Third Krai Party Conference in March 1927, Syrtsov spoke of the confusion which had arisen from the rivalry between the 'two administrations' that had emerged in the Kraistatotdel.[19] As statistics on peasant differentiation gained in political significance in the course of 1927 an increasingly acrimonious public debate on the issue developed in the regional party and state press and at party meetings and conferences. The argument at the Siberian level followed a similar pattern to that of the Left–Right split in the central party leadership but was made more intense by the scale of kulak activities in the region. The essential function of Kavraisky and like-minded pro-NEP economists and statisticians in Siberia was to provide empirical evidence to justify the policy of the party leadership regarding the general growth in prosperity of all peasant strata and give Syrtsov ammunition to offset criticism from the Left. From this time forward the careers of Kavraisky and his associate Nusinov were hinged to Syrtsov in much the same way that the latter's was tied to Stalin's.[20]

In Siberia the studies of peasant differentiation fall, both methodologically and chronologically, into two groups: firstly, to the end of 1926 the main indicator of differentiation used was the size of the sown area of households; secondly, from early 1927 a broader range of indices were employed, involving the size of sown area plus ownership of animals, implements and machines (the 'means of production'), and engaging in commercial enterprise and exploitative activities (hiring labour, leasing land, hiring out the 'means of production'). The latter included the more sophisticated devices of the 'dynamic studies', which were probably the best material on the countryside collated in the 1920s. The results of these studies had an importance which went beyond the merely local for, as we shall see, they made a significant political impact on the intra-party disputes at the centre.

The sown area indicator

Although the size of the sown area of a peasant household was used as the basic indicator of differentiation in the years 1924–6, there was no agreed standard established for which social strata of peasants should be included in a given category of sown area. Consequently, studies employing this indicator produced widely divergent conclusions, varying according to political requirements and the categorisation adopted. In Siberia the sown area methodology was used by I. V. Iarovoi, the regional plenipotentiary of TsSU, in a study conducted in 1924 and published as a brochure in 1926. His method of social categorisation of the peasantry (as shown in Table 1) led him to conclude that the central figure of the countryside was the bedniak and that NEP had 'not facilitated a revival in the well-off and rich peasantry'.[21] Nevertheless, his work was sensitive for the party leadership in that he designated a significant proportion of peasant households as either poor or well-off rather than middle peasants, who were officially supposed to be the 'central figure' in the countryside.

It is very likely that these were the statistics which provoked the acrimonious exchange between Lashevich and Kosior at the Fourteenth Congress in December 1925. In the build up to the congress the 'Leningrad Opposition', led by Zinoviev, raised the spectre of a 'kulak danger' and Lashevich, newly arrived from Siberia as Deputy Commissar of War, provided details of Iarovoi's sensitive Siberian statistics on differentiation. Zinoviev published them on 16 December in *Leningradskaia pravda* as an illustration of the 'bedniakisation' of the countryside and the growth of the kulak. Unnerved by this political bombshell the party leadership no doubt turned to Kosior, as the Siberian Kraikom Secretary, for a rebuttal and at the congress it fell upon Kosior to make the official response. He angrily rejected the figures put forward

Table 1. *Social categorisation of Siberian peasantry, 1924*

Group	Size of sown area (in *desiatinas*)	% of households
bedniak/weak	with none up to 4	60.5
seredniak	from 4.1 to 10	24.0
well-off/rich	10.1 and above	15.5

Source: I. V. Iarovoi

Table 2. *Social categorisation of Siberian peasantry, 1925*

Group	Size of sown area (in *desiatinas*)	% of households
bedniak	up to 2	40
seredniak	from 2.1 to 10	57
well-off	10.1 and above	3

Source: S. V. Kosior

by the Opposition as flawed and denounced Lashevich for having 'frightened the Leningrad workers' about 'our Siberian kulak'.[22] He presented an alternative configuration of Siberian statistics, recently prepared by TsSU with 'corrections' by Kuibyshev, which restored the seredniak to his official position of dominance, minimalised the strength of the kulak stratum and thereby confirmed the success of the party policy of encouragement for private peasant farming. This much more acceptable result from the leadership's viewpoint had been achieved by a manoeuvre which amended the sown area categorisation for each group (see Table 2). This episode proved that in the event of political dissension over data, the statistical goalposts would be moved and new methodologies devised to produce the desired outcome. Given its control of the government statistical organs, in such circumstances the party leadership held the trump cards.[23]

In early 1925 an extensive programme of research into peasant differentiation and the implementation of party economic measures in the countryside was carried out by local rural commissions supervised by the centre. The results of the Siberian rural commissions differed considerably from district to district and produced highly conflicting conclusions on the role of the 'kulak' in local agriculture. Mesiatsev, the neo-populist chairman of the Kraikom Rural Commission, told a conference on the state of agriculture held in Omsk that he had 'hardly found a kulak, but only disenfranchised (*ispravnykh*) farmers', while the report of researchers in the Rodinsk, Muromtsev and Poltava Raions of Omsk Guberniia bitterly declared: 'There are kulaks in the countryside, mainly in a hidden form. The supportive instruments in the birth of the kulaks are primarily taxation and a number of political obstacles.'[24] In stark contrast, the report of the commission investigating Zalarinsk Raion, Irkutsk Guberniia, in late 1925 was forthright in its condemnation of kulak witch-hunting and forcefully observed that:

The real kulak, the spider, usurer, trader, exploiter, actively strug-
gling for power and influence in the countryside, the open enemy of
our party, the presence of whom we read about in the leading party
press, we did not find in the countryside. There is also no ideological
influence from the well-off, better cultivated (*kul'turnyi*) farm, which
was the first to begin improved tilling of land and which serves as an
example for the whole countryside to imitate.[25]

This view was echoed at the Second Krai Party Conference in November when Kosior summed up the general view of the reports by stating
the 'Comrades have come from the countryside and told us: on the
whole there are no kulaks there', and Parfenov, a leading local advocate of the party's pro-peasant policy pointedly declared: 'There is
the secret kulak, the hidden kulak, the draft kulak, the prospective
one, but a real kulak does not exist.'[26]

Such contrasting conclusions may be explained not only by differences in the political approaches of the authors and their desire to
establish patterns of differentiation to suit political ends, but also, at a
more basic level, by the absence of common methodologies in the data
gathering process in the localities. This is illustrated by the report of the
Biisk Okrug Rural Commission on differentiation in 1926, which
voiced strong opposition to the very idea of creating a nebulous category of 'well-off' farms because it would lead to confusion in delineating the real kulaks. With disparaging references to a raikom which
had counted 30% of its farms as belonging to the kulak category, the
commission made it clear that in its view: 'The kulak can and must be
distinguished on the principle of exploitation not only of hired labour,
but also the unscrupulous exploitation of bedniaks by machines, in
enterprises and so on.'[27] An awareness of the growing role of machines
in kulak exploitation was registered in a Kraikom statement of March
1925 which noted that, in the main, 'the kulak grows in a hidden form,
through hidden forms of leasing land, renting out equipment ... and
hiring working labour. The growth of an exploitative peasantry via
machines is particularly striking.'[28]

However, at the local level an ambivalent attitude to the kulak
question continued to pervade the work of the rural commissions
which gathered data on the renting of farm equipment and hiring of
labour. Many of their reports rejected talk of exploitation in this context
and claimed that these kinds of economic relations were frequently no
more than 'friendly', 'neighbourly' or 'family help'. For example, the
report from Pokrovsk Raion, Rubtsovsk Okrug, spoke of well-off farms
lending their equipment 'gratuitously' to bedniaks. On the other hand,

Table 3. *Social categorisation of Siberian peasantry, 1926*

Group	Size of sown area (in *desiatinas*)	% of households
bedniak	with none up to 2	27.6
seredniak	from 2 to 8	57.5
well-off	8 and above	14.9

Source: V. Diakov

in Rodinsk Raion, Slavgorod Okrug, a researcher recognised that the size of sown area was not an adequate measure of a kulak farm and, referring to agricultural equipment, commented that 'the presence of it on a farm serves as a real indicator of a powerful farm'. He revealed that to rent a mowing machine cost 2 puds of grain or 4 days labour per desiatina, and a thresher (without a horse or an operator) cost 5 roubles per day. The levying of rental charges in terms of workdays and grain reflected both the strong non-monetary element in the rural economy and the premium placed on field workdays given Siberian conditions. The short Siberian harvesting season meant that the bedniaks were forced by circumstances 'to agree to any conditions' set by the owners of machines or face losing much of their crop. In any case they usually had to wait until the well-off owners of mechanised equipment had completed their own harvest.[29]

A similar situation was disclosed by the commission working in Staro-Bardinsk Raion, Biisk Okrug, where bedniaks rented machines, took seed and grain loans from the 'strong seredniaks and well-off', and sometimes borrowed money. In this district owners charged 3 days work at harvest time for the hire of a plough, 4 days field-work for the hire of a plough with horses, and for each desiatina of land ploughed charged 5 puds of wheat. This report concluded that the 'hidden kulak' was growing 'through machines' and lamented that 'everyone rents them out, including communists'. It was estimated that a thresher earned its owner 8–10 tons of grain in rental charges during an average season and a mower up to 5 tons. Given average yields of around 50 puds (0.9 tons) per desiatina, this type of machinery produced in rental charges alone the equivalent of twelve and six desiatinas of land respectively, and these earnings were tax-free. On a more general level, it is worth noting the gains in terms of productivity that came with the use of mechanised equipment, for example, a mechanised harvester was up to four times more productive than the

scythe and a steam thresher as much as sixteen times faster than hand
threshing and flailing. At this time of enthusiastic support for NEP and
the development of private peasant agriculture the Krai Land Administration under Mesiatsev ignored the issue of kulak exploitation of
machines since, as Iarovoi explained, 'for the bedniaks to have advanced equipment for just a small share of production is not
advantageous'.[30]

The differentiation debate in Siberia took a new turn with the publication of an article by a local Leftist party statistician, V. Diakov, in the
Kraikom daily newspaper *Sovetskaia sibir'* on 30 November 1926. Once
again Siberian statistics on this issue impinged upon political events at
the centre as Diakov's data were cited by Zinoviev at the Central
Committee plenum of 29 July–30 August 1927 as evidence of the
emergence of a class of 'kulak' petty-capitalist farmers in the countryside. Diakov based his results on the 10% selective spring census
conducted in the countryside of south-west Siberia in 1926, and using
the sown area indicator he tabulated a new set of classifications (Table
3). This categorisation gave a startling view of peasant differentiation
in Siberia compared with the rest of the country. The bedniaks were
reckoned to have a minimal role in agricultural production in as much
as they held just 6% of the total sown area, a little over 13% of working
animals, 18.4% of cows, around 1%–2% of advanced machines and
6.3% of leased land. The share of the seredniaks was substantial as
they accounted for over 54% of the sown area, almost 60% of working
animals, 58.5% of cows, 50% of various types of advanced equipment
and over 35% of leased land. Nevertheless, Diakov asserted that their
economic importance as the central figures in agriculture was declining
compared with 1925 since: 'Both by sown area and working animals,
and by cows, the proportion of the seredniak group, in spite of its
quantitative growth, has decreased.'[31]

These conclusions were roundly criticised by the leading krai statisticians, Kavraisky and Nusinov, and also from the Left by Brike (discussed below, pp. 78–81). Kavraisky and Nusinov, concentrated their
fire on the personal and political dimensions, deriding Diakov as a
'Siberian representative' of the Trotskyite Opposition and claiming
that a 'fraction at the centre' had set him the task of 'establishing the
presence in the Siberian countryside of 15% kulaks'. They accused him
of conducting 'statistical exercises' to exaggerate the numerical
strength and economic power of the well-off peasants by including
part of the bedniak strata (those sowing from 2 to 4 desiatinas) among
the seredniaks, and by counting many seredniaks (those sowing from

8 to 12 desiatinas) in the well-off category. By Diakov's estimates, the 14.9% of households in the well-off group accounted for almost 40% of sowings, and owned over 27% of working animals and 23% of cows. Most significantly, they owned a huge share of advanced agricultural equipment: almost 78% of seeders, over 61% of harvesters, 46.4% of mowers, over 55% of threshers, almost 50% of winnowers, and were responsible for the bulk of leased land at over 58% of the total. As an immediate consequence of these results the Kraikom ordered a fresh series of studies of the countryside in the spring of 1927. These new studies marked a turning point in that they eschewed the reliance on the size of sown area as the basic indicator of differentiation and instead utilised a broader and more sophisticated series of indices, with particular importance attached to variables of regional significance such as the ownership of machines.[32]

Brike's studies: the 'means of production' indicator

In early 1927 the Diakov article was lambasted in a series of publications by Brike.[33] He investigated the mass of data which had been gathered in censuses and spring surveys in 1920–6 in south-west Siberia (Altai). This made it possible for him to review changes in the economic position of farms over a period of several years. The main thrust of Brike's analysis was that Diakov's methodology was flawed because the sown area of peasant households was by itself an insufficient means of indicating differentiation. Brike believed that the 'primary' factors in peasant stratification were the combination of the distribution of farm equipment and animals, and the extent to which farms leased out their equipment and used hired labour, in addition to size of sown area. He argued that the use of the size of sown area as the basic indicator of differentiation was a 'practical and political mistake' because it was the main factor in direct taxation and consequently peasants habitually concealed the true extent of their sowings, from 25% to 75% according to some estimates. Further, many peasants with a small sown area engaged in kulak-type exploitation through ownership and leasing of advanced agricultural machines or operating small commercial enterprises. For Brike, the observable growth under NEP of the groups with large sown areas was occurring, 'not so much on account of new accumulation by these groups, as much as on account of the exposition of their means of production which in the years of crisis and collapse had been converted into dead capital'.[34]

The prodrazverstka campaigns of 1920–2, concurrent with a series of bad harvests, had plunged Siberian agriculture into a crisis as the peasantry sharply decreased sowings and went over to subsistence farming. In 1920 over 52% of households had sown 4 or more desiatinas (of which 15.3% sowed 10 or more) but by 1924 this had slumped to just over 29% (of which only about 3% sowed 10 or more). The worst year was actually 1922, after the introduction of NEP, when those sowing 10 or more desiatinas had fallen to around 1% of farms. Evidently, the Siberian peasantry were slow to appreciate that NEP signalled a meaningful change in Bolshevik policy. The most obvious sign of subsistence farming was that households with no sown area virtually disappeared in the years 1921–4 because declining opportunities for the poor peasants to eke out a living as farm labourers forced them to cultivate small plots of land for food. The absence of a general levelling campaign in the post-revolutionary Siberian countryside enabled the well-off farms to retain their farm equipment and to a large extent also their livestock. Brike illustrated this by highlighting the significant increase in the possession of ploughing implements held by households in the lower sown area categories during the critical years 1920–4. In this period the number of peasant households sowing up to 2 desiatinas which owned no ploughing implements fell from over 77% in 1920 to a little over 50% in 1924, and then rose again to almost 82% by 1926. This could only be accounted for by a temporary contraction on the activities of well-off farms.[35]

According to Brike, the pattern of differentiation assumed two distinct forms as the agricultural recovery proceeded in 1925–6, the apogee of NEP in the countryside. Firstly, there was a process of what he termed the 'return home', as those farms which were better technically supplied with equipment and animals expanded their sown area and quickly restored their production to 1920 levels. This was clearly evident among the middle peasant category (sown area from 4 to 10 desiatinas) which had accounted for almost 37% of households in 1920, 26% in 1924, rising to over 36% in 1926. At the same time the poorer groups (sowing up to 4 desiatinas) shrunk in size as their 'alien guests' returned up the socio-economic ladder, with the number of households sowing up to 2 desiatinas falling from 38.7% (1924) to 27.6% (1926), and those sowing from 2 to 4 desiatinas declining from 32% (1924) to 27.4% (1926). There were concomitant losses in the shares of these groups in the total sown area, and ownership of livestock and equipment. Meanwhile the well-off farms (10 desiatinas

or more) had increased from 3.2% (1924) to 8.8% (1926) of all households, which was just over half their share in 1920.[36]

Brike foresaw that the process of differentiation would continue on
the basis of 'new accumulation' through the exploitation of machines,
but that this would be at a slower pace than that of 1920–6. The political
implications of his analysis was that he sought to undermine Diakov's
thesis that the seredniak was being squeezed and the countryside
polarised into rich and poor classes. Given the prevailing party definition of the seredniak as an economically independent but non-
exploitative farmer, Brike demonstrated that Diakov was mistaken to
include those farms with a sown area of 2 to 3 desiatinas in this
category since in 1926 only 32% of such households worked their land
exclusively with their own equipment, about half had no plough and
almost 60% had no horse or only one. Therefore, the great mass of
these farms were dependent on their well-off and better-equipped
neighbours for essential implements, animals and machinery. Similarly, of those households sowing from 3 to 4 desiatinas, less than half
had their own animals or equipment, which again required a stretching of the term seredniak for them to be included in this category. In
light of the above, Brike counted as bedniak households the 55% of
farms sowing up to 4 desiatinas. More importantly from the political
perspective, he slashed the content of Diakov's well-off category by
removing those farms in the 8 to 10 desiatina sown area category which
owned less than three horses and three cows, and produced a politically less embarrassing figure of 8.8% for this group.[37]

One of Brike's principal objections to Diakov's work was that it
focussed on the sown area indicator and ignored the paramount importance of implements, machines and working animals in Siberian
agriculture. The presence of 'hard' soils in many areas of western
Siberia and the extensive nature of farming made it virtually imperative that a peasant farmer have at the very least good iron implements
and at least two working animals (preferably horses). Normally,
households with only one animal were forced to hire a second, particularly in the spring and autumn when farm work was at its most
intensive. As noted earlier (pp. 5–6), it was precisely then that climatic
conditions of frequent rain showers compelled the peasantry, if they
were to avoid serious crop losses, to harvest grain and mow their hay
simultaneously in an intensive period of about three weeks. In this
situation mechanical harvesters, mowers and threshers were indispensable, and those without such machines had to wait until their

well-off neighbours had finished their field-work and were prepared to rent them out.[38]

The mass of Siberian peasant farms, both the poor and middle strata, were at the mercy of the well-off owners of machines. The increasing mechanisation of Siberian agriculture under NEP has been discussed in detail in chapter 1, but that this development was concentrated in the well-off stratum at one pole must be set against the general absence of basic implements and animals in a large number of poor farms in many okrugs: 40% in Kamensk, over 42% in Barnaul, almost 49% in Rubtsovsk, about 32% in Novosibirsk and Barabinsk. One source states that research conducted in a village in Barnaul Okrug in 1926 revealed that 8% of households owned all the threshing machines and 88% of the others hired them out.[39] This evidence explains why Brike believed that farm equipment, particularly advanced machines, were the 'basic instruments of exploitation and accumulation' in the Siberian countryside and, consequently, they constituted the 'basic indicator of differentiation (not the only)'.[40] Brike drew political conclusions from his work which were highly critical of NEP, for he attributed the increasing productive capacity of the well-off farms in Siberia to the encouragement given to small-scale private farming by Soviet government policy: 'revolutionary legality, NEP in the countryside, the Temporary Rules and so on'.[41] From the spring of 1927, as the Left Opposition stepped up its campaign against 'kulak growth', the differentiation issue moved to the top of the political agenda and the mass of statistical data gathered in the countryside over previous years assumed major political importance. A reflection of the political sensitivity of this question was that from this time forward it was increasingly party political figures rather than statisticians who assumed the responsibility for public pronouncements on the issue. In Siberia, Diakov's work and Brike's critique created a political storm and acted as the catalyst for a wide ranging debate on differentiation which absorbed the attention of the regional party leadership for most of 1927.

The kulak issue on the eve of the grain crisis

A measure of the heightened political importance of statistical data on differentiation was the convocation by the Kraikom, from 27 February to 3 March 1927, of a special Krai Conference on Rural Affairs to evaluate the work of the rural commissions which had been operating in the countryside since mid-1926. The conference was attended and addressed by Syrtsov and other leading regional party officials, no doubt to ensure that the correct political assessment was drawn in its resolutions and final report. Consequently, the conference report was optimistic and glowing in its praise of the impact of NEP in the Siberian countryside and dismissed negative analysis of peasant differentiation. It asserted that: 'there is a significant increase in the level of all peasant farms and in the transition of these to higher, stronger groups' and concluded that, 'there is no economic decline or impoverishment of weak farms and there is no erosion of the seredniak group'.[42] Brike warned the conference of 'kulak growth' and repeated his views on the crucial role played by the ownership and renting out of the 'means of production' in the acceleration of differentiation. He rejected the lumping together of kulaks and seredniaks into a generic 'well-off' category and defined kulak farms as those 'which have a surplus quantity of animals and agricultural machines and who exploit these on the side'.[43] Several delegates emphasised the need for applying a broad series of indicators in establishing peasant social categories and cited many examples where the sown area indicator had failed to unmask kulak farms. For example: in Abakansk Raion, Minusinsk Okrug, a kulak farm sowed only 1 to 2 desiatinas, owned two horses and two cows, but employed two batraks on a permanent basis and the main sources of its income were money-lending, seed loans, and the hiring out of machines to other farms. In Irkutsk Okrug, a kulak farm had an income from sowings of 680 roubles p.a., but this was supplemented by 100 roubles from butter-making, 200 roubles from sorting and cleaning seed, 90 roubles from harvesting and 200 roubles from other work, an extra amount estimated to be equivalent to approximately the income from 17 desiatinas of sowings.[44]

Hitherto, Kraikom resolutions had taken an ambivalent position in the differentiation debate but tended to minimalise the significance of kulak activity. For instance, in a statement of December 1926 it warned against the use of the ambiguous term 'well-off' because there was a tendency to incorporate part of the seredniak stratum with the kulaks. In his speech to the Conference on Rural Affairs Syrtsov defended the party's policy with great vigour, affirming his full support for the development of private peasant farms and declaring that, 'it would be a crime to put a seredniak, be he the most well-off, in the same category as the kulak'.[45] Focussing on the need to raise the productivity of agriculture he forcefully exhorted the peasantry to take full advantage of NEP, and it was on this occasion that he displayed his Rightist credentials by issuing a call for the well-off to 'accumulate and good luck to you'. Syrtsov reassured his audience that the party was not opposed to accumulation *per se*, and had disenfranchised the kulak 'not because of accumulation, but because of his unscrupulous exploitation of the bedniak and seredniak'. This assumed that there was an acceptable level of exploitation. That the speech was received enthusiastically at the time is an illustration both of the support in the Siberian party organisation for the encouragement of private peasant agriculture and the unpopularity of the demands of the Opposition for the imposition of restrictions on unbridled accumulation by the well-off peasantry.[46]

Shortly afterwards, from 25 to 30 March, the Third Krai Party Conference convened and a few delegates were critical of the Syrtsov slogan exhalting peasant accumulation. In delivering the political report of the Kraikom Syrtsov moderated his earlier exhortations and presented a carefully drafted analysis of the differentiation issue. He repeated the claim that the growth of economic differentiation in the countryside had not led to 'appreciable impoverishment of the lower strata' and accounted for changes in the economic status of lower groups as a process of 'natural destruction'. In discussing the methodology of defining peasant groups Syrtsov stressed the need to distinguish the well-off and seredniak farms from the kulak type. He asserted that it was essential to consider a wide range of factors and sources of income because the sown area indicator on its own led to the counting of many seredniaks with large families as kulaks. The use of tax assessments in delineating groups must also be exercised with due care as often the seredniak paid high taxes. Even the use of hired labour was by itself an insufficient measure of kulak status, according to Syrtsov, since the seredniak farm often did this, but 'as a general rule he does not systematically exploit'. He believed that only broader and more complicated mechanisms could satisfactorily evaluate differentiation. As for the kulak, he was distinguished mainly by exploitative activities: leasing land, renting out machines, employing hired labour, operating small-scale industrial enterprises.[47]

Syrtsov proceeded to criticise those party and soviet organisations who underestimated the political dangers of a wrong assessment of the differentiation process but he did not clarify whether he was more concerned with overassessment or underassessment of particular groups. Certainly, he reproached those who were reluctant to name kulak farms, those who said 'this farm is a labouring type, this farmer is a hard worker, how can he be a kulak?' In Syrtsov's eyes this was 'slipping into SR'ism' for 'when the spider sucks blood from a fly, he also works hard'. He excluded the possibility that there were raion size kulak-free oases in Siberia but accepted that there might be such individual villages. At the same time, if a raion turned up a figure of 10% kulaks this also would be 'losing the scent'. He firmly ruled out the use of 'administrative pressure' to counteract kulak growth and bluntly informed the delegates that they must resign themselves to differentiation in the countryside as part and parcel of NEP: 'It is inevitable that there will be a certain level of differentiation, it is inevitable that there will be some growth of capitalist elements.'[48]

Syrtsov's speech provoked a furious reaction in the conference hall and lobby and set the scene for an acrimonious debate on the Kraikom report on agriculture delivered by Eikhe. Speakers argued over whether the term 'well-off' was too nebulous. One delegate proposed that the seredniaks with 'kulak tendencies' be given a special name, and yet another turned the whole argument on its head by arguing that it was the kulaks who got mixed up with other categories of peasants, not the other way round.[49] In his report Eikhe attempted to prove the efficacy of NEP by demonstrating that data gathered in the countryside of western Siberia in 1920–6 revealed that there was either a process of general upward mobility among all groups of farms or a pattern of stability, with only 5% to 12% of farms in various groups (by sown area) moving down the scale. He supported Syrtsov's plea for a more exact definition of peasant groups and attacked those who engaged in the 'mechanical snipping off of higher groups' for this was 'a factor which holds back the development of the productive strength of agriculture'. However, Eikhe relied on the same statistical material as that used by Brike in his studies and, consequently, he arrived at similar conclusions regarding the strength of the well-off farms: 8.8% sowed 10 or more desiatinas, 8.8% owned 4 or more horses and 13.7% owned 4 or more cows, and there was likely to be an overlap between these categories.[50]

A fierce clash ensued between Eikhe, Nusinov and Brike over these statistics. Nusinov claimed that Eikhe's figures assisted the Opposition because they essentially confirmed Brike's assessment of substantial kulak growth, while Brike gave a scathing indictment of the complacent approach of the Kraikom leadership, asking why the question of kulak exploitation of the 'means of production' had not been given prominence. He reiterated his recently published conclusions to the assembled delegates, emphasising that the well-off 8.8% of households held 28% of the total sown area, 17% of the horses, 15% of the cows and one-third to two-thirds of the advanced agricultural machinery depending on the type. He also reminded the conference that the rapid growth of the well-off peasantry in Siberia compared with other parts of the country could be explained by the absence of de-kulakisation by the Kombedy during the civil war in the region. Syrtsov responded by labelling Brike 'the central figure of confusion at our conference' and spoke of the need to 'fire on the Left' (*ogon' nalevo*). In a barely veiled threat, he mentioned in an aside that some comrades wanted Brike's removal from the Rural Commission of the Kraikom but that he felt the latter still served a useful function there. At this point, perhaps ruffled by Brike's statistical evidence, Syrtsov exposed his incomprehension and impatience at the complexities of the differentiation question by characterising the difference between the kulaks and the well-off as 'the kulaks are disenfranchised, the well-off are not': clearly a political distinction rather than an economic one. This throw-away remark illustrates the difficulties encountered by a party politician when confronted in open debate by an experienced statistician.[51]

The resolutions approved by the conference supported the Syrtsov–Eikhe analysis. It was determined that the process of reconstruction in the countryside had resulted in 'a general economic strengthening of the countryside and a move by all socio-economic groups upwards to stronger categories'. In addition, it was affirmed that 'as a rule the process of economic decline (impoverishment) of bedniak farms is not occurring, also the erosion of the seredniak is not occurring, and the latter remains the central figure in agriculture'. However, the tempo of growth of farms was recognised to be unequal and the *verkhushka* stratum was growing quickest of all, by a process of 'systematic exploitation'.[52] In an article published shortly after the conference Syrtsov still maintained that differentiation would be overcome by 'the granting of the widest possibilities of development for the seredniak including the strong seredniak farms', by overcoming the 'exploitative appetites of the kulak *verkhushka*', and by state assistance to the bedniaks. An attack on the use of the term 'well-off' remained central to his argument and he claimed that those estimates which had counted 12% to 14% kulak farms in Siberia had achieved this only by including seredniak farms 'distinguished by a certain economic well-being'.[53]

In the summer of 1927 the question of peasant differentiation in Siberia moved to the centre stage of Soviet politics. At the joint plenum of the Central Committee and Central Control Commission which met from 29 July to 9 August Zinoviev and Evdokimov provoked unease in the central party leadership when they cited the Siberian data to

Table 4. *Social categorisation of Siberian peasantry, 1927*

Group	Size of sown area (in *desiatinas*)
kulaks	with 16 or more
strong seredniaks	from 10 to 16
seredniaks	from 4 to 10
weak	from 3 to 4
bedniaks	with none to 3

Source: S. A. Bergavinov

lambast the policy of concessions to small-scale peasant farming and bolster the Opposition's case for tighter restrictions on kulak growth. The publication of Brike's findings in the June issue of *Na agrarnom fronte*, the journal of the Agrarian Section of the Communist Academy, made an official party rejoinder to the Left's use of this data politically indispensable. There followed a sequence of discussion articles in *Bol'shevik*, the theoretical organ of the Central Committee.[54]

The first of these was published in July 1927 by S. A. Bergavinov, a Central Committee instructor, who had recently returned from Siberia where he had supervised the expulsion of Opposition supporters from the Omsk party organisation. As someone with recent experience of working in the region, Bergavinov was an obvious choice for the Central Committee Secretariat to delegate the task of refuting the Left's interpretation of the Siberian data. He dismissed Diakov's estimates of differentiation as exceptional and irrelevant to the course of NEP in the country as a whole given the distinctive nature of Siberian agriculture. He highlighted the specific peculiarities in Siberian development which had led to the emergence of an economically strong peasantry: the absence of *pomeshchiki* and land hunger; the role of the state as a major landholder in the pre-revolutionary period; the scarcity of re-divisional communes; and the fact that there was no 'general levelling' after the revolution, especially in 'dead equipment' (i.e. implements and machines). For the most part, however, he merely repeated the bland assertions contained in the resolutions of the Kraikom and the Third Krai Party Conference regarding the 'general movement upwards of all farms' and the central role of the seredniak. Bergavinov based his analysis on the spring sample dynamic censuses of 1925 and 1926 in south-west Siberia and, in order to achieve the political task of deflecting the charge of a 'kulak danger' made by the Left, he re-arranged the sown area indicators (as shown in Table 4).

By this mechanism, he numbered the kulak verkhushka in Siberia at just 2% of households and concluded that the evidence showed that 'the basic mass of farms, sown area and means of production, including complicated equipment are concentrated in the hands of the seredniak group'. Although he admitted that kulak exploitation of machines was significant, the fact that they were growing faster than other groups had no 'terrible' repercussions, and was an 'inevitable' feature of the transitional period of economic recovery in the countryside. He discounted the Opposition claims about the seriousness of differentiation in Siberia as simply 'fairy tales'.[55]

The following month, the Left Opposition was given the right of reply with an article by G. Safarov, the Zinovievist leader of the Komsomol, rather provocatively titled 'The offensive of capital in the Siberian countryside (The blatant facts)'. The distinctive features in the development of Siberia which Bergavinov had enlisted as an apology for the rapid growth of the well-off peasantry, were branded by Safarov as the very root of the danger, for it was precisely these circumstances 'which allow capitalist tendencies to develop in the Siberian countryside at a much quicker tempo and in a more open manner than in the central areas'. He alleged that the Siberian research on differentiation had revealed 'the defects and deficiencies of our peasant policy', and they cried out about 'an American tempo of growth of the well-off kulak farm' on the basis of exploitation of machines. The rarity of the redivisional commune in Siberia was characterised by him as 'landlordism without the landlord'. Quoting copiously from the reports of several Siberian okrug rural commissions, he constructed a picture of a kulak assault on what he called 'the commanding heights' of the countryside: machine supply and credit facilities. Safarov sharply rebuked the Siberian party organisation for its failure to combat the 'industrialisation' of the kulak verkhushka. It was, he declared, gripped by the 'Ustryalov ideology' and 'Ustryalov–Kondratiev' ideas and in the process of 'degeneration'. This was a clever use of the 'guilt by association' technique by linking the Siberian leadership, and Syrtsov in particular, with the discredited policies of the far Right.[56]

This article represented the most comprehensive and politically incisive Leftist critique of Siberian rural developments and the regional party leadership published thus far. Syrtsov was under pressure to produce a satisfactory response and it is not surprising that the same issue of *Bol'shevik* carried a lengthy rejoinder by him which attempted to allay party fears of the 'Siberian kulak' and dispel suspicions about the political soundness of the regional party organisation and his leadership. His approach was long on rhetoric and short on detail as he attempted to belittle Safarov's article (he described it as 'hysterical bawling') and avoided dealing with the main issues at stake. He earnestly reassured the party that the previously stated positions of the Kraikom on the scale of differentiation, the increase in the strength of all farms and no squeezing of the seredniak were accurate. Yet, in an apparent contradiction, he acknowledged that a degree of impoverishment of the bedniak stratum had occurred. This was rather limply explained by the arrival of poor peasant immigrants in the region. The allegation of an 'American tempo' of development among the well-off Siberian peasantry was completely rejected and although Syrtsov admitted that there were deficiencies in the implementation of restrictions on kulak growth, particularly with regard to the supply of machines, he noted that the krai party conference had only recently adopted a series of corrective measures to improve this situation. Safarov's claims looked impressive but, according to Syrtsov, he had simply manipulated the data by citing the reports from those areas of south-west Siberia where the situation was exceptionally bad. Syrtsov was sure in his belief that the main concern of the party was to avoid including part of the seredniaks among the kulak verkhushka, as this had led to instances of excessive disenfranchisement in the countryside.[57]

While the party was absorbed in polemical debates on peasant differentiation during the summer of 1927, a sample census of farms was being carried out in Siberia, under the supervision of Kavraisky and Nusinov at the Kraistatotdel. The results were anxiously awaited by the Kraikom leadership as it was expecting a definitive rejection of the Opposition case for 'kulak growth' in the region. On the contrary, the publication of the analysis of the data served only to arouse new controversies over the process of differentiation in the region.

The studies of Kavraisky and Nusinov

With the increasing political importance of statistical material in party debates, attempts were made by the leadership to extend and tighten its political control over the collection and analysis process. After the completion of the Soviet demographic census of 1926, plans were laid for a reorganisation of the Siberian statistical network, particularly at the lower level. In May 1927 the Second Siberian Statistical Conference met (including representatives from TsSU) and approved a number of measures refining the methods of collecting statistical material. The main aim of this reorganisation was to increase the quality of local statisticians. While the bulk of the work-load continued to be shouldered by raion and okrug statistical officials, a more diffuse and socially representative network of voluntary correspondents was installed at the local level. A uniform methodological approach in the conduct of research was established by the Kraistatotdel, and there was to be close cooperation with the TsSU of the RSFSR and USSR. Finally, given the political significance of statistics, more funds were demanded to finance the collection of material.[58]

In the spring and summer of 1927 there were two programmes of 'dynamic studies' conducted in the krai: a 10% Spring Selective Agricultural Census, under the central supervision of V. S. Nemchinov, and a sample cluster (*gnezdovoi*) census of farms in south-west Siberia carried out by the Kraikom Rural Commission. The latter involved a survey of approximately 12,354 (about 3%) of peasant farms in the area and it was on the basis of this material that Kavraisky and Nusinov made their analysis. Their conclusions were published in preliminary form in an article in *Sovetskaia sibir'* on 29 October 1927, and their main study followed in book form in November, at the very moment when the struggle with the Opposition reached its denouement.[59] The political importance of their work for the Kraikom, and an indication of the close relationship between Syrtsov and the authors, is evident in the fact that he wrote a glowing foreword to their book and described it as the most sophisticated rebuttal of the Opposition case (especially Safarov's). The authors also recognised the political significance of their study and spent some time attacking the Siberian Leftist statisticians, Diakov and Brike, whose work had provided the foundation of the Opposition critique. The book was intended as a practical guide for party and soviet political, economic and cooperative officials and, because 'introducing intermediary groups frequently confuses our officials in practice', it laid out peasant groups in the simplified, familiar form: bedniak, seredniak and kulak. Syrtsov held up this study as a decisive move away from the counting of kulaks 'by eye' (*na glaz*), a practice he condemned by quoting the saying: 'Try to do something well, and in an instant you will be pointed out as a kulak.'[60]

The methodology devised by Kavraisky and Nusinov to delineate peasant groups utilised a complicated series of indices. Firstly, farms were divided into five categories according to their main source of income: (1) agriculture; (2) hired labour; (3) self-operated small-scale industrial enterprises; (4) the same with the employment of hired

labour; (5) services and other. These five categories were then subdivided on the basis of economic wealth, the main indicator used being
the value of the 'means of agricultural production' owned. The 'means
of production' was defined as all livestock, agricultural equipment
(tilling, harvesting, transport etc.) and farm buildings (excluding living
quarters). By this means thirteen sub-groups of farms were distinguished, from a bottom stratum owning up to 50 roubles worth of
'means of production' to a top one possessing over 2,500 roubles
worth. These thirteen sub-groups were further allocated into seven
categories of farms by size of sown area. Thus, three basic indicators of
differentiation were employed: main source of income, value of means
of production owned and size of sown area. This type of sophisticated
classification produced several hundred possible permutations ($5 \times 13
\times 7 = 455$), all of which indicated real economic differences. However,
establishing the limits of each of the three main categories of farms
(bedniak, seredniak and kulak) was a much more arbitrary process.
Kavraisky and Nusinov quite reasonably decided that the 'absolutely
indisputable' indicators of a kulak farm were: (a) hiring manpower; (b)
renting out complicated equipment; (c) leasing land (*arenda*); (d) industrial activity dependent on the use of hired labour; and (e) trade as the
main source of income. Bedniak farms were defined as those with no
sown area or sowing up to 3 desiatinas with 300–400 roubles worth of
means of production, depending on whether they were farmers or
rural labourers, and 100–200 roubles worth if they had a small business
(without hired labour). All other peasant households were counted as
seredniaks.[61]

By using these intricate parameters they assessed the relative
strength of each of the main peasant categories in south-west Siberia as
follows (as a proportion of households): bedniak (38.9%), seredniak
(54.8%), kulak (6.3%). This pattern of differentiation was much less
acute than the one claimed by the Opposition but was still significant.
The estimate of 6.3% for kulak households compared with a figure of
3.2% for the country as a whole proposed by Nemchinov in early 1928.
Furthermore, the economic power of the Siberian kulaks far outweighed their numerical strength as they accounted for 16.4% of the
total value of the means of production (of which almost 53% was
animals and about 30% equipment), 14.5% of the sown area (an average of about 12.5 desiatinas per farm) and almost 25% of leased land
(an average of 8.5 extra desiatinas per farm). From the Bolshevik
viewpoint, the key indicator of capitalist class relations in the countryside was the hiring of wage labour, and Kavraisky and Nusinov

revealed that over 85% of kulak farms availed themselves of this, with over 64% employing it on a long-term basis (over 150 days p.a.). Kulak farms also profited greatly from renting out their equipment to other peasants (over 65% did this). Nevertheless, according to the study the seredniak remained the 'central figure' in the countryside, with over half of all farms falling into this category and holding over 70% of the 'means of production' (by value) and over 68% of the total sown area. Many seredniaks also engaged in exploitation but on a lesser scale to the kulaks: approximately one-third used hired labour and rented out their equipment, and they leased almost 65% of all *arenda*. The bedniak farms, on the other hand, while accounting for about two-fifths of all households were emaciated in terms of economic strength, owning a little over 12% of the value of the means of production, only 17% of the sown area and employing less than 14% of batraks, mostly on a short term basis.[62]

Kavraisky and Nusinov regarded the sown area indicator on its own as a fundamentally flawed method of discerning differentiation. In fact, by their procedures almost 92% of seredniak farms fell into the 8 to 12 desiatina category, which was a common standard for recognising a kulak farm, and over 28% of kulak farms sowed less than 8 desiatinas, an amount normally used as the upper limit of the seredniak farm. As an illustration, Kavraisky and Nusinov drew a striking comparison of two farms; firstly that of the bedniak Bakhov, a household of three members, with 3 desiatinas of sowings, two horses and a cow, and a total annual tax of 18 roubles; secondly, the farm of the kulak Petr which had four family members, 3 desiatinas of sown area, a horse, two cows and an annual tax of 16 roubles. The second farm was placed in the kulak category, even though it had a small sown area and a low tax, because it owned a mechanised thresher which yielded an annual income of 280 roubles from rental charges. In addition, this peasant secretly supplemented his income by leasing land from bedniaks and acting as a loan shark (dealing in cash and grain).[63]

Given that the use of hired labour was an accepted touchstone of a kulak farm, Kavraisky and Nusinov paid particular attention to this factor. Official estimates of the number of agricultural labourers in the krai varied from 156,000 to 185,000 but the consensus was that it was growing steadily. The batraks were usually employed on a casual or seasonal basis, worked long hours (ten to fifteen-hour days) with an average pay of about fourteen roubles per month (in cash and kind), women and children workers receiving substantially less. Nearly one-quarter of bedniak farms were indistinguishable from batraks as they hired out their labour for long periods (150 to 210 days p.a.), and almost 59% worked as labourers at some time in the year. A particularly oppressive form of exploitation of bedniaks was the 'partnership' (sic) method (*supriaga*) which supposedly originated in Siberia. In theory this meant joint working of land and use of equipment but in practice served as a cover for exploitation. A bedniak with no land or equipment rented them and borrowed seed from a well-off neighbour and would then pay off this debt by labouring on the farm of the latter and handing over a share of his own harvest in lieu of payment. This was a convenient method for the well-off peasant to secure cheap hired labour and avoid paying tax for extra sowings. In 1927 the Head of the Krai Land Administration, I. A. Kharlamov, claimed that as many as one-quarter of Siberian farms were involved in supriaga.[64]

Poor peasants would also be drawn into debt to well-off neighbours by building up credit for purchasing *samogon* or food supplies, or rental payments for the use of equipment (ploughing, threshing and so on). Frequently, the only way a bedniak could clear such debts would be to lease part of his landholding to the creditor. For example, a bedniak in the village of Chistiun'ka, Barnaul Okrug, did not have any agricultural equipment and was forced to lease 10 desiatinas of his holding to a kulak neighbour. In payment for the lease the kulak ploughed just 1 desiatina of the bedniak's remaining land. Considering that the standard charge for ploughing 1 desiatina was 6 roubles, the cost incurred by the kulak for leasing this land was a paltry 60 kopecks per desiatina.[65]

Kavraisky and Nusinov completed their attack on the Left by disparaging Brike's studies of sown area changes as 'mathematical exercises'. They asserted that there had been no decrease of the bedniak sown area, rather the farms sowing up to 4 desiatinas had increased their total sown area by 37% in 1926/7. They claimed that the Kraikom line that all farms were increasing in prosperity was substantiated by their findings, and they concluded that 'for the present' both the poor and the kulaks were growing in strength 'in parallel'.[66] However, if anything, their figures on the numerical strength and economic power of the kulak stratum tended to reinforce rather than assuage the fears raised by the Opposition about the growth of an exploitative kulak class in Siberia, and the publication of their study immediately stirred up a fresh controversy in the Siberian party organisation over this issue. At the end of November an issue of the recently founded journal of the Kraikom, *Na Leninskom puti*, was devoted to several discussion articles on peasant differentiation. An article by Syrtsov again derided the Left's claims and lavished praise on Kavraisky and Nusinov for their 'comprehensive analysis' of differentiation and for puncturing once and for all the 'sowing mythology'.[67] Syrtsov must have hoped that the lower rate of differentiation (in comparison with that claimed by the Opposition) established by Kavraisky and Nusinov would effectively mute the criticisms levied against the Kraikom on this question. In fact, the opposite proved to be the case as he found himself under sustained attack for not having 'a correct line' on differentiation in a counterbalancing article by a Leftist economist, L. Kleitman, in the same issue.

Kleitman's article contained a detailed challenge to the Kavraisky and Nusinov analysis. He analysed the material gathered in the Siberian countryside between 1924 and 1926 which was overly reliant on the sown area indicator) and concluded that the idea that all farms were rising in prosperity was misplaced. Rather than diminishing, he alleged, 'class antagonisms' were growing in the countryside because the kulak group was expanding its economic power by exploitation across the board. Kleitman believed that the process of differentiation was accelerating in the Altai in particular, the key grain producing area of Siberia. In support he cited statistics which revealed that between 1924 and 1926 in Rubtsovsk Okrug the percentage of farms in the large sown area group (sowing 10 desiatinas or more) had risen dramatically from 6.5% to 22.3%, and their share of the total sown area had rocketed from 2.3% to 50.4%. Similarly in Biisk Okrug, over the same period, this group surged from 9.7% of households holding 26.9% of the sown area to 15.9% with 41.6% of all sowings. Kleitman was not so much concerned by the numbers of farms rising to the well-off category as by their economic power. This not only extended to a vast share of the sown area but also to ownership of a substantial proportion of machines and animals. In 1925, 24% of households in south-west Siberia owned four or more cows, accounting for over 52% of the total herd, while in 1926 the 8.8% of households in the large sown area group owned over 30% of mowers, 45.6% of harvesters, almost 40% of threshers and over 66% of seeding machines. It was through the exploitation of advanced agricultural machines by the well-off peasantry that Kleitman saw the 'proletarianisation' of the countryside occurring.[68]

The intra-party conflict over peasant differentiation reached its climax at the Fifteenth Congress in December 1927. During the main debate, Syrtsov preceded Kamenev at the rostrum and a large part of his speech was taken up with repudiating the claims of the Opposition about an 'American tempo' of development among the peasant verk-hushka in Siberia. His speech is of particular interest since he adopted a much more hard-line stance before the central party leadership than he had hitherto exhibited in Siberia and spoke of a process of 'sharp differentiation' in the region and of a kulak verkhushka which had 'grown significantly in recent years'. One possible explanation for Syrtsov's shift in emphasis and tone is that he had recently become aware that Stalin's attitude to NEP was becoming more negative and that he was moving to the Left on industrialisation and agrarian policy. Syrtsov may have felt, quite sensibly, that his political debt to Stalin's patronage required him to pitch some of his speech in the direction of the new line. Nevertheless, he still maintained that 'growth in produc-tive strength is not at all tantamount to, not at all synonymous with the growth of kulak farms'.[69] Embarrassingly, the fact that the Siberian party leadership was not unanimous on the kulak issue was made clear to the delegates when N. N. Zimin, the Irkutsk Okruzhom Secretary and political rival of Syrtsov, delivered an outspoken and fervent critique of the 'capital accumulation' of the Siberian kulaks, and claimed that 70% of their basic capital was in the form of advanced machinery and that 30% of their income came from trade and domestic industries. This was a hint of the bitter conflict which was to flare up shortly between these two men over the manner in which the krai leadership should deal with the grain crisis of 1927–8.[70]

After the end of the congress the question of peasant differentiation was overshadowed as the focus of party attention and activity was concentrated on resolving the grain crisis. Before we examine the nature of this crisis of NEP we should mention the post-script to the differentiation debate in Siberia. The figures produced by Kavraisky and Nusinov in late 1927 were those that were subsequently deployed by the Kraikom against the Left and they influenced events at the time. However, in early 1929 they published a follow-up study, again with a foreword written by Syrtsov, employing an even more complicated statistical mechanism and including data collated in sample spring cluster censuses over the two year period 1927–8. In assessing differen-tiation this study attached particular importance to those indices which were of regional significance given the peculiarities of Siberian agricul-ture. In Siberian conditions they established these as the hiring of labour and the renting out of advanced agricultural machines, in addition to the size of sown area. These indices were then combined with the value of the sum total of all elements of means of production (i.e. all property) held by farms. A statistical 'sliding scale' was drawn composed of the coefficients of the number of days a farm rented out its machines and the number of days it hired labour. In this case, it was calculated that the income from one day's rental of a machine was equal to the income from fifteen days' use of hired labour. The peasantry was divided into a seven-fold classification, and accordingly, Kavraisky and Nusinov revised their previous estimates of the level of differentiation of farms for 1927 and 1928 (Table 5). It should be noted that this study was published at a time when the party had become actively engaged in suppressing the kulaks. Nevertheless, for the first time in Siberian analyses of peasant differentiation an attempt was made to examine 'organic processes' in the character of peasant farms (sub-division, migration, merger and liquidation of farms, family size), and the 'social structure' of the harvest. The latter is important because it illustrated the relative economic power of each category of farms in the marketing of grain, and will be discussed in chapter 4.[71]

The main conclusion of Kavraisky and Nusinov as regards the 'organic processes' among Siberian peasant households was that the kulak group was the least stable in terms of maintaining its economic position. Between 1927 and 1928 almost 42% of farms in this group declined to the seredniak level. Concurrently, there was actually an overall 7% increase in the number of kulak farms in the same period, largely as a result of the inclusion of seredniak farms whose prosperity had significantly risen. In 1928 these new arrivals from the seredniak stratum accounted for over 45% of total kulak strength. Kavraisky and Nusinov revised their previous assertion of 'parallel' growth of kulaks and bedniaks and now provided the statistical backing for the

Table 5. *Social categorisation of Siberian peasantry, 1927 and 1928*

	Number of households(%)	
Group	1927	1928
agricultural labourers	7.9%	5.7
other labourers	3.5%	2.9
bedniaks	28.5%	27.9
seredniaks	53.0%	56.0
agricultural entrepreneurs: kulaks	6.5%	7.0
traders	0.3%	0.1
owners of industrial enterprises	0.3%	0.4

Source: Kavraisky and Nusinov

resolution of the March 1928 plenum of the Kraikom which had ominously declared that: 'The accumulation of the kulak verkhushka in the
countryside is approaching the utmost limits at which the economic
usefulness of their productivity will be tolerable in Soviet conditions.'
This reflected the anti-kulak line adopted by the party during and after
the grain crisis of 1927–8 in response to what was seen as 'kulak
sabotage' of the grain procurements.[72]

This more detailed analysis revealed the tremendous complexity of
class relations in the countryside and demonstrated that there was no
clear dividing line between the kulaks and the well-off seredniaks,
confirming the view expressed earlier that social mobility in the Siberian countryside was largely a cycle of interchange between the well-
off seredniak and kulak strata.

4   The crisis of NEP

In this chapter we shall be concerned with the causes of the grain
procurement difficulties in the last quarter of 1927, which erupted into
a full scale crisis of NEP in January 1928. In particular, we shall examine
the extent to which there were regional variations or peculiarities in the
impact of the factors contributing to the crisis. In fact it should be said
that this crisis was simply the climax to a series of convergent crises
which had been gathering steam in the course of the mid-1920s and,
indeed, one scholar described it as the *'coup de grâce'* to NEP.[1] The grain
crisis of 1927/8 was not an isolated incident in the history of the
mid-1920s, for of the four grain procurement campaigns between 1924
and 1927 only one, that of 1926/7, proceeded without a crisis of some
sort.

The nature of the difficulties encountered by the Bolsheviks in their
relations with the peasantry in this period lay in the explosive mix of
political and economic ingredients which formed NEP. The fundamental principle of NEP was the *smychka* and, as we have seen in earlier
chapters, this involved the party making political and economic concessions to the peasantry: subordinating the pace of industrial investment to the development of agriculture in order to stimulate
peasant production and accumulation, and encouraging the peasants
to join the party, soviets and cooperatives. Notwithstanding this, the
fact was that NEP had been introduced by Lenin in March 1921 as a
tactical temporary retreat to defuse peasant unrest and consolidate the
revolution, and the Bolsheviks in no way abdicated from their long-
term ambition of overall central direction of the economy in order to
'build socialism'.[2] While the party retained central control over the
'commanding heights' of the economy, including large-scale industrial
production, trade and financial organs and economic planning, the
regulation of the peasant economy was a more complicated matter. In
this respect the party attempted to exert an influence by a number of

levers, the most important of which were the price scissors, manufactured goods supplies and taxation.

In manipulating these levers the regime had two policy goals in
mind. Firstly, it sought to transfer resources from the agricultural
sector to finance industrialisation. Secondly, it aimed to determine the
nature of agricultural production itself by the setting of preferential
prices. In practice, the peasant economy proved to be less amenable to
state control because of contradictions in government policy and in the
way NEP operated. NEP allowed the free market to exist alongside that
of the state and the peasants were permitted to dispose of their produce as they saw fit, in other words, on the most profitable basis.
Consequently, the peasants' incentive to produce and sell was determined by the price obtainable and as this fluctuated from year to year
so peasant production and marketings alternated according to what
was profitable. The scale of peasant marketings was largely determined by the availability of manufactured goods for purchase and in
the event of shortages the peasants withdrew from the market rather
than accumulate cash which they could not spend. This feature
became more pronounced as NEP progressed and the growth of peasant income in real terms outpaced the ability of industry to satisfy rural
consumption of goods. In such circumstances the state policy of
moving the price scissors (the ratio between the price of manufactured
goods and agricultural produce) in favour of the peasantry actually
aggravated the situation by adding to peasant income, further deplet-
ing goods stocks and causing a price inflation spiral. The state could
have absorbed some of the growth in peasant income by applying
more penal tax measures but in the mid-1920s the Bukharinist pro-
peasant policy held sway and it was only in the spring of 1926 that the
government began to levy a more progressive and heavier agricultural
tax burden.[3]

In Siberia these difficulties took an especially sharp form. Although
traditionally grain was cheap in the region and prices remained low in
comparison with other areas of the country throughout the NEP
period, the problem of price imbalances was particularly disruptive to
state procurement plans because the mixed nature of dairy, livestock
and grain farming gave the Siberian peasantry a large degree of flexibility in deciding how to deal with both the state and free market.
Furthermore, the distance of Siberia from the central industrial areas
was a handicap when it came to the allocation of scarce manufactured
goods. Given that the Siberian peasantry were prospering under NEP
and seemed to be more active politically than in other areas of the

country it is no surprise that attempts by the Bolshevik regime to interfere and direct the rural economy of the region met with considerable resistance.

Grain campaigns during the heyday of NEP

As we saw in chapter 1, the delayed introduction of NEP in Siberia combined with the prodrazverstka campaigns of 1921–2 to plunge agriculture in the region into subsistence farming. The peasantry were slow to recover from this onslaught and the first signs of a return to surplus production in Siberian grain farming came during the grain campaign of 1924/5. The government fixed low state grain procurement prices in the autumn with the aim of accumulating finances for industrial investment. However, when faced with a surge in private trade in grain at free market prices, it was compelled to capitulate and by May 1925 state procurement prices were double those of the preceding December. Some restrictions were applied against private traders but the regime was unwilling to resort to a policy of general coercion against the peasantry to force them to sell grain at the official prices and, reluctantly, it was forced to bite the bullet of curtailing industrialisation plans.[4]

In Siberia the procurement campaign was reasonably successful as 40.5% of the planned 45% of the yearly plan had been collected by 1 January 1925. But in the main planned procurement areas of south-west Siberia the figures were disastrous due to the fact that private trade in grain flourished. For example, the proximity of the grain growing Omsk Okrug to the industrial consumer areas of the Urals meant that private traders and speculators proliferated in this area and, consequently, only 28% of the yearly state plan was fulfilled while private traders accounted for about 40% of all grain procured. State procurement was further de-stabilised by private traders from other grain deficient areas pouring into the area and buying up grain at high prices. As a result, in December 1924 the Kraikom resorted to emergency powers to restrict free trade and banned the transport of grain out of Siberia by private traders. Although procurement prices in Siberia increased in the spring they did not double as in the rest of the country. It would seem that the increase in prices was of less importance for the course of the grain collections in Siberia than the imposition of administrative restrictions on private trade, for December and January were the peak procurement months. In the end the annual plan of just under 819,000 tons was fulfilled by 97.6% but this was achieved by a huge increase in procurements in eastern okrugs, which overfulfilled their plan to 128% and compensated for shortfalls in the main grain surplus areas of the south-west, where plan fulfilment had stalled at 76% of the total as the peasantry either sold their surplus on the free market or hoarded it for the next year.[5]

The grain campaign of 1925/6 developed into a crisis as a result of the depletion of manufactured goods stocks in the countryside because of low prices and the failure of the state to match output to the pent-up rural demand. Once again the party leadership felt that the only solution was to raise grain prices to stimulate peasant marketings and, for the second year in a row, was forced to abandon plans to finance a higher tempo of investment in the industrial sector from the hard currency earnings of grain exports. In Siberia the grain harvest was the best on record at over 5.5 million tons yet this was not reflected by an increase in state procurement. In November and December 1925 the region suffered severe shortages of manufactured goods resulting in rampant speculation by private traders. Apparently even the state regional trade organ (Sibtorg) was reduced to buying manufactured goods at inflated prices from private traders and wholesalers. By December peasants preferred to barter their grain than sell it for cash, and when A. Enukidze, Secretary of the Presidium of VTsIK, came to the First Krai Congress of Soviets he was met on each of his railway stops by delegations of peasants demanding manufactured goods and machines. Whereas state grain procurement prices were increasing in the autumn and winter of 1925/6 in most areas of the country, in Siberia prices actually fell (by 10% for wheat). This unfavourable price scissors between high manufactured goods prices and low grain prices was a major disincentive to peasant marketings of grain and led to a resumption of widespread hoarding.[6]

The crisis led to public disagreements among Siberian party and state officials. In December 1925, Mesiatsev, the Narkomzem plenipotentiary in Siberia, called for a substantial increase in state procurement prices and D. Petukhov, an official in the Krai Land Administration, went even further and advised the peasants to withhold their grain until state prices were raised significantly or to feed it to their livestock. The Kraikom came out strongly against an increase in grain prices, with Eikhe in the forefront. In an article published in January 1926 he put the blame for the crisis squarely on the shoulders of 'local speculators' and the well-off peasants and kulaks who, following the experience of the previous year, were hoping to force the state to raise prices in the spring. Eikhe warned that an increase in grain prices would cause an inflationary spiral in the economy, lower the real income of workers and threaten plans to build up the foreign currency reserves of the state. Although he admitted that the crisis was an economic one, he offered few concrete alternatives to raising prices other than improved party and soviet political work among the peasants, eliminating competition between grain procurement agencies (which fuelled price inflation) and increasing the delivery of manufactured goods to rural areas (an unrealistic proposal given the severe shortages). He bitterly observed that 'grain surpluses are many', yet state grain exports, 'the fulfilment of which will determine to a significant degree the tempo of our economic growth', were threatened by the refusal of the peasantry to deliver. What was needed, he asserted, was heavier taxation on the peasants to force them to sell their grain for cash.[7]

The determination of the regional party leadership to curb price inflation was elaborated in the Kraikombiuro report on the grain campaign to the plenum of the Kraikom in March 1926. This acknowledged that the fundamental issue for the peasantry was 'the question of prices' but the Kraikombiuro had taken a hard line against a price rise in order to protect the interests of the poor peasants who had sold their grain at the lower state prices in the autumn and would be buying grain for food in the spring. There was also a fear that an increase in grain prices in the spring would set a precedent and would lead to a similar outcome next year. Yet, despite the strong rhetoric to the contrary from krai leaders, state prices did rise marginally (by 2 kopecks per pud of wheat) but still remained well below prices offered in October 1925. As a result the grain procurements were a complete failure. The initial planned target for Siberia was set at just under 1.4 million tons but in December this was revised down by as much as 30% to about 983,000 tons. The actual total procured for the year was just 855,037 tons (61% of the original plan, 87% of the revised plan). A significant feature of the collections was that the south-western areas of the krai had sharply increased their share of the total, from 43% in 1924/5 to 54% in 1925/6. This indicated that NEP was taking hold in the Siberian countryside and that, with the expansion in sown area, an agricultural recovery was underway. It was also an illustration of how the expansion of wheat growing in the steppe belt stretching from Omsk to the Altai was displacing the traditional Siberian emphasis on dairy farming.[8]

The exception to the series of procurement crises in the mid-1920s was the campaign of 1926/7, which was an outstanding success across the country and marked the high point of NEP. This success may be attributed to several factors. The harvest of that year was a post-revolutionary record at 76.8 million tons, indeed it approached the record level of 1913, and the countryside was awash with grain. The government had also made adequate preparations by making it a priority to boost the output of manufactured goods in the spring and summer of 1926, and thus ensured that there were plentiful supplies throughout the campaign to stimulate peasant sales. Moreover, peasant wealth was subjected to heavier and more progressive taxation, with fixed periods established for its prompt collection, and in this way excess peasant revenues were absorbed early in the campaign. Finally, a reorganisation of the state procurement agencies implemented in April 1926 provided a more efficient framework for the conduct of operations, with state procurement concentrated in Khleboprodukt and the cooperatives. At the same time private trade in grain was severely restricted by punitive railway charges and some nationalisation of private mills. The outcome was that state grain procurement for the whole country rose from just over 8.4 million tons in 1925/6 to over 10.6 million tons in 1926/7, and as prices remained stable throughout the year a steady flow of grain on to the market was secured.[9]

In Siberia the success was even more pronounced. There was another record grain harvest, amounting to over 6.5 million tons, and record procurements totalling over 1.3 million tons, a massive 54% increase on the amount procured in 1925/6. The Siberian leadership was taken by surprise by this outcome for at the outset of the campaign a moderate plan of 819,000 tons (the same as in 1924/5) had been set, but this was soon revised up to 983,000 tons after the initial results proved encouraging and by August 1926 even the revised targets had been exceeded by 34%. In the autumn of 1926 a prolonged period of favourable weather, with a general absence of the bad roads season greatly facilitated the collections and the quarter October–December accounted for almost half the total of grain procured during the whole year. There were several distinguishing features of the campaign in the region. Firstly, although the burden of taxation on the peasantry had increased by almost 50% over the previous year, from 16.8 million roubles to 24.2 million, periods of heavy grain collections did not necessarily correspond with periods of high tax receipts. For example, in October about 164,000 tons of grain and over 3.7 million roubles in taxes had been collected, followed in November by almost 240,000 tons and about 2.5 million roubles of taxes, and in December by over 250,000 tons and over 5 million roubles. Grain collections also far outstripped supplies of manufactured goods to the krai. In the peak procurement period of October to December, goods supplies had increased by 8.4% whereas marketings had more than doubled in comparison with the same quarter of 1925/6. These factors suggest that peasant marketings were stimulated by other means.[10]

A major reason for the surge in peasant marketings of grain was the fact that the regional leadership had been resolute and not substantially increased prices in the spring and summer of 1926. The large stocks of grain held over from previous years by the peasantry coupled with the bumper harvest in the autumn of 1926 produced a huge glut and with no prospect of a rise in prices peasants flooded the procurement points with their grain. One source explained the huge increase in the collections by the new-found confidence of the peasantry in the Soviet regime, asserting that the peasantry were transferring from natural wealth accumulation to monetary and that the banks and credit cooperatives were being overwhelmed with peasant deposits. In addition, the new restrictions on private trade in grain meant that the state and cooperative procurement organs had virtually a free hand in a buyers' market. In 1925/6 they had taken 89.6% of all grain procurements in the region but in 1926/7 they accounted for almost the total amount. The exclusion of private traders from the grain campaign was assisted by the remoteness of Siberia and its limited rail network which made rigid state control of movements of goods and people feasible.[11]

Another striking feature of the campaign in Siberia was the extent to which the south-western okrugs had realised their potential as a grain surplus area and outpaced north-eastern okrugs in the collections. About 80% of all grain procured came from the south-western okrugs, with Omsk Okrug and the Altai region accounting for over 70% of the total. Furthermore, the proportion of wheat in the procurements had risen sharply, to 76% of the total (compared with 36% in 1924/5 and 51% in 1925/6). This year Siberian wheat was of major significance in satisfying both internal demands and state exports of cereals. In particular, given that the region accounted for over one-third of Soviet exports of wheat in this year, Siberia was now an important source of the hard currency earnings that were central to Bolshevik plans for the industrialisation of the country. There were some problems caused by the lack of infrastructure in the krai, with bottlenecks at collection points, wharves and railway junctions, and the deficiency of grain storage facilities, which meant that there were heavy losses in quantity and quality of shipments. Nevertheless, the campaign was a tremendous success and raised the regime's expectations for a similar outcome to the harvest of 1927. By the autumn of 1927, such high hopes were gripping the Stalinist element of the party leadership that they began to heighten their demands for a more ambitious approach to industrial investment plans.[12]

The grain crisis of 1927/8 (October–December)

The grain procurement campaign of 1927/8 opened with much promise. The prospects for the harvest were good and the Central Committee looked forward to the establishment of a state grain reserve of 819,000 tons (50 million puds). The total first quarter planned procurements significantly exceeded the corresponding figure for the previous record year. Amid mutual back-slapping, and with a new confidence in their agrarian policy, the party leadership began the process of the expulsion of the Left. The initial euphoria quickly dissolved when a slight fall in the procurements at the end of September deteriorated into a slump in October. In November and December the collections plummeted with a second quarter total of just over half that in the equivalent period in 1926/7. By January 1928 only 4.9 million tons of grain had been procured by the state against over 7 million in the same period of the previous year. The total was not only well below state expectations for building a grain reserve and exports but was disastrously short of the minimum required to feed the towns and the Red Army.[13]

Due to climatic conditions Siberian grain was normally harvested in late August and early September, much later than in other regions of the country, and therefore grain procurement campaigns in the region did not usually get under way until the middle of September. Following the record collections of 1926/7 the planned target for Siberia this year was raised to an ambitious 1.34 million tons (about 2% up on the total procured the previous year). The early returns augured well as the amount procured in September (at 29,330 tons) exceeded that of the same month of 1926 by about 3,500 tons. By comparison with 1926/7, the decline in the collections began in October and by the end of December had reached crisis proportions. By 1 January 1928 the shortfall in grain amounted to over 265,000 tons less than had been collected in the same period of 1926/7. The krai party leadership must have been stunned by these figures for they indicated that there had been a fall of over 50% in Siberian grain procurement compared with about 30% in the USSR.[14]

The reasons for the fall-off in grain procurement elicited an intense debate in the party. Stalin provoked controversy by emphasising the political nature of the crisis, describing it as kulak 'sabotage' and claiming that they had deliberately withheld their grain surpluses and influenced the seredniaks to do likewise with the aim of forcing the state to raise grain prices. In effect, according to Stalin, the state was being blackmailed into abandoning its plans for financing increased industrial investment from grain exports. Furthermore, the speculative aims of the kulak had been assisted by poor political and organisational work by the party and state organs and grain procurement agencies at the local level. For the Right, Bukharin rejected the 'fairy tales' about speculation and hoarding of grain by peasants and asserted that the main problem was low production of grain, while the crisis in the winter of 1927/8 was due to specifically economic factors, the main ones being: low prices for grain in comparison with other agricultural produce and manufactured goods shortages. As we shall see later, in the immediate aftermath of the crisis the April joint plenum of the Central Committee and Central Control Commission met and the party leadership patched over its divisions and decided on a delicate compromise analysis of the crisis, which incorporated the positions of both Stalin and Bukharin.[15]

The causes of the grain crisis continue to excite considerable debate among Western scholars. Conquest has stated that the deficit in grain in January was 'by no means a "crisis" or "danger"' but was something of a figment of the imagination of the party leadership. He believed that, 'it was no more than a temporary disequilibrium in the grain market, easily correctable if normal measures had been applied'. By 'normal measures' he meant a rise in the state procurement price of grain. Davies, on the other hand, has suggested that from the autumn of 1927 elements in the party leadership centred on Stalin were moving outside the constraints of the mixed economy framework of NEP. He views the grain crisis as the 'decisive test' where the conflicting ideological approaches of 'planning through the market' and 'planning by overcoming the market' clashed. The Fifteenth Congress decisions for a 'reinforced offensive against the kulak' and the placing of collectivisation as 'the main task' of the party in the countryside were evidence, in his opinion, of the new harsher attitude of the regime towards NEP. The new militant approach of Stalin and others precluded a price rise which would mean the postponement of plans for industrialisation. Therefore, the only alternative to ditching economic plans and the starvation of the towns and army was for the government to coerce the peasantry to sell their grain at the fixed state prices.[16]

The Western academic dispute over the nature of the grain problem in the 1920s is centred on the reliability of Soviet statistics on grain production and marketings. Jasny asserted that the statistics produced in the mid-1920s (1925–9) were the most reliable ever produced in Russia: 'the right people were given a real chance and they did an excellent job'.[17] However, others have maintained that the degree of professional competence and overall reliability of statisticians was 'fairly low' and thus the statistics represented no more than 'an order of magnitude'.[18] One can only speculate as to the extent to which local officials, engaged in the gathering and assessment of statistical data, deliberately falsified results or misunderstood and erroneously fulfilled their tasks. A contemporary observer stated that local officials, overwhelmed by the sheer weight of statistical material being gathered at the time, admitted that they 'just put down the first thing that comes into our heads'.[19] Whatever the accuracy of the statistics, throughout this period critical political decisions were based on them, and after all they were (and remain) the only statistical data available.

Western scholars have outlined several contributory factors in the grain crisis: low productivity and increased peasant consumption, price imbalances, manufactured goods shortages, increased peasant income in real terms, the inefficiency of the grain procurement organs, poor party and state supervision of the campaign, and the war scare of 1927. These factors were identified to a greater or lesser extent in party pronouncements in the aftermath of the crisis but Stalin's post-mortem assessment of the reasons for the crisis singled out one additional element as the key explanation: kulak sabotage. How accurate are these general assumptions about the causes of the crisis in the country at large and are they substantiated when viewed from the regional perspective of Siberia?

Low productivity and increased peasant consumption

A fundamental problem in the relationship between the regime and the peasantry was that the regime had high expectations of a return to the grain export levels of the pre-war period in order to finance its plans for industrialisation, while grain production and marketings had not regained pre-war levels. In 1927 production of grain in the USSR, at 72.3 million tons, was several million tons lower than the 1926 record (76.8 million tons) and well below the estimated levels of 1913 (77 to 94 million tons). The absence of precise information on marketings in the pre-war period makes a comparison with the mid-1920s difficult. The so-called 'Nemchinov table', used by Stalin to illustrate the economic power of the kulak stratum, estimated that grain marketings as a percentage of total production had fallen by half between the pre-war period and 1926/7, from 26% to 13%. The latter figure was almost certainly too low as the TsSU handbook on agricultural statistics published in 1929 gave a figure for marketings of 20.7% for 1926/7 and 21.8% in 1927/8. However imprecise the statistics it was widely recognised that marketings had fallen substantially and the general conclusion was that the growing rural population and livestock were eating better than in the pre-revolutionary period and were consuming a substantial proportion of what was once exported. The situation was further exacerbated by the demographic trend of a growing urban population which meant that urban consumption of grain was steadily rising in the mid-1920s, and eating habits were changing to increased consumption of wheat bread as opposed to the traditional staple of rye bread. The upshot of all this was that exports of grain had fallen from about 9.6 million tons in 1913 to around 2.1 million tons in 1926/7.[20]

The impact of low productivity on decreased peasant marketings of grain was not applicable in Siberia. As we saw in chapter 1, when we discussed the rise of the Siberian grain industry, there was a rapid expansion in grain production and marketings in the region during the mid-1920s and of premium quality wheat in particular. The gross grain harvest in Siberia in 1926 at 6.52 million tons was a 28% increase on that of 1913 (5.1 million tons). Much of this increase was due to the fact that there were an additional 2.43 million acres sown to wheat by 1927 (45% of the total sown area) compared with 1913. In parts of the Altai the share of wheat as a proportion of the total sown area was even greater: for example, 76% of the total in Slavgorod Okrug. Nevertheless, the harvest of 1927, at just over 5.8 million tons, registered a shortfall of 710,000 tons (11%) compared with that of the previous year, mainly as a result of a harvest failure in some okrugs (Tarsk, Tulunsk) and, more importantly, in several raions of the main grain areas of Omsk, Slavgorod and Biisk. Thus, there was less grain to sell while procurement targets and state expectations of marketings in the region had risen. The high expectations of the state turned into desperate demands once it became evident that there had been a more serious harvest failure in the Ukraine and North Caucasus, the bread basket of the country, and the regime looked to the Eastern grain producing regions, notably Siberia, to make good the shortfall. Although the Siberian harvest was down on 1926 levels while peasant consumption of grain was rising, there remained a huge marketed surplus and it is very likely that this was supplemented by grain reserves hoarded from previous years. Therefore, we must look to other reasons for the development of the grain crisis in the region.[21]

The price factor

It has been argued that the grain crisis of 1927/8, 'was due much more to price relationships, which were very unfavourable to grain, than to any other single cause in the short run'.[22] This price imbalance was caused by the decision of the government in September 1927, as the harvest came in, to lower grain prices and at the same time increase the procurement prices for industrial crops and livestock produce. The aim was to correct a disequilibrium in prices which in the previous year had discouraged peasant production and marketings of the latter products. In practice, the measure had the unintended impact of stifling the flow of grain to the procurement points, since peasants sensibly sold those products which raked in the greatest profit. This is borne out by survey data collated in the grain areas of the RSFSR in early 1928 which revealed that peasants regarded low grain procurement prices as the primary reason for their reluctance to sell.[23]

An examination of Siberian agricultural data confirms that price imbalances were indeed central to the grain crisis. A comparison of agricultural price indices in Siberia for 1927/8 with those of 1913 reveals that the price of wheat, which was the region's main crop, lagged far behind increases for other products. If 1913 prices equal 100, then prices in 1927/8 were as follows: wheat 133.7, large hides 140.7, milk 145.7, beef 154.5, pork 155.6, lamb 177.2, small hides 186, wool 209.7. In the autumn and winter of 1927/8, the highly advantageous prices for livestock produce, especially meat and hides, meant that Siberian procurement agencies found themselves in the unusual position of fulfilling their annual plans for these several times over in a remarkably short period of time: for example, the Biisk Okrug Agricultural Credit Union fulfilled virtually its whole seasonal procurement plan for meat in December alone. Procurement of livestock products was usually highest in West Siberia, where many of the okrugs were typified by a mixture of livestock and grain farming, but the levels of 1927/8 were unprecedented and demonstrated that the ratio of products procured in these areas radically altered between 1926/7 and 1927/8.[24]

The surge in peasant marketings of meat and a whole range of other livestock products in the winter of 1927/8 was obviously directly related to high prices for such products in comparison with grain. In fact, the high price of second and third grade meat (milch cows), coupled with a shortage of fodder in some areas of West Siberia caused a significant increase in the slaughtering of milch herds. These losses had a serious effect on the krai procurements plan for butter which was under-fulfilled by 40% on 1 January 1928, and in the okrugs where meat sales were particularly high this shortfall was even greater. For example, meat procurements in Rubtsovsk Okrug to 1 January 1928 were up by 590% in comparison with the same period of 1926/7, yet the butter procurements plan had only been fulfilled by 28%. Butter collections were also undermined by the priority allocations of consumer goods to grain raions and to peasants who sold grain. By the end of the campaign the share of meat in the Siberian procurements had risen by over 56% in comparison with the previous year, with similarly impressive increases in procurements of other livestock products. To a striking degree, this evidence confirms that price imbalances between grain and other agricultural products was of crucial significance in deterring peasant marketings of grain in Siberia.[25]

Manufactured goods shortages

In the Soviet countryside of the mid-1920s a truly self-sufficient peasant household was rarely encountered. The peasantry depended on state, cooperative and, to a lesser extent, private traders for many basic household items, as well as the more expensive products such as ironware implements, farm equipment, construction materials and cloth. Trotsky had once described the smychka as 'an endless ribbon of cloth which is stretched out between town and country. A cloth conveyor.'[26] The essence of this statement was that NEP rested on a bilateral duty of the state to provide the peasantry with consumer goods and the peasantry to yield its marketable surpluses in exchange. The problem was that shortages of manufactured goods had been endemic in the Soviet economy since the First World War, and in the mid-1920s the Bolshevik regime had to struggle to ensure that manufacturing industry produced sufficient output to satisfy the minimum demands of the prospering peasant economy. In the spring of 1927 the party decided to reduce the prices of industrial goods by about 10% by June, with the aim of closing the 'scissors gap' between agricultural and industrial goods prices in favour of the peasantry and thereby undercut speculation in scarce goods by private traders. It was a decision of great folly given the existing dearth of goods and the inability of the state to raise output to a level which satisfied the current rural demand, never mind an artificially inflated one. To add to an already deteriorating situation the price reductions were badly timed to come into effect just before the summer period, when production was at its annual nadir due to workers' holidays and maintenance work in factories. It is to this period, the last quarter of 1926/7, that the goods shortages of 1927/8 may be traced.[27]

The shortfall in planned goods supplies to Siberia for this quarter were serious, amounting to 30% of woollens and 15% of ironware amongst others, and the diminished stocks were further depleted by the reallocation of some supplies for industrial use. As in other parts of the country, in August and September goods stocks were quickly bought up by the peasantry and by 1 October nearly all types of goods had become scarce (*defitsitnyi*). In the first quarter (October–December) of the economic year 1927/8 supplies did not even match the minimal levels required, never mind satisfying the surge in peasant demand. The Narkomtorg target of planned deliveries to Siberia for this quarter was 518 wagons of manufactured goods but by early December 239 (46%) of these had failed to materialise. By the end of the last quarter of 1927 about 400 wagons of manufactured goods had been delivered, but this was still well short of planned targets and needs. Meanwhile, an article in *Na Leninskom puti* in late November complained that the 10% reduction in manufactured goods prices was being implemented in an erratic fashion, with some okrugs failing to enact it while others exceeded the limit (Rubtsovsk 12.9%, Barnaul 12.5%, Slavgorod 11.3%).[28]

Matters were not helped by the inefficient distribution of goods, with no overall coordination between the party's aims for high grain procurements and priority allocation of scarce goods to the grain areas in order to stimulate peasant sales. In this respect the distance of Siberia from the manufacturing centres of the country put it at a severe disadvantage. As we shall see later, once manufactured goods were directed to the grain areas of the region there was a sharp decline in procurements in those areas specialising in dairy farming, for there was nothing to buy in the stores. A further drain on rural supplies was the fact that goods were first delivered by rail to the large urban centres for distribution, and frequently supplies to rural areas were held up or otherwise seized to satisfy urban demands. Delays in distribution were added to by traffic congestion at major junctions and railway workers either were overwhelmed by the burden of organising shipments of grain and other products or simply showed a lack of urgency for the task. The result of all this was that from October 1927, faced with bare shelves in state and cooperative stores, the peasants increasingly sold meat and agricultural products other than grain at high prices. In this way they were able to pay for taxes and other outgoings without drawing on their grain stocks.[29]

Increased peasant income

The growth in real terms and accumulation of peasant income during NEP was assisted by a series of good harvests, the high procurement prices offered by the state and a reduced overall tax burden together with changes in the tax structure which were very favourable to the peasantry, while the irresolute collection of taxes by government officials allowed vast sums in arrears to mount. In the case of Siberia, the sum of agricultural tax fell from 24.2 million roubles in 1926/7 to 22.3 million in 1927/8, and the general rise in the prosperity of the countryside was such that a Soviet historian has estimated that the purchasing power of the peasantry rose by about 20% between 1926 and 1928. Not surprisingly, the peasantry were not under any significant financial pressure to sell grain.[30]

A main feature of the 'Platform of the Left' of September 1927 was the call for a sharply progressive rise in peasant taxation, which would penalise the well-off in particular, in order to finance a higher tempo of industrial investment. However, the party leadership rejected this proposal as an attack on the smychka, though this was before the acute nature of the grain crisis had become apparent. In mid-November 1927, at the height of the intra-party struggle, Eikhe described the Leftist idea that industrialisation could be financed through 'a tightening of the tax screws' as 'massive demagogy'.[31] Yet in the absence of effective government action peasant tax arrears continued to mount and by 1 November only 1.8 million roubles were paid in Siberia compared with 4.8 million in the same period of 1926. By 1 January 1928, the target date for the completion of the tax collection campaign, only 49% of the plan (10.4 million roubles) had actually been raised.[32]

Given the mixed nature of farming in West Siberia, with widespread ownership of livestock by grain farmers, the reduced tax ratings for animals introduced by the Bolsheviks in 1925 were especially lucrative. For example, in Siberia the annual tax rate for cattle had been reduced from 16 roubles per head to 13 roubles 72 kopecks by 1927/8. Clearly, this reduction was of greatest benefit to the well-off farms owning many head of cattle and other livestock. The well-off peasants were also the main beneficiaries of the tax reform of April 1926 which established a system based on 'norms' of income from land and live-stock divided by the number of 'mouths' in a household. This system took no account of earnings from the renting out of machines and implements, which was widespread amongst the well-off in the region, and the division of the total income by the number of 'mouths' benefited those households with big families, and over 75% of well-off farms had six or more members. The state further contributed to peasant revenues by the freeing of the 35% poor and weak households from all agricultural taxation to celebrate the tenth anniversary of the October Revolution. This populist measure undoubtedly had the effect of discouraging the mass of peasants from paying taxes. A party plenipotentiary from the centre working in Siberia at this time told of how when he toured a village with a raikom secretary, the latter was anxiously apologising for the fact that he had not conducted a campaign amongst the local peasants to explain the government order on freeing the poor peasants of taxation. However, when they got to the village reading room the librarian explained that word of the order had spread like wildfire in the village and *everyone* had filled out an application to claim the tax exemption.[33]

In addition to tax arrears, peasants lagged in a whole series of other payments: insurance, self-taxation, credit repayments and cooperative share payments. The upshot of this combination of low taxation and arrears was that vast amounts of cash were retained in the countryside. The well-off peasants were particularly well-placed, as in their study of peasant farms in south-west Siberia Kavraisky and Nusinov revealed that the kulak farms investigated paid a total of 54,600 roubles in tax but that this was almost cancelled out by the 47,500 roubles which they received in payment for the leasing out of their machines and implements to other peasants. Another research study conducted in the same area in late 1926 revealed that 45% of the well-off peasants paid their agricultural taxes without selling any grain whatsoever. A modern Siberian historian has claimed that most of the approximately 12 million roubles in Siberian tax arrears were held by the kulaks and well-off peasants who represented the 13% of households in the krai that accounted for 48.6% of total taxes payable each year.[34]

The coincidence of widespread shortages of consumer goods, low prices for grain and buoyant peasant incomes meant that the peasantry had no incentive to sell their grain for cash. While these economic factors were important, elements in the party leadership, especially Stalin, were quick to look elsewhere for the causes of the peasant withdrawal from the grain market. In Stalin's view the blame for the crisis could be laid at the door of party and state organisations that had performed poorly, with the added ingredient of deliberate kulak sabotage of the party's economic programme. How accurate were these assessments?

The inefficiency of grain procurement agencies

Stalin condemned the inefficiency of the grain procurement agencies on two grounds. Firstly, he accused them of complacency at the beginning of the campaign, allowing the procurements to come in spontaneously (*samotek*: literally, by drifts) because of their over-confidence after the success of the campaign in the previous year. Secondly, once the crisis unfolded and began to gather pace at the end of 1927, they had been guilty of all sorts of malpractices and poor management. In particular, they took panic actions usually described as agiotage, that is to say, grain procurement agencies competed with each other's purchase prices in order to fulfil targets and thereby caused an inflationary price spiral.[35]

At the beginning of the campaign in October the Kraiispolkom attempted to rationalise the grain procurement apparat. This year only agricultural and consumer cooperatives and the state agencies, Khleboprodukt and Sibtorg, would be allowed to procure grain in the countryside while milling trusts (*Mel'trest*) were permitted to procure grain only at their own mills. Detailed orders fixing prices were drawn up and, in order to coordinate prices throughout the region, okrispolkoms were instructed not to tamper with these. The consumer cooperatives were placed in a highly advantageous position from the outset. They had about 1,750 procurement points (74.4% of the total) in the krai compared with 528 for agricultural cooperatives and 77 for Khleboprodukt. More importantly, the consumer cooperative network extended into the remotest areas of the countryside, employed a large staff of workers and volunteers and, crucially, dominated the supply of manufactured goods to the villages via their chain of local retail stores. The cooperatives were also assisted by the territorial division of the procurement plan to match the hierarchy of soviets, given that they existed side by side in the villages and had overlapping membership.[36]

The consumer cooperatives were frequently accused of using the 'manufactured goods bait' in the campaign, whereby they would only sell these (scarce as they were) to those peasants who sold grain at their procurement points. Those peasants who did so were given receipts which qualified them for purchases in the cooperative stores. Not only was the competition in prices between the different procurement agencies intense, but in some areas they engaged in deceit and cut-throat methods to outdo each other. In Slavgorod Okrug consumer cooperatives secretly procured grain under a Khleboprodukt sign, seemingly because it was more popular with the peasants. Sibtorg representatives waylaid peasants on the roads and offered to buy their grain, and Khleboprodukt printed declarations listing the advantages of selling grain to it rather than to other agencies. Some cooperatives were simply unable to compete because they lacked the disposable cash to pay for grain and many had no goods to entice the peasants with. Drunkenness was a perennial problem, especially during the religious holidays of early January, and there were many reports of cooperative officials being too drunk to open up the procurement points when peasants came to sell, while others were too officious, only procuring certain types of grain at set times. In Kansk Okrug, cooperative officials, who regarded their job as 'receiving grain', thought it beneath their dignity as cooperative chairmen to go to peasant farms and ask for grain. One Kraikom member, denouncing the inability of the Kansk authorities to discipline the lower cooperative network described it as 'a state within a state'.[37]

The effect of the chaotic conduct of the campaign by the official agencies was to encourage the peasants to hold back their grain in expectation of further price rises. It also encouraged private speculators (*skupshchiki*) to operate in the countryside, buying up grain at inflated prices for resale at extortionate mark-ups in towns and grain deficit rural areas. In early January 1928 in Barnaul private traders bought just under 100 tons of grain and flour in one day and almost 500 tons in the first five-day period, while Sibtorg and Khleboprodukt together procured less than 5 tons over the first ten-day period, and in the same area the Chairman of the Shakhovsk Credit Cooperative was arraigned for selling grain procurements to private individuals.

Their advantageous position meant that the cooperatives dominated grain procurement. By 1 January 1928 consumer cooperatives accounted for 38.7% of the total grain procured in Siberia, agricultural cooperatives 34%, Khleboprodukt 18.1% and others 9.1%. As we shall see later, the abuses and inefficiency surrounding the campaign continued in January and February of 1928, even after the party had launched itself into an all out offensive to obtain grain. In the first half of the campaign official attention to organisational deficiencies was fairly lax as party leaders at all levels were distracted by the climax of the struggle with the Left.[38]

The complacency of the party

That the Siberian party organisation was absorbed with matters other than grain procurement is illustrated by the fact that there were no anxious articles on the matter published in local journals before January 1928. In the latter months of 1927 the attention of Siberian Bolsheviks, as with all other party organisations in the country, was consumed by the struggle with the Left Opposition and the build up to the Fifteenth Congress. A German traveller described the scene in the region in late December 1927:

> Nobody in authority bothers about the purchase of grain. For weeks no papers, directives etc ... come from the centre to the village. All the party bosses, the authorities, are in Moscow for the party congress, for the jubilee celebrations, for the soviet sittings and other things, and the lower party bosses, the youth organisations and the village correspondents have only the anniversary of the revolution in their heads. The peasant feels neglected and left to his own devices. Thus the grain prices rise slowly.[39]

Although these observations were later confirmed by Syrtsov, there were other organisational and human failings in the party's performance. From the outset the organisation of the grain campaign was flawed in one basic aspect: the grain procurement plan was drawn up by the Sibstatotdel based on the estimates of sown area and harvest yield on a krai scale. There was no detailed breakdown of the plan by okrug and raion and no consideration allowed for area variations in yield. Frequently, by the time the plan reached down to the lower levels it had been distorted out of all proportion to the original by each tier of the hierarchy, sometimes even doubled. By the end of November the first murmurings of unease were being voiced by the Kraiispolkom and on 30 November its Presidium despatched a cable to the central government warning of the 'chronic under supply of manufactured goods to Siberia'. Narkomtorg had promised Eikhe that the shortfall in the goods supplies planned for the quarter October–December 1927 would be made up by 3 January 1928 and that the planned totals for the second quarter would be increased from 542 to 750 wagons. But such promises were illusory at this stage as there was no prospect of them being realised.[40]

One of the most serious shortcomings in the management of the campaign by the regional authorities was in its organisation of shipments of grain from procurement points to rail junctions and then by rail within and outside the krai. On 1 January 1928 only 45% of planned shipments from Siberia had been achieved, yet it was estimated that 24,570 tons of grain remained in the system, often stored in the open at railway junctions and procurement points. In the preparations for the procurement campaign the Kraiispolkom had requested 5 million roubles from the central government to refurbish the railway network, wagons and engines but was allocated just 2 million. The Krai Railway Administration further requested an additional seventy-three steam engines for the campaign but only twenty were spared from other regions. There seems to have been a complete breakdown of the Siberian rail network at this time, with trains delayed as far away as the Urals and Bashkiria waiting from six to eight weeks before being called for and delays of up to three times the normal between Irkutsk and Tomsk. In Bersk, Novosibirsk Okrug, when grain was collected and ready for shipment it was discovered that twenty-four of fifty-two wagons allocated were unfit for use and had to be repaired. Similar transport problems were experienced on the waterways. The rivers of the region were used extensively for shipping grain but were only navigable for a short period in the summer and autumn, and since the grain crisis struck in winter were not available to relieve pressure on the railways. Besides, many river vessels had been destroyed in the civil war and these losses had still not been made good by 1928. In 1926/7 it was estimated that 65% of steamboats in the krai were completely wrecked.[41]

At the Fifteenth Congress in late December 1927, Eikhe was one of the few delegates to voice concern at the prospects for the procurements. While Mikoyan and Rykov played down the extent of the difficulties, Eikhe forewarned that the campaign would only be concluded successfully if the party adopted 'a certain amount of shock tactics', particularly as Narkomtorg was now placing great hopes on the Siberian procurements.[42] On 24 December *Pravda* made one of its first references to problems in the campaign when it announced that a member of the Siberian Kraiispolkom had been sent to each of the nine most important grain okrugs in the region to concentrate the attention of the local authorities and coordinate the campaign. A contemporary observer of the Siberian political scene connected the new vigour instilled into the campaign in the region with the return of the regional party leaders from the congress, where no doubt they had been briefed on the gravity of the situation and received appropriate hard-line instructions from Stalin. However, the new approach did not have immediate results as some rural cells displayed a hostile attitude to it. When the chairman of a raikom in Biisk Okrug reproached the secretary of the village cell in Shul'gin-logskii about poor tax collection the response was: 'Why have you come here? This isn't 1920, when you could push the *muzhik* around.' It was only in mid-January that the party went over fully to 'shock tactics' and, as we shall see in chapter 5, that was wholly due to Stalin's intervention.[43]

The 'war scare' and incidental local factors

From late 1926 the USSR lived through a period of heightened international tension with a real fear of invasion. In September 1926 there was a threat of an attack on Lithuania by Poland followed in the spring of 1927 by the 'China crisis' and the bloody suppression of the Chinese Revolution. In May 1927 Britain broke off diplomatic relations after the raid on *Arcos*, and this was followed in June by the assassination of the Soviet ambassador to Poland. The culmination of the war fears came in mid-September when there was renewed strain on Franco-Soviet relations over the repayment of tsarist debts.[44]

The threat of war and state of panic which gripped the country at this time was whipped to an even higher pitch by the party press which served to spread rumour and counter-rumour among the peasants suggesting that war was looming. The Siberian press published many articles on this topic from the summer of 1927. At the June plenum of the Kraikom and Krai Control Commission the danger of war was a major preoccupation. In Omsk, Barabinsk and Rubtsovsk, mass meetings were called and local party officials delivered reports on the current international situation and collected funds for a government war chest. In June a 'Defence Week' was held in the region, with army reservists called up and military exercises conducted in Kansk. The fact that Siberia was on the front line with China caused even greater nervousness in the region. In July Syrtsov published a brochure in which he stated that a campaign being waged against the Soviet Union by foreign imperialists was 'approaching its climax' and warned that 'the storm will definitely break in the near future'. He also made some disparaging remarks about the activity of the kulaks in the face of the war scare noting that, with the urban 'White intelligentsia', 'the kulak takes advantage of these setbacks, profits by them, gloats to himself about the war danger threatening the country and at the moment of this danger he will try to drive a wedge between the party and Soviet power on the one hand and the bedniak–seredniak mass on the other'.[45]

Rumours of war were given further substance by letters from Red Army men to their families in the villages telling of military preparations. In Biisk Okrug a rumour went around the countryside that 'Kuznetsk had been taken by the Chinese' and a correspondent was told in conversations with peasants that radio broadcasts from Moscow had said that war had started, others mentioned the stories in the press, and one even noted that 'speakers have said that the Soviet authorities are trying to procure grain and stockpile it in expectation of war'.[46] As the grain procurements slumped official sources increasingly blamed kulaks for spreading fear and encouraging the mass of peasants to hoard their grain. During the 'Defence Week' kulaks in Barnaul were accused of spreading war rumours and saying 'if there is war, we must, above all, kill the communists' or 'if there is war, we must, above all, suppress the *bednota*, before long the *bednota* will serve us'.[47] In many areas the attitude of the peasants to the grain campaign was typically, 'it makes no sense to hand it over, it's better to store it up. It's obvious that there will be famine again.'[48] The effect of all this scaremongering was that by the autumn of 1927 the countryside was gripped by war fever, wild rumours and panic. It not only discouraged peasants from selling grain, but also caused a rush of panic buying of everything in consumer cooperative stores in the autumn and, in the process, added to existing goods shortages. For the peasantry had learned from experience to think as far ahead as their pockets permitted and one thing they knew was that paper money would lose much of its value and goods supplies would vanish in the event of war.

In periods of political instability or low prices peasants by tradition increased their home consumption of grain by either feeding it to their livestock, turning it into bread flour or distilling it into *samogon* (moonshine). In Siberia in 1927/8 over 130,000 tons of grain were estimated to have been used in samogon production. Detailed information on this was provided by a research study by Tsentrospirt conducted in the spring of 1927. This revealed that approximately 844,000 farms (60.6%) made their own samogon using 121,300 tons of rye flour and 59,300 tons of wheat flour, with a value of 11.58 million roubles. Understandably, the authorities were concerned not only at the quantity of grain being used for samogon production, but also at the wave of drunkenness which soaked the countryside, particularly over the Christmas holiday period in early January at the very moment that the party leadership was demanding maximum attention to the procurements. As we shall see later (p. 157), as part of the general stepping up of the campaign from January 1928, measures were taken to restrict illicit distilling.[49]

Finally, one of the most important contributory factors in unsettling the procurements in many parts of Siberia was the spell of unusually bad weather conditions in late 1927 and early 1928. There was a prolonged season of bad roads from October which brought transport and movement in the countryside to a virtual standstill. This was followed at the end of December and early January by severe frosts and strong blizzards which further obstructed grain collections. However, whilst these incidental factors undoubtedly had a significant impact on delaying procurement operations they were largely overlooked by the party leadership in its assessment of the causes of the difficulties. Stalin in particular characterised the crisis as politically motivated 'kulak sabotage' of the state plan and this stance remains an important element in Soviet historians' analyses of the crisis as they usually describe the crisis as a 'kulak grain strike'.[50]

'Kulak sabotage'

In considering Stalin's claim of a deliberate and organised attempt by kulaks to sabotage the grain procurements we need to establish a number of standards by which we can judge its accuracy. A useful starting-point is to determine the 'social structure' of the harvest, i.e., the relative share of each peasant stratum in the gross grain harvest and marketings, in order to evaluate the strength of the kulak hold on grain stocks. Secondly, there is a considerable amount of evidence of acts of peasant resistance and obstruction of the state procurement campaign, but it is less clear to what extent these actions were coordinated by the well-off stratum, who had most to lose from the party's grain offensive in the countryside, or indeed whether the motivation for resistance was economic or political. In this respect, we need to draw a distinction between kulak-led peasant actions in the period up to early January 1928, which may be more readily regarded as responses to an unfavourable economic situation and will be dealt with in this section, and those carried out at the height of the party campaign of emergency measures from mid-January onwards, which often assumed a pointedly anti-Soviet political character and will be considered in chapter 6.

The only analysis of the social structure of the grain harvest in Siberia currently available is contained in the study by Kavraisky and Nusinov published in early 1929. In defining the social structure of the harvest they assessed the consumer norms of households, livestock feed requirements, seed reserves and the average yield per desiatina. No account was taken of grain reserves held at the beginning and end of the economic year and thus their estimations are only of gross and marketed production from the harvest of 1927. It should be noted that the amount of peasant grain reserves (as family food, livestock feed, seed stocks and marketable surplus) is an important indicator of the economic strength of a household and its capacity to accumulate, and the absence of data on reserves held over from previous and current harvests is a serious shortcoming and serves to underestimate the real economic power of each stratum.[51]

In terms of the gross grain harvest there was an approximate parity between the relative shares of each peasant stratum and the sown area held. Poor farms accounted for 16.9% of the sown area and 14.4% of the gross harvest, kulaks 16% and 16.7%, while seredniaks dominated with about two-thirds of the sown area and gross grain production. However, there was a great disparity in the respective grain yields and outlays of each stratum, and this had a crucial bearing on their potential to accumulate wealth. Batraks (who in south-west Siberia often had a small sown area) only produced about 58% of their grain requirements. They had three main ways of making good this deficit: they could buy grain from other peasants or elsewhere on the free market, they could work either in exchange for grain or for cash to buy it, or they could apply for state assistance in the form of seed loans. In 1927 about two-thirds of the batrak deficit was made up by purchases on the free market, only 5% was met from the state seed fund, while the remainder was obtained from payment-in-kind for work. The bedniak farms had a deficit in grain which was equivalent to 9.3% of their overall needs and therefore they also depended, though to a lesser degree, on seasonal work and state aid to make up shortfalls in their production. At the other end of the scale, the seredniaks had a grain surplus averaging about 25% of their gross harvest, but the kulak surplus was a massive 41%. It follows that the well-off farms had greater stocks available for productive outlays (for seed and animal feed) than poor farms. On average a seredniak farm in this part of Siberia produced a grain surplus of 1.55 tons per annum, and a kulak farm had almost 5 tons. Consequently, in the procurements year of 1927/8 the marketable grain surplus of seredniak farms included in the study amounted to 7,835 tons (72.3% of the total), of kulaks just under 3,000 tons (27.7%) and the poor peasants had a deficit of 1,069 tons.

This compared with USSR figures of about 80% from the bedniaks and seredniaks and 20% from the kulaks.[52]

More importantly, according to Kavraisky and Nusinov, kulaks in south-west Siberia were involved in widespread hoarding of grain. According to their study, 42% of planned collections had been realised by early January 1928 almost exclusively from seredniak sales of grain. Meanwhile, the kulaks had increased their share of the marketable grain surplus from 27.7% to almost 50% of the total, and were holding on for high spring prices on the free market. The increase in the kulak share was due to the fact that when other peasants sold their surpluses earlier in the campaign the kulaks bought up grain on the village markets at higher prices than those offered by the state agencies, speculating on a price surge in the spring. This caused rampant inflation: for example, in Barnaul Okrug grain speculation by kulaks and Nep-men inflated the prices of all types of grain products by 50%–100%. A Siberian historian has suggested that the kulaks were being joined by some seredniaks in withholding marketable grain surpluses and cites in her support figures from the Altai region which show that the share of the seredniaks in sales of grain had fallen sharply from 60% in January 1927, to 30% in the same month of 1928. However, this evidence is incomplete and could be explained by higher than average seredniak sales of grain in the autumn.[53]

It seems clear that the main reasons for the hoarding of grain at this stage of the campaign were economic in that it was instigated by low state prices and goods shortages combined with the insecurity aroused by the war scare and wild rumours in the countryside. This is illustrated by Kraikombiuro reports of the views of kulaks who refused to deliver grain to the procurement organs: 'There are no goods and there will not be any for a while so we shall not sell grain for money', 'You don't give us manufactured goods, so like hell you won't get any grain. We don't need them at the moment, but here's the grain you need, as you can see nicely ripened.' The Kraiispolkom listed cases where kulaks brought wheat to procurement points and taunted officials with jibes: 'Look at this juicy wheat only it's not for sale. You pay too cheap. In the spring you will come to us and you will pay dearly.' By the autumn of 1927, in the aftermath of the war scare there were reports that peasants were hiding their grain in pits, and it was at this time that Rightist elements in the Siberian party organisation, such as Parfenov, were attributing difficulties in the procurements to a 'go slow' (*ital'ianskaia zabastovka*) (a term which suggests premeditation) by the well-off peasantry in response to the restrictions on their economic activities imposed by the party.[54]

Even before the grain crisis erupted a strong undercurrent of tension existed between the Bolshevik authorities and the well-off peasants in the Siberian countryside. At the Third Siberian Party Conference Syrtsov had acknowledged that there was a growth in the violent activities of kulaks, 'which show that the hostile attitude of the kulak sometimes exceeds the bounds of legality, becoming actions against Soviet power, in the form of individual cases of kulak terror against party and non-party officials'. He laid the blame for these acts of kulak terror at the door of those party organisations which wanted to 'seize the kulaks by the gills'.[55] Such acts of terror took many forms from murder to assaults, arson attacks on property, intimidation and others. It has been estimated that between January 1925 and August 1927 there were 1,838 acts of terrorism in the countryside against party and soviet officials, rural correspondents (sel'kori), peasant informers and others, of which 571 (almost one-third) were committed in Siberia. However, another source states that the number of terrorist acts in Siberia fell from 256 cases in 1926 to 226 in 1927.[56] Nevertheless, in Irkutsk Okrug, we are told that 'bands operated, and rural communists were forced to arm themselves with guns when working in the fields', and a German traveller in south-western Siberia at this time reported that rural party members were frequently assaulted and in danger of being killed by the well-off peasants who, the party claimed, operated out of churches.[57]

Once the peasantry realised that the party meant business in its grain offensive on the countryside, fears of a return to civil war methods involving prodrazverstka by armed detachments served to assist kulaks and private traders in buying up grain from the nervous and from those unable or reluctant to store or hide their surpluses. From January 1928, as party pressure in the countryside intensified and emergency measures were adopted to deal with the crisis, violent acts of resistance by peasants increased. The oppressive and urgent nature of the campaign conducted by the party inevitably meant that the mood of the well-off peasantry, those who were large-scale grain holders, would become more politically hostile to the regime.

5   The end of NEP

Moscow's response to the grain crisis

The indications are that even as late as mid-December 1927 the central authorities were still unaware of the full extent of the grain crisis. The Politburo was absorbed by the struggle with the Left and polemics on the launch of the new party slogan of a 'reinforced offensive' on the kulak, which aimed to take the venom out of attacks by Zinoviev, Trotsky and other Oppositionists on the supposedly 'pro-kulak' policy of the leadership. While the Left cited the fall-off in the grain procurements as a vindication of their stance, leading party and state officials complacently played down the scale of the difficulties, characterising them as a transitory phenomenon. At the Fifteenth Congress (2–19 December) the looming crisis went almost completely unnoticed as it was overshadowed by the main business of the expulsion of the Left.

Only Mikoyan, Head of Narkomtorg USSR, and Rykov addressed themselves directly to the unsatisfactory state of grain procurement and they cited the price imbalances and shortages of manufactured goods in the countryside as the main reason for the difficulties. Mikoyan referred to the effect of the war scare on peasant hoarding and argued for the resolution of the problem 'in the most painless way', by transferring goods from the towns to the countryside even at the cost of 'a temporary (for a few months) denuding of the town markets'. He also called for a new sowing campaign to raise grain production: a proposal that was reminiscent of famine-relief measures taken by the Bolsheviks during the civil war. Later in the proceedings, Rykov tentatively warned the delegates that 'this partial difficulty can grow into a general economic crisis', and supported 'additional measures to develop grain cultivation' (without specifying what these might be). Eikhe was one of the few delegates to mention the procurement difficulties at the congress and the only one to demand 'shock methods' to resolve problems, in particular, the drastic under-supply of manufactured goods to Siberia.[1] In fact, the call for increased goods supplies was in line with the policy decision adopted by the Central Committee in April 1926, in the aftermath of the procurements crisis of 1925. This held that in the event of future procurement difficulties, supplies of manufactured goods to the countryside would be increased and, if necessary, that hard currency reserves would be expended on importing raw materials and even finished manufactured products from abroad in order to satisfy peasant demand.[2]

Just when the decision to use emergency coercive measures to overcome the crisis was taken, and by whom, is still a matter of great conjecture among historians of this period and is an unresolvable issue given the restricted access to Soviet archives. Medvedev has asserted that there was unanimous consent in the Politburo to enact emergency measures and that Rykov had cooperated with Stalin in drawing up special instructions on grain procurement in December 1927, though Stalin was left in charge of their implementation. Similarly, while he dates the Politburo decision to the beginning of January 1928, Cohen has argued that Bukharin, Rykov and Tomsky regarded the decision to use coercion against the peasantry as a temporary measure and envisaged a quick campaign on a limited scale but Stalin subsequently exceeded their parameters and pursued a broader and harsher offensive in the countryside. He described this move as 'the pivotal event' which opened a new political schism in the party leadership.[3] The impression of an American newspaper correspondent in Moscow at this time was that the party was mobilised for emergency methods on Stalin's initiative, and this is a theme that has been taken up by some Western historians. Nove believed that the decision to use emergency measures was 'a great turning-point in Russian history . . . the first time that a major policy departure was undertaken by Stalin personally, without even the pretence of a Central Committee or Politburo decision'. Lewin agreed that the measures were adopted at 'Stalin's personal instigation', though he believed that the Central Committee 'were no longer interested in the use of NEP methods' to resolve grain procurement difficulties. He saw the campaign as essentially the re-enactment of a civil war atmosphere in the countryside through actions which Carr described as 'kindling the class war'.[4]

The signs are that the Central Committee began to issue a series of urgent directives from the middle of December 1927, ordering regional party organisations to make it their priority task to tackle the grain crisis without delay. The main worry of the central authorities was that unless there was a rapid improvement in the flow of grain to the towns, industrial centres and the Red Army there would be famine in the spring. Time was of the essence since reserves of grain had to be stockpiled in the towns before the spring thaw made the countryside impassable to heavy traffic. In addition, the crisis put in jeopardy the ambitious new plans for industrial investment, advocated by the Stalinist wing of the party leadership, as this was to be partly funded by increased grain exports. In the midst of this calamity the Bolsheviks would almost certainly have recalled the contribution hunger had made to the successful overthrow of the *ancien régime* in February 1917. Stalin himself just a few years previously had recalled Lenin's dictum that 'a revolution is impossible without a national crisis (affecting both the exploited and the exploiters)', and it seemed that without a dramatic, pre-emptive and decisive intervention by the government, such a national crisis was imminent for the spring of 1928.[5]

At the height of the Fifteenth Congress, on 14 December, a special directive on grain procurement was sent by telegram to all party organisations. This highlighted the exceptionally serious grain shortage facing the country and ordered the party, especially those organisations in important grain surplus areas, to make the procurement campaign their top priority, and emphasised the necessity of taking speedy measures before the spring thaw made roads impassable. By this juncture Stalin was taking a leading part in organising the campaign, as is illustrated by his decision to appoint one of his clients in the Central Committee apparat, A. A. Andreev, to the post of First Secretary of the North Caucasus Kraikom, a crucial grain growing region. Sometime during the party congress, he approached Andreev and asked if he would like the position, declaring 'we have weak leadership there'. Two days later, Andreev agreed and the next day he was on a train to the area.[6] It seems that Stalin's conduct had already caused a split to develop in the Politburo by this stage, for Voroshilov was quite precise when he later spoke of how 'literally on the second day after the Fifteenth Congress Rykov, Tomsky and Bukharin revealed their true face before our eyes and began to swing to the Right and came out against the policy of the Central Committee'.[7]

On 23 December a telegram to regional ispolkoms from the Deputy-Chairman of Sovnarkom RSFSR, G. A. Chukhrit, gave effect to Mikoyan's recommendations for the coordinated use of economic measures to deal with the crisis by ordering the immediate despatch of goods stocks to the countryside with priority delivery to grain producing areas at the expense of towns and non-grain areas. There was to be the minimum of delay in holding, storing and transporting goods and at the local level members of consumer cooperatives were to be given first choice. The next day saw a significant escalation of the campaign. A new telegram-directive to the local party organisations from the Central Committee ordered that leading party and soviet officials at the regional level be urgently assigned to the okrugs and raions to supervise the conduct of the campaign. All officials sent to the localities in this way were encharged with plenipotentiary powers to override decisions of local party and soviet organs which conflicted with Central Committee and regional committee decrees on the procurements, and the right to issue orders independent of local organs. The same day, *Pravda* carried a small unobtrusive announcement by Mikoyan, tucked away in a back page, that officials from the Narkomtorgs of the USSR and RSFSR had been sent to assist with the grain procurements and with fulfilling export tasks in a number of provinces and regions: the Ukraine, Central Asia, Urals, Bashkiria, North Caucasus, Tambov, Voronezh, Kursk, Saratov, Astrakhan, the Crimea, Vologda, Arkhangel'sk, and Belorussia. Curiously, every main grain area was covered except Siberia and yet this region along with the North Caucasus and the Urals was regarded by the authorities as the main source for wheat procurements. This would tend to suggest that the Siberian region had been reserved for a special campaign.[8]

In the last week of December 1927 and first weeks of January 1928 the pressure on the government mounted as the crisis unfolded and its serious nature became apparent. There was a massive transfer of goods supplies from the industrial centres of the country to the main grain areas, and from Leningrad alone between 27 December and 15 January the volume of cotton textiles despatched to Siberia, the Urals, Ukraine, Volga regions and North Caucasus doubled as the textile factories of Moscow and Leningrad worked flat out to meet new government targets. One critical element weighing on the government was the need to increase grain supplies to regions of the country specialising in technical crop production. It was feared that if sufficient supplies did not reach these areas before the spring sowing season the peasants would switch their production to food crops. Representations from party leaders in these areas to the central government further heightened the pressure. For example, at the end of December the gubkom secretary of the flax growing Smolensk region came to Moscow to plead for more grain supplies and warned that the panic at food shortages in the countryside could lead to serious public disorder.

The potential for disruption and unrest was also high in the Central Asian cotton growing belt as it received only 40% of its total planned grain requirement in January 1928. The threat of interrupted technical crop production raised the prospect of serious dislocations of economic plans, with reduced supplies of raw materials for certain industries, particularly textiles and food processing, and ultimately the possibility of large-scale urban unemployment.[9]

For the moment the government's nerve held and, in keeping with its economic approach to dealing with the crisis, it announced a new state loan (*zaem*) by which it was hoped to raise 100 million roubles for developing the economy, 10% of which would be spent on local needs. This was the first in a series of acts designed to soak up excessive peasant cash revenues in the countryside. However, while the next issue of *Pravda* complained of lax collection of agricultural taxes and insurance payments, it also introduced publicly for the first time the notion of 'kulak speculation' in grain and decried their ability to buy up goods stocks in the countryside with large surplus revenues. At the same time official circles in Moscow were giving Western reporters off the record hints that the government was thinking beyond the use of strictly economic methods to overcome the crisis and threatening to apply 'the most drastic measures to pump grain from the peasants'.[10]

A turning point in the regime's ambivalent handling of the campaign came on 6 January 1928 when, following a resolution of the Politburo, a third Central Committee directive on grain procurement was sent to all regional party organisations. It was evidently the most significant yet for Stalin later revealed that, since the earlier directives had not elicited 'the desired effect', the new order was 'quite exceptional both as regards its tone and its demands'. It instructed that a series of measures be taken in order to bring about 'a revolution in the grain collections' in the shortest possible time. While it reaffirmed the use of economic methods, including the immediate transfer of manufactured goods stocks from towns to the countryside, an intensification of collections of rural payments (taxes, insurance, self-taxation) and a more resolute fight against speculation, it went much further than previous directives by demanding that local organs employ 'all means' to complete the procurements, and in particular they were to stringently apply Soviet laws against sabotage and speculation (such as Article 107 of the Criminal Code of the RSFSR). If this implicit sanction of the application of coercive methods against the peasantry was a shock to regional leaderships, they must have been aghast that the directive concluded 'with a threat to the leaders of party organisations in the event of their failure to secure a decisive improvement in grain procurement within a very short time'. By making local party leaders personally responsible for the success of the campaign the central leadership was guaranteed not only vigorous actions but also a sharply increased likelihood of excesses and abuses against the peasantry.[11]

As each day passed the headlines and space in *Pravda* devoted to the grain campaign grew though, as Bukharin and a circle of young followers controlled the editorial board, the crisis was explained primarily in terms of economic imbalances and organisational deficiencies. Nevertheless, the day of the new Central Committee directive marked the beginning of a major press campaign and henceforth a militaristic tone was adopted in the daily reports from the 'grain front'. On 8 January Mikoyan gave an interview to *Pravda* in which he blamed inertia in the party-state apparat and called for 'all attention to the grain procurements', and in the following issue he inaugurated the first sowing campaign by the party since 1921. His strategy of economic measures had by now caused a major rift in the central state organs and ministries between non-party and party officials because the huge increases in manufactured goods output and deliveries to the countryside entailed a massive cutback in planned allocations to the consumer industry sector.[12] The scope of the authorities in absorbing the excessive revenues of the well-off peasantry was substantially widened on 10 January by a new law on self-taxation by the communal gathering. This gave okrispolkoms and raiispolkoms a discretionary power to permit a simple majority of the village gathering to impose a progressive levy on all peasant households, amounting to a sum in excess of the standard rate of 35% of the total agricultural tax of the village. The introduction of this procedure constituted the first attempt by the government to stir up social antagonisms within the peasantry by setting the poor against the well-off and was the prototype for the measures of 'social pressure' incorporated into the 'Ural–Siberian method' of grain procurement in the spring of 1929.[13]

A revealing insight into Stalin's attitudes to the crisis was disclosed in a series of telegram exchanges with Syrtsov in early January 1928. In one instance, Stalin informed Syrtsov of his outrage at a telegram that he had received from Frumkin, who was on grain procurement duties in the Urals, about the situation in Siberia. Frumkin had sensibly proposed that official bartering of manufactured goods for grain should be introduced immediately in Siberia but this was rejected outright by Stalin in the strongest possible terms:

We hold that this is a road to panic, to the raising of prices, the worst form of barter when it is clearly impossible to meet the needs of a countryside full of peasants with marketable grain stocks, it strengthens the capacity of the powerful stratum of the countryside to resist, it is the use of received goods beyond the norms of individual demand for the strengthening of the economic position of the re-surgent private trader, demoralising the bedniak–seredniak strata and the cooperatives. The fulfilment of the Politburo directive: 'Com-plete the agricultural taxation campaign by the first of March' – inevitably involves a change in the legal procedures for taxation periods. The *Sibkraikom* and *Kraiispolkom* decrees of 29 December and 4 January broke the law – they changed the periods. We consider this correct. The peasant will not hand over his tax on the basis of a *Pravda* editorial – for him binding periods are essential. *Narkomfin* protests against the change in the periods and legal procedures, but this infringement can be answered for after the campaign, we ask you to ensure that there are no bureaucratic hindrances in this area whilst the collection of taxes is being carried out.

From this telegram it is evident that by early January Stalin's frus-tration with the peasantry had reached the point where, his patience exhausted, he was prepared to abandon the strategy of economic measures to resolve the crisis and resort to illegalities and coercion. Indeed, the derisory comment about the lack of effectiveness of the Rightist-dominated editorial board of *Pravda* was a slight on Bukharin and an indication of the political animosity that was emerging in the party leadership over the conduct of the campaign. Yet the fact remains that at this stage Stalin continued to view the failure to procure grain mainly in economic terms and did not consider it as evidence of 'kulak sabotage':

> Less goods were received this year than last. Many cooperatives have empty shelves (in the absence of goods it is difficult to make them a key factor of influence on the grain procurements) . . . A partial reason for the weakening of the procurements in the current period is the holidays, no party discipline will eliminate this fact.[14]

The most dramatic development in the central government's hand-ling of the crisis was the Politburo decision to despatch contingents of urban party cadres, headed by senior officials, to the main grain areas to assist the local authorities with the procurements. Between January and March 1928 about 4,000 guberniia and okrug party officials and as many as 26,000 from uezd, raion and volost organisations, drawn from 'the staunchest and most experienced Bolsheviks' (read: the most hardened and disciplined) were sent into the countryside to get grain.[15] The mobilisation of urban worker-communist brigades for grain procurement duties has been seen not only as an attempt to overcome rural cadre shortages and lacklustre work but also as an attempt by the regime 'to circumvent a politically suspect rural officialdom in policy implementation'.[16] The organisation of the 'grain front' recalled the darkest days of the food campaigns in the countryside during the civil war. Leading members of Sovnarkom and the Central Committee Secretariat personally toured the provinces where the situation was most critical. Mikoyan repeatedly visited Siberia, the North Caucasus and other areas, Kirov went to western districts, Zhdanov to the Volga region, Shvernik to the Urals, Kosior and Postyshev to Siberia, the Ukraine, Urals and elsewhere.[17]

In the provincial party apparats a network of emergency grain 'troiki' was established from the top down to rural cell level and they assumed direct authority for the conduct of the campaign. At the highest level troiki were usually composed of local party secretaries, soviet chairmen and chekists or trade officials. They appointed local plenipotentiaries (*upolnomochennie*) with emergency powers to override decisions of lower level organs. As we noted above, the roving officials and party leaders sent from the centre also acted in this capacity, armed with plenary powers to issue decrees locally on any subject in the name of the Central Committee and Sovnarkom. On their tours they were accompanied by a large entourage of assistants (chekists, technical experts, propagandists, typists) from the offices of the Secretariat of the Central Committee in Moscow. While in the provinces, they not only invigorated the procurements but attempted to instil enthusiasm among local party and soviet officials for the development of collectivisation and political work among the poor and middle peasants.[18]

On 8 January *Pravda* published the first report of the use of Soviet laws against speculation and emergency coercive measures by the OGPU against private traders and 'speculators' in grain in Odessa. According to a Western news report from Moscow, an official announcement declared that the government intended to hold several showtrials to demonstrate to the general public and lower soviet apparat the penalties for obstructing the grain procurements, with 'specially urgent cases' to begin immediately. Already by 14 January 500 persons had been arrested in the Ukrainian city of Kharkov alone, and of these 176 were textile and 192 leather goods traders who were detained for 'disturbing the state collection of raw materials'.[19] Such operations by the OGPU so early in the campaign seem to have been concentrated in the Ukraine and North Caucasus, where hundreds of cases of speculatory violations of Soviet law were opened. A Soviet historian revealed that about 200 'speculators' were brought to trial by the middle of January with huge quantities of concealed grain confiscated. Speculators who bought up hundreds of tons of grain to transport to consumer areas were also arrested. A hoard of almost 500 tons of grain was confiscated in Kharkov Okrug and one of 164 tons seized from a kulak in Armavirsk Okrug in the North Caucasus, while seizures of over 100 tons were common elsewhere. On 13 January *Pravda* reported that a kulak hoard of 328 tons of barley was uncovered in Cherkass with the assistance of local bedniaks.[20]

From this evidence it is clear that the use of anti-speculation laws and the secret police were already features of the campaign in many areas of the country from early January 1928. Western correspondents reported the closure of private flour mills and the seizure of grain from private traders or 'sackmen' (*skupshchiki*) by special detachments. In late January came the first official acknowledgement of an execution arising out of the grain crisis. The Head of the Transcaucasian Narkomtorg, L. Novikov, was summarily executed by the OGPU for accepting commission payments from a private grain company. The execution was laconically described by the OGPU as a 'simplified method' for dealing with such abuses and was no doubt intended as a warning to others. Around this time, Andreev described how the use of emergency measures had got out of control in the North Caucasus:

> Our *apparat* and people, who were at first hard to stir for shock work, now in a number of places have stirred themselves up in such a way that is so excessive that we have to grab hold of their shirt tails . . . Not having considered the policy of the party in relation to the peasantry, they think they are striking at the kulak but hit the seredniak and bedniak, as a result there is a very alarming mood in several areas.

He was forced to give orders to control the over-use of force even though this offended some officials who wanted a 'free rein' to deal with the peasantry.[21]

As far as is known, Stalin was the only full member of the Politburo to personally lead an expedition to the provinces to supervise the implementation of the Central Committee directives on the grain campaign. His decision to visit the countryside is certainly indicative of the gravity with which he perceived the crisis but why did he choose to go to far off Siberia and when did he make this decision? These are questions that are impossible to answer satisfactorily given the secrecy surrounding these events. Presumably Stalin's decision to go to Siberia was taken at least a week before his departure simply to prepare the expedition from the logistical point of view and it may well be that the absence of Siberia from the list of regions to be visited by central officials announced in *Pravda* on the 24 December meant that Stalin had already singled it out for his special attention. The decision to depart for a two-week tour of Siberia on 15 January 1928 is particularly surprising considering that the struggle with the Left Opposition was then at the delicate stage where its leaders were being expelled from Moscow and Leningrad into internal exile. That same day Radek and several others were forcibly removed to the Urals and Trotsky was dragged off two days later and deported to Alma Ata. One would have thought that Stalin, as General Secretary, would have preferred to monitor this operation *in situ*. On the other hand the expulsions were a highly emotive issue in the party and were likely to be messy affairs given the refusal of the Opposition leaders to cooperate with the orders. Stalin, the astute tactician as always, may well have decided to leave this matter to Rykov and Bukharin and timed his departure to coincide with the expulsions in the hope that he could avoid tarnishing his carefully cultivated image as the leader of the centre-ground of the party.[22]

There were important economic reasons for going to Siberia, since a grain harvest failure in parts of the Ukraine and North Caucasus meant that the country greatly depended on successful procurements in the region and yet these were lagging behind target. In addition, we should remember that high quality Siberian wheat had accounted for about one-third of Soviet wheat exports the previous year and planned grain procurement in the region had been significantly increased this year. Thus, a successful campaign in Siberia would not only make a major contribution to warding off the threat of famine in the towns and Red Army but was also crucial to the realisation of the regime's industrialisation goals. Siberia was also an obvious choice of destination for Stalin for personal and political reasons. He had a deep emotional attachment to the region arising from the happy experiences of a four-year period of exile spent there in 1913–17 and his daughter has recorded that, 'he loved Siberia, with its stark beauty and its rough, silent people'. Moreover, from the political perspective, the Siberian party secretary, Syrtsov, was a trusted supporter and protégé and could be relied upon to carry out Stalin's instructions without question.[23]

Stalin, no doubt, acquainted himself with the procurements situation in the region and the personnel records of the key figures in the local party leadership. He would have also formulated a plan of action and itinerary for the trip and picked close associates from his staff to accompany him and supervise the Central Committee 'patrol brigade' of worker-communists assigned to the region. Just two days before he left for Siberia, on 13 January, he met with leading officials of Sel'skosoiuz, Khlebotsentr, Khleboprodukt and Narkomtorg USSR (the main grain procurement agencies of the state) to discuss the crisis and put together a package of measures to deal with it. It would be reasonable to assume that this meeting provided Stalin with an up-to-date assessment of the extent of the crisis facing the country. By now it must have been clear that, given the decision not to raise state prices for grain, only a campaign of coercion would produce the sudden transformation of the situation necessary to avert a nationwide catastrophe.[24] While there is no direct evidence that Stalin left Moscow with this kind of premeditated plan of wholesale terror against the peasantry, it must have been uppermost in his mind that the last time he had embarked upon this type of political expedition to the provinces was over nine and a half years ago, in July–August 1918, during the civil war. Then, under similar circumstances, he had been sent by Lenin to Tsaritsyn to secure grain supplies and it was largely due to his unflinching conduct of a reign of terror in this area that famine was averted in the capital. At that time he had written to Lenin saying, 'You may rest assured that we shall spare nobody, neither ourselves or others, and shall deliver the grain in spite of everything.' As he set off on the two-day train journey to Siberia these past experiences must have been churning over in Stalin's mind. The procurements had to be secured 'at all costs'.[25]

The response of the Siberian party

On their return from the Fifteenth Congress at the end of December 1927, the Kraikom mobilised the regional party apparat to deal with the emergency along the economic and organisational lines outlined by the Central Committee directives of 14 and 24 December. In late December a Kraiispolkom decree, titled 'It is essential to achieve a decisive turn-around', described in detail the measures to be adopted by the procurement agencies in order to secure a breakthrough and ensure that the annual target of 1.34 million tons (73% for the centre and 27% for local needs) was fulfilled. It stated that A. N. Zlobin (Head of Sibtorg) had been to Moscow to consult with Narkomtorg and that these discussions had been taken into account in the framing of the decree. Following these 'consultations' with the central government it was decided to sacrifice Siberian grain needs in order to augment deliveries to the centre to the maximum, and only a minimum of grain stocks would be reserved for local supplies. Shipments of grain were to be despatched on the orders of the Kraikom without delay and it was forbidden 'on any account to reserve grain stocks for local needs'. Likewise the okrispolkoms were refused permission to alter the plan of supply of manufactured goods set by Sibtorg, which directed that goods were to be channelled, as a priority, to the grain surplus raions and local officials were to ensure that shipments were not syphoned off to other areas. The aim was to sell the bulk of goods stocks as quickly as possible and thereby soak up peasant cash savings. To assist this cooperatives were even encouraged to take down payments on future goods deliveries. The decree was emphatic that on no account were grain prices to be raised and all competition between procurement agencies, particularly the price wars raging in the countryside, was to cease forthwith.[26]

To enhance the effectiveness of this decree and stiffen the resolve of the lower level officialdom, senior krai leaders were assigned to super-visory duties in the localities. At the end of December and early January nine members of the Kraiispolkom were sent to the nine most important grain okrugs: Omsk, Slavgorod, Rubtsovsk, Biisk, Barnaul, Kansk, Achinsk, Minusinsk and Krasnoiarsk. Another eighty-four leading krai officials were sent to assist particular local party and soviet organs during the campaign. In the main grain areas, enlarged plenums of party committees and *actifs* were convened to discuss and prepare strategies for the campaign. Posses of party and komsomol plenipotentiaries were raised (in Omsk Okrug alone 200 were recruited) and formed into 'agitational-brigades' to converge on the countryside as shock troops in the struggle for grain. In the main, these plenipotentiaries were mobilised from among the urban working-class party cadres, those who were bearing the brunt of the hardship being wrought on the towns by the peasants' refusal to sell grain. They were in no mood for the conciliatory economic methods required by NEP and were ready for a hard-line campaign of coercion.[27]

In addition to these measures the Kraikom and Kraiispolkom re-sponded to Stalin's orders for an intensification in the collection of rural payments, including legal prosecution and the use of distrain-ment and fines to ensure prompt settlement of outstanding debts. Other measures to stem the purchasing power of the peasantry in-cluded a campaign to sell the new state loan shares, the raising of the price of the membership dues of the cooperatives to 10 roubles and tightening up on their collection, and the placing of new restrictions on access to credit in the countryside. A deadline for the collection of all rural payments was set for 15 February 1928 and, following the example of the central press, Siberian newspapers and journals carried daily reports warning the peasantry of the consequences of non-payment.[28]

Stalin's telegram to Syrtsov of early January, ordering the Siberian authorities to cut through 'bureaucratic obstacles' and infringe the law if needed to collect outstanding rural taxes and payments, caused great concern in the regional leadership. Some months later, Syrtsov revealed that the Kraikom had been reluctant to follow Stalin's new harsh line and 'protested against a whole series of directives from Moscow'. He singled out those instructions regarding the collection of agricultural taxes and other payments, admitting that they had been disregarded.[29] Given this kind of obstructionism at the regional level, it is not surprising that Moscow found it necessary to issue the extraordinary decree of 6 January. The Kraikom later acknowledged that 'essentially the turning-point in the work only began after the Central Committee directive of 6 January'. Syrtsov stated that the clarity of the directive lay in its explicit threat that 'for all mistakes in the grain procurements the corresponding okruzhkom secretaries would pay with their posts' and it demanded that they use 'all means' to secure the flow of grain to the state. He aptly described the arrival of this *lex talionis* as like 'the crack of a whip' to those party officials who were unprepared or 'pottering around' with the problem.[30] The directive effectively dictated a paramilitary organisation of the campaign in the provinces. In compliance with central instructions to simplify the chain of command and provide for a more operative and flexible crisis management team at the top, an emergency grain 'troika' was formed in the Kraikom on 10 January, with subordinate troiki at the okrug and raion levels. The Kraikom troika consisted of Syrtsov, Eikhe and A. N. Zlobin, the Head of Sibkraitorg, and it directed the Siberian grain campaign from a military style headquarters (*shtab*) in Novosibirsk.[31]

A shock assault on the countryside to fulfil grain procurement targets with the utmost speed involved overcoming severe logistical problems, not least of which was eradicating the chaos on the railway network. The immediate priority tasks were to transport to the centre the grain already collected and now lying at procurement points, wharves and rail junctions and simultaneously to distribute the new shipments of manufactured goods which were beginning to arrive in large quantities. The means by which this was to be achieved were a draconian combination of personal threats, scapegoating and summary justice. Once the positions of party secretaries were put on the line and their future careers depended on a successful campaign, they passed the threat down to lower level officials and made them 'personally responsible' for the fulfilment of orders from above. To instil the appropriate sense of urgency and to combat slipshod work and inefficiency in the transport system, the Kraikom circulated a directive on 4 January making the Board of Administration of the Siberian Railways personally accountable for the efficient operation of the network, and delays in services were henceforth regarded as 'proof of economic crime' and punishable accordingly. On 12 January the party organised a meeting with 700 railway workers in Novosibirsk to discuss the crisis and impress upon them the need for shock work in relation to the grain shipments. At this stage not one train to Omsk was leaving on schedule and delays were blamed on 'a fall in labour discipline', namely, drunkenness and absenteeism. There was also a dire shortage of essential equipment and spare parts, as a result of which the Head of the Railway Administration announced the first official casualties of the campaign with the dismissal of three senior apparatchiki whose remit included these areas.[32]

The Kraikom troika drew up a detailed plan of action with fixed monthly and ten day plans for procurements, and no less than 80%–85% of the annual plan to be completed by 1 April. A grain procurement target of 254,000 tons was set for January (63% in West Siberia and 37% in East Siberia) but the results of the first and second ten-day periods of procurement in West Siberia were terribly disappointing, with under 80,000 tons collected. For the plan to be met required that a similar amount be procured in the last ten-day period alone. A similar disastrous shortfall occurred in the shipments of grain from the krai to the centre. A target of 163,000 tons for the month had only been fulfilled by 48% on 20 January because Sibtorg shipped only 25% of its plan and the agricultural and consumer cooperatives and Khleboprodukt achieved about 44% each. The failure to meet plan targets and deadlines was not the result of poor grain procurement work but rather the slowness of the system to move grain stocks. One estimate put the quantity of grain stockpiled in the agricultural cooperative system alone on 20 January at 28,260 tons, of which 14,820 tons were at railway stations and 13,440 on wharves, and these stocks had been reduced by an incredible 18.6% from the level of 1 January.[33]

Meanwhile, manufactured goods were flooding into Siberia as fast as the railway system allowed. Compared with the previous quarterly

period, when approximately 400 wagons were delivered, in the first
ten-day period of January about 250 wagons of manufactured goods
arrived and over the month Siberia received 425 wagons of goods with
a value of around 3 million roubles. The bulk of these supplies was
distributed in West Siberia, and in some areas goods deliveries were so
intensive in these weeks that, after a while, certain trade organisations
refused to receive any more. Peasants who sold grain were to be given
first preference in the purchase of manufactured goods and the headlines in the regional press constantly reiterated this message. Some
press advertisements were aimed directly at the well-off peasantry, as
for example: 'If you want to receive new agricultural machines and
parts for these, seed cleaners etc . . . in the spring – hand over grain
right now.' However, there was no consistency in the way that local
party officials interpreted their orders. Some instructed that goods
could be sold only to those peasants who delivered grain even when
supplies were plentiful, while others rationed goods irrespective of the
amount of grain delivered. In Omsk goods in short supply were sold to
fully paid-up cooperative members to a value of ten roubles per month
while other members could only buy 2 or 3 metres of cloth. In Kuznetsk
Okrug it was impossible to buy goods without a cooperative membership card or receipt for selling grain to a state agency. Here, grain
deliverers were given special vouchers, instead of cash, which could be
exchanged for goods in the cooperative stores. In the middle of January, probably in response to Stalin's rejection of this type of 'bartering',
a new Kraiispolkom directive ordered the restoration of normal market
relations in goods sales but, given that demand vastly exceeded supply
and the goods were a lure to attract grain sellers, this instruction was
disregarded as a 'squandering' of supplies in some areas. This factor
together with the general sluggishness in the distribution and trade
system meant that by 1 February there were millions of roubles worth
of extra goods in stock compared with 1 January.[34]

It was into this convoluted scene of crisis management by the Siberian party leadership that Stalin launched himself like a *deus ex ma-
china* determined to bring the grain crisis to a speedy and satisfactory
conclusion, and to test the reaction of the regional party apparat to his
vision of the future economic development of the countryside.

Stalin's Siberian tour

The prospect of Stalin's visit must have thrown the Siberian
leadership into a terror-stricken panic to get their act together. Syrtsov

must have been particularly concerned as, being well-acquainted with Stalin, he would have known that 'the boss' (*khoziain*, as Stalin was called by his clients in the party) did not lightly leave Moscow on political matters, and may have realised that the visit was a portent of a sea change in policy. Shortly before Stalin's arrival, in the middle of January, Syrtsov made a special trip to Barnaul and Rubtsovsk Okrugs to check that their party organisations were prepared for the General Secretary's tour of inspection. There, to his horror, he encountered reluctance among local party officials to step up the pressure on the kulaks, even though they knew Stalin was coming. The *émigré* writer, A. Avtorkhanov, claims to have learned of events in Siberia at this time from I. I. Sorokin, a Central Committee official assigned to emergency duties in the krai, and he relates how the impending arrival of Stalin shook the Siberian leadership into setting their house in order by organising, in the best traditions of Russian officialdom, 'Potemkin' peasant villages for the General Secretary to review.[35]

Around the middle of January detachments of Central Committee 'patrol brigades' of experienced worker-communists from the Moscow and Leningrad regions, began to arrive in Siberia in advance of Stalin's group. The total complement of these harbingers of the new militant line against the peasantry was 100, with 50 drawn from each region. Stalin's expedition left Moscow by train on 15 January and arrived in Novosibirsk on 17 January, for a stay of just over two weeks. He was supported by an entourage of personal aides and officials from the Central Committee Secretariat, though there are conflicting accounts as to the exact identities of his accompanying party. We know for sure that he arrived with A. I. Dogadov, a long-standing member of the Orgbiuro and Secretary of the Central Trade Union Council, who may have assisted in assessing the performance of local party cadres and settling the labour problems in the railway system. Stalin also brought along A. N. Poskrebyshev, his aide-de-camp, and probably included other *pomoshchniki*: the retinue of political assistants, security advisers and household staff that formed his secret personal chancellery in Moscow. The inclusion of Poskrebyshev was significant because he was Stalin's link with the OGPU, an organ that was playing a major role in the offensive against grain speculation by Nepmen and kulaks.[36]

By the time of his arrival in Siberia, Stalin had come to the conclusion that the grain crisis was a premeditated political challenge to the Soviet government by 'kulak saboteurs'. This and other anti-NEP statements made by Stalin in the course of his tour were so controversial, at a time when NEP was still official policy, that they were not made public. In fact, even twenty years later only an edited and composite record of these speeches and his itinerary was published in his collected works. Given the content of the Central Committee directive of 6 January and the exchange of telegrams with Syrtsov, the Siberian leadership were sensitive to the fact that Stalin was likely to demand punitive measures against the peasantry which contravened their pro-NEP inclinations. Evidently, Syrtsov and other Siberian leaders by now accepted that some form of assault on the sacred cow of NEP, the right of the peasantry to free trade in grain and other produce, would have to be tolerated, however objectionable, and that they must move fast to precipitate any proposals from Stalin. Consequently, immediately prior to Stalin's arrival on 17 January, the Kraikombiuro issued directive No. 101 which provided for limited repressive measures against the kulaks. It ordered that a quota of four to ten of the 'most clearly anti-Soviet' kulak farms with large grain stocks be singled out and arrested by the OGPU in each grain producing raion, and L. M. Zakovsky, the OGPU plenipotentiary representative in Siberia, gave the localities the command: 'start the operation immediately'. It was considered politic to unveil this decree in Stalin's presence at his first general meeting with regional officials in Novosibirsk on 18 January, when an enlarged session of the Kraikombiuro and representatives of the main Siberian procurement organs, was convened.[37]

Stalin opened this meeting with the kind of disarmingly short, informal and matter of fact speech at which he excelled. He briefly described the nature of the crisis and informed the Siberian leaders that he had come not only to assist them fulfil the grain procurement plan but also, in accordance with Central Committee instructions, to discuss with them 'the prospects for the development of agriculture, the plan for expanding the formation of kolkhozes and sovkhozes'. He outlined the predicament facing the government and explained that the huge state grain deficit threatened the towns, industrial centres and the Red Army with famine. To prevent this from happening those regions with good harvests, notably Siberia (where although the grain harvest was down on the previous year there was still a huge surplus), would not just have to fulfil their grain procurement plans but overfulfil them. He wanted to know what action the Siberians were taking to resolve the crisis. Syrtsov followed with a report detailing the extent of the grain crisis in the region and the measures taken by the Kraikom to improve the situation. At this point the new Kraikombiuro decree was formally laid before the meeting. Later in the year Syrtsov, with hindsight, was at pains to explain that the Siberian leadership had acted independently, that a 'measure such as the necessary blow against the kulak was clear to us from the very beginning', and he avowed that the new decree had been promulgated by the Kraikom-biuro on its 'own responsibility and risk'. However, he also admitted that:

> Comrade Stalin significantly added to the directive, reminding us of what we had failed to take into account. We had been relying only on the GPU *apparat*, counting on its exactitude, but comrade Stalin made corrections on the lines of a greater use of revolutionary legality. This of course, was absolutely correct and a new stage in the grain procurements opened.

Stalin's intervention forcing the Siberians to amend the decree along the lines of his recent statement to the Fifteenth Congress, when he had disowned the use of OGPU 'administrative methods' against the kulak and favoured economic restrictions and the use of 'revolutionary legality', specifically recommended that Article 107 of the Criminal Code of the RSFSR be applied against peasants hoarding large stocks of grain who refused to sell to the procurement agencies.[38]

Stalin's proposals, and indeed the decree itself, were neither accepted immediately nor without question. There was a debate during which he 'resolutely dispelled the doubts of local leaders on the expediency of introducing emergency measures'.[39] One Siberian party member S. I. Zagumenny, Chairman of Sibsel'kredit, particularly irked Stalin with his vocal opposition to the use of Article 107, claiming that it would not only produce bad results but would actually lead to a deterioration in the situation in the countryside. Stalin was accustomed to the compliant obsequiousness of the apparatchiki of the Central Committee and unused to contradiction of his opinions except in the highest party circles. Therefore, he quickly lost patience with this type of persistent questioning and nagging doubts, and to the Siberian party officials who complained that the use of Article 107 was an extreme measure and contrary to the spirit of NEP his exasperated response was 'so what'. He assured them that it had already been applied in other regions and districts of the country (probably thinking of events in the Ukraine and North Caucasus) and yielded 'splendid results'. Stalin's political instincts had convinced him that there was a dynamic of pressure from below, among the lower level officialdom and party rank and file, for abandoning NEP in favour of a policy of coercion against the well-off peasantry. Soon after his arrival in Siberia he told Syrtsov of his belief that 'if we gave a signal to pressurise and to fall upon the kulak, they [the party activists] will be more than enthusiastic about it'. Having encountered the leading representatives of the Siberian nomenklatura, Stalin's confidence in his instincts must have been shattered. Shocked and irritated by the repeated questioning and hostile reception given to his orders to apply Article 107, he began to interpret this sort of resistance as indicative of widespread political degeneracy at the regional level which required purging.[40]

The outcome of the meeting of 18 January was a Kraikombiuro decree which was a compromise between the Siberians' desire for controlled repressive measures on a limited scale and Stalin's demand for the immediate use of Article 107 against all large-scale grain holders. Firstly, it provided for a number of intimidatory organisational measures to be taken. The fulfilment of the planned grain shipments to the central government was declared to be 'absolutely binding' for the regional party organisation. Given the urgency of the situation, Zlobin was instructed to break down the plan by okrug and raion for each grain procurement agency and set targets for each five-day period from 25 January. To guard against complacency among party officials, 'individual responsibility' for meeting grain targets was imposed. Labour problems were to be resolved by the Krai Trade Union Council in the shortest possible time, and to heighten the level of discipline among railway, industrial and state employees some of its officials were to be sent out to supervise work in important areas. The Omsk and Tomsk Railway Boards, responsible for sections of the Trans-Siberian Railway that were most critical for the success of the grain campaign, were singled out for particular criticism and chastened for not implementing the Kraikom circular of 4 January on the fight against inefficiency. To maintain the pressure on those involved in procurement work a campaign was to be launched in the regional press to expose scandals and shortcomings, while Kisis and Eikhe were to draw up a list of additional Kraikom and Kraiispolkom officials to be sent to the localities and attached to departmental organisations. Importantly, to ensure an element of flexibility in the response of the apparat at all levels, troiki were permitted to supplement the instructions in the decree, while procurement and local organs were prohibited from questioning the scale of their targets for the duration of the quarter.

The key measures to combat kulak grain speculation centred on a surgical application of Article 107 against a carefully selected kulak elite *pour encourager les autres*. Rather than unleash the OGPU, the quota of 4–10 kulak cases in each raion were to be handled by the procuracy and publicly tried under Article 107 as 'malicious speculators' by special courts without any 'formalities'. The kulaks selected for trial were to be invited to deliver their grain surpluses immediately at government prices and if they refused were to be prosecuted and their grain confiscated. The use of Article 107 and other coercive measures will be discussed in chapter 6, but it should be noted at this point that the limited scale of the operation suggests that Stalin had to accept the more restrained approach preferred by the Siberian leadership, who hoped that a few public trials in the localities, with wide press coverage given to the sentences, would intimidate the kulaks and other peasants into selling their grain.[41]

Stalin proposed a significant addendum to the decree by advising that 25% of all confiscated grain be distributed among the poor and 'economically weak' middle peasants at low state prices or in the form of long-term loans. This was a master-stroke designed to stir up class antagonisms in the countryside and encourage collaboration, recriminations and informing to the authorities. Subsequently, a Kraiispolkom decree of 26 January gave full effect to this measure. The 25% of confiscated grain was to be turned over to the raion Krestkomy as long-term loans to be repaid on advantageous conditions over three to five years at an annual interest charge of 6%. They were to redistribute the grain to their village branches as seed loans for socialised plots, collectives, and individual farms of Red Army families, invalids and bedniaks. Thus, as one writer put it, the poor peasants were incited to cooperate in the campaign as 'government contractors on a percentage commission'. Another measure aimed at winning the poor peasantry to the side of the government and tightening the pressure on the well-off was the issue of a joint circular by the President of the Krai Judiciary Department, the Krai Procurator and the Head of the Labour Department of the Kraiispolkom on 19 January. In language reminiscent of Stalin's telegrams to Syrtsov, this ordered the elimination of 'bureaucratic obstructions' in the implementation of legislation designed to protect batraks from exploitation.[42]

After the plenum Stalin set off on a hectic rail tour of Siberia accompanied by Syrtsov. On 22 January he chaired an inter-okrug conference on the crisis held in Barnaul and attended by party, soviet and cooperative leaders from Barnaul, Biisk and Rubtsovsk. The following day he spoke to a meeting of the Rubtsovsk Okruzhkombiuro on the progress of grain procurement in the area, and on 27–8 January he visited Omsk to address the okruzhkom there. If one report of his visit to Barnaul is accurate and typical, then Stalin's visits were shrouded by secrecy, probably for security reasons given that the Siberian peasantry were regularly assassinating party and soviet officials, and he met only with the most senior apparatchiki.[43] At some stage during his stay Stalin travelled into the countryside and what he witnessed there caused an immediate crystallisation of his hard-line position on the crisis and left him in no mood for further comradely debate with the local party elite. The personal impressions gleaned from what could only have been a fleeting sojourn among the Siberian party and peasantry was to be the backdrop for all Stalin's future thinking on the state of the regional party organisations and the peasant question. In fact, according to Khrushchev, this was the last time that he ever visited a peasant village.[44]

Stalin's own edited record of these events contains some inconsistencies and factual errors but it makes clear that his experiences left him angry and embittered, and had reawakened the latent hostility to the peasantry which had lain dormant in many Bolsheviks since the introduction of NEP in 1921. He had taken 'the opportunity to see for myself that your people are not seriously concerned to help our country emerge from the grain crisis', and been outraged by the complaints of local leaders that the grain plan was too heavy and impossible to fulfil. Siberia had produced a 'bumper harvest' (actually it was about 11% below the previous years level, though there was still a huge surplus) yet the procurement plan was almost the same as last year (it had actually been increased by over one-third but was slightly more than the total state procurement in the region in 1927). Moreover, he claimed that the kulaks had surpluses approaching 1,000 tons per farm (a wild exaggeration, a few hundred tons was exceptional) and their barns and sheds were so crammed full that grain was lying out in the open under pent roofs. Most ominously, Stalin now interpreted the Siberians' trenchant criticism and questioning of his orders and reluctance to use Article 107 as a sign of support for the kulaks. Local party officials that he encountered constantly took issue with him about the kulak complaint of low state prices for grain but Stalin cut them short. As far as he was concerned, the problem was 'unbridled speculation' by the kulaks who were demanding, he claimed, a threefold increase in state prices and such a hike was politically unacceptable since the poor and middle peasants had already sold their grain at the regular prices in the autumn. He tauntingly enquired of those officials who wavered in applying coercion, in a statement which revealed as much about his state of mind as it presaged ill for them: 'Is it that you are afraid to disturb the tranquillity of the kulak gentry?'[45]

Stalin reserved his most contemptuous rebukes for the local procuracy and judicial officials who vehemently opposed the emergency measures. He claimed to have seen several dozen of these officials, nearly all of whom 'live in the homes of kulaks, board and lodge with them and, of course, are anxious to live in peace with the kulaks'. When questioned by Stalin about this they had replied that the housing and food was better with the kulaks. Later, in more considered evaluations of his experiences, he was to describe these officials and communists as elements alien to the party:

> who are not alive to the class problem in the countryside, who do not understand the basis of our class policy and who are endeavouring to conduct affairs in such a way that no-one in the countryside is offended, and to live in peace with the kulaks and generally maintain their popularity amongst 'all strata' in the countryside.[46]

It was undoubtedly to these communists that Stalin referred in October 1928, in his first major public attack on the pro-Nepist wing of the party, when he claimed that he 'came across exponents of the Right danger in our lower party organisations during the grain procurement crisis last year, when a number of communists in the volosts and villages opposed the party's policy and worked towards forming a bond with kulak elements'.[47] In Siberia he had demanded that these 'gentry' be purged immediately from their positions and replaced by 'honest, conscientious Soviet-minded people'.[48]

According to Avtorkhanov's second-hand version, after Stalin went off to the villages with his aides in search of grain and to explore the situation on the ground for himself, he became convinced that in the areas where the grain procurement plans had been fulfilled the targets had been set too low, while the areas where procurement was lagging behind were actually the richest in grain. In response, Avtorkhanov claims, Stalin ordered that meetings of poor and middle peasants be called, from which the kulaks were excluded, to allocate 'self-imposition of delivery quotas' and the levying of 'hard and fast commitments' on the kulak households, with non-fulfilment punishable by confiscation of grain under Article 107.[49] In fact, in February 1928, Stalin admitted that the 'imposition of grain delivery quotas on individual households' had occurred (though he does not state where), but he condemned this as an excess to be 'resolutely eliminated'.[50] The levying of such quotas in Siberia during the period of Stalin's visit is not confirmed from other sources and it may be that Avtorkhanov, like some Western historians, has confused the emergency measures en-

forced in early 1928 with the 'Ural–Siberian Method' of grain procurement in the spring of 1929.[51] In a similar vein, the Avtorkhanov account
tells of how Stalin was personally humiliated on one of his village stops
when 'a kulak came up with a pipe in his mouth and said, "Do us a
dance, lad, and then I will give you a *pud* or two."' Interestingly, this
incident corresponds with an anecdote related by Stalin in his attack on
the 'Right deviation' at the joint plenum of the Central Committee and
Central Control Commission in April 1929, though he ascribed it to a
party activist in Kazakhstan. That such an insult was suffered by Stalin
personally is questionable; that such an episode had a marked negative
influence on Stalin's outlook towards the well-off peasantry is
incontrovertible.[52]

In his Siberian speeches Stalin dealt not only with the immediate
measures to be taken to secure a speedy resolution of the crisis, but also
addressed himself to the overall direction of party policy in the
countryside in the light of the resolutions of the Fifteenth Congress
and to the question of collectivisation in particular. The congress had
affirmed in its resolution on 'Work in the Countryside' that the formation of collective farms must be made the party's 'main task in the
countryside', though no timescale or deadlines were mentioned and
no one seems to have understood this as anything other than the usual
rhetorical deference to its long-term goal of a socialist transformation of
the countryside.[53] One would have expected Stalin to pay lip-service to
this policy when speaking to a provincial party audience, however,
what he actually propounded was nothing less than a radically new
approach to the peasant question and a fundamental reappraisal of
NEP.[54]

Stalin wove a pattern of links between the current grain crisis, the
existence of petty-capitalist kulak farmers, and the problem of 'building socialism' through industrialisation in conditions of capitalist en-
circlement. The kulak was portrayed as the bogeyman in the grain
procurement difficulties and the onset of the crisis was attributed to
'kulak sabotage'. Although he believed that the emergency measures
would rectify the situation this year there was no guarantee that 'kulak
sabotage' would not recur in the future because 'it may be said with
certainty that so long as there are kulaks, so long will there be sabotage
of grain procurement'. To put the procurements on a secure footing
required 'other measures', namely: the development of kolkhozes and
sovkhozes. These large-scale collective farms employed machinery
more efficiently and produced larger marketable surpluses than the
well-off kulak farm. Given the increasing rate of industrialisation and

urbanisation in the country, the demand for grain was set to rise annually and only collective farms provided the high level of marketings needed to meet this. A continuous flow of cheap grain to the state was essential for the economic development of the country and this could not be jeopardised by 'the whim of the kulaks'. Stalin affirmed that the kulaks would be relegated to the background in the procurements as collective farms were to be expanded rapidly 'to the utmost, sparing neither energy or resources' in order that they would be in a position to supply the state with at least one-third of its grain needs within three or four years, and thus effectively displacing the role currently played by the kulaks.

Looking to the future, he envisaged that the partial collectivisation already alluded to was insufficient. What the country needed was 'the socialisation of the whole of agriculture', 'gradually, but unswervingly', in all areas of the country 'without exception'. The successful completion of this task, he pronounced, would determine the fate of Soviet socialism, and he made this clear by posing the following question: 'today the Soviet system rests on two heterogeneous foundations; on united *socialised* industry and on the *individual* small-peasant farm based on the *private* ownership of the means of production. Can the Soviet system survive for long on these heterogeneous foundations? No it cannot,' (emphasis in the original). 'We must realise', Stalin declared, as if to leave his audience in no doubt as to the meaning of his speech, 'that we can no longer make progress on the basis of small-scale individual peasant farms.' He outlined several other advantages that would arise from complete collectivisation. Apart from assisting in the process of eliminating 'all sources that engender capitalists and capitalism', the collectives would also provide a secure basis for the procurement of foodstuffs and act as political bastions of support for the party's political and economic control of the countryside: 'a single and firm socialist basis for the Soviet system, for Soviet power'. Attuned to the political sensitivity of his prognosis Stalin drew on the authority of Lenin to illustrate the sound credentials of these proposals by citing statements in favour of collectivisation made by Lenin during the period of War Communism prior to the retreat to NEP in 1921. Ominously, Stalin's conclusion framed the goal of collectivisation in terms of an ideological imperative left unfulfilled by the party from the days of War Communism, and the suggestion was that the time was now ripe for an advance in this area.

Fervent advocates of the development of small-scale private farming through NEP, like Syrtsov and most of his colleagues in the Siberian party leadership, must have been horrified by the militant tone of Stalin's rhetoric, never mind the implicitly anti-NEP substance of his blueprint for agriculture. By starkly informing the Siberians that small-scale private peasant farming had effectively outlived its usefulness and must be transcended quickly, Stalin had essentially reversed the party's official line that NEP was the only viable long-term course of development for the country. In so doing, he directly contradicted his previously orthodox pro-NEP stance, only recently restated to the Fifteenth Congress in late December, that the socialist transformation of the countryside would come about, 'slowly but surely . . . not as the result of pressure, but of example and conviction . . . there is no other way.'[55] The proviso in regard to the voluntary nature of collectivisation was now nowhere to be seen.

A Western scholar has recently cast doubt on the accuracy of the report of Stalin's statements in Siberia, arguing that the editors of Stalin's *Collected Works* 'were improving on the record of the Siberian trip in order to sustain the image that later became part of his myth'.[56] Yet the new Stalin line was immediately reflected in Siberian party journals which from the end of January 1928 suddenly began to publish numerous articles calling for rapid large-scale collectivisation as an economic and political necessity. Stalin's speeches may have been considered too radical for widespread dissemination at the time but the editorial in the issue of *Na Leninskom puti* published in late January 1928, if not written by Stalin personally, certainly constituted the first public statement of his new thinking. In a major break with its previous position on the peasant question the journal declared that the 'small-scale, dispersed, individual farm is by its very nature reactionary. On this basis the further development of the productive strength of the country, which is indispensable for us, is impossible. On the basis of small-scale peasant farming we cannot overcome class contradictions in the countryside.' The answer to this problem was collectivisation, and this could only be carried out in conditions of 'class struggle'. These sentiments were incorporated into the resolutions of the March plenum of the Kraikom which called for an acceleration of collectiv-isation.[57]

Whether Stalin had worked out the content of his speeches before arriving in the region is not known, though it would be reasonable to assume that the basic propositions on the future of agriculture were prepared in advance. However, it is possible that they were modified in the light of his Siberian experiences and given a more pointed and sharper edge. What is certain is that it was in Siberia in the last two weeks of January 1928 that Stalin first publicly disclosed the details of a plan for Soviet agriculture which evolved into an *idée fixe* that only a crash programme of mass collectivisation and the physical elimination of the kulaks as a class would solve the peasant question and secure the building of socialism in the USSR. A programme that was ultimately enforced with cataclysmic consequences for the countryside from late 1929. In this sense the genesis of Soviet forcible mass collectivisation and the Stalin 'revolution from above' may be traced to the grain crisis of 1927–8 and Stalin's Siberian tour.

Shortly before his departure from Siberia, Stalin left the local party leaders with a display of his consummate political skill. The details were revealed by Syrtsov in his report to a session of the Kraikom in Novosibirsk on 31 January. Syrtsov had just returned from seeing Stalin off at Omsk and, in what may have been an attempt to reassure his colleagues of Stalin's commitment to NEP, told them of the repudiation and summary dismissal of A. Povolotsky, Chairman of Omsk Okruzhkom grain troika. Povolotsky had ridden roughshod over the local party's reluctance to deploy the OGPU to deal with the crisis and had bragged that 'NEP had been practically abolished' and prodrazverstka was again party policy.[58] It was a signal that while Stalin was prepared to exhort local party officials to adopt extreme measures, he was careful to distance himself in public from the excesses that inevitably resulted from his pressure. Stalin may have been already looking ahead to the political confrontation with the pro-NEP elements of the party leadership and such a gesture was a simple expedient to assuage the fears of the Siberian party and quash precipitate overt talk of the abandonment of NEP until he had fully secured his political position. Shortly afterwards, Stalin lulled the Right into a false sense of security by soothingly describing Povolotsky's type of talk as 'counter-revolutionary tittle-tattle' and foreswearing that 'NEP is the foundation of our economic policy, and will continue to be so for a long period of history.'[59] This rhetorical flourish was double-tongued for the struggle with the Right was already under way.

6   The emergency measures

Revolutionary legality under NEP

The idea of the 'rule of law' had only the most tenuous of roots in the Russian political tradition. For the Bolsheviks this principle was an absolute anathema not only on grounds of dogma, since they regarded it as a tenet of 'bourgeois ideology', but also as a result of their harsh experiences at the hands of the tsarist secret police. The Marxist–Leninist idea of law as an instrument of *realpolitik* was one with which they were more familiar. This approach was encapsulated by Lenin's statement at the Seventh Party Conference in April 1917 when he contemptuously dismissed the use of regular judicial procedures declaring that, 'for us it is the revolutionary deed which is important, while the law must be its consequence'.[1] Of course, in any state the application of impartial and regularised legal and judicial procedures is usually one of the first casualties in the event of a political emergency. The bloody events of the civil war reinforced Bolshevik impatience and disdain for 'bourgeois' legal practices and their hold on power was consolidated by *force majeure*, though they euphemistically termed it 'administrative methods'. The new Soviet government ruled by decree and delegated plenipotentiary powers to party and soviet officials, and particularly the Cheka. The standard guiding principle in the application of the law by government agents was 'revolutionary' or 'class consciousness'.[2]

The end of the civil war and the introduction of NEP in 1921 inaugurated what one scholar described as an era of 'significant social pluralism within the authoritarian framework of the one-party dictatorship.'[3] Bolshevik toleration of social and cultural diversity and the limited restoration of free market economic relations required regularised legal and judicial procedures to function effectively. Thus, in 1922 a new system of criminal and civil courts was established to replace the

149

revolutionary tribunals, new legal codes were promulgated and the Cheka was reorganised into a state ministry (the GPU) and restricted to the political sphere. Lenin spoke of a 'sea of lawlessness' at the local level and the party leadership increasingly emphasised the slogan of 'legality' in official acts. In May 1922 a VTsIK decree established the office of State Procurator with the power to decide whether to prosecute cases and amend or annul any legal or administrative decision which it held to be in contravention of the law. This office was a highly centralised legal watchdog and, in theory, independent of local soviet control as the procurators were ultimately responsible to and financed by the Peoples Commissariat of Justice of the USSR (Narkomiust) in Moscow. Lenin's aim was to create a central procuratorial office of 'about ten reliable communists' who would work closely under party control.[4]

The reorganisation of the judiciary was carried out in a VTsIK decree at the end of October 1922 which established People's Courts presided over by People's Judges. Unlike the procuracy, judicial organs were placed firmly under local control and were part of the nomenklatura of local party committees. Judges were to be selected for a term of one year and be subject to recall by provincial ispolkoms. Any enfranchised citizen who had three years practical experience working in soviet legal organs or two years as a party, government or trade union official was eligible for selection. Formally, nominees were proposed jointly by the ispolkoms and the senior judges at each level and only from the provincial level upwards did Narkomiust have the right of confirmation, though this was normally automatic. Once appointed their activities were closely monitored by the GPU to ensure that they adhered to the proper 'class line' in their decisions and check for personal or political lapses such as drunkenness and ties with the well-off peasantry. The main obstacle to the development of a legal culture among such officials was their deficiency in general education, never mind professional legal training. The party recognised and, to a certain extent, took advantage of this state of affairs by expecting law officers to rely on their 'class instincts' in a given case, rather than legal and procedural norms.[5]

In 1927 the Siberian judiciary and procuracy were reorganised into territorial circuits, with 224 judges and 55 district procurators dispersed over the 293 raions in the krai. Party control was absolute over the procurators, all of whom were communists, and about 80% of them had joined the party before 1921. Similarly, only 8% of judges in the region were non-party and 58% had joined during the post-1921 NEP years. Reflecting the high level of peasant participation in party and state bodies in Siberia, over one-third of procurators and 38% of judges were peasants by social status and this must have had a prejudicial impact on their willingness to uphold laws and directives penalising the peasantry. The general symptomatic problems of low education and poor training were strongly in evidence in the region, as only one judge and two procurators had completed higher education and the bulk (92%–93%) of their colleagues had only lower level or home education. Despite the government commitment to the spread of legality little was done to raise legal standards as only one-third of Siberian judges had undergone a training course by 1928. Poor legal standards could have been offset by relevant work experience but this was hindered by the high turnover of law officers. For example, in the year to October 1927, 34% of judges left office or were replaced and less then 20% of judges and 10% of procurators had tenure of more than three years.[6]

As a counterpart to the Bukharinism which dominated the party's political thinking from 1925, the central leadership campaigned vigorously to ensure that provincial law organs complied with the concept of 'revolutionary legality' and stamped out 'administrative caprice'. Such a campaign was held to be an indispensable corollary of the new pro-peasant economic and political policies and slogans of the party: the 'get rich' slogan, the 'Face to the Countryside' and 'Revitalisation of the soviets' campaigns. Bukharin in particular championed the ideals of 'normalisation' in government and 'scrupulous regularity' in administration, especially with regard to the party's relations with the peasantry. This attempt to imbue the apparatchiki with a respect for the law met with uneven success and during the crisis of 1927–8 procurators and judges seeking to uphold NEP legal norms clashed with party officials who, accustomed to unrestrained authority in their own demesnes and under pressure from Stalin to resolve the crisis quickly by applying emergency coercive measures, interpreted 'revolutionary legality' in a way that conflicted with the fundamental principles of NEP.[7]

The application of Article 107

It is a general practice to make speculation of any kind a criminal offence in a state emergency, and the severe penalties introduced by the Bolshevik authorities to combat speculation during the civil war were not exceptional. However, NEP was designed to usher in an era of civil peace, conciliation and economic recovery, and the Bolshevik government found itself confronting the grey area of what constituted speculatory activities under normal commercial conditions. Consequently, the legislative enactments against speculation passed during the NEP period were suitably ambiguous both in wording and intent. The RSFSR Criminal Code of 1922 banned attempts to inflate prices by agreement between traders or by withholding goods from sale, though both of these crimes were notoriously difficult to prove. In November 1926 a new version of the RSFSR Criminal Code was instituted (to be enforced from 1 January 1927) and, in response to grain procurement problems the previous year, a more comprehensive statement of anti-speculation legislation was incorporated in Article 107. This made it an offence, punishable by one year's imprisonment with confiscation of part or all property, to engage in 'malicious raising of prices of goods by means of bulk-buying, concealment or hoarding of such from the market'. In addition, any activity regarded as leading to the establishment of traders' agreements was an offence punishable by three years imprisonment with confiscation of all property.[8]

The freedom of the peasantry to dispose of its agricultural surpluses being one of the pillars of NEP, it is clear that this article was intended to curb speculation by private traders, the so-called Nepmen. In particular, the authorities aimed to eliminate the proliferating speculatory activities of the 'sackmen' (*meshochniki*), for the most part urban traders, who travelled to the countryside and bought up grain and flour from the peasantry to resell at exorbitant prices in the towns and rural areas deficient in grain. At the same time, Article 107 was drawn up against the background of procurement difficulties in the countryside and framed in such ambivalent language that its provisions could be legally applied against peasants who hid or hoarded grain in expectation of a price rise. The operative *mens rea* in this respect was 'malicious' intent.[9]

The decision to apply Article 107 against peasants was a turning point in Soviet history, for it contradicted the policy of conciliation of the peasantry on which NEP rested. Undoubtedly, it was for this reason that Stalin's demands for its application met with such vociferous opposition from Siberian party officials. His demands were also fiercely resisted by those responsible for upholding Soviet legality in the region: the judges and procurators. The Siberian procuracy was especially vocal in its complaints from the very beginning and, refusing to be intimidated by Stalin, it firmly adhered to its responsibility for protecting the public from administrative abuses of the law. A contemporary commentator states that in January 1928 the Siberian procurators exhibited a distinct 'lack of enthusiasm' for the emergency measures and issued 'a flood of protests' against the enactments of local soviet organs that pressurised the peasantry to deliver grain. Stalin made it absolutely clear to the Siberians that the law must be interpreted from the viewpoint of 'class interests', as a weapon against 'the exploitative minority – the nepmen, the kulaks, etc . . .' and against 'kulak speculation'. In typically blunt and sardonic style he cut through the legal gordian knots presented by the local procurators with the declaration that, 'laws written by Bolsheviks cannot be used against Soviet power'. One does not know whether the irony of this statement escaped Stalin, but it was a strikingly conventional response in the tradition of Russian officialdom and virtually mirrored the maxim of Nicholas I's chief of security police, Count A. K. Benckendorff, that 'laws are written for subordinates, not for the authorities'.[10]

Stalin may have been demoralised by the unexpected lack of enthusiasm of the Siberian leadership to embrace his call to fall upon the kulak but his belief in a dynamic from below in favour of harsh measures was not implausible. A report on the grain procurement situation in *Sovetskaia sibir'* on 28 January 1928 by O. Barabashev, formerly a Zinovievist komsomol journalist in Leningrad and possibly transferred in the course of the intra-party struggle, supported Stalin's assessment of the grass roots' mood of the party: 'Stalin is right in saying that the party is ready for the slogan of dekulakisation . . . pressure on the kulak implants in the lower party ranks a mood for dekulakisation in the old way. In this thought Stalin was right.' Admittedly, Barabashev's opinion was biased in favour of the Left, but he based his observations on the passions prevailing in a closed meeting of the predominantly working-class party cell in the important rail junction of Isil'kul', Omsk Okrug. His account of the discussion described the sense of fear felt by these workers in the face of food and goods shortages and demonstrated that powerful pent-up urban antagonisms against the peasantry were being released by the crisis.[11]

The members of this cell were divided over how the crisis could be resolved but the common theme in the views expressed at the meeting was that force should be used. As one of them asserted, 'If the kulak is cleared out then grain will come immediately.' Some protested at the preferential delivery of manufactured goods supplies to the countryside while others wanted a return to prodrazverstka and demanded that the kulak be hedged in by higher taxation. A voice advising caution raised the possibility of increasing grain imports from abroad and one speaker went to the heart of the matter by posing the crux question, 'Is it really possible to force the kulak to hand over grain without infringing NEP?' But these reservations about the use of force were drowned out by a huge cheer when someone pointed out that *Sovetskaia sibir'* had published an order declaring that the concealment of grain was a criminal offence. The meeting became animated and there were shouts of 'hear, hear, it's about time'. These worker-communists were mainly worried by the rampant price inflation of flour and bread, and rumours of further increases on the way. 'Fulfil the grain procurements with guns in our hands', cried one worker. Many demanded the arrest of 'kulak speculators', asking 'Why is Malafeev walking the streets? Hasn't he enough money.' Others indignantly claimed that the kulaks were saying 'The communists are showing the white feather.' Barabashev's conclusion caught the atmosphere of the cell by noting that 'There's a fighting mood amongst the lads.' It was precisely from cells like this that the party recruited hardened worker-communists to go into the countryside to assist with the procurements and they were clearly tearing at the leash to hit the peasantry.[12]

The Kraikombiuro directive of 18 January ordering the limited application of Article 107 raised several difficulties for the local authorities. Firstly, the instruction that a quota of four to ten of the most anti-Soviet 'kulak-speculators' be immediately arrested and tried publicly left a considerable element of variation in purely numerical terms of prospective kulaks to be prosecuted (it goes without saying that the possibility of a fair trial and acquittal was not entertained by the party leadership). Secondly, the application of this article against the peasantry was highly controversial and its implementation depended on the cooperation of the local judiciary and procuracy. Stalin had already denounced the krai judiciary for succumbing to 'kulak bait' by opposing the use of Article 107 against peasants and for the close personal relations between some judges and the kulak stratum in the countryside. This criticism was borne out to some extent as many law officers in the localities simply refused to cooperate and there were many cases when kulaks were acquitted by the courts.[13] The procuracy contributed to the confusion in the campaign with its attempts to prevent the application of Article 107 against peasants. On 22 January, just four days after the Kraikombiuro directive, the Krai Procurator, I. D. Kunov, published an article in *Sovetskaia sibir'* which specifically confined the use of Article 107 to private traders dealing in manufactured goods.[14] Thirdly, the manner in which the krai party leadership presented the campaign against the kulaks, particularly in the press, encouraged an over-zealous mood among workers sent into the countryside to get grain. The innumerable arbitrary abuses and excesses which resulted were to cause an intense intra-party debate after the worst of the crisis had passed and these will be discussed in a later section.

In his speech to the March plenum of the Kraikom, Syrtsov made it clear that the flexible quota of kulaks to be arrested had been set in order to take account of local variations in peasant differentiation. The work of Kavraisky and Nusinov had shown that there were a large number of kulak farms with huge grain surpluses in south-western Siberia, in comparison with other areas, and thus it was expected that the largest number of arrests would occur there. He also disclosed that the Kraikombiuro had considered the legality of these measures to be so shaky that, as part of the abandonment of 'formalities', it instructed that the kulaks were to be tried without the right of a defence counsel because it was feared that the state prosecutors would not be able to win their case. Some party organisations refused to follow this in-struction but where adversarial trials were held the kulaks were often convicted anyhow. The greatest confusion in the application of Article 107 surrounded the procedure for selecting the kulaks to be arrested and tried. The Kraikombiuro directive, based on Article 107, spoke of the most 'malicious' speculators without clarifying exactly how this was to be defined on the ground.[15]

Stalin's directive to all party organisations of 13 February 1928 ha-rangued them for abuses and excesses in the application of the emer-gency measures and attempted to clear up the confusion by ordering that, while general pressure on the kulaks was to continue, Article 107 was to be reserved for 'particularly malicious elements who hold surpluses of 2,000 puds [about 33 tons] or more of marketable grain'.[16] Syrtsov went a stage further than this on 17 February when he deliv-ered an important speech to the Novosibirsk party *actif* in which he differentiated two types of kulak: the 'pernicious' (*zlovrednykh*), against whom Article 107 must be applied; and the 'decent' (*poriadochnykh*) who although not politically sound were not to be repressed by the emergency measures. He defined the 'pernicious' as those large-scale grain hoarders who refused to sell to the state, while the 'decent' were those kulaks who 'sold grain willingly, did not evade their tax burdens, and paid their debts to the credit unions punctually'. He illustrated these types with some examples of kulaks from Rubtsovsk Okrug. Here, Article 107 had been applied against the 'pernicious' kulak Teplov who held a stock of about 246 tons of grain accumulated over a series of years and other speculators with many tens of tons and hoards of manufactured goods. This was counterbalanced with the example of the 'decent' kulak Kornienko, who had sold grain from the beginning of the year and had already delivered over 57 tons. After the newspapers had announced that Article 107 would be used against grain hoarders, Kornienko had cooperated by selling more grain, purchasing the state loan and warning other kulaks to sell grain otherwise things would go badly for them.[17]

Only sparse details are available as to the course of the trials under Article 107 and the punishments dealt out to those convicted. For publicity purposes the Siberian press coverage highlighted the trials of the big kulaks such as Teplov, as did Syrtsov in the information he supplied to the central party press. What is clear is that Article 107 was not employed against the mass of kulaks, never mind other peasants, but was for the most part carefully targeted and applied on a very limited scale. According to Syrtsov, less than 1,400 Siberian kulaks were brought to trial under Article 107 to the end of February 1928. A modern Soviet historian has revealed that in all, to the end of June 1928, Article 107 was applied against 1,589 kulaks and the great mass of trials were conducted in the period from mid-January to the end of February, during and immediately after Stalin's Siberian tour. That the success of Article 107 lay more in its terrorising effect on the well-off peasant grain hoarders than in its impact on increasing the overall procurement total with confiscated grain may be gauged by the fact that from those convicted only approximately 11,500 tons of grain were confiscated, i.e., less than 1% of the total amount of Siberian grain procured that year.[18]

Another Soviet source has stated that 922 kulaks were tried in West Siberia at this time, of whom only 545 were convicted. Many of these were given a high profile by the party as substantial grain stocks were often confiscated. For example, in the Pokrovsk Raion, Rubtsovsk Okrug, twenty-one kulak farms were brought to trial (an infringement of the Kraikombiuro quota of four to ten kulaks per raion) and some of the largest grain hoards in Siberia were discovered on the farms of those arrested, including: Teplov (mentioned above, 246 tons), Balyn (115), Zharikov (82) and Polik (65.5). However, such vast stocks were wholly exceptional as only just over one-third of those convicted in south-west Siberia had more than 1,000 puds (16.4 tons). The low conviction rate would suggest that, in interpreting the law, many judges refused to be browbeaten by the party, but whether they acted out of sympathy with the kulaks, to preserve their credibility in their locality or uphold their independence is impossible to say. The conflict between judges acting in the best interests of the peasantry and the party's use of emergency measures to overcome the crisis is also evident in the massive crackdown on illicit distilling in the krai which by 24 February had seen about 25,600 persons prosecuted (95% of whom were peasants) and over 3,400 stills confiscated. The courts nullified the hard work of the militia by treating the offenders lightly and imposing fines ranging up to 44 roubles against the 500 roubles laid down by the law of 2 January. Such behaviour may have been popular in the countryside but it reaffirmed Stalin's belief that the Siberian judges were treacherously sympathetic to the kulak cause and must be purged and subverted to rigid party control.[19]

A detailed sample of cases under Article 107 was provided by Kavraisky and Nusinov in a study written at the end of 1928. They analysed a total of 400 cases from four of the main grain okrugs of south-west Siberia. These okrugs had some of the wealthiest kulak farms in the region and this was reflected in the large size of grain stocks confiscated: an average of about 16.4 tons (over 26 tons in Rubtsovsk) and a total of 6,942 tons, well over half of all grain seized under Article 107 in Siberia. The number of kulaks brought to trial varied by okrug, broadly in compliance with the quota of four to ten set out by the Kraikombiuro. Curiously, fewer cases were held in Rubtsovsk (an average of 6.6 per raion) where average grain stocks confiscated per farm were the highest, compared with Kamensk where an average of 10.6 trials per raion were processed and average grain stocks seized were relatively low (about 14.6 tons per farm). In addition, farms prosecuted in Rubtsovsk were more wealthy, with 68% owning means of production with a value of over 1,500 roubles against 54.3% in Kamensk. Certainly, in terms of average grain stocks per farm and value of means of production, on the whole those brought to trial in these four okrugs were from the kulak verkhushka. Nevertheless, there were instances when seredniaks and even poor peasants were prosecuted under Article 107 and we shall discuss these later when we examine the excesses committed in the course of the campaign. Here, we shall be concerned with the cases of 'kulak speculation' brought under Article 107.[20]

The procedure by which kulaks were selected for trial, and who exactly picked them out, is not clear. Rural soviets kept lists of disenfranchised kulaks which was probably the starting-point for party plenipotentiaries to select a quota of known or suspected large-scale grain holders. In many cases this must have been an arbitrary and random process but where the collaboration of peasant informers was available it would have been most effective. The selective nature of the arrests inevitably added to the resentment of those prosecuted and the fear of the surrounding peasantry. Syrtsov recalled how in many villages the arrested kulaks would plead, 'Why do you only seize me, why don't you set up a commission which can go through the village and see who has surpluses.' Such was their acrimony that they frequently named other peasants who were hiding grain.[21] To maximise the intimidatory impact on the peasantry, trials of kulaks were held in public, in the presence of crowds of peasants and with the proceedings reported widely in the local press.

The trials of the kulak grain barons of Rubtsovsk were given the widest press exposure both locally and at the centre since they demonstrated the general lesson that the most powerful elements in the countryside were being brought to heel. The case which excited the most interest was that of Teplov from the village of Pervaia Karpovka, Rubtsovsk Okrug; a case which Syrtsov admitted, as we noted earlier, was entirely exceptional. This seventy-year-old patriarch headed an extended family with large property assets which included 3 houses, 5 barns, 50 horses, 23 cows, 108 sheep, 12 pigs, many machines and, as we noted above, a huge store of 246 tons of grain. At his trial, Teplov adamantly told the judge 'better to let it rot, than for me to cart it in for sale' and was explicit that the principal reason for his refusal to sell grain to the state was in retaliation for the government ban on the sale of tractors to individual farmers. If he could buy a tractor, 'it would be another matter'. Teplov received an eleven-month prison sentence with the confiscation of 213 tons of his grain stocks, but the court generously allowed him to retain the not inconsiderable amount of 33 tons, though half of this was rotted oats.[22]

Another case under Article 107 involving a wealthy kulak farmer was that of E. F. Rukavkin in Barnaul Okrug. His 'kulak' status dated from before the revolution, and his property included a full array of implements and machines, 10 horses, 8 cows and 70 sheep. In 1925 he expanded into the buying and selling of cattle and horses and every year drove herds from the Altai mountains. The following year he journeyed to Kharkov in the Ukraine and brought back 4 threshing machines and resold them to other wealthy villagers. It was even said that he made a speech to the factory workers praising the smychka. He sowed 58 desiatinas to grain in 1927 but after the harvest he was not satisfied with the prices offered and so refused to sell the bulk of his grain stocks. During the winter he sold 49 tons but despite this he was prosecuted under Article 107 and had 33 tons confiscated. By his own accounts, the income of Rukavkin's farm in 1927/8 was about 5,000 roubles. The prosecution of wealthy kulak farmers such as Teplov and Rukavkin was exceptional in most raions, even in the grain growing districts of south-west Siberia, though the confiscation of grain hoards of many tens of tons from kulak traders was less uncommon. In general, the quota of kulaks convicted under Article 107 had smaller, but still significant, grain surpluses of 10 to 15 tons.[23]

The squeeze on peasant income

From the middle of January 1928 the Siberian authorities exerted increased pressure on the peasantry for the settlement of outstanding payments and debts to state and cooperative agencies. Forms of social pressure were applied through rural organisations such as the village commune, rural soviet, cooperatives and party cells. At the behest of party plenipotentiaries resolutions would be passed setting deadlines for the fulfilment of all payments. The fact that the Kraikombiuro was under instructions from Stalin to conclude the tax payments campaign in the shortest time possible, even if it entailed breaking the law, meant that the local authorities in turn were given strict orders to meet the completion date of 15 February. In some places effective but time consuming legal methods were taken to pursue tax evaders, as for example in Omsk Okrug where kulaks were prosecuted for non-payment of taxes and penalised by the courts with a doubling of their original assessment.[24] However, given the pressure from above, most local officials disregarded such procedures and resorted to coercive methods to impose a monetary squeeze on the peasantry.

In furtherance of its aim of isolating and pressurising the well-off peasantry the party stepped up its attempts to organise and control the bednota and manipulate it as a cohesive social base of support for the party in rural institutions. The resolutions of the Fifteenth Congress ordered party committees at all levels to establish poor peasant groups in the soviets and cooperatives that would meet in periodic confer- ences at the village and raion level, and to supervise and coordinate their work a new bureaucratic tier was created in the party apparat: departments for work in the countryside. The Siberian leadership was slow to act on these resolutions and it was only at the end of January 1928, while Stalin was still present in the region, that it decided to put them into operation by 15 February. At the same time, to facilitate the regional party leadership's control of this aspect of the work of okruzhkoms, the Kraikom Secretariat was reorganised and its

Agitprop Department subdivided into five territorial groups: Western, Altai, Eastern, Mining-Industrial, Nationalities.[25]

The first priority of the Agitprop groups was the organisation of a huge propaganda exercise involving mass meetings of poor peasants to demonstrate their support for the party's grain procurement and payments campaigns. In the period January to March 1928 over 380,000 peasants participated in about 12,000 meetings held across Siberia, and throughout the spring and summer 239 raion and 20 okrug conferences of poor peasants were convened. The success of such a large-scale operation was hindered by the organisational weakness of rural party cells in a region as vast as Siberia and the fact that the rural poor constituted the least educated and most inarticulate, depressed, demoralised and intimidated section of the peasantry militated against their solidarity with the party in countering kulak authority in the villages. The party itself admitted that its task was made difficult in many places by the deep-rooted peasant suspicions of its motives and resistance to the emergency measures. In areas of Slavgorod Okrug seredniaks were aggrieved at the party's work with the poor and the kulaks felt that their hegemony over the countryside was threatened by the renewed activism of the Krestkomy. Typically, the kulaks responded by undermining and discrediting the party's measures by putting forward their own lists of peasant proxies to be elected to bednota conferences and the Krestkomy.[26]

The bednota meetings and conferences discussed the whole gamut of issues affecting the countryside: the agricultural tax, self-taxation, the state loan, credit, elections to soviet and cooperative organs and so forth, in addition to the grain procurement campaign. On occasions they did not proceed as the party expected. At the Kamensk Okrug Conference the local party secretary insisted on checking the tax lists of the delegates to verify that they were really poor, such was their hostility to the measures adopted by the party, and he claimed that 'their heads are at the disposal of the kulaks'. In this instance the peasants were afraid that if all the surplus grain was taken from the kulaks they would have no one to turn to in the spring to buy grain.[27] A similar mood was in evidence at the Barnaul Okrug Conference where delegates reported that in many villages the poor had come out against the party's demands.[28] Mindful of the need to stir up social antagonisms in the countryside, and in the process win over the poorer sections of the peasantry, Stalin emphasised in his letter, of 13 February, to local party organisations that highly progressive rates of self-taxation must be applied by the village gatherings against kulaks and well-off sections of the peasantry, while the poor should be exempted and the economically weak farms and Red Army families be given a reduced burden. When the Kraikom issued a directive on 22 February giving effect to Stalin's orders it noticeably toned down the demands of the original instruction and ordered that the increased rates of self-taxation were to be applied only against 'outright kulak farms' while seredniak 'big sowers' were specifically excluded, even if they had entered the higher tax category and to all intents and purposes were kulak farms. This once again illustrated the manner in which directives from the centre were moderated by the pro-peasant Siberian leadership.[29]

Demagogic competition for control of rural institutions between the well-off peasantry and the party intensified from early 1928 and was given an added urgency by the introduction of progressive self-tax-ation. The well-off peasants were outraged that the party was organis-ing the bednota to advance its goals and, if they had no tangible success in infiltrating the poor peasant groups, often demanded that they be excluded altogether from the deliberations of the communal gathering. For example, in the village of Ukrainka, Omsk Okrug, the poor peasants met as a caucus prior to the meeting of the communal gathering to work out a platform for progressive self-taxation but later their spokesman poorly presented their case by portraying the tax as being for the exclusive needs of the state and failing to mention the benefits for the village. Consequently, he lost the support of most of those assembled and when he proposed that payments be levied according to the agricultural tax assessment starting with the poor paying 5 kopecks in the rouble and increments thereafter up to 33 kopecks for the well-off, the kulaks objected and demanded that everyone pay a flat rate charge of 10 kopecks and called for those who did not pay taxes (i.e., the poor) to have no vote on the matter. The unpopularity of the progressive levy was such that the party repre-sentatives in attendance had to intervene and force it through, though how this was achieved is not recorded and one must presume that force was used. On the other hand, in the village of Dubrovino, Kamensk Okrug, the kulaks were more successful and a standard per capita charge of 1 rouble was imposed throughout the village. In addition the plenipotentiary to collect the levy was appointed from one of their number and he went around collecting money from the poor first and ignoring the kulak farms.[30]

On the whole, the Siberian party was successful in the campaign to soak up surplus peasant revenues. By the deadline of 15 February the collection of the agricultural tax had been fulfilled by 96.3% and by the end of March the annual plan of 22 million roubles had been exceeded by 0.5%. The subscription to the state loan was especially successful and by 1 April about 58% of the loan obligations allocated to Siberia had been bought, amounting to a sum of over 11.2 million roubles. The sale of the loan was particularly impressive in Barnaul Okrug, where the plan of 380,000 roubles sold out very quickly and another 100,000 roubles worth was taken up in February. In their eagerness to appease the party and show their 'decent' credentials wealthy kulaks in this okrug bought hundreds of roubles worth. The campaign for progress-ive self-taxation did not fare so well. A total sum of 8.42 million roubles had been set for Siberia (37% of the region's total agricultural tax), with 50% to be collected by 15 March. In reality only about 34% of this plan was achieved though there were wide intra-regional variations, pre-sumably depending on the efforts, exactitude and coercion employed by the local party organisation: for example, the figures for the neigh-bouring okrugs of Rubtsovsk and Slavgorod were 60% and 18% respectively.[31]

Rural communists and the emergency measures

The speed with which the emergency measures were imple-mented by Stalin caught the Siberian party and state officials un-prepared and off guard. The Kraikom had no time to instil a sense of activism in the lower level officialdom with a preparatory agitational-propaganda campaign, rather the localities were swamped by an ava-lanche of concurrent campaigns and expected to fall into line quickly. The pressure on the countryside intensified dramatically from the last week of January as the impact of Stalin's visit made itself felt at lower levels and a horde of party plenipotentiaries from the centre, Kraikom, Kraiispolkom, okrug and raion authorities descended on the villages to quicken the tempo of grain sales. Some advance political work among rural activists might have eased the impact of the campaigns but in the event a large number of rural party, soviet and procurement officials sided with the peasantry and reacted with open hostility to the emer-gency measures.

Writing in *Na Leninskom puti* in the middle of February, the Kraikom Second Secretary, Kisis, supported the Stalin line of blaming the poor performance of many officials on their political ties with the kulak stratum in the countryside and he was forthright in castigating the performance of the rural party. He stated that 'the majority of rural party cells were distinctly neutral in the carrying out of grain confiscation from kulaks, in distributing the peasant loan, collection of taxes, in the recovery of overdue loans, the fight against samogon and the implementation of other measures'. Kisis described how peasant communists had placed their loyalties to their social class above their allegiance to the party and felt that they should not 'fall out' with the peasantry. Some openly resisted and thwarted party measures, especially those with large farms and big grain surpluses, and there were even instances when party members hid kulak grain on their farms to save it from confiscation by the authorities.[32] Syrtsov paid lip-service to this theme at the March plenum of the Kraikom when he derisively described the lower level officials as 'Rotten elements in our apparat, outright kulak accomplices' who had been 'splendid allies' of the kulaks and a 'trump-card' in their favour.[33]

The lack of political will among Siberian officials to deal with the kulaks was also commented upon by the Leftist journalist Sosnovsky in a series of letters to Trotsky reporting on the events in Siberia at this time. He disclosed that prior to the unfolding of the grain crisis in early 1928 party officials in the region were complacently saying that the decision of the Fifteenth Congress to step up the offensive against kulak farms would remain a dead letter so long as grain procurement proceeded without difficulty. He viewed the reluctance of the Siberian party to support the renewed offensive against the kulak as the direct result of the purge of Left Oppositionists from the regional party in late 1927 which allowed supporters of a pro-kulak policy to dominate the regional apparat. It was only after the arrival of Stalin in mid-January that the Siberian press began to publish articles exposing these so-called 'kulak-communists'. Many were not only supporters of a policy in favour of the kulaks, or kulak 'yes-men' (*podgoloskie*) but fully fledged kulak farmers themselves, concealing many tens of tons of grain, owning advanced agricultural machines and using hired labour. In *Sovetskaia sibir'* a 'rogues gallery' of such communists was published, including secretaries of cells and raikom members. One raikom instructor was reported to have spoken out at a village meeting and railed against the 'extortionist' policy of the party while others of those mentioned had dealings with town speculators in grain. The many cases where rural party cells were the first to hand over grain as an example to the other peasants were pushed into the background as the press hounded the rural communists and made them scapegoats for the failures of the campaign.[34]

The lack of enthusiasm and hostile mood of rural communists to the emergency measures is illustrated by a newspaper report of the meeting of the Irbeisk Raion party *actif* held in the grain growing area of Kansk Okrug on 24 January 1928. The raikom justified the poor grain procurement level by claiming that their plan was 'unreal' since half the grain harvest had been ruined by frost and hail showers. It was recognised that only the kulaks had grain but, in a response typical of rural officials, the local leadership was afraid that if they were cleaned out the other peasants would have nowhere to turn for grain and seed in the spring. The raikom secretary stated that no grain would be procured in many areas because the peasants had a shortfall and were already meeting their own demand by carting it in from elsewhere. He dismissed the party's directives on the procurements as 'double-dutch'. The report spoke of peasant communists holding grain surpluses who were reluctant to sell, saying: 'Others keep grain, why am I worse?', 'I'm free to dispose of my own surpluses and sell them at a profit, to whom and whenever I want.' Others took their hostility to its logical political conclusion, declaring: 'The party is oppressing us, it wants to take grain at a fixed price only in the interests of the workers. We need to organise a peasant party. Let them start to reduce the high wages in the towns and then they can force us to deliver grain.' Several of these rural communists, including chairmen of the boards of cooperatives and rural soviets, had grain surpluses of 5–8 tons. Given such blatant anti-party sentiments among rural communists it would be reasonable to assume that ordinary peasant attitudes were even more hostile and we noted earlier that it was just this kind of resistance that outraged Stalin during his visit to the region.[35]

A common excuse used by rural party cells and soviets for not applying Article 107 was to claim that there were no kulaks in their jurisdiction. In the village of Mezhevo, Krasnoiarsk Okrug, the soviet and party cell asserted that there were no kulaks, only 'well-off seredniaks' who, following Syrtsov's guidelines on the kulak issue, were divided into 'good' (those selling grain to the state) and the 'bad' (those who refused to sell or only sold small quantities). According to an official report the members of the soviet included clear kulak farmers with large numbers of animals and machines, who hired labour and held considerable grain stocks which they refused to sell to the procurement organs. In other areas peasant communists were threatened with Article 107 if they did not sell their grain and indeed sometimes were actually prosecuted, like the communist from the Novoselovsk Raion, Krasnoiarsk Okrug, who had 150 sacks of flour confiscated. In the key grain surplus Rubtsovsk Okrug many party cells rejected the instruction to mobilise the rural poor, regarding them as 'good-for-nothings'. When Article 107 was applied against a kulak in the village of Berezovsk, Pokrovsk Raion, the secretary of the local party cell, and member of the raikom, spoke in his defence at the trial and the court acquitted him.[36]

There were other more practical means by which rural communists obstructed the use of the emergency measures in the procurement campaign as for example, in Tat'ianovsk, Omsk Okrug, where members of the party cell refused to allow their sleighs to be used in the carting of grain confiscated from local kulaks. No doubt, they felt it better to suffer a temporary scolding from a plenipotentiary than the indelible stain of collaborating in the pillaging of their well-off neighbours. Given the close-knit nature of peasant communities and the strength of the well-off peasantry in the social profile of the rural party organisations, family and neighbourly ties frequently proved to be a crucial factor in softening the blow of the emergency measures. A typical case in this respect was that of the kulak Matskevich from the village of Kalichenko, Tomsk Okrug, whose son was a prominent local communist and rural soviet secretary. The son assisted his father by under-assessing the tax burden of his farm and protecting his 33 tons of flour from the grain procurement organs. There were exceptions, of course, as in the Gutovsk Raion of the same okrug a member of the Komsomol turned in his father to be prosecuted under Article 107 for hiding over 13 tons of grain.[37]

Certain district party organisations were singled out by the Kraikom for particularly strident criticism for their reluctance to adhere to the application of the emergency measures and were used to illustrate the endemic nature of this problem. In Slavgorod Okrug, party activists were accused of falling in behind the kulaks, obstructing the campaign and even of anti-Soviet acts. They objected to the anti-NEP character of the campaign: 'They gave us this plan out of thin air and force us to plunder the peasant. But this is just like War Communism, if not worse.'[38] The Barnaul Okrug party organisation was the target of press attacks because of its indulgence to the kulaks. At the height of the grain campaign in February, the okruzhkom newspaper *Sel'skaia pravda* published a provocative article headlined 'The grain has been taken away by a *razverstka* front.' It praised 'labouring peasants' such as the wealthy kulak P. P. Chuikov, who bought 750 roubles worth of state loans and delivered 82 tons to the procurement organs. It was this episode that forced Syrtsov to clarify that although such kulaks were not to be prosecuted under Article 107, they were not to be treated favourably, as politically acceptable or of 'labouring' status. Apparently one Barnaul raikom secretary had even had his photograph taken with the above mentioned kulak and this had been printed in the newspaper for the purpose of taking advantage of the authority of the kulak in the countryside to persuade other peasants to follow suit. Syrtsov harangued this as a political error for it only served to strengthen the position of the kulaks and gave the impression that they were acceptable to the party and cooperating with its policies.[39]

The party employed the full weight of its propaganda machine in the attempt to forestall rural party cells from non-implementation of the orders from above. It organised 'red trains' of cart loads of procured grain decked out with red flags, buntings and slogans which, accompanied by groups of peasants, were driven off to the nearest town or raion centre to be greeted with as much pomp and circumstance as the local party and soviets could stage-manage. One of the first in Siberia was a shipment of 300 wagons to Srostki in Biisk Okrug on 12 January. Important political holidays such as Lenin's death (21 January), and Red Army day (23 February) became an excuse for the organisation of 'red trains' across the country. In the towns and cities factory workers and trade unionists were induced to participate in welcoming ceremonies in a manufactured reaffirmation of the smychka between workers and peasants.[40]

A more dependable method by which the party secured the cooperation of the bednota at least, was Stalin's suggestion that a 25% share of confiscated grain be delivered to the Krestkomy for use as a lure in the form of seed loans or food grants. Any peasant over 18 years old and not disenfranchised could join a Krestkom and their main function was to provide social welfare for the poor and families of Red Army men. In 1927/8 there were about 6,400 Krestkomy in Siberia, with a membership of almost 2.4 million peasants, organised around the rural soviets but only covering about 54% of villages. The evidence of a huge increase in the seed assistance distributed by the Krestkomy in Siberia between 1926/7 and 1927/8 suggests that their activities were considerably expanded by the party during the grain crisis. Until their mobilisation in January 1928 the Krestkomy had largely been a dormant feature of party influence in the countryside. In 1927 the Siberian Krestkomy had dispensed just 213 tons of grain seed in the assistance of poor farms whereas in the course of 1928 almost 5,000 tons were given out, of which over 3,300 tons came from confiscated grain and was issued in the form of seed loans to the bednota. The latter figure amounted to about 28% of grain seized under Article 107 in the region, evidently more generous than Stalin had intended. Nevertheless, its delivery to the poor was a vital demonstration of the party's good faith and acted as an inducement for the future cooperation of the poor with party attacks on the well-off peasantry. At the same time there was a massive rise in the level of general state seed assistance to the Siberian peasantry from 9,337 tons in 1927 to 36,839 tons in 1928, reflecting the efforts of the government to ensure a successful sowing campaign in 1928.[41]

When party, soviet or procurement officials and plenipotentiaries arrived in rural areas one of the most widespread difficulties they faced was a breakdown in communications between the regional centre and localities. Frequently, the local authorities either had not received important directives or had not been convinced of their urgency. At the okrug level it was usually bureaucratic inertia while at the raion level and below the sheer scale of distances and poor administrative capabilities of rural officials hindered the speedy implementation of orders from above. These elements were clearly in operation in Tulunovsk Okrug, where the okrugtorg had allocated grain procurement plans to the raions at the beginning of the campaign. On 13 January, in the wake of the emergency directives of the Central Committee and the Kraikom, the Tulunovsk Okruzhkom ordered an inspection of the extent of plan fulfilment in the raions, but it was another two weeks before any officials were sent to the localities. When these inspectors arrived they could only find out the sketchiest of information about how the procurements were proceeding. Local leaders were naturally quick to blame the delays in the campaign on apathetic, corrupt, inefficient or uncooperative lower level officials, rather than assume responsibility themselves and party and press reports reflected this.[42]

The Kraikom leadership contributed to an already poor organisational situation by often sending its plenipotentiaries into the countryside with no specific agenda or concrete tasks and usually no fixed period of stay. Even in Novosibirsk, the communications heart of the krai, it was reported that at the end of January many procurement organs had not been fully mobilised for crisis action and in the middle of February the chairman of a consumer cooperative in Slavgorod Okrug could still complain that he did not know that the procurement campaign was now being conducted on a 'shock basis'.[43] As the pressure filtered down to the localities from the higher echelons of the regional leadership the immediate effect was to further exacerbate the problem of competition between grain procurement organs and different raions to fulfil their plans. L. S. Strikovsky, the Head of the

Kraisoiuz, described the competition between procurement agencies in detail at the March plenum of the Kraikom. Rival agencies put up signs with slogans offering advantages to sellers, consumer cooperatives sent out 'patrols' to search out and buy grain from peasant farms, and price inflation was rampant. In some areas cooperative officials labelled Khleboprodukt as a 'private capitalist organisation' and rural soviets gave orders that grain could not be sold to it. One of the most common abuses in Siberia was the issue of vouchers by the cooperatives to those who sold grain to them and without which they refused to sell manufactured goods to the peasantry. The enmity between these agencies was so fierce that the Head of Achinsk Consumer Cooperatives claimed that 'War was declared [by Khleboprodukt] and a systematic offensive was conducted against us.' The issuing of more severe orders by the authorities, in the middle of January, threatening officials with removal and prosecution for 'nonfulfilment of grain procurement tasks', served only to intensify competition between rival agencies.[44]

The fear of loss of office and prosecution produced a hysterical panic-stricken reaction among some lower level officials. In Achinsk Okrug, several rural soviets attempted to meet their grain targets by purchasing it with the proceeds of the self-taxation funds because the consumer cooperatives had no money or goods. In many okrugs grain designated for internal use was shipped out in order to meet krai targets or simply because in the confusion okrug authorities did not exercise sufficiently stringent control over the movement of grain. The first wave of sackings came in late January at a meeting of Sibsel'sko-soiuz when several okrug officials were removed and others reprimanded for slipshod work. Then in early February the Presidium of the Kraiispolkom and the Kraikombiuro issued a joint decree publicly reprimanding the leaders of the main krai grain procurement organs; M. T. Zuev (Sibtorg), F. N. Baranov (Khleboprodukt) and L. S. Strikovsky (Sibkraisoiuz) and dismissing the Deputy Chairman of Sibsel'sko-soiuz, Vedeniapina, with referral of her case to the Party Control Commission.[45]

The scale of the purge in the procurement apparat in Siberia was substantial as in the course of the grain campaign in 1927/8 1,370 soviet and cooperative workers in 10 okrugs were dismissed for inactivity or inefficiency, 612 of whom were prosecuted. Most were tried under Article 111 of the RSFSR Criminal Code which stipulated that officials guilty of abrogating their duties and showing a 'neglectful ... and unconscientious attitude to entrusted tasks' could be sentenced to up to three years imprisonment.[46] In Tomsk Okrug alone 713 officials were prosecuted under Article 111 in 1928. In Biisk Okrug, 13 out of 18 raiispolkom chairmen were brought to trial, and 149 out of 277 (53%) chairmen of rural soviets were replaced and 54 prosecuted. In Irkutsk one-third of chairmen of rural soviets were prosecuted and in Kansk, to 1 March, 54 chairman were removed. As with those prosecuted under Article 107 the trials of these officials were given wide publicity in the press as a means of terrorising the others. In one case, the ex-Chairman of the Board of Smolianinsk Credit Union in Omsk Okrug received six years in a strict regime prison and four years' loss of all civil rights. In the space of ten months he had lost over 15,000 roubles by giving out loans to kulaks (even from the bedniak fund). During the grain campaign in early 1928, he had gone off to Omsk for weeks and consequently had only fulfilled his grain plan to 15%.[47]

The pressure from above for a quick end to the crisis recreated an atmosphere in the countryside akin to that which had prevailed during the civil war and led to arbitrary abuses by officials who feared the ramifications of failure or breach of duty. The real threat of removal and prosecution for non-fulfilment of plans, no matter what the circumstances, inevitably meant that many officials simply resorted to the method of order fulfilment with which they were most familiar in times of crisis and which had produced speedy and positive results during the civil war, namely, coercion. Past experience had demonstrated that once the party resorted to the use of emergency coercive measures all kinds of abuses and excesses resulted.

Coercion and excesses against the peasantry

The degree to which Stalin was personally responsible for abuses committed in the course of the party offensive to overcome the grain crisis has been a subject of much debate, even among Siberian historians in the pre-*glasnost* era. One scholar has argued that when Stalin and Poskrebyshev came to Siberia they demanded that the procurements be achieved 'by any means' and issued telegrams and circulars to local party and soviet organs by which they were 'compelled to go over to administrative pressure'. However, this view has been specifically refuted by another Soviet historian who has asserted that documents exist which show that Stalin spoke out against the use of administrative methods while in Siberia. As we saw earlier, one of Stalin's last acts before leaving Siberia had been the removal of Povolotsky, Omsk Okruzhkom Secretary, for advocating a policy of razverstka and declaring that NEP had been abandoned by the party leadership. Such an ambiguous and even contradictory approach to political problems was central to Stalin's style and a reflection of his political astuteness. By such actions and statements he covered himself for all foreseeable outcomes and eventualities. If the emergency measures were a success he could claim the credit for saving the country from disaster, and if his instructions produced excesses and overreactions on the ground he could shift the blame onto over-zealous lower level officials. It was a ploy later used to great effect in March 1930 when his 'dizzy with success' article in *Pravda* castigated lower officialdom for excessive zeal in forcing the rapid all-out collectivisation drive which had been launched with his approval.[48]

While Stalin's radical policy of pounding the well-off peasantry into submitting to the economic strategy of the state may have been responsible for official excesses in the application of the emergency measures, the Siberian party leadership took its cue from his condemnation of Povolotsky in Omsk. From early February 1928 the local press published many articles exposing officials who had perpetrated abuses against the peasantry and calling for an end to such activities. When Stalin condemned such excesses in his letter to party organisations of 13 February, an editorial in the *Na Leninskom puti* on 15 February followed suit. It spoke of the need to correct distortions in the campaign and stated that they had arisen 'either as a result of an incorrect understanding of leading directives or as a result of personal initiative or simply in the urgent conditions of the work'. The focal point for criticism was the 'prodrazverstka deviation' that had been observed in many areas and included the levying of fixed grain delivery quotas among villages and households by rural soviets, often because they had been set compulsory targets by raiispolkoms. Local party and soviet officials were denounced for 'an extreme enthusiasm for administrative methods of pressure while ignoring economic measures of influence'. In some places the bazaar had been closed, permit orders were needed to transport grain and milling quotas were allotted, all of which were 'a legacy from the time of forced seizures' during the civil war. The editorial went on to reveal that measures were being taken locally to eradicate these errors, but it recognised that such moves would have little impact since the real reason for official excesses, the pressure from above for quick results, was not being alleviated. An article in the same issue described how some lower party *actifs* had preferred to engage in 'one administrative swoop' rather than use economic methods of pressure and it delivered a dire warning against the current trend towards coercion: 'We cannot organise the economy to the sound of a militiaman's whistle.'[49]

Despite Stalin's attempt to squash 'tittle-tattle' in the party about the end of NEP, in Barnaul some communists bragged that 'NEP is out' as rumours of armed food detachments and a return 'to 1920' swept the villages, and some party members in Slavgorod talked of 'proletarianising' the countryside. The secretary of the party cell in Katunsk, Biisk Okrug, described targets set by the raiispolkom as no better than a 'Dawes plan' for the countryside. Typically, when plenipotentiaries arrived in a village, they forcibly entered peasant barns, decided by eye how much grain there was, allocated an amount to be delivered by a fixed date and made the peasants sign a promissory note.[50] In some areas the 25% share of confiscated grain intended for the Krestkomy was shipped out by over-zealous procurement officials fearful of failing to meet their delivery targets. In these circumstances the issue of grain to the bednota was a lesser priority and consequently it was frequently delayed until the last possible moment. A village correspondent from Shestakovka, Odessa Raion, Omsk Okrug reported that 35% of the local peasants had no seed grain to sow in the spring yet the raion Krestkom delivered less than 1 ton against the nearly 6 tons ordered. Demands for additional supplies were buried in bureaucratic delays.[51] The most damning critique of official abuses came in an article by Nusinov in *Na Leninskom puti* in late February 1928 titled 'Grain procurement swindling'. He lashed out at the Rubtsovsk party organisation for acting in a 'frenzy of administrative actions'. They had conducted fifteen campaigns concurrently, all of which could be summed up in one word: 'Give! Give grain, taxes (before they are due), insurance, credits, shares, loans, self-taxation, seed fund.'[52]

Syrtsov's speech to the Novosibirsk party *actif* on 17 February 1928 was intended to both curb the excesses unleashed by the pressure from above and outline the correct methods for the conduct of the campaign. In particular he sought to clarify Stalin's directives and distinguish those kulaks to whom Article 107 was to be applied. As we discussed previously, he categorised the kulaks into the 'pernicious' and the 'decent': a bold elucidation of Stalin's approach which tarred all kulaks with the same brush and recognised no such phenomenon as the 'decent' kulak. Syrtsov again fundamentally diverged from Stalin's thinking on the application of Article 107 since this had been surrounded by the most confusion and worst abuses. Not only did he distance himself from the use of this measure against peasants, calling it one of the 'hard revolutionary laws', but also vented a barely veiled

rebuke to Stalin and others who favoured coercion: 'We are not relying
on Article 107 alone. We know that we will not resolve the issue by
Article 107 nor by any measures of an administrative or judicial order.
Those comrades who think that socialism can be built with the help of
cudgels are mistaken.' Such were the rumours sweeping the party in
the wake of the abuses being perpetrated, that he was compelled to
stress that 'we are not pursuing a policy of dekulakisation', and that
NEP was not being abandoned. He followed Stalin's lead by describing
the current campaign as 'an examination' (*proverka*) of the whole party.
But whereas Stalin viewed the performance of the party during the
crisis as a test of its commitment to the 'class line' Syrtsov urged the
membership to 'observe the law' and threatened to 'prosecute those
over-zealous officials who take it into their heads that they can apply
prodrazverstka, that they can enter homes and demand surpluses to
be handed over'.[53]

It was in this speech that Syrtsov made his only reference to the
cohort of party activists sent by the Central Committee to assist the
Siberians with the procurements. He acknowledged that they had
shown a 'fervent intention to help with grain procurement', but laid
the blame for many of the abuses on them.[54] One report described the
terroristic operational methods of these 'shock workers'. On arrival at a
village they informed the chairman of the soviet that he was being
arrested and taken away to the town because he had not fulfilled the
grain and payments collections. After some argument he was allowed
to remain in the village for one more day on condition that he fulfilled
the plans. In Kamensk and Novosibirsk Okrugs, plenipotentiaries
went to villages and, threatening the peasants with revolvers,
demanded that grain be handed over. Inevitably, this type of conduct
created a mood of terror in the countryside although usually once the
plenipotentiaries departed the village activists eased off the pressure
and the intensity of the campaign slackened.[55]

The clear divisions in the krai party elite over the application of
Article 107 to the peasantry that had been evident at the time of Stalin's
visit, were not resolved by the General Secretary's threats of purging
those who did not fall in behind the new radicalism, or indeed even by
Syrtsov's attempt to clarify the policy within the framework of NEP.
Syrtsov attempted to demonstrate his commitment to punishing official violations of NEP in a Kraikombiuro circular of 18 February, the
day after his Novosibirsk speech, which denounced the Kuznetsk
Okruzhkom troika for applying Article 107 to a quota of two seredniaks
per raion in addition to Kulaks.[56] This signalled the beginning of an

official backlash by the Siberian leadership against the emergency measures in which the regional procuracy and judicial officials were in the forefront. In March the head of the Krai Procuracy, Kunov, wrote an article for one of the main regional peasant journals titled 'The law watches over the interests of the peasantry.' Criticising the use of Article 107 he regretted that 'in places this article was taken as a method for intimidating entirely Soviet-minded parts of the countryside'. He went on to reveal that some judges had ordered the confiscation of all property of those convicted as well as the article of speculation: grain. In April one of Kunov's subordinates, Leonidov, warned that those who 'exceeded their authority' under Article 107 would be prosecuted under Article 110 of the Criminal Code for breach of duty and would, if convicted, be liable to a six-month sentence in a strict regime prison or even to execution in extreme cases.[57]

The Stalinist counter-attack on such views came at the March plenum of the Kraikom when Zimin and the Irkutsk Okruzhkom leaders vigorously defended their ruthless implementation of Article 107 and called for Syrtsov's removal as regional party secretary. As we shall see later, what was remarkable about this plenum was the way that the Irkutsk officials were isolated in their stance. Indeed, it was only much later, at the end of 1928, when the local party organisations drew up their annual reports against the background of Stalin's triumph over the Right, that there was blanket condemnation of the failure of the party, and in particular of legal officers, to impose the emergency measures with sufficient resolve. The annual report of the Barnaul Okruzhkom was typical in this respect as it derided the performance of local judges and procurators during the crisis as displaying 'a completely uncommunistic fear before the formal "shackles" of jurisprudence, to the detriment of the revolutionary-proletarian thought behind our laws'. It claimed that the judiciary had demonstrated a lack of 'political keenness' and a 'hard proletarian line' in their work and required purging.[58]

On 3 June 1928 a special Kraikom 'grain conference' was convened and attended by Kosior and Poskrebyshev as representatives of the Central Committee. At this sensitive juncture when the party leadership was bracing itself for a likely showdown between Stalin and Bukharin at the Central Committee plenum in July over the handling of the grain crisis, and given their positions as leading Stalin clients in the apparat, Kosior and Syrtsov were naturally anxious to secure resolutions that affirmed the efficacy of the emergency measures in a region where Stalin had played a central role, in spite of Syrtsov's reservations about their use. The ensuing Kraikom report issued on 5 June 1928 reviewed the application of Article 107 during the campaign and asserted that only three bedniaks had been tried (two in Omsk and one in Biisk) and that 93% of cases had involved 'kulak-exploiters'. The many cases involving so-called seredniak farms were more problematic given the often blurred dividing line between the well-off seredniak and the kulak. These trials were most prevalent in Omsk (over 10% of cases), Biisk (over 10%), Irkutsk (over 15%) and Kuznetsk (over 20%). One section of the report was devoted to criticising okrug party organisations where there had been 'massive rescinding' of sentences on judicial appeal, including the acquittal of 'clear kulaks'. Consequently, Kunov as Krai Procurator and Kozhevnikov of Kraisud were instructed to reexamine all cases where it was suspected that bedniaks or seredniaks had been convicted (with restoration of grain, and where possible, property, or compensation if not) and, in a further extension of party control of the judiciary, it was ordered that convictions under Article 107 could only be rescinded with the approval of the relevant okruzhkombiuro. On the whole the application of Article 107 was deemed to have been 'satisfactory'. In mid-July, following the ending of the emergency measures by the Central Committee, Kozhevnikov sent a circular to the okrug authorities in which he emphatically stated: 'It is categorically forbidden, henceforth, to permit a single case of the application of Article 107 in the grain procurements.' All cases pending were to be closed forthwith.[59]

Peasant resistance

Over one year after the grain crisis, at the Sixteenth Party Conference in April 1929 when the leadership was stoking the fires of the anti-kulak hysteria in the country, Syrtsov made a curious speech which not only blatantly contradicted his concerns in early 1928 but was highly ambivalent about the active opposition of the Siberian kulaks to the emergency measures and the political threat they posed to the regime. He stated that the emergency measures had been instituted only once it had become apparent that 'significant amounts' of seredniak grain had been bought up by kulaks. Citing the figures drawn up by Kavraisky and Nusinov, he revealed that by the end of January 1928 kulaks held about 50% of marketable grain in the krai and the party was confronted by 'collossal' kulak resistance to the procurements. He argued that state prices for grain and other agricultural produce were not the real issue, rather it was a political question for the

kulaks demanded not only the freedom to purchase advanced agricultural equipment but also political rights. Yet one source states that
Syrtsov was very conscious of the price issue in early 1928, having been
harangued by the peasantry about the preposterous price policy of the
regime on his village trips.[60]

According to Syrtsov the kulaks aspired to the overthrow of the
Bolshevik government in order to eliminate 'the regime under which
the kulak finds himself politically isolated in the countryside'. The root
of the kulak's antagonism to the party was that they had developed
their farms to a level where their further growth was hindered by
Soviet legal restrictions on the hiring of labour, ownership of land and
purchase of advanced equipment. He asserted that 'every pud of grain
left in kulak hands would be turned into guns to be used against Soviet
power and aid the restoration of capitalism'. On the other hand, as
during the crisis of early 1928 when he had been adamant that 'the
kulak has no prospects for political power', he gave short shrift to the
view that the kulak posed an immediate political threat to the regime.[61]
For although the kulak had gained a whole series of toeholds in the
lower levels of the party and state apparatus and there was a certain
growth in kulak 'consciousness as a class', he did not possess 'the
necessary organising ability, he had no nationwide organisation, no
platform which can legitimately organise such a movement on an
All-Union scale and he has no authoritative individuals in his ranks to
support him in this matter'. Moreover, these were the very features
that determined the weakness of the peasantry as an organised social
and political force.

In Siberia the most common form of kulak resistance to the emergency measures was the destruction of grain rather than delivering it to
the state and a common kulak slogan was 'neither mine nor to the
Soviet power'. Syrtsov reported that coercion had proved effective and
'where we broke kulak resistance after obstructive demonstrations
(volynki), we observed that a steady flow of grain began immediately,
as if a cork had been removed'. The scene described by him was of
politically motivated resistance to the grain procurements by one section of the peasantry only: the kulaks. This acceptance of the political
nature of the grain crisis and recognition of the success of the emergency measures from a man who had bitterly condemned both the
previous year must be seen in the context of Soviet leadership politics
at this time. By early 1929 Stalin's consolidation of his power at the
centre demanded that upwardly mobile officials show support for his
radical shift of policy to the Left and the acute hostility of the party

towards the role of the kulak in agriculture. This kind of adept, Janus-faced act by Syrtsov, with the embracing of a genuinely 'soft' pro-peasant line at the regional level and a fake 'hard' Stalinist line when making speeches at the centre, was a political necessity for career promotion given his factional ties to Stalin.[62]

In the event, in Siberia, as in the rest of the country, no coordinated large-scale politically motivated peasant resistance to the party materialised during the crisis of 1928. Rather, the evidence confirms Syrtsov's confidence regarding the political impotence of the kulaks as potential leaders of the peasantry. What emerges is a chaotic picture of isolated, and usually spontaneous, armed or violent attacks by groups of peasants against officials, plenipotentiaries and peasant collaborators, with widespread passive resistance and some instances of peasant infighting which the party played up as class war. However, the party generically branded all such acts of peasant resistance as evidence of 'kulak terrorism', a slogan which conveniently justified the use of 'counter-terror' in the countryside. At the same time, it should not be forgotten that since the driving force behind the actions of the peasantry was a general disgruntlement with the economic measures adopted by the party it was frequently the case that discontent assumed a political direction. Concealment of grain hoards by the peasantry was endemic throughout the krai and to confuse the authorities and reduce the likelihood of peasant informing, kulaks sometimes dispersed their grain surpluses around poorer neighbouring farms in return for a share. Often kulaks refused to sell grain to the bednota unless they rejected the party's promises of assistance and backed the resistance to the emergency measures. After the application of Article 107 the kulaks tended to be more circumspect in their opposition and often gave grain to the poor on credit as this was another useful way of dispersing stocks liable to seizure by the state. An added burden for the party was the close tie between the kulaks and rural officialdom: as noted earlier, kulaks were frequently members of the local party cell and rural soviet or had close relatives in them, or could easily bribe the underpaid and disaffected rural officials, and this severely handicapped the activities of outside plenipotentiaries who depended on the rural representatives of Soviet power for local knowledge.[63]

An example of the close ties between kulaks and the local authorities was the establishment of an informal committee or 'shatkom' (*komitetom shataiushchiksia*) in a village of Shipunovsk Raion, Rubtsovsk Okrug, by kulaks who had been disenfranchised and excluded from the boards of cooperatives. The local party cell considered it to be a 'useful *actif*' and acceded to its demand not to raise the level of self-taxation. In the village of Zakharov, the kulak Akimov frequently attended sessions of the rural soviet even though disenfranchised. He described himself to one plenipotentiary as 'the head of the vanguard' of the village (he was an ex-soldier) and offered to deliver 2.5 tons of grain and buy 200 roubles worth of loans if his voting rights were restored. The problems encountered by party plenipotentiaries in areas where local officials were hostile to the campaign is illustrated by the following case. In the villages of Tikhoretsk and Rakitakh, Novo-Uralsk Raion, Omsk Okrug, there was no party cell and the rural soviet and local cooperative were run by a group of kulaks, the three brothers Shentiapinyi. Grain procurement in the area was low, there was no self-taxation, machines were sold to kulaks and collective farmers were excluded from credit facilities. The brothers were prosecuted under Article 107 when a plenipotentiary arrived in the district, and the local bednota attended the trial. But as soon as the plenipotentiary left kulaks broke up the poor peasants group, called a meeting of the commune, got peasants drunk and secured a vote to acquit the brothers.[64]

A potentially more threatening development for the party was the unsuccessful attempt by peasants in several okrugs of south-west Siberia to revive the anti-Bolshevik and SR inclined 'Siberian Peasants' Union' under whose banner the well-armed peasant revolt of 1921–2 occurred. It would be reasonable to presume that many of the arms used in this revolt were kept hidden by the peasantry and, by comparison, what is striking about the level and nature of peasant resistance to the emergency measures in 1927–8 is just how rare and uncoordinated the acts of armed resistance were. Across the krai, between January and June 1928, only 204 cases of what the party termed 'kulak-terrorism' were recorded and although this was almost double the same figure for 1927 it must still be regarded as a feeble response in terms of violent peasant opposition to the party's 'grain offensive'. This would suggest that the party's strategy of a limited application of Article 107 against clearly kulak farms and the reward of a 25% share of confiscated grain to the poor, paid dividends in terms of stirring up social divisions among the peasants and prevented a coordinated peasant response such as that of 1921–2. Indeed, a Soviet historian has revealed that it was only where bedniaks and seredniaks were caught in the net of Article 107 that 'open hostilities' resulted, presumably in the form of armed clashes between the peasantry and the authorities.[65]

Most of the violent incidents involved cases of individual terror. For example, a teacher in the village of Martiushevo, Tarsk Okrug, was shot because she campaigned for the rural soviet to collect kulak surpluses. A kulak in Volotinsk Raion, Tomsk Okrug, stabbed the raion militia chief while under interrogation about hidden grain. In the same raion three chairmen of rural soviets were murdered and as one was shot he was told 'Here's your grain procurements, here's your loan and here's your cheating measures.' In the village of Permiakove, Kuznetsk Okrug, a bedniak was hacked to death for informing the authorities of the ties between the rural soviet and local kulaks. Kulaks in the village of Vagaitsevo, Biisk Okrug, enticed local collective farmers to sell their grain to them, but they were enraged when the collective purchased a mechanical thresher with the proceeds because it threatened to end the kulak monopoly of machines. They attacked the farm, beat up the peasants and destroyed the thresher.[66]

Some kulaks were conscious of the political nature of the struggle and saw their fight against the party as a return to the unfinished battles of 1921–2. One caught with over 8 tons of grain and a rifle retorted: 'I know very well that this is what class war is all about.'[67] The more devious among them took clever measures to avoid suspicion, for example, by making a token contribution to a 'red train' and hoisting a red flag over their sledge. A particularly worrying feature for the regime was the flood of letters which inundated the army from the peasantry protesting at the exactions of the party in the countryside. It was precisely this kind of action that had provoked the Kronstadt revolt against the Bolsheviks in 1921. At the March plenum of the Kraikom Syrtsov told of how Red Army men showed these letters to their political commissars and demanded answers and he reported that one garrison of 5,000 men had received as many as 6,000 protest letters in one day! Sosnovsky reported that up to 5% of Red Army ranks in some garrisons were branded kulaks and discharged, some of whom were party members, and it may well be that these soldiers were purged for complaining too vociferously about the treatment of their fellow peasants.[68]

A prominent feature of the peasant resistance to the emergency measures was the leading part played by women in organising disturbances. One of the most serious of these co-called 'women's riots' (*babii bunty*) occurred in Karasuksk Raion, Slavgorod Okrug, in May 1928. The trouble began when angry and hungry peasants from six villages held a demonstration to complain about grain shortages and the apparent reneging by the local Krestkom and cooperative on a promise to deliver supplies. On 14 May a crowd of 120 women surrounded the raiispolkom office in Karasuk and demanded grain. Under pressure the chairman drew up a list and within a few days about a third of a ton was handed out. This climbdown by local officials was a cue for the unrest to spread and in the following days women throughout the district ransacked cooperative barns and stores or seized carts on the roads and distributed the spoils. As men stayed out of the disturbances it was difficult for the authorities to use physical force to stop them. Eventually, as looted grain defused and satiated the pent-up frustration of the peasantry, order was restored and an investigation into the causes of the affair was launched. It was discovered that the unrest had been sparked by rumours of outsider plenipotentiaries forcing poor peasants to deliver grain to the state and claimed that only a handful of those peasants involved were actually short of grain.[69]

In contrast to the armed rebellion of 1921–2, the best resistance the Siberian peasants offered in the spring of 1928 were acts of individual terrorism or 'women's riots'. Even by the rather loose interpretation of 'kulak terrorism' set by the party, there were only a couple of hundred violent acts whereas the vast majority of peasants seem to have retained their faith in the party's commitment to NEP and sought redress of their grievances by orderly appeals to higher authorities. In time honoured fashion the mood of the uncomprehending peasantry seems to have been that the abuses perpetrated against them were the result of the excessive zeal of the local authorities and junior officials rather than a predetermined plan set by the centre. In such circumstances a common but invariably futile response was to flood the leading governmental figures with letters detailing the miscarriages of justice at the grassroots. Siberian peasants swamped Moscow and Novosibirsk with complaints of abuses while letters and telegrams of a similar vein were sent in their thousands by rural party organisations to Stalin, Molotov, Kalinin, Syrtsov and Eikhe. When this avalanche of complaints arrived in Moscow in the wake of Stalin's Siberian tour it caused an uproar in the Politburo as Bukharin, Rykov and Tomsky were outraged at the infringements of NEP. The scene was now set for a new schism in the party leadership.[70]

The success of the emergency measures

A breakthrough in the grain crisis was already apparent before Stalin departed from Siberia on 30 January 1928. In the fourth (16–20) and fifth (21–25) five-day periods of January about 41,000 tons of grain were collected in total, but during the sixth period (26–31) alone the procurement points were inundated with over 49,000 tons. This was in spite of the unusually adverse winter weather conditions, with strong blizzards hampering the campaign in many okrugs. In February grain procurement peaked at just under 31,800 tons for the month; a massive trebling of the total achieved in February 1927. On the basis of these results Stalin could rightly claim, on his return to Moscow, that there was a direct correlation between the surge in peasant sales of grain and the application of the emergency measures, and he testified to a 'decisive victory for the party'.[71]

The turn-around in grain procurement was confirmed by newspaper reports from the Siberian countryside. From Omsk, Barabashev reported that grain convoys of forty to fifty wagons could be seen on the roads and that peasants were queuing up with their carts to sell grain to the procurement agencies. He described how only 7.5 tons had been obtained in one raion in the period 20–23 January, but in the next three days (23–25) 119 tons had come in and in the last two days (26–27) almost 344 tons. Barabashev believed that the peasantry was now selling grain because the arrival of manufactured goods had 'squeezed' it out of the seredniaks, while the kulaks and well-off were handing it over because of the repressive measures.[72] Flooded by deliveries, the main problem now facing local procurement officials was the sheer volume of sales and the lack of storage facilities. Similarly, in the village of Aliesk, Barnaul Okrug, only about 82 tons had been sold to the procurement agencies by 23 January but immediately after three 'speculators' were prosecuted on 24 January the local peasantry delivered over 245 tons within a few days. This kind of sudden transformation in the fortunes of the campaign was repeated in other areas of Siberia and throughout the country and undoubtedly averted a major food supply crisis for the government before the spring thaw.[73]

In a flush of elation at the successes of February the Kraikom set a new target of 85% fulfilment of the yearly grain procurement plan of just over 1.34 million tons by 1 April. This was somewhat optimistic given that March was normally one of the most difficult months in the Siberian grain collections each year as the spring thaw increased the humidity of grain and made good storage and speedy shipment essential to avoid rotting, yet transport became bogged down on the muddy roads. Nevertheless, about 191,646 tons were procured in March and consequently the target was almost reached and 82.6% (just over 1.11 million tons) of the annual plan was achieved by 1 April. By this time the law of diminishing returns began to take effect and, partly as a result of an easing of the pressure on the countryside as the zeal of those involved in the campaign became exhausted, and partly because most peasants had sold their available surpluses by this stage, procurement levels began to subside once again. In April only about 14,742 tons were delivered and in early May peasant sales slumped to a paltry 737 tons for the first ten-day period.[74]

Stalin and other members of the Politburo contributed to the more relaxed atmosphere in the localities by the conciliatory tone advanced at the April joint plenum of the Central Committee and Central Control Commission. Following the strongly worded condemnation of abuses in the application of the emergency measures which were included in the resolutions of the plenum, a series of articles on this theme appeared in the central press. This reinforced the message to the party apparat that the time had come to ease the pressure on the peasantry. Yet it was precisely at this point that the fall off in grain procurement once again assumed crisis proportions because the failure of the winter grain harvest in the Ukraine and North Caucasus left a severe shortage not only of food grains in these regions but also of seed grain. This threatened to ruin the spring sowing and darken the prospects for the following year's harvest. The regime was forced into a sharp u-turn and the orders went out for the reapplication of the emergency measures and the pressure on the peasants in grain surplus areas resumed. Consequently, when Kosior attended the Siberian Kraikom 'grain conference' on 3 June 1928, the former party leader in the region conveyed orders from Stalin that the Siberian authorities must 'increase the pressure', persist with the application of Article 107 and continue to pursue the policy of politically organising the poor peasants against the kulaks. To make good some of the shortages currently being experienced in the central industrial regions due to the crisis in the Ukraine and North Caucasus, Stalin demanded that the Siberians supply about 82,000 to 90,000 tons of grain by the end of June 'at all costs'. Whether this was a supplement to the annual plan or a demand to find part of the shortfall in its fulfilment is not clear, but the exceptional tone of the order put it in the same category as the earlier emergency directives from Stalin and it opened the way for a return to the punitive exactions of early 1928. There is a curtain of silence in the sources as to the scale of the reapplication of the emergency measures in the summer of 1928, their effect on the peasantry and whether or not the specific task set by Stalin was achieved. The most reliable modern Siberian historian of this period has stated that upwards of 1.3 million tons of grain was procured in the region in 1927/8 (almost 98% of a very ambitious annual plan), and around 792,600 tons of planned grain shipments from the region (80% of the plan) were achieved.[75]

Once the scale of the shortfall in butter procurement became known to the Siberian authorities, they decided to denude the regional market in order to reserve the maximum quantity for planned shipments out of Siberia. Although this policy must have further exacerbated food shortages in the towns it ensured that the targets for Siberian deliveries to the centre in this sector survived relatively intact and, according to one historian, 37,273 tons of butter were shipped from Siberia in 1927/8; a modest 5.5% fall from the level achieved in 1926/7. In spite of the problems faced by the Siberian authorities during the crisis of 1927/8, procurement plans for grain and butter were almost completed. This was a remarkable achievement given the circumstances, and considering that local targets had been set against the background of the record procurement levels of 1926/7 while the gross harvest of 1927/8 was actually 11% lower and there had been a general decline in dairy marketings throughout the decade. The Siberian contribution to Soviet food procurement in 1927/8 was significant: accounting for 11.3% of grain, 16.3% of wheat, 44% of butter, and 12.1% of meat. One area where the crisis had a disastrous impact was in wiping out the foreign currency earnings derived from grain exports which were vital for the realisation of the planned increases in industrial investment. Nowhere is this clearer than in the virtual elimination of the Siberian contribution to the Soviet grain export drive as its share of 345,000 tons of wheat exported in 1926/7 fell to a meagre 5,700 tons in 1927/8. However, the region continued to be the main source of Soviet butter exports, accounting for about 75% of the total this year.[76]

That the grain crisis was resolved primarily as a direct outcome of the application of the emergency measures is indisputable. Article 107 was a legal measure as opposed to an emergency method but one that hitherto was without precedent as regards its use against peasant speculation. The Siberian authorities intended that this statute should be applied in a sophisticated manner by targeting a limited number of key kulak farmers in each raion and, for the most part, this was adhered to. Clearly, it was more the intimidatory effect of the very public threat of the use of Article 107 which persuaded those peasants with grain surpluses to sell to the state. Nevertheless, the use of 'revolutionary legality' on its own was not sufficient to produce the sudden surge in grain procurement that occurred in late January and early February 1928, but rather it was the combination of law, terror and arbitrary coercion. In Siberia, Stalin had privately pressurised local officials into resorting to the use of illegal methods of coercion when necessary while at the same time he sought to avoid any political fall-out by publicly distancing himself from their disagreeable results. He consistently maintained that the grain was to be obtained 'at all costs' not only in his personal orders in January but also through his emissary, Kosior, in June and this was after his supposed return to a moderate pro-NEP line at the April joint plenum. By now it was clear that Stalin's radical breach with NEP was not a transitory phenomenon but a permanent fixture of his outlook and as a consequence a new round of factional infighting broke out in the party elite.

7 The 'Irkutsk affair'

The March plenum of the Kraikom

Tension had been building up in the krai party leadership in the first months of 1928 in the wake of Stalin's severe reprimanding of their conduct of affairs and the intensification of the 'grain offensive'. When the Kraikom plenum convened from 3 to 7 March to review the regional party's performance during the procurement campaign, this tension cracked under the strain of heated debates and mutual recriminations over the application of Article 107 and the party's role in the arbitrary excesses committed in the emergency situation. Syrtsov's previously well-aired public support for 'accumulation' by the well-off peasant farms, and his tolerant approach to the kulak question, created difficulties for him in the light of Stalin's new anti-kulak radicalism and demands for a punitive policy in the countryside. Now Syrtsov found himself in the invidious position of having to politically adjust to Stalin's line and justify the application of Article 107, while at the same time do justice to his own consistently pro-NEP instincts and reassure the like-minded majority of the regional party elite by suitably condemning the excesses perpetrated against the peasantry. Given his lukewarm support for the emergency measures during the grain crisis, in particular his ambivalent attitude to the use of Article 107, the scene was set for a challenge to the authority of Syrtsov from hardliners in the regional party leadership.

Not surprisingly, the challenge came from the area that had most to gain from disarray in the Kraikom leadership: Irkutsk. The Irkutsk Okruzhkom Secretary, Zimin, used the plenum as a platform to question Syrtsov's ability to remain as regional party secretary following what was considered to be inept crisis management and the inherent political unsoundness, and even dubious allegiances, demonstrated by his dealings with the kulak. The political uncertainty in the Kraikombiuro in the wake of these charges provided Irkutsk with a window of opportunity for it to revive its undiminished ambitions for secession from the Siberian Krai. Zimin presented the plenum with an ultimatum that demanded the removal of Syrtsov as the price of Irkutsk remaining within the krai. As is often the case with the reopening of old political scars, the ensuing debate saw unprecedentedly bitter exchanges between Zimin and the regional duumvirate of Syrtsov and Eikhe, with Zimin accusing Syrtsov of a 'half-hearted' approach to the policy of pressurising the kulaks, and Syrtsov and Eikhe denouncing the Irkutsk leadership with conspiring to leave the jurisdiction of the Kraikom and a series of political errors. The breech was irrevocably personal and political, and in the weeks following the plenum it degenerated into what became known as the 'Irkutsk affair', though its political significance went beyond the merely local arena.[1]

It was apparent from the opening minutes of the March plenum that it would be a contentious arena of debate. Zimin immediately demanded that the order paper be suspended and the meeting proceed straight to the salient issue – Eikhe's report on the party's performance during the grain crisis. After all, he asserted, 'everyone's mind is now focussed on grain procurement' and nobody had given any thought to the cultural development of the krai (the first subject on the agenda). Syrtsov was clearly irritated by this attempt to preempt the discussion and unsettle him, and he successfully opposed it. In a warning of things to come, he held up Zimin's motion as a typical example of the 'one-sided' approach which had led to over-zealousness in the grain campaign.[2]

When the session reached Eikhe's report on the grain campaign, from its title ('On shortcomings and distortions in the grain procurements') one would have expected him to dwell at length on the arbitrary official excesses and abuses perpetrated against the peasantry. On the contrary, the report echoed many of Stalin's earlier comments and criticisms of the Siberian party that had been repeated in the broader context of his directive of 13 February to all party organisations. Eikhe lavished praise on the use of Article 107 and the emergency measures, minimalised the excesses in their implementation as exceptional and chided as 'unfit' and 'alien' to the party those communists who had obstructed the campaign against the kulak. His analysis of the nature of the crisis took its lead from Stalin by asserting that the tightening of economic screws on the peasantry applied by the party at the beginning of the campaign had failed to achieve the requisite breakthrough because the kulak had exerted his authority in the countryside to influence the rest of the peasantry not to sell grain to the state. The reasoning for this was as follows: the kulak has 'an iron roof on his house, he has plenty of grain, a good horse, he has a thrifty mind which means he manages his farm correctly', and therefore if he tells the seredniak that grain prices will be higher in the spring then the latter holds on to his grain. This characterisation of a kulak farmer by the second most important political figure in the krai showed that Eikhe's thinking and understanding of peasant social stratification had not progressed beyond the simplistic stereotypical images of the Bolshevik civil war experience. It was essentially a gut rejection of the whole NEP concept of developing the peasantry into 'civilised cultivators' and a slap in the face to those, like Kavraisky and Nusinov, who had produced sophisticated breakdowns of rural stratification just a few months previously. Moreover, in the Siberian countryside of the late 1920s such criteria for defining the kulak could be applied to the seredniak mass of peasants.[3]

In a ringing endorsement of the use of Article 107 Eikhe argued that its real value lay in the immediacy of its intimidatory effect on kulaks, who even when they had only heard about the trials of speculators brought in their grain to sell to the procurement agencies. The brunt of his criticism was reserved for those lower level officials who had displayed 'negative features' in their work and who, in applying Article 107, 'in certain localities they looked but could not find a kulak'. This was hardly the kind of admonishment of the over-zealous approach that had been consistently condemned by Syrtsov. Rather, Eikhe vigorously pursued Stalin's line and pointedly questioned the reliability of rural communists in the region, claiming that many of them 'by their ideology and material position were close to the kulak stratum and were themselves large-scale grain holders'. This interlocking of the rural communists with the well-off peasantry meant that there was an unwillingness to expose kulaks in some areas and in certain places the rural authorities even joined in outright opposition to the party's directives. The lesson to be learnt, he confirmed, was that Stalin was right and the Siberian party organisation must 'decisively purge itself of unfit elements'.

When he considered the question of excesses in the application of Article 107 Eikhe singled out Zimin and the Irkutsk Okrug authorities and named them as the worst offenders as regards the over-enthusiastic approach in conducting a great quantity of trials under Article 107. Whereas western okrugs (the main grain areas where, according to official statistics, there was the highest density of kulak farms) had tried 70–80 cases per okrug, so far Irkutsk had heard 123 cases (with 13 raions in the area, this worked out at an average of just under the permissible maximum of 10 per raion). He acknowledged that there were kulaks and kulak areas in Irkutsk but the trial figures were excessive, given that agriculture was not highly developed in the okrug, and Zimin was to blame. Arguably, this attack on the Irkutsk leader had an ulterior purpose in that it was motivated less by concern to stamp out abuses against the peasantry than to serve as a pretext for pursuing the political differences between the Kraikom and the independent-minded Irkutsk elite. Eikhe denounced the Irkutsk nomenklatura for its 'secessionist mood' (*samostiinoe nastroenie*), and questioned the political reliability of the Irkutsk intelligentsia by citing their under-subscription to krai party journals and newspapers. In fact, he provoked general derisory laughter by commenting that the Irkutsk leadership was so detached from the Kraikom that only one person in the area subscribed to the regional party journal *Na Leninskom puti* and that was a non-party person.[4]

Moving on to more general abuses Eikhe drew attention to the 'harmful tendency' to widen the circle of those to be arrested under Article 107 to include seredniaks, though given his earlier definition of a kulak farm one can understand how lower officials were confused about this. He claimed that this sort of abuse was most prevalent in the areas where there was initial reluctance to prosecute kulaks; the implication being that this was a deliberate wrecking move by some rural communists. Another cause of concern was the unreliability of the judiciary who had passed 'very soft' sentences, with many instances of convicted kulaks being left with 10 tons or more of grain. When he tentatively widened the net of those guilty of abuses beyond the Irkutsk party by mentioning a case from Kansk Okrug, the meeting became agitated and there were shouts of denial as, naturally, there was resistance on the part of the responsible secretaries to join Irkutsk as scapegoats. As far as Eikhe was concerned, a court which left a kulak with an amount approaching 15 tons of grain was giving a signal to the other peasants to the effect that this was an acceptable norm to hold. 'If kulaks are brought to trial', he declared, 'they must be tried in earnest.'

He also condemned instances when property other than grain was confiscated by the courts or the OGPU. Many of these were petty examples, as in the case where a raikom secretary ordered the local militia chief to find and confiscate a sewing machine so that he could give it to the women's section. Where agricultural machines were seized, he revealed that there was a sharp drop in sales of these because peasants believed it was illegal to own them. Such was the confusion over party directives, even among senior officials, that the Omsk Okruzhkom Secretary, N. A. Filatov, asked if it was permitted to sell tractors to kulaks. In exasperation, Eikhe pointed out that the party had previously issued a directive forbidding this over a year earlier and he ordered that machine cooperatives be reregistered to exclude those run by kulaks. He recognised that some party officials had approached the grain procurement campaign like 'an area bombardment', returning to prodrazverstka methods as in 1919–20, seizing all grain stocks, closing down the bazaar and arresting anyone involved in private trade in grain. These actions had created a volatile and difficult situation in the countryside that would be defused, Eikhe insisted, once free trade in grain was restored in the spring and not infringed. He concluded by pronouncing that the grain crisis had been 'a test (*proverka*) of our whole apparat' and had demonstrated the necessity for a purge. In particular, the judicial organs were 'insufficiently firm and insufficiently qualified' and personnel changes in this department were the 'number one priority task'. Similarly, it was necessary to purge the procurement agencies and rural party organisations of the politically unreliable and deadwood 'kulak yes-men'. Reflecting Stalin's impressions and intentions during and after his Siberian tour that the party needed a reinvigorating influx of 'new revolutionary personnel', Eikhe observed that what the grain crisis had revealed above all was that the Siberian party needed an infusion of *new blood*.[5]

Syrtsov's speech to the plenum was markedly different in substance and tone from Eikhe's ready approval of the use of Article 107 and downplaying of abuses and administrative methods. Confronting directly the main issue of 'the future offensive against the kulak', Syrtsov was much less willing to accept the new Stalin line that had been faithfully followed in Eikhe's speech. Rather he reiterated the theme of moderation which he had made his own in the course of 1927 and appears to have understood Stalin's militancy as a temporary aberration and example of overblown rhetoric in the panic attempt to achieve a rapid breakthrough in the grain crisis. He noted with regret that a mood had developed among local communists to the effect that the current policy of the party was no different from the aims of the Left Opposition; 'nothing could be more wrong', he assured them. Resolutely rejecting the use of force to decide the kulak question he told the plenum that 'the task of an offensive on the kulak cannot be decided by means of naked administrative methods', and he warned them of the harmful consequences of Stalin's line of thought (without mentioning him by name) which held that 'the economic roots of the kulak can be seriously undermined by Article 107'.[6]

The message to his audience was a clear reminder that it was precisely the policy of prodrazverstka which had brought the party to the brink of disaster in 1921, and the regime had been saved by the introduction of NEP to placate the peasantry. Syrtsov appealed for a return to a more sophisticated approach in dealing with the kulaks as opposed to the 'over-simplified way' of Article 107. Henceforth, he stated, Article 107 would not figure so prominently in the party's measures and he hoped that there would be no future need for emergency measures. In fact, he proposed that there would be some relaxation in the directives of the Central Committee for the application of emergency measures, particularly with regard to Stalin's 2,000 pud limit, so that a combination of 'economic, judicial and administrative methods would be employed against the kulaks'.[7] Turning to the criticisms made by okruzhkom secretaries of the failure of the Kraikombiuro to issue detailed guidelines on the use of the emergency measures, Syrtsov explained that the blame for any chaos, ambiguity or misunderstandings rested squarely with the Central Committee Secretariat since the Kraikombiuro itself had not been given clearly detailed directives but had been obliged to pass on those orders it received to the okrug authorities. He admitted that the lack of clarity had resulted in occasional situations when the Kraikombiuro had issued instructions that had later been contradicted by those sent from the centre, but he dismissed complaints with the rather tetchy and inauspicious remark that 'in leadership you always risk "your head"'. For Syrtsov, the primary cause of the confusion was the intense pressure from the centre for quick results, because it created conditions where 'mistakes were inevitable given the panic with which we were seized and the abundance of directives on different topics which came from Moscow'. Although he admitted that the Kraikom leadership had made many mistakes in dealing with the crisis Syrtsov refused to accept his culpability and rejected the attacks of certain secretaries, notably Zimin and Filatov, who had accused him of complacency towards grain procurement at the end of 1927 and of indecisiveness in dealing with the crisis in the first weeks of 1928.[8]

The talk of ambivalency in the attitude of the Kraikom leadership to the offensive against the kulak was an indication that Siberian party politics were beginning to refract the 'Stalinist–Rightist' divide emerging in the Politburo. However, the very insistence with which Syrtsov branded the talk of 'Right–Left' divisions in the Siberian party as nothing more than 'Opposition terminology' and an attempt to sow confusion would seem to confirm that such polarisation was occurring. Indeed, he contradicted himself by using these terms to describe the political divisions that had emerged in the regional party during the crisis and he observed that 'if the introduction of barter is a Right deviation, then the ideas that we can seize grain through GPU force, that the kulak has all the grain, these are Left deviations'. Evidently, such labels and accusations had been a feature of the grain campaign in Siberia, for Syrtsov noted that there had been ridiculous situations where some party organisations or individual communists had been accused of both deviations in the space of a single day.[9]

In his analysis of the grain campaign Syrtsov, like Eikhe, singled out the activities of Zimin and the Irkutsk Okrug authorities, and denounced them for a plethora of abuses ranging from excessive use of judicial methods to 'a tendency to dekulakize'. Earlier in the debate Zimin had goaded Syrtsov for the 'vagueness' in his attitude to the application of Article 107. Now, flouting his earlier rejection of the labels 'Right' and 'Left', Syrtsov responded with a verbal assault on Zimin's 'Leftism' in his attitude towards the peasantry (a charge that could carry the penalty of expulsion from office and the party), and in his infringement of the Kraikombiuro directives on the application of Article 107 by the excessive use of the statute. He followed this up with a sharp personal jibe at Zimin's bending of the Central Committee directives and ignoring of the 2,000 pud limit for prosecuting peasants: 'he is a lawyer and as regards legal chicanery he can lose me for sure'. Syrtsov claimed that, unlike Zimin, he approached the kulak question and the use of Article 107 as 'an economist and a politician'. He therefore relied on the research of Kavraisky and Nusinov which had shown that kulaks were more numerous in south-west Siberia and, thus, common sense dictated that the number of trials should be higher there than in other areas. This was the rationale behind the Kraikom decision to set a broad category of four to ten kulaks per raion to be tried under Article 107. However, while Syrtsov denounced Zimin for taking up to the agreed limit of ten kulaks and ignoring telegrams from the Kraikom warning him to desist from this practice, there was no balancing criticism of okrugs in south-west Siberia, such as Barnaul and Rubtsovsk, which had fallen substantially short of their permitted quota of trials.[10]

In his address to the plenum Zimin forcefully defended the strategy followed in Irkutsk. His attitude was that the emergency measures and Article 107 were implemented with exceptional thoroughness because this was precisely the kind of enthusiastic dedication to the offensive against the kulak that Stalin had asked for during his stay in Siberia. The rigorous approach in Irkutsk might also be explained by Zimin's personal style since as a former 'distinguished chekist' coercion was probably intrinsic to his implementation of policy. Syrtsov's many condemnations of the activities of the OGPU in the countryside indicates that he was particularly disturbed by their tactics but for Zimin this was only further evidence of Syrtsov's soft-pedalling approach to the 'offensive against the kulak'. The underlying tension of intra-regional rivalries over status and claims to investment resources was never far below the surface, as was demonstrated by Zimin's sensitivity to one speaker's description of Irkutsk as the cultural centre of Siberia. Zimin angrily rejected this term and demanded that Irkutsk, as the largest town in the region, be accorded the status of a major industrial base, the equal of Novosibirsk and other towns. To no avail, for evidently matters had progressed too far and in the course of the plenum Zimin's comments were alternatively scorned and laughed at. This reception, together with the exclusivity of the criticism and humiliation levied at the Irkutsk leaders by Syrtsov and Eikhe, no doubt strengthened their sense of isolation at the plenum and made them more determined to break away and form a separate jurisdiction from the Siberian Krai.[11]

The vitriolic exchanges between the Kraikom and Irkutsk leaderships at the March plenum were not simply an exercise in scapegoating for shortcomings in the procurement campaign, rather they were rooted in complex, long-standing intra-regional personal, political and territorial rivalries which were being reshaped and moulded to take account of the emerging framework of new political divisions in the central party hierarchy. Certainly, one would have expected an awareness among the Siberian party elite of the tide of events at the centre and of the extent to which Stalin's attitude to NEP had been radicalised by the grain crisis, especially since they had been personally lectured and cajoled by him on the need for emergency measures, the offensive against kulaks, the stepping up of collectivisation and industrialisation, the purging of the party and so forth. This new thinking was enthusiastically embraced and put into effect by Zimin, who instinctively favoured an escalation of the repression of the kulak and was prepared to take advantage of Stalin's policy contortions to undermine the authority of his main regional rival Syrtsov. On the other hand, although Syrtsov was one of Stalin's clients in the apparat his commitment to the continuum of the NEP road of development was unshaken by the outbursts of his patron. Nevertheless, he was obliged to protect his position as a senior member of the party nomenklatura and client of Stalin from Zimin's attempt to inculpate him with 'Rightism'. For Eikhe the problem was even more delicate in that while he sympathised with Stalin's new hard-line approach in the countryside, he found it politically unpalatable to side with his old rival Zimin against his erstwhile colleague Syrtsov.

Consequently, the resolutions of the plenum reflected a balancing act by Syrtsov and Eikhe and for the most part they blandly restated the substance of Stalin's statement of 13 February on the nature and handling of the grain crisis. The reasons for the crisis were attributed primarily to economic and organisational shortcomings: the goods shortage, price policy imbalances, increased peasant income, the inertia of the grain procurement agencies and the complacency and insufficient attention of the party to the problem. The opposition of the kulak to state planning and regulation of agriculture was acknowledged and it was claimed that the kulaks had conspired with town speculators to 'disorganise the grain market and wreck our price policy'. However, there was also an unusual and ominously vague resolution, that sat uneasily amid the others, to the effect that 'the accumulation of the kulak upper stratum of the peasantry has reached the limits at which the economic benefits gained from their production, on the basis of private capital, have become troublesome in Soviet conditions'. Neither Syrtsov nor Eikhe had hinted at any such idea in their speeches to the plenum and this statement appears to be a more ambiguous wording of Stalin's declarations in Siberia that kulak influence on the peasant economy would be eliminated sooner rather than later. Most noticeably, and unlike Stalin's statement of 13 February or the later resolutions of the April plenum of the Central Committee, there was no mention of the efficacy of Article 107 or the emergency measures. Rather, the successful breakthrough in the procurement crisis in Siberia was ascribed to the application of economic and organisational measures in conjunction with what was vacuously termed 'the application of pressure' on the kulak and heightened political work with the rural poor.[12]

The resolutions also contained a section under the heading 'Distortions in the party line' that condemned abuses in the application of the emergency measures in a much more expansive fashion than had been presented in Stalin's statement. In fact, the only mention of Article 107 in the document comes under this heading. By and large the criticism was even-handed and both 'naked administrative actions' (prodrazverstka, closure of markets, bartering and so on) and deviations from the 'class line' of the party (pro-kulak communists) were denounced. More important, from the viewpoint of future policy in the countryside, was the recognition of Syrtsov's cautious pro-NEP line that the kulak could only be overcome 'step by step' through economic measures and by a sophisticated and flexible implementation of party policy.

In recognition of the new Stalinist emphasis on collectivisation, it was decided to expand collective farms across the board during the new spring sowing campaign. Local party organisations were given direct responsibility for fulfilling this task with rural communists ordered to take the lead in joining collectives. Hereafter the policy of raising the cultural-economic level of individual peasant farms was to be subordinated to the development of socialised collective farms. In addition, a number of organisational changes in the grain procurement organs were recommended, including the merger of Sibmeltrest with Khleboprodukt and the ending of independent procurement by Sibtorg. These changes foreshadowed those introduced by the April plenum of the Central Committee and must have been initiated by Moscow. Finally, a purge of the regional party, state and procurement apparats was ordered and indeed was launched at the plenum itself with the removal of the Omsk Okruzhkom Secretary, Filatov, for failure to halt a 'systematic decline' in grain procurement in his area. Filatov may also have been paying the penalty for his forthright criticism of the failures of the Kraikom leadership and his dismissal was a message to the other local secretaries that there were limits to this kind of insubordination.[13] However, checking the secessionist tendencies of Zimin and the Irkutsk leadership and bringing them to heel was a more thorny problem for the Kraikom. Moreover, since Zimin portrayed the nature of his challenge to the Kraikom in highly sensitive politicised terms, it made the operation fraught with danger for Syrtsov.

The 'Irkutsk affair'

The relations between the Irkutsk Okrug authorities and the Kraikom had been troubled from the formation of the Siberian Krai in 1925. The root of the problem was, as we discussed in chapter 2, the strong sense of regional identity in Irkutsk that found expression in a popular movement for political and economic autonomy and opposition to union with the krai. Consequently, when the Irkutsk demand for autonomy was rejected by VTsIK in late 1924 and the region was incorporated into the Siberian Krai, its leaders tended to ignore Krai-kom decisions and pursue an independent course of action whether dealing with local problems or relations with the central government. Relations with the Kraikom were further strained by the way industri-alisation plans for Siberia had been thrown out of balance by the claims for a greater share of investment made by Irkutsk, a development that particularly angered Eikhe. But it was the pursuit by the Irkutsk Ok-ruzhkom of a radically more hard-line policy towards the peasantry than was advocated by the Kraikom during the grain crisis of 1927/8 that brought the tense relations between both authorities to breaking-point.[14]

Following the clashes at the March plenum of the Kraikom Zimin was determined to bring his grievances to the attention of Stalin. Shortly afterwards he drafted a letter, with the support of his okruzh-kombiuro, charging the Kraikom leadership, and Syrtsov personally, with a series of political errors, and he despatched it to the Central Committee. Echoing the sort of indictments of local party officials made by Stalin in his letter of 13 February, Zimin recommended that Syrtsov be replaced as regional party secretary due to his 'failure to understand the class policy of the party in the countryside', his poor selection of party secretaries and cadres and breaches of the party line. Until such time as their demands were met the Irkutsk Okruzhkom decided to secede from the jurisdiction of the Kraikom. Stalin must have been exasperated by this full-blown political crisis in Siberia at the very moment when he was distracted by turbulence within the Polit-buro over the grain crisis. There is no reason to assume that he was unaware of the underlying intra-regional rivalry in the matter but it was not a run of the mill local crisis or one from which he could easily extract political gain. In fact, it was a situation that required great political dexterity on Stalin's part because all the protagonists were members of the party elite who supported his leadership and included one of his senior client provincial party chiefs whose vote in the Central Committee was crucial to his own survival in the looming struggle with the Right. Furthermore, they were bandying about some highly sensi-tive political charges of the type being reserved by Stalin for the Right. Clearly, the best course was for the Siberians themselves to resolve their differences as quickly as possible and with the minimum of fuss and that may have been the instruction given to Syrtsov when he came to Moscow for the plenum of the Central Committee that met on 6–11 April. Meanwhile, an Orgraspred instructor, A. I. Sedel'nikov, was sent to Irkutsk at the head of a commission of inquiry to verify the activities of the local party. Some weeks after this in late April and early May 1928 Syrtsov and two senior Kraikom officials, M. I. Kovalev (Krai Control Commission Secretary) and V. F. Sharangovich (Chairman of the Krai Trade Union Council), travelled to Irkutsk and spent ten days in an unsuccessful attempt at comradely reconciliation with Zimin and his colleagues.[15]

On 23 May the Kraikombiuro moved in a more forceful manner to reassert its authority and passed a motion of censure against the Irkutsk Okruzhkom, accusing it of a wide range of political mistakes, notably systematic non-cooperation with and ignoring of Kraikom decisions, encouraging separatist tendencies in the area, failures in the grain campaign and a lack of firmness in dealing with both the Left Opposition and 'petty-bourgeois' elements. Since Zimin's post was on the nomenklatura of the Central Committee the Kraikom needed its sanction for his removal and a request to that effect was sent to Stalin. This action may also indicate a note of caution by Syrtsov and his colleagues as they were aware of Zimin's letter against them and, confronted by Stalin's new militant agrarian policy, it was only prudent to distance themselves from the charges this contained and represent the break with Irkutsk in terms of a serious lapse of party discipline. Meanwhile, Eikhe led a high-powered delegation to the area with an order that the okruzhkom appoint him temporary secretary in Zimin's place (Sharangovich later replaced Eikhe and L. V. Roshal was subsequently appointed). Zimin was to be brought to Novosibirsk for his case to be heard by the Krai Control Commission. The Central Committee gave its approval for Zimin's dismissal in early June, at the precise moment that Stalin was launching the campaign for self-criticism in the party, and on 13–16 June a joint plenum of the Irkutsk Okruzhkom and Okrug Control Commission met to ratify the change formally. Evidently this meeting did not go smoothly as after four days of discussion the Kraikom decided to reselect the entire okruzhkombiuro.[16]

The circumstances of the 'Irkutsk affair' give rise to a number of intriguing questions. At first sight it seems strange that Stalin would have sanctioned the dismissal of a senior party official like Zimin on the grounds of an over-zealous implementation of Article 107. On the other hand, as the Povolotsky case demonstrated, Stalin did not hesitate to sacrifice those who had willingly embraced the new anti-kulak radicalism when he considered it necessary in order to preserve an outward appearance of outrage at flagrant abuses of the principles of NEP. The question remains, just how well informed was Stalin of the problems between Irkutsk and Kraikom? It may well be that he decided that political capital could be derived from the matter if it was regarded primarily, as the Kraikom wanted, in terms of a breach of party discipline through 'local separatism' for which the responsible officials must be called to account under the slogan of self-criticism. Certainly this interpretation was suggested by the directives published by the Central Committee on the affair in early August, based on Sedel-'nikov's report of his investigation, and signed by A. Smirnov, a Rightist member of the Secretariat. They focussed on the 'absolutely intolerable' disparaging attitude of the Irkutsk party leadership to the Kraikom and its irresolute stance against 'old *chinovnik*' influences but also criticised the Kraikom for its failure to prevent the crisis from developing. It recommended that a wholesale purge of the party and state apparat in Irkutsk be carried out. What is striking about the directives is the absence of any reference to 'Leftism' in Irkutsk and the downplaying of the political conflict in the Siberian party elite over the handling of the grain crisis and policy towards the peasantry. Stalin may have reasoned that this central aspect of the affair, like his own Siberian speeches, was much too sensitive to be given a public airing in the party at large since his support for Syrtsov and sacking of Zimin would convey the wrong impression that the new hard-line agrarian policy was discredited. Besides, as we shall see shortly, he planned to rehabilitate Zimin and bring his expertise to the radicalisation of the central party leadership in the struggle with the Right.[17]

The exiled Left Oppositionist, Sosnovsky, revealed that the 'pearl' of the Kraikom case against Irkutsk was the failure of the okrispolkom to suppress a movement among local businessmen and traders for the restoration of their political rights, a return to the principle of 'free competition' in the economy and equal treatment with the cooperatives in respect of tax and credit privileges.[18] This would explain why the Central Committee directives on the affair gave prominence to the charge of 'petty-bourgeois' influences in the Irkutsk party. Sosnovsky believed that the Kraikom had singled out the Irkutsk and Kuznetsk party organisations as scapegoats in pursuit of the campaign for self-criticism in the party that had been initiated by Stalin in the aftermath of the Shakhty scandal in May–June 1928. The Kuznetsk Okruzhkom Secretary, Z. Ia. Novikov, was outraged by this 'discrimination' against him and had initially threatened his local critics with the OGPU but confessed to political errors when he realised that the Kraikom had masterminded the attack. Thus, in attacking the Irkutsk and Kuznetsk leaderships the Kraikom paid lip-service to the slogan of self-criticism and simultaneously removed irritating sources of regional political and economic instability that had revealed Leftist sympathies.[19]

The 'Irkutsk affair' has parallels with the better-known crises of local authority that emerged in other regions during the grain crisis of 1927/8. For example, the central feature of the 'Smolensk affair' of spring 1928 was the removal of Gubkom Secretary D. A. Pavliuchenko and a purge of the local party under the slogan of self-criticism for their mishandling of the procurements. However, unlike in Siberia, the Smolensk case was used by Stalin as a cover for the removal of an 'NEP faction' in the regional party leadership. In fact, it has been argued that the entire self-criticism campaign was devised and manipulated by Stalinists as 'a legitimate way to attack and mobilise support against the entrenched Rightist leaderships'.[20] The events in Siberia in the first half of 1928 demonstrate that the above view of the self-criticism campaign is an oversimplification of a very complex political process. While the 'Irkutsk affair' was an intricate web of intra-regional rivalries, personal antagonism and political differences, it was also a clear instance when an orthodoxly pro-NEP krai party leadership, headed by a secretary sympathetic to the policies of the Right, acted against okrug party committees which had eagerly acted upon Stalin's call for a radical, pseudo-Leftist hard-line policy in the countryside.

The post-crisis purge in Siberia

A purge was launched in the months following Stalin's Siberian tour and took its toll of hundreds of officials in the Siberian party and state apparat. No allowances were made for previous good service and the purge included former partisans, Red guards and sailors, and those recruited in the Lenin enrolment. The scale of this purge is difficult to measure accurately but its direction was against 'class alien' elements and the main force of its blow fell on rural party cells. Sosnovsky's contemporaneous report estimated that up to 25% of rural communists were expelled in some raions whereas a modern Soviet source suggests that the purge was of a minor scale and only 427 party members were expelled between April and October 1928.[21] Siberian leaders persisted throughout 1928 in denouncing 'alien' communists who had infiltrated the party, which would indicate either that the purges were not having the desired effect or that the specification of elements 'alien' to the party was being constantly modified to suit changing political circumstances. For example, in December 1928 Syrtsov was heckled by delegates at the Tomsk Okrug Party Conference who opposed, he said, 'the right of the working class to lead the country'. At the Barnaul Okrug Party Conference in November, local leaders attacked rural communists who had not learnt from the mistakes of the previous year and 'who still hardly know the class enemy and who are unwilling to fight'.[22]

The softness of the post-crisis purge is illustrated by events in Irkutsk Okrug where, although it had been singled out by the Kraikom as an area with the most severely degenerate apparat, just 141 persons were called to account in the purge. Of these there were 22 party members, 50 soviet officials, 8 employees in the economic apparat, 47 trade union officials and 14 others (66 communists altogether). During the purge 18 were tried and convicted, 39 were removed from their posts, only 10 were expelled from the party and 32 received sharp reprimands (54 other cases were not specified). Later in the year a further 27 party members were expelled for 'Rightism' and there was a more punitive purge of non-party specialists from the soviet apparat, involving 304 persons from 72 institutions and offices, and including 90 office holders.[23]

The Siberian state apparat was particularly susceptible to charges of class alien infiltration given the low representation of party members in leading offices, particularly in economic departments. In the spring of 1928, before the Shakhty scandal hit the headlines, articles in *Na Leninskom puti* attacked the role of 'specialists' in Siberian economic departments. It was revealed that of the 40–50 leading krai economic posts an 'insignificant number' were held by communists. The cooperative apparat was brandished as the worst example: of 380 employees of Sibkraisoiuz, 95 were described as 'non-Soviet elements', in other words ex-members of 'anti-soviet' political parties, former whites and nobles and 45 of these worked in the headquarters. Only 40 employees were in the party or komsomol. In Sibsel'skosoiuz offices only 30 out of 150 employees were party or komsomol members and in Sibmaslosoiuz only 3 of the 25 senior posts were held by communists. In the aftermath of the grain crisis the crescendo of criticism of the cooperatives was so intense that Strikovsky, the head of Sibkraisoiuz, complained of at first 'a gallop' and then 'a cavalry charge' on the whole system.[24] Given the very bitter nature of the attack by Stalin on the Siberian judiciary and procurators during his tour, it is not surprising that a considerable purge was pursued in these departments. In early 1928 the Siberian Rabkrin investigated local judicial processes and recommended a purge of local legal institutions and the adoption of 'simplified' methods to speed up a backlog of cases. Over the next year

17 procurators (about one-third of the total) and 45 judges (one-fifth of the total) were removed from their posts and attempts were made to increase the party content in these departments.[25]

Thus, despite much rhetoric from Stalin and Siberian party leaders about the impact of and need for a purge in the region, the practical effect by late 1928 seems to have been minimal (apart from in the judiciary and procuracy). On 21 December 1928 a Kraikombiuro decree was still talking of the need 'to decisively purge all party organisations of pro-kulak and estranged communists', and reminding the localities that party members deprived of their electoral rights must be immediately expelled.[26] At the same time it was decided to launch a campaign to recruit 3,000 batraks into the party by the time of the Fourth Krai Party Conference in February 1929. This campaign was a dismal failure in many okrugs as the conference subsequently recognised. It was only from early 1929 that more incisive purges were carried out and from 10 to 25 June 1929 a well organised wave of expulsions swept the krai and cleared out almost 18% of party members and candidates. Considering the strongly pro-peasant feelings of the Siberian party it would be a reasonable assumption that it suffered proportionately heavy losses when Stalin moved against the Right.[27]

The most radical turnover in personnel occurred at the pinnacle of the party establishment in Siberia: in the Kraikom and the Krai Control Commission. At the Fourth Siberian Party Conference in February 1929 sweeping changes were made to the membership of these bodies as elected at the previous krai conference in March 1927. Of the 68 members and 32 candidates of the Kraikom chosen in 1927, 36 (53%) and 25 (80%) respectively were removed. Similarly, in the Control Commission 27 (58%) of 43 members and 12 (75%) of 16 candidates were replaced. A lack of information on the composition of the leading positions in the organs elected in 1927 makes a direct comparison with those of 1929 impossible. However, in the Siberian party elite as a whole there were many casualties in the aftermath of the grain crisis as the following notables departed from office and lost their seats on the Kraikom or Krai Control Commission: Kalashnikov (Chairman of the Control Commission), Kunov (Krai Procurator), Kozhevnikov (head of Kraisud), Strikovsky (head of Sibkraisoiuz) and several okruzhkom secretaries: Filatov (Omsk), Novikov (Kuznetsk) and Zimin (Irkutsk). One of Syrtsov's local protégés, Kavraisky, was a main beneficiary of this purge as he moved rapidly up the regional hierarchy, from the Head of Sibstatotdel in 1927 to candidate membership of the Kraikombiuro and Secretary of the Department for Rural Affairs in 1929.[28]

Stalin and the 'Irkutsk affair'

Zimin's views on the need for a more rapid tempo of industrialisation and a punitive offensive against the kulak were much closer to Stalin's new thinking of early 1928 than the pro-NEP Rightist approach of Syrtsov, which in many respects harked back to the long-repudiated heyday of Bukharinism in 1925. Stalin had been disturbed by what he had seen at first hand in Siberia and he ended his tour of the region with the shouts of opposition to his instructions from local officials and peasants reverberating in his head. Perhaps the most enduring picture, and certainly the most worrying, that Stalin took back from Siberia was of a 'degenerate', recalcitrant and politically suspect local party, tainted by its ties with kulaks and its resistance to the application of emergency measures. In ordinary circumstances, Syrtsov, as regional party secretary, should have fallen victim to Stalin's wrath at this state of affairs and been removed at the first opportunity, as was Pavliuchenko in Smolensk. All the more so, given Syrtsov's outspoken support for accumulation by small-scale private peasant farmers and his hostility to the repression of the kulak by non-economic means, never mind his hostility to those of his subordinates who implemented the policy of coercion favoured by Stalin. Why then did Stalin support Syrtsov in the conflict with Zimin? To answer this question we must look more closely at the aftermath of the 'Irkutsk affair', and Stalin's relationship with Syrtsov and Zimin. For what emerges from Stalin's handling of this crisis serves to further illustrate his consummate adroitness at exploiting any event for political advantage.

One would expect that Zimin's career would have been terminated after his removal as okruzhkom secretary and the disgrace of a Krai Control Commission investigation, though whether the latter process occurred is not known. On the contrary, Stalin recognised Zimin's talents as representative of the corps of 'new men' that he believed had been brought to the fore in the party by the grain crisis and who were equal to the task of renovating the apparat and advancing his new programme of rapid collectivisation and industrialisation. Zimin was ordered back to Moscow where he was promoted to Deputy Head of the Orgraspred. This was the key department of the Central Committee Secretariat, responsible for overseeing the nomenklatura system and making senior appointments, and as such was Stalin's chief institutional instrument for consolidating his power base in the party by the promotion of people on whom he could rely. Another factor in Zimin's promotion may have been his connections with the

Moscow party organisation, for at this time Stalin was beginning to deploy the Orgraspred to contain, outmanoeuvre and break up Rightist cliques in the apparat, and N. A. Uglanov's leadership in the Moscow party organisation was a prime target. Zimin's move from the periphery to the heart of the party machine was ironic in two respects: firstly, it placed him in much the same kind of direct patron–client working relationship with Stalin, where he could be groomed for higher office, that Syrtsov had enjoyed in the early 1920s, and secondly, one of his new functions was to supervise the investigations of Central Committee instructors, including Sedel'nikov who had been partly responsible for his dismissal as the Irkutsk party leader.[29]

The turning point in the fate of Bukharin and the pro-NEP line of slow growth of socialism came at the Central Committee plenum in July 1928 when, as with the defeat of the Left, Stalin's control of the nomenklatura system ensured that key influential party secretaries and functionaries sided with him. This factor, combined with the tactical and organisational incompetence of the leading figures of the Right, meant that they were relatively easily outflanked and politically defeated.[30] However, in recent years some Western scholars have offset the significance of control of the apparat in the factional struggles of this period and argued that 'machine politics alone did not account for Stalin's triumph', rather argument and programmatic choices were also central to his success. According to this interpretation, Stalin had to lobby and win the support of members of the ruling oligarchy in the party through 'effective argumentation on other than power grounds', and by presenting a 'politically persuasive programme'.[31] Thus, Stalin's ability to wield his bureaucratic power was constrained by the need to build a consensus over policy within a caucus of Central Committee members composed of high party officials and regional secretaries, including Syrtsov, most of whom 'were not his mindless political creatures, but important, independent-minded leaders in their own right'.[32]

The fact is that this caucus of influentials in the party elite, who determined the course of Soviet historical development, are depicted as rather shadowy figures in the studies of this period and we know very little about them. Nonetheless, the above explanation for Stalin's victory is not borne out in Syrtsov's case. Syrtsov's policy preferences leaned clearly to the Right and *ipso facto* could not have been a factor in his continued allegiance to Stalin. If policy considerations are excluded, then Syrtsov's support for Stalin must have rested on the only other decisive issue at stake – the leadership question. It was not that

Syrtsov favoured Stalin's unique blend of toughness and pragmatism, for after all he had been highly critical of Stalin's coercive style during the grain crisis and derided the attempt to 'build socialism with cudgels', but rather that their relationship was based on patron–client career ties. Syrtsov had held high office under Stalin in the central party bureaucracy for five years in 1921–6 and, working closely together, they seem to have established a symbiotic political relationship and personal rapport which outweighed policy differences. From that time forward the political careers and ambitions of both men were interlocked by the loyalties of party machine politics.

At this point in time, what mattered above all else for Stalin was Syrtsov's continued allegiance in the leadership contest. Nevertheless, the manner of Zimin's promotion and the way that Stalin now moved against the Right must have confirmed to Syrtsov that his future career prospects required that he show enthusiasm for the new militancy and abandon his pro-NEP convictions. In this respect Syrtsov had the foresight to mould himself to events and not only did his political support for Stalin remain firm in the course of the struggle with the Right in 1928–9 but he also exercised self-censorship of his own Rightist views during this period. Indeed, for good measure he even engaged in some vitriolic kulak-baiting. For example, at the Fourth Krai Party Conference in February 1929 he agreed that the growth of kulak farms was now top of the political agenda and postulated the question in stark terms: 'kulak grain brings with it the question of kulak power tomorrow. He who puts a stake on the kulak farm, inevitably must put a stake on a bourgeois-democratic refashioning of the USSR.' He also denounced the doubters in the party, those who had 'lost faith' in the party's ability to overcome difficulties, and compared them to 'those soldiers who at the decisive moment, hesitate and doubt victory, flee from the battlefield in panic, capitulators, deserters who are shot'. His speech to the Sixteenth Conference in April 1929 was similarly hard-line.[33]

This homage to the new radicalism was evidently deemed satisfactory by Stalin and in May 1929 Syrtsov was rewarded by being brought back from Siberia and appointed to head the Sovnarkom of the RSFSR in place of Rykov. This promotion seems to have boosted Syrtsov's self-confidence and in late 1929 and early 1930 he reverted to overtly expressing his former moderate opinions at party gatherings and consistently voiced his concern at the unrealistic pace of industrialisation and collectivisation. Yet his rise within Stalin's closely knit ruling clique continued unabated and after the Sixteenth Congress in

July 1930 he was coopted as a candidate member of the Politburo.[34] It was then, at the very moment when Syrtsov's influence was at its zenith in Moscow, that a final twist to the 'Irkutsk affair' occurred. The long-standing demand of the Irkutsk party for regional autonomy was met by the centre and the Siberian Krai was divided into East (capital Irkutsk) and West (capital Novsibirsk) regions. At the same time the Orgraspred was completely reorganised and Zimin was again reassigned to Siberia, this time as head of the Orgbiuro of the East Siberian Krai (Eikhe headed the West Siberian Kraikom), and at the First East Siberian Krai Congress of Soviets in February 1931, he was selected Chairman of the Kraiispolkom.[35]

Syrtsov's membership of the highest echelon of Stalin's ruling clique proved to be a brief interlude before the sudden demise of his career. Stalin's toleration of his carping criticism and public dissent was finally exhausted by a speech Syrtsov made on 30 August 1930 to a joint meeting of Sovnarkom and the Economic Council of the RSFSR in which he poured scorn on the disastrous way that rapid collectivisation and industrialisation had been carried out.[36] In late October, the process of Syrtsov's removal began with an attack on two of his close associates, Kavraisky and Nusinov, whom he had brought with him to Moscow from Siberia. They were expelled from the party along with M. N. Riutin and A. N. Slepkov for Rightist 'double-dealing fractional activities' and branded as 'kulak agents'.[37] Syrtsov was dismissed from the Chairmanship of Sovnarkom in early November and at a Siberian Kraikom plenum Eikhe denounced him for blaming the party leadership for the economic crisis facing the country. On 1 December 1930 an official resolution announced that he had been expelled from the Politburo and Central Committee for his part in forming a '"Left"–Right bloc' based on a 'common political platform, coinciding in all fundamental aspects with the platform of the right-wing opportunists'. In fact, his involvement in the so-called 'Syrtsov–Lominadze affair' had amounted to nothing more than some tentative discussions about curbing Stalin's policy excesses.[38]

The 'Syrtsov–Lominadze affair' is an important indication that Stalin's victorious patrimonial political machine was itself vulnerable to factional infighting but, in my view, it has been inaccurately described as the first example of 'officials who had stood with Stalin against all the oppositions and who now, precisely when the latter's defeat was complete, could be moved by their concern over Stalin's policies to come out in criticism'.[39] On the contrary, the evidence presented in this study demonstrates that Syrtsov's policy disagreements with Stalin's

Left turn' began over two years previously. The significance of this affair lies less in the fact that Stalin's patience with Syrtsov's nagging disagreements wore thin and he decided to remove him, but rather that the nature of Stalin's hold on power had become so unassailable between early 1928 and late 1930 that he could afford to dispense with the services of the more troublesome among his senior party clients.

Conclusion

The Pyrrhic victory in the civil war and the collapse of the War Communism strategy for a quick transition to socialism left the Bolshevik party engulfed by several critical problems; the country was on the verge of economic and social disintegration, the party was becoming increasingly isolated from any social base of support, and a culture of authoritarianism gripped the political administration. In order to temporarily alleviate these problems and secure the tactical survival of the goals of the October Revolution, Lenin imposed the NEP model of development on the party at the Tenth Congress in March 1921. This combined an entrenchment of the party's political monopoly with a retreat to a mixed economy of extensive state ownership coexistent with small scale capitalist enterprises and a market relationship with individual peasant producers. As for Lenin's conceptualisation of NEP, it is clear that he regarded it as a stopgap prescription for the difficulties facing the new regime and envisaged that at some future point, once the economy had been sufficiently resuscitated, the advance on the road of 'building socialism' would be renewed. In the meantime, the aim of party policy towards the peasants was to capture and subject them to political control by expanding state authority, party membership and cooperative institutions in rural areas.

The Siberian countryside under NEP

The peculiarities of Siberian agriculture in the 1920s were a double edged sword for the party. In contrast to other regions, the conditions in Siberia were ripe for a rapid resurgence of agricultural production under NEP because of the healthy economic state of the local peasantry. Siberian peasants were the best provided in the country in terms of land, animals, implements and machines (crucial to profitable farming in the region because of the climatically induced

205

short sowing and harvesting seasons), while the virtual absence of the redivisional commune was an added incentive to the spirit of self-reliance that imbued the local culture and characterised this frontier and immigrant society. Furthermore, the rural economy had largely escaped the deprivation and havoc wrought by the civil war in other areas, and this placed the long established and extensive network of Siberian cooperatives in a good position to reap the benefits from the advantages offered by NEP. Equally, the strength of the enterprising, technically advanced, and indeed often mechanised, Siberian kulak farms meant that the policy of 'enrichment' implied in NEP revived the growth of social stratification and economic differentiation in the countryside, and nurtured the proto-capitalist and petty-capitalist peasants who were among the social strata potentially most hostile to socialist construction.

The revolutionary levelling of farms in the region conducted by the party in 1920–2, which concentrated on the redistribution of land and animals and effectively ignored agricultural capital (machines and implements), consecutive with prodrazverstka campaigns and poor harvests, instigated a slump in production as the peasantry went over to subsistence farming. In 1924–7, as the incentive effects of NEP took hold, with soaring state procurement and market prices and a low burden of agricultural taxation, peasant output recovered rapidly to 1920 levels, and from 1926 far exceeded them. A worrying aspect for the government was that the success of NEP in raising productivity was not matched by a corresponding increase in peasant marketing of output, and Siberia was among the worst performers in this respect. Among the most important deleterious factors contributing to this situation were the substantial demographic growth in the Siberian rural population and the recuperation of livestock numbers which absorbed through increased consumption a large part of what might have been marketed, while, at the same time, the reduced burden of taxation meant that the peasants were under less financial pressure to sell. Arguably, the most significant impact was made by the regular imbalances in state procurement prices, particularly as the mixed nature of livestock and grain farming in the region allowed the peasantry a large margin of manoeuvrability in the market.

In the mid-1920s, the heyday of NEP, Siberia emerged as a grain surplus area, especially of high quality wheat, of vital importance to the country, once pre-war prohibitive financial penalties on grain producers (such as the Cheliabinsk grain tariff) had been removed, land reserves were brought under cultivation, and the nature of

agriculture in the region shifted away from the primacy of dairy farming following the break up of the large cattle herds by the Bolshevik
levelling process. By 1926/7 as much as 35% of Soviet wheat exports
originated in Siberia and the region was distinguished as a main source
of valuable agricultural exports at a time when the party leadership
placed increasing reliance on the accumulation of foreign currency for
industrial investment.

    Further departures from the norm are also evident in the Siberian
political scene in the 1920s. The destruction of its home grown Bolshevik leadership by Kolchak and the popular support for separatist
movements displayed during the civil war meant that not only was
Moscow preoccupied with rebuilding the regional party apparatus,
but found it imperative that firm central control be reestablished by
breaking the regional party's commitment to local elites. Consequently, experienced party outsiders – Kosior, Lashevich, Syrtsov,
Eikhe, Zimin *inter alia* – activists whose loyalty to the centre was
presumed to be above question, were appointed to the leading nomenklatura posts in the krai in these years. Irritatingly for Moscow, this
tactic did not always produce the desired trouble-free monolithic behaviour, as even the outsiders became embroiled in political in-fighting
over institutionalised intra-regional rivalries, the most notable of
which was the competition between the centripetal interests of the
Kraikom, supported by Syrtsov and Eikhe, and the centrifugal pressures of the Irkutsk Okruzhkom, defended by Zimin.

    The overwhelmingly rural foundation and markedly high peasant
representation in the social profile of the reconstructed Siberian party
organisation were additional contours that set it apart from the rest of
the country. Such was the flood of Siberian peasants into the ranks of
the party as a result of the recruitment drives under NEP that by 1928
over two-thirds of party cells were based in the countryside, and in the
wheat growing okrugs of south-west Siberia over one-third of party
members were working peasants. Party studies of this trend tentatively suggested that kulak incorporation into rural party organisations
and soviets was endemic in the region, and this aroused fears among
some local leaders that a situation of 'dual power' was emerging, as
kulak family cliques used their control of rural institutions (the commune, rural soviet, party cell, cooperatives) to secure for themselves
preferential treatment in the supply of state credits, machines and
other goods, and prevent remedies against their abuses of laws restricting the hiring of labour and leasing of land.

    The notion that the exceptionally fast economic recovery of Siberian agriculture under NEP was probably kulak-led was given statistical backing by Brike's studies in 1927, which demonstrated that kulaks were exploiting their ownership of capital equipment that had lain dormant on their farms during the lean years of the early 1920s. This and other reports of the vitality of petty-capitalist farming and the widening of peasant economic differentiation in the region, as kulaks cultivated large tracts by operating modern machines and hiring labour on a widespread and long-term basis, caused political tremors in Moscow when the Left Opposition cited them to illustrate the negative impact of NEP. The enthusiasm with which the krai party leadership, and Syrtsov in particular, embraced the extreme Bukharinist version of NEP as a device to promote accumulation by the well-off peasantry, made for a reluctance to acknowledge the significance of the kulak threat or conform to the more punitive anti-kulak policy forged by the centre in response to the sustained criticisms of the Left regarding the 'kulak danger'.

The search for a definitive rejection of the Left's claims about kulak accumulation led the Kraikom to sponsor Kavraisky and Nusinov's investigation of economic differentiation among the Siberian peasantry, published in late 1927. Employing a sophisticated methodology similar to that devised by Nemchinov for his country-wide survey, they calculated the proportion of kulaks at 6.3% of the peasantry (twice Nemchinov's figure for the USSR), owning 16.4% of the means of production (by value) and 14.5% of the sown area, holding 25% of leased land, and 64% of whom hired labour on a long-term basis. The economic importance of the kulaks in the grain sector was made even clearer in their analysis of data for early 1928, which revealed that this stratum held 16% of the sown area, accounted for 16.7% of grain production and 27.7% of the marketable grain surplus, with the latter figure rising to 50% in early 1928. Rather than dispel suspicions about the growth of the well-off and kulak peasant, the conclusions drawn by Kavraisky and Nusinov substantiated that they were indeed a power to be reckoned with in Siberian agriculture.

The grain crisis and the end of NEP

The unravelling of NEP during the grain crisis of 1927–8 owed less to the specifically situation-determined problems of that particular economic year – low grain productivity, increased peasant consumption, state procurement price imbalances, manufactured goods shortages, higher peasant incomes, the inefficiency and complacency of the party and state organs, the war scare, bad weather, and a premeditated peasant withdrawal from the market (kulak sabotage) – many of which affected Siberia in an exacerbated form, than to the fact that the fundamental flaw in the whole NEP package, as it applied to the countryside, finally tore the policy asunder. The prime years of NEP, 1924–7, witnessed the congruence of a cumulative series of converging crises the resolution of which rested upon the outcome of a struggle in the party between two irreconcilable ideas; on the one hand, there was the instinctive ideologically determined antipathy of mainstream Bolshevism towards NEP in preference for a policy of financially squeezing the peasantry by means of the price scissors in order to accumulate resources to finance the 'building of socialism' via a rapid tempo of industrialisation; and on the other, the compromisingly restrained approach of Bukharin that advocated capitulation to the peasant market and the contraction of industrial investment plans as and when necessary to preserve the economic and social equilibrium of NEP as an evolutionary road to socialism.

Essentially, the latter policy was followed in 1924–6, but the bumper harvest in 1926/7 sent grain prices tumbling and fed the ambitions of the embryonic Stalinist majority in the Politburo for a more ambitious programme of industrialisation that would be largely funded by exports of cheaply procured agricultural products. At the same time, growing urbanisation meant that the state was increasingly concerned with ensuring a regular supply of low-cost food, especially grain, to the towns; however, this was not always possible given the fluctuations of the market and, consequently, urban discontent was on the rise. The Bukharinist agricultural strategy began to disintegrate when there was a renewed upsurge of grain procurement difficulties at the end of 1927, and the majority of the party leadership decided to abandon market forces and adopt a hard-line solution of using coercive emergency measures against the peasantry to break the deadlock. This spelt the end of NEP and a return to the methods of War Communism.

A central theme of this book is that Stalin's command of the paramilitary assault on the countryside to secure grain supplies, culminating in his two-week tour of Siberia in January 1928, was the decisive turning-point in the radicalisation of his approach to the problem of party–peasant relations. In his discourse with local party and state officials during his Siberian expedition Stalin depicted the crisis in stark terms and, for the first time, described NEP as a catalogue of political errors and debilitating economic trends. He crudely simplified the complexity of the problems generated by NEP, focussing his criticism on the way that it had 'engendered' the growth of petty-capitalist kulaks who, under market conditions, posed an immutable block to the party's plans for an industrial take-off and were using their economic leverage to threaten the party's attempt to exercise political hegemony over rural areas. Stalin's remedy for the uncertainty of state control of the countryside entailed a crash programme of collectivisation and the speedy elimination of *all* small-scale individual peasant farming, and as such must be viewed as the precursor of his 'revolution from above' launched in late 1929.

The intellectual revolution in Stalin's outlook towards NEP was accelerated by his experiences of distinct Siberian conditions. He was alarmed by the demonstrable economic power of the well-off peasant stratum in the region, and perceived with horror the uncooperative attitude of the local party and state officialdom in the implementation of directives emanating from Moscow ordering the use of emergency measures. He viewed this as symptomatic of the failure of devolved power in the regions and indicative of a system of neo-traditional collaborative politics at the local level that was undermining control from the centre and effectively determining the pace of change in the country. Moreover, he must have been doubly irked on his return to Moscow in early February 1928, not only by the general recalcitrance of many Siberian officials in applying Article 107, including Syrtsov who had proved a hindrance rather than the asset he had expected from a client regional party secretary, since for the most part it was carefully targeted on selected kulak farms and highly successful in breaking the grain crisis with the minimum of violent peasant resistance, but also by his adversaries on the Right of the party leadership who demanded a return to the market equilibrium of NEP.

Stalin's Siberian experiences must be viewed in the wider political context of his moves to establish a personal dictatorship in the party leadership, but given the evidence it is impossible to assess with any exactitude the relative weights of each in Stalin's motivations. What is clear is that by the end of January 1928 he had crossed the Rubicon and was inexorably determined to implement his revolutionary agrarian programme, a task that he felt could only be achieved by the purging and rejuvenation of the entire party and state apparatus. Indeed, some features of the campaign encouraged him to believe that there existed a spontaneous dynamic from below in favour of such changes: for example, the willing participation of urban worker-communist militants, mobilised to spearhead the party's attack on the kulaks, in enforcing the new line; the social cleavages stirred up in the peasantry

by the doling out to the rural poor of a bounty of 25% of grain confiscated under Article 107; and most significantly, the positive response
to the new radicalism of some regional party leaders, such as Eikhe and
Zimin in Siberia, though admittedly to different degrees.

The 'microhistorical' approach to the study of political developments in Siberia in the aftermath of the grain crisis, concentrating on
the schism in the Siberian Kraikom during the 'Irkutsk affair' of March–
June 1928, reveals the intricate complexity of Soviet regional politics in
this period. Ostensibly, the breach between the Kraikom, headed by
Syrtsov, and the Irkutsk party elite, under Zimin, was provoked by
Syrtsov's moderation in dealing with the kulaks; however, there were
more deep-seated antagonisms and pluralistic tendencies underlying
the episode, primarily: conflicts of interests over territorial boundaries,
political jurisdiction, economic investment and prestige, as well as
personal rivalries. The circumstances surrounding the 'Irkutsk affair'
illuminate our understanding of both the operation of centre–periphery relations and Stalin's patrimonial political machine in the party
hierarchy on the eve of his 'revolution from above'. It has parallels with
more well-known contemporaneous political crises in other regions,
for example in Smolensk, but the argument postulated by Cohen and
Brower that Stalin manipulated such events to oust pro-NEP Rightist
regional leaderships and install his own allies does not stand up in the
case of Siberia. Similarly, Tucker's thesis that Stalin's rise to power
rested on a patron–client network of party secretaries built on programmatic cohabitation is not borne out by the Stalin–Syrtsov
relationship.

From early 1928, Stalin and Syrtsov clearly diverged on the major
policy issues of the day, in particular, regarding the efficacy of coercive
measures against the peasantry and the reversal of NEP, without
breaking their political alliance. Indeed, their mutual allegiance, which
had been cemented in the early 1920s when Syrtsov worked directly
under Stalin's patronage in senior positions in the Central Committee,
was reaffirmed following the grain crisis when Stalin supported Syrtsov against Zimin in the 'Irkutsk affair', though he later promoted both
to Moscow, and likewise Syrtsov sided with Stalin in the leadership
battles with the Right. This kind of interdependence illustrates just
how vulnerable Stalin's hold on power was at this time, as programmatic conformity took a back seat to personal loyalty and the appor-
tionment of patronage.

Appendix

Table A.1. *Grain marketings and procurement in the USSR, 1925/8 (as % of gross production)*

AREA	1925/6		1926/7		1927/8	
	marketed production	procurements	marketed production	procurements	marketed production	procurements
Siberian Krai	19.1	14.6	21.9	18.8	25.2	19.6
USSR	20.8	11.9	20.7	14.8	21.8	15.0
RSFSR	20.7	12.1	20.6	15.1	20.9	13.8
Ukraine	23.0	14.7	23.5	18.0	27.0	21.8
North Caucasus	37.1	25.5	37.9	29.3	37.3	22.7
Lower Volga	24.1	12.9	27.3	21.9	25.8	16.2
Middle Volga	21.9	12.0	25.9	22.0	21.5	14.9
Central Black-Earth Zone	16.3	8.5	17.5	10.4	22.4	18.3

Source: *Sel'skoe khoziaistvo SSSR, 1925–1928*, pp. 294–5

Table A.2. *Grain production and state procurement in Siberia, 1913 and 1925/9 (in million tons)*

	Production	% 1913	% 1925
1913	5.1	100.0	n/a
1925	5.53	108.4	100.0
1926	6.52	127.9	117.9
1927	5.81	113.9	105.1
1928	7.49	146.9	135.5
	Procurement	As a % of previous year	As a % of 1925/6
1925/6	0.854	100.0	100.0
1926/7	1.32	154.0	154.0
1927/8	1.31	99.8	153.6
1928/9	1.79	129.5	209.6

Source: Gushchin, *Sibirskaia derevnia*: production – table 15, p. 102; procurement – table 18, p. 105

Table A.3. *Changes in the ratio of procurements in areas of West Siberia 1926/8 (for the quarter October–December)*

A. GRAIN AS % OF TOTAL PROCUREMENTS (by value)

	1926/7	1927/8
Omsk	87.2%	42.5%
Slavgorod	89.8%	59.1%
Biisk	78.6%	49.2%

B. MEAT AS A % OF TOTAL PROCUREMENTS (by value)

	1926/7	1927/8
Omsk	6.0%	39.8%
Slavgorod	7.0%	39.8%
Biisk	15.7%	43.9%
Barnaul	12.5%	81.6%
Krasnoiarsk	39.0%	79.0%

Source: NLP, 1–2 (31 January 1928), 15–16.

Table A.4. *Data on cases held under Article 107 in areas of south-west Siberia (end January 1928–15 April 1928)*

Okrug	No. of raions	No. of farms tried under A.107	Aver. no. of trials per raion	Value of means of production (in roubles) of farms tried under A.107 (as % of total)						% of farms with grain stocks of (puds)		Aver. grain stocks per farm (puds)	Total grain confiscated (puds)
				up to 500	500–1,000	1,000–1,500	1,500–3,000	3,000–6,000	over 6,000	up to 1,000	over 1,000		
Rubtsovsk	10	66	6.6	1.5	3.0	27.3	37.9	27.3	3.0	30.3	69.7	1607	106,062
Biisk	18	147	8.2	8.2	12.3	17.0	44.9	13.6	4.0	56.5	43.5	1018	149,646
Barnaul	14	60	4.3	11.7	16.7	26.6	36.7	8.3	–	56.7	43.3	911	64,660
Kamensk	12	127	10.6	–	15.0	30.7	37.8	15.7	0.8	66.9	33.1	893	113,411
Total	54	400	7.4	5.0	12.25	24.5	40.25	15.75	2.25	55.5	44.5	1107	423,779

Source: Kavraiskii and Nusinov, *Klassy i klassovye otnosheniia*, p. 82

Glossary

Agitprop Sektsiia agitatsii i propagandy (Agitation and Propaganda section)

Arcos Vserussiiskoe kooperativnoe aktsionernoe obshchestvo (All-Russian Cooperative Joint Stock Company)

Artel A producers collective enterprise

batrak An agricultural labourer

bednota/bedniak The poor peasantry / a poor peasant

Cheka Chrezvychainaia komissiia po bor'be c kontrrevoliutsiei, sabotazhem i spekuliatsiei (The Secret Police 1917–22). See (O)GPU

Gosplan Gosudarstvennaia planovaia komissaia (State Planning Commission)

Ispolkom Executive Committee of a soviet. Thus, Kraiispolkom, okrispolkom and raiispolkom

Khleboprodukt Aktsionernoe obshchestvo torgovli khlebnymi i drugimi sel'sko-khoziaistvenymi produktami (Joint Stock Company for Trade in Grain and Other Agricultural Products)

khutora A peasant farmstead fully enclosed outside of the commune

Krai A large territorial province subdivided into okrugs (districts) and raions (areas)

Kraikom (biuro) Krai komitet (biuro) (Krai Party Committee and its Bureau). Thus, okruzhkom in okrugs, raikom in raions

Krestkom Krest'ianskii komitet obshchestvo vzaimopomoshch' (Peasant Committee of Mutual Aid)

kulak The rich peasant, rural trader or entrepreneur defined by the party as a 'petty-capitalist peasant'

Maslosoiuz Soiuz maslodel'nykh artelei (Union of Butter-making Artels)

Narkomfin Narodnyi komissariat finansov (People's Commissariat of Finance)

Narkomiust Narodnyi komissariat iustitsii (People's Commissariat of Justice of RSFSR)

Narkomprod Narodnyi komissariat prodovol'stvie (People's Commissariat of Food Supplies)

Narkomtorg Narodnyi komissariat vneshnei i vnutrennoi torgovli (People's Commissariat of External and Internal Trade of USSR)

Narkomzem   Narodnyi komissariat zemledeliia (People's Commissariat of Agriculture of RSFSR)

(O)GPU   (Ob'edinennoe)   gosudarstvennoe   politicheskoe   upravlenie (United) (State Political Administration) The Secret Police (1922–34)

Orgbiuro   Organizationnoe biuro (Organisational Bureau of the Central Committee)

Orgotdel   Organizatsionnyi i instruktivnyi otdel (Organisational and Instruction Department of the Central Committee)

Orgraspred   Organizatsionno-raspredelitel'nyi otdel (Organisation and Assignment Department of the Central Committee)

otruba   A peasant farmstead with land only enclosed outside of the commune

prodrazverstka   Forced confiscation of agricultural produce from peasants

Rabkrin   (RKI)   Narodnyi   komissariat   raboche-krest'ianskoi   inspektsii (People's Commissariat of Worker's and Peasant's Inspection)

Sel'skii skhod   Village gathering. A rural assembly of all enfranchised peasants over 18 years old

Sel'skosoiuz   Vserossiiskii soiuz soiuzov sel'skokhoziaistvennykh i kreditnykh kooperatsii (All-Russian Union of Agricultural and Credit Cooperative Unions)

seredniak   A middle-stratum peasant

Sibbiuro   Sibirskoe biuro (Siberian Bureau of the Central Committee)

Sibkraisoiuz   Sibirskii krai soiuz kooperativov (Siberian Krai Union of Cooperative Societies)

Sibrevkom   Sibirskii   revoliutsionnyi   komitet   (Siberian   Revolutionary Committee)

Sibsel'skokredit   Sibirskii sel'skokhoziaistvennyi i kreditnyi bank (Siberian Agricultural and Credit Bank)

Sibtorg   The Siberian department of Narkomtorg

Sovnarkom   Sovet narkodnykh komissarov (Council of People's Commissars of the USSR)

SDPLR   Social-Democratic Party of the Latvian Republic

Smychka   The political 'link' or alliance between the working class and the peasantry

SR   Social-Revolutionary Party

Toz   Tovarishchestvo po obshchestvennoi obrabotki zemli (Association for common cultivation of land)

Tsentrosoiuz   Vserossiiskii tsentral'nyi soiuz potrebitel'skikh obshchestv (All-Russian Central Union of Consumers' Societies)

TsSU   Tsentral'nyi statisticheskoe upravlenie (Central Statistical Administration of RSFSR)

Uchraspred   Uchetno-raspredelitel'nyi otdel (Records and Assignment Section of the Central Committee)

VTsIK   Vsesoiuznyi (Vserossiiskii) tsentral'nyi ispolnitel'nyi komitet (All-Union [All-Russian] Central Executive Committee of Soviets)

zemel'nyi skhod   Communal gathering. Peasant assembly of the heads of farm households of a village or group of villages

Notes

Abbreviations

BSE	Bol'shaia sovetskaia entsiklopediia
IS	Izvestiia sibkraikoma VKP (b)
Izv. Ts. K. VKP(b)	Izvestiia tsentral'nogo komiteta VKP(b)
NAF	Na agrarnom fronte
NLP	Na Leninskom puti
SS	Soviet Studies
SSE	Sibirskaia sovetskaia entsiklopediia
SSKK	Sibirskaia sel'sko-khoziaistvennaia kooperatsiia
ZS	Zhizn' sibiri

Introduction

1 The pioneering study was: M. Fainsod, *Smolensk under Soviet Rule* (Cambridge, Mass., 1958). The following works are a selection from this Western scholarship: O. Narkiewicz, *The Making of the Soviet State Apparatus* (Manchester, 1970); J. Arch. Getty, *The Origins of the Great Purges* (Cambridge, 1987); L. Viola, *The Best Sons of the Fatherland: Workers in the Vanguard of Soviet Collectivisation* (Oxford, 1987); H. Kuromiya, *Stalin's Industrial Revolution: Politics and Workers* (Cambridge, 1988). For a lively debate on the merits of this approach see the discussion articles in *Russian Review*, 45, 1986, 357–427, and 46, 1987, 375–431.

2 The standard interpretive works of this period are: E. H. Carr, *Foundations of a Planned Economy, 1926–1929*, 2 vols. (vol. 1 with R. W. Davies) (London, 1969–71); M. Lewin, *Russian Peasants and Soviet Power: A Study of Collectivization* (London, 1968); A. Nove, *An Economic History of the USSR* (London, 1969); A. Erlich, *The Soviet Industrialization Debate, 1924–1928* (Cambridge, Mass., 1967). Stimulating analyses of 'high politics' are also provided by: S. Cohen, *Bukharin and the Bolshevik Revolution: A Political Biography 1888–1938* (London, 1974), chapters 8–9, and R. C. Tucker, *Stalin as Revolutionary, 1879–1929* (London, 1974), chapters 8–11. The major studies by Siberian scholars are: N. Ia. Gushchin, *Sibirskaia derevnia na puti k sotsializmu* (Novosibirsk, 1973); N. Ia. Gushchin and V. A. Il'inykh, *Klassovaia bor'ba v sibirskoi*

219

derevne, 1920-e – seredina 1930-x gg. (Novosibirsk, 1987); and for a critique of the Western scholarship see N. Ia. Gushchin and V. A. Zhdanov, *Kritika burzhuaznykh kontseptsii istorii sovetskoi sibirskoi derevni* (Novosibirsk, 1987).

3 Getty, p. 206.

1 The Siberian peasant utopia

1 N. Baranskii, *An Economic Geography of the USSR* (Moscow, 1956), pp. 242–4, 252.

2 *Sibirskaia sovetskaia entsiklopediia* (hereafter *SSE* refers to this work), 3 vols. (Novosibirsk, 1929–32), vol. 2, p. 82.

3 H. J. Ellison, 'Peasant colonisation of Siberia. A study on the growth of Russian rural society in Siberia with particular emphasis on the years 1890–1918' (unpublished Ph.D. thesis, University of London, 1955), p. 42; W. S. Vucinich, *Russia and Asia: Essays on the Influence of Russia on the Asian Peoples* (Stanford, 1972), p. 309. G. T. Robinson, *Rural Russia Under the Old Regime* (London, 1932), p. 251. For a study of peasant settlement of Siberia in this period see D. W. Treadgold, *The Great Siberian Migration: Government and Peasant in Resettlement from Emancipation to the First World War* (Princeton, 1957).

4 M. Phillips Price, *Siberia* (London, 1912), p. vii.

5 W. K. Matthews, *The Structure and Development of Russian* (Cambridge, 1953), p. 106. Over 430,000 returned to Russia in 1905–9; Treadgold, *The Great Siberian Migration*, pp. 71–3.

6 Treadgold, *The Great Siberian Migration*, pp. 159, 239–46; M. A. Novomeiiskii, *My Siberian Life* (London, 1956), p. 15.

7 H. Seton-Watson, *The Russian Empire 1801–1917* (Oxford, 1967), p. 657.

8 D. W. Treadgold, 'Russian expansionism and Turner's American frontier', *Agricultural History*, 26, 4 (October 1952), 150; see also Treadgold, *The Great Siberian Migration*, pp. 206–20. The Siberian saying is cited in S. Brike, 'Zapadno-sibirskaia derevnia (kamenskii okrug)', *Na agrarnom fronte* (hereafter *NAF*), 6 (1927), 121.

9 Ellison, 'Peasant colonisation', p. 79; Gushchin, *Sibirskaia derevnia*, pp. 26–8; Treadgold, *The Great Siberian Migration*, pp. 229–30, 256; *SSE*, vol. 2, p. 85.

10 Treadgold, *The Great Siberian Migration*, pp. 213–15, and 231–2 citing V. V. Soldatov's investigation of the commune in the Altai in 1919. For the Siberian commune in this period see Ellison, 'Peasant colonisation', ch. 3.

11 S. Brike, 'Ekonomicheskie protsessy v sibirskoi derevne', *Zhizn' sibiri* (hereafter *ZS*), 1 (1927), 13–14; S. A. Bergavinov, 'O tempe i kharaktere rassloeniia sibirskoi derevne', *Bol'shevik*, 13–14 (1 July 1927), 81–3; Gushchin, *Sibirskaia derevnia*, pp. 37–9: *SSE*, vol. 2, p. 109.

12 Gushchin, *Sibirskaia derevnia*, pp. 44–5.

13 As note 11 above.

14 *Sel'skoe khoziaistvo SSSR 1925–1928* (Moscow, 1929), pp. 2–3, 6–7; N. Ia.

Gushchin (ed.), *Problemy istorii sovetskoi sibirskoi derevni* (Novosibirsk, 1977), p. 64; G. Cleinow, *Neu-Siberien* (Berlin, 1928), pp. 267–8. According to the *Soviet Union Yearbook 1928* (London, 1928), p. 24, only three towns had populations in excess of 100,000: Irkutsk, Omsk and Novosibirsk. For industrial output see *III sibirskaia kraevaia partiinaia konferentsiia VKP(b), stenograficheskii otchet*, vol. 1 (Novosibirsk, 1927), pp. 70 (Kanaev), 95 (Kornev); *Pravda*, 13 December 1925, 4. For a breakdown of urban employment in Siberia see *SSE*, vol. 1, p. 712.

15 *Sel'skoe khoziaistvo SSSR*, p. 17; Gushchin (ed.), *Problemy istorii*, p. 98; Gushchin, *Sibirskaia derevnia*, p. 95; E. H. Carr, *Socialism in One Country 1924–1926*, vol. 1 (London, 1958), pp. 524–5.

16 Gushchin, *Sibirskaia derevnia*, pp. 77–81; *Propagandist* (Novosibirsk), 1–2 (1928), 39. For the impact of the Land Code of 1922 on the Russian commune see D. J. Male, *Russian Peasant Organisation Before Collectivisation* (Cambridge, 1971), pp. 12, 57–65.

17 *Statistika sibiri, sbornik statei i materialov*, vol. 1 (Novosibirsk, 1930), p. 21; *SSE*, vol. 2, p. 142. In some areas of Slavgorod Okrug communes had not undergone a redivision for over twenty years; S. I. Syrtsov, 'Neudachnoe nastuplenie tov. Safarova', *Bol'shevik*, 15–16 (31 August 1927), 109.

18 Gushchin, *Sibirskaia derevnia*, pp. 85–6; *Sel'skoe khoziaistvo SSSR*, pp. 154–6, 158–61; Ellison, 'Peasant colonisation', pp. 346–7; V. P. Timoshenko, *Agricultural Russia and the Wheat Problem* (Stanford, 1932), pp. 41, 198–9.

19 Gushchin, *Sibirskaia derevnia*, pp. 80–1. Data gathered in Saratov Guberniia in 1927 suggested that the costs of fieldwork doubled when the distance to outlying strips exceeded 9.2 kilometres; V. P. Danilov, 'Zemel'nye otnosheniia v sovetskoi dokolkhoznoi derevne', *Istoriia SSSR*, 3 (1958), 113. See also Male, pp. 9–10.

20 *Sel'skoe khoziaistvo SSSR*, pp. 154–61; Gushchin, *Sibirskaia derevnia*, p. 127.

21 For equipment purchases see *Istoriia sibiri*, vol. 4 (Leningrad, 1968), p. 229; I. Rettel', 'Mashinosnabzhenie i posevnaia kampaniia', *Na Leninskom puti* (hereafter *NLP*), 5 (20 March 1928), 19–23; V. A. Il'inykh, 'Klassovaia bor'ba v sibirskoi derevne v usloviiakh Nep'a (1924–1927 gg.)' *dissertatsiia kandidata istorii nauka* (Novosibirsk, 1985), p. 234. For the role of tractors see A. K. Kas'ian, 'Zapadnosibirskaia derevnia v 1926–1929 gg.' in *Istoriia sovetskogo i kolkhoznogo stroitel'stva v SSSR* (Moscow, 1963), p. 121; Carr and Davies, *Foundations*, p. 210; N. Ia. Gushchin, *Soiuz rabochego klassa i krest'ianstva sibiri v period postanovleniia sotsializma 1917–1927 gg.* (Novosibirsk, 1978), pp. 31, 226.

22 V. I. Lenin, *Polnoe sobranie sochinenii*, 5th edn, 55 vols. (Moscow, 1958–65), vol. 45, pp. 369–77.

23 See also, for example, I. V. Stalin, *Sochineniia*, 13 vols. (Moscow, 1946–51), vol. 8, p. 79. For an analysis of Bukharin's views on peasant cooperation see Cohen, pp. 195–8. The failure of Bolshevik policy in this respect is described in R. F. Miller, 'Soviet agricultural policy in the twenties: the failure of cooperation', *Soviet Studies* (hereafter *SS*), 27, 2 (April 1975), 220–44.

24 Carr, *Socialism in One Country*, vol. 1, pp. 276, 429–30. See also pp. 49–50 above.
25 *SSE*, vol. 3, p. 311; Ellison, 'Peasant colonisation', pp. 352–9; I. Vasil'ev, 'Sibirskaia potrebitel'skaia kooperatsiia', *ZS*, 8 (1927), 54; Gushchin, *Sibirskaia derevnia*, Tables 48 and 49, pp. 203–4.
26 *SSE*, vol. 1, pp. 135–6; *Istoriia sibiri*, vol. 4, p. 231; Gushchin, *Sibirskaia derevnia*, p. 207.
27 Gushchin, *Sibirskaia derevnia*, p. 208; K. Lunev, 'Novyi etap v razvitii sibirskoi s.-kh. kooperatsii', *ZS*, 11 (1928), 95; Vedeniapin, 'Sibirskaia derevnia na putiakh kollektivizatsii', *NLP*, 1–2 (1928), 25.
28 Gushchin, *Sibirskaia derevnia*, p. 93; *SSE*, vol. 1, pp. 17–18 (specialists) and vol. 3, p. 690 (literacy levels). For infrastructural deficiencies see: V. S. Davidenkova, *SSSR po raionam: Sibir'* (Moscow–Leningrad, 1927), p. 82; Ellison, 'Peasant colonisation', p. 370; I. Trelin, 'Tovarooborot i zagotovki v 1927–28 g.', *ZS*, 9–10 (1927), 109; M. I. Reminnyi, 'Iz ekonomicheskoi zhizni okrugov sibirskogo kraia', *ZS*, 11 (1927), 101; M. Lebedev, 'Sostoianie i perspektivy razvitiia elevatornogo khoziaistva v sibkrae', *ZS*, 2 (1928), 34; *Sibirskaia sel'sko-khoziaistvennaia kooperatsiia* (hereafter *SSKK*), 5 (25 March 1928), 13, 64, and Inzh. Prokhorov, 'Gotovim elevatory i sklady', *SSKK*, 11 (10 September 1928), 17.
29 Brike, *ZS*, 1 (1927), 15; A. Povolotskii, 'Narodnoe khoziaistvo sibirskogo kraia po kontrol'nym tsifrom na 1927–1928 gg.', *ZS*, 9–10 (1927), 7; N. S. Vasil'ev, 'Kolichestvennye protsessy v sibirksom sel'skom khoziaistve i perspektivy na 1927–28 god', *ZS*, 9–10 (1927), 29; *III sib. part. konf.*, pp. 181–3; *SSE*, vol. 1, p. 940; Gushchin, *Soiuz rabochego klassa*, p. 217.
30 Gushchin, *Soiuz rabochego klassa*, p. 217; Gushchin (ed.), *Problemy istorii*, p. 98; *III sib. part. konf.*, p. 183 (Eikhe); *Sel'skoe khoziaistvo SSSR*, p. 17; Vasil'ev, *ZS*, 9–10 (1927), 31. For state prices policy see pp. 97–103, 108–9 above.
31 Gushchin, *Sibirskaia derevnia*, p. 31.
32 See V. L. Mote, 'The Cheliabinsk grain tariff and the rise of the Siberian butter industry', *Slavic Review*, 35, 2 (June 1976), 304–17.
33 *SSE*, vol. 3, pp. 310–23; vol. 1, p. 916; vol. 2, pp. 696, 1058; Ellison, 'Peasant colonisation', pp. 372–3; Davidenkova, pp. 62–3.
34 *SSE*, vol. 3, p. 314; *III sib. part. konf.*, pp. 24–5; Gushchin, *Sibirskaia derevnia*, p. 119.
35 Davidenkova, pp. 84–5; *SSE*, vol. 2, p. 1058; vol. 3, pp. 313, 324–8.
36 *SSE*, vol. 2, p. 62; vol. 1, p. 916; N. Jasny, *The Socialized Agriculture of the USSR*, (Stanford, 1949), p. 535; Mote, 'The Cheliabinsk grain tariff', 311.
37 Ellison, 'Peasant colonisation', p. 371; *SSE*, vol. 1, pp. 749, 916; Gushchin, *Sibirskaia derevnia*, p. 108.
38 Gushchin, *Sibirskaia derevnia*, p. 62.
39 V. I. Shishkin, *Revoliutsionnye komitety sibiri v gody grazdanskoi voiny 1919–1921 gg.* (Novosibirsk, 1978), pp. 19, 33, 90–1. A leading participant in this campaign was M. I. Frumkin, who later broke with Stalin over the use of emergency measures against peasants in 1928. In fact, at this time he wrote a handbook for prodrazverstka activists; *Prodovol'stvennaia politika v svete*

obshchego khoziaistvennogo stroitel'stva sovetskoi vlasti, sbornik materialov (Moscow, 1920), pp. 257–60. For his clash with Stalin see p. 236 n. 14 below. For the organisation of the prodrazverstka campaign see *Sobranie uzakonenii i rasporiazhenii*, 1920, no. 6, article 298, pp. 315–16; Frumkin, pp. 261–3; Gushchin, *Sibirskaia derevnia*, Table 1, p. 66.
40 For the uprising, see Gushchin and Il'inykh, *Klassovaia bor'ba*, pp. 63–6.
41 Vasil'ev, *ZS*, 9–10 (1927), 28–9; Gushchin (ed.), *Problemy istorii*, p. 93; Gushchin, *Sibirskaia derevnia*, Table 16, p. 102.
42 A. Tel'tevskii, 'Mesto sibkraia v sel'skom khoziaistve SSSR', *ZS*, 3–4 (1927), 66–7; *Vneshniaia torgovlia SSSR za 1918–1940 gg., statisticheskii obzor* (Moscow, 1960), pp. 110–13; Gushchin, *Sibirskaia derevnia*, pp. 105, 108; V. G. Botvinik, 'Khlebozagotovki', *ZS*, 1 (1927), 38; Il'inykh, 'Klassovaia bor'ba', p. 240; *Sel'skoe khoziaistvo SSSR*, p. 486.
43 R. W. Davies, *The Industrialisation of Soviet Russia*, vol. 1, *The Socialist Offensive: The Collectivisation of Soviet Agriculture 1929–1930* (London, 1980), pp. 16–18; M. R. Dohan, 'Soviet foreign trade in the NEP economy and Soviet industrialization strategy' (unpublished Ph.D. thesis, Massachusetts Institute of Technology, 1969), pp. 345, 382, 445–7.
44 See Table A.1, p. 213 above.
45 P. Dominique, *Secrets of Siberia* (London, 1934), p. 237.
46 Vasil'ev, *ZS*, 9–10 (1927), 29–31; Gushchin, *Sibirskaia derevnia*, p. 104.

2 The party and the peasantry

1 For changes in the party's organisation in this period see L. Schapiro, *The Communist Party of the Soviet Union*, 2nd edn (London, 1970), part 2; R. Service, *The Bolshevik Party in Revolution: A Study in Organisational Change 1917–1923* (London, 1979), especially pp. 104–11, 123–6; J. R. Adelman, 'The development of the Soviet party apparat in the civil war; center, localities and nationality areas', *Russian History*, 9, 1 (January 1982), 86–110.
2 Schapiro, pp. 243–6; Service, pp. 126–9, 171; *KPSS v rezoliutsiiakh i resheniiakh s"ezdov, konferentsii i plenumov Ts. K. (1898–1986)*, 9th edn (12 vols., Moscow 1983–6), vol. 2 (1917–22), pp. 104–6, 579.
3 Schapiro, pp. 242–4, 252–4, 319–24; Service, pp. 170–1. For the development of the nomenklatura system see T. H. Rigby, 'Staffing USSR incorporated: the origins of the nomenklatura system', *SS*, 40, 4 (October 1988), 523–37. Stalin's patrimonial power is discussed in G. Gill, 'Ideology, organisation and the patrimonial regime', *Journal of Communist Studies*, 5, 3 (September 1989), 292–4. The phrase 'circular flow of power' was coined by R. V. Daniels in J. W. Strong (ed.), *The Soviet Union under Brezhnev and Kosygin: The Transition Years* (New York, 1971), p. 20.
4 I. A. Moletotov, *Sibkraikom* (Novosibirsk, 1978), p. 27; O. H. Radkey, *The Election to the Russian Constituent Assembly of 1917* (Cambridge, Mass., 1950), pp. 28–9. For the SR party in Siberia see the *émigré* memoir of a leading activist; P. Dotsenko. *The Struggle for a Democracy in Siberia, 1917–1920* (Stanford, 1983), p. 155.

5 For the divisions in Siberian Bolshevik ranks see R. E. Snow, *The Bolsheviks in Siberia, 1917–1918* (London, 1977).

6 Moletotov, pp. 32–3; Carr, *Socialism in One Country*, vol. 2, pp. 273–80, 290–1.

7 Moletotov, pp. 29, 32–4; Carr, *Socialism in One Country*, vol. 2, pp. 283–4.

8 *Sobranie uzak. i rasp.*, 1925, no. 38, article 268, and no. 85, article 651; *Vserossiiskii TsIK XII sozyva, II (vtoraia) sessiia, postanovleniia*, 1925, pp. 25–61. See map, p. xiv above, and pp. 193–7 above.

9 Siberian party casualties are discussed in Adelman, 'The development of the Soviet party apparat', 99. For Kosior's career see *Sovetskaia istoricheskaia entsiklopediia*, 16 vols. (Moscow, 1961–76), vol. 7, pp. 990–1; *SSE*, vol. 2, pp. 961–2. For Lashevich see *SSE*, vol. 3, p. 28. The Kraikombiuro membership details are in Moletotov, p. 31, and the congress is mentioned in *Pravda*, 13 December 1925, 4.

10 Moletotov, pp. 38–40.

11 For these changes see Carr, *Socialism in One Country*, vol. 2, pp. 119, 136, 166–7, 170. I. Deutscher, *The Prophet Unarmed, Trotsky 1921–1929* (London, 1959), pp. 260–1 states that Lashevich became political commissar of the Leningrad military region; *(XIV) Chetyrnadtsatyi s"ezd VKP(b), 18–31 dekabria 1925 g., stenograficheskii otchet* (Moscow, 1926), pp. 310–14 (Kosior).

12 See I. Deutscher, *Stalin: A Political Biography* (London, 1949), pp. 362–4. For the impact of the civil war on the shaping of a new kind of authoritarianism and the emergence of a Stalinist cohort in the party see R. C. Tucker, *Stalin as Revolutionary 1879–1929* (London, 1974), pp. 395–420, and his article 'Stalinism as revolution from above' in Tucker (ed.), *Stalinism: Essays in Historical Interpretation* (London, 1977), pp. 91–2; S. Fitzpatrick, 'The civil war as a formative experience' in A. Gleason, P. Kenez and R. Stites (eds.), *Bolshevik Culture: Experiment and Order in the Russian Revolution* (Bloomington and Indianapolis, 1989), pp. 57–76.

13 The biography is drawn from the following sources: *Izvestiia sibkraikoma VKP (b)* (hereafter *IS*), 5–6 (25 March 1929), 4; *(XI) Odinnadtsatyi s"ezd RKP (b) 27 marta – 2 aprelia 1922, stenograficheskii otchet* (Moscow, 1961), pp. 157, 248, 852; *Bol'shaia sovetskaia entsiklopediia* (hereafter *BSE*), 3rd edn, 30 vols. (Moscow, 1970–8), vol. 25, pp. 410–11; B. Levitsky, *The Stalinist Terror in the Thirties. Documentation from the Soviet Press* (Stanford, 1974), p. 467; J. L. Wiecsynski (ed.), *The Modern Encyclopedia of Russian and Soviet History*, 51 vols. (Gulf Breeze, Florida, 1976–85), vol. 38, pp. 146–7.

14 R. A. Medvedev, *On Stalin and Stalinism* (Oxford, 1979), p. 25. See also B. Bazhanov, 'Stalin closely observed' in G. R. Urban (ed.), *Stalinism. Its Impact on Russia and the World* (London, 1982), p. 17, where Syrtsov is described as 'Stalin's propaganda chief'. For the expansion of the Central Committee apparat see Rigby, 'Staffing USSR incorporated', 525.

15 B. Souvarine, *Stalin: A Critical Survey of Bolshevism* (London, n.d. [1938]), p. 517.

16 The career details are in *IS*, no. 5–6 (25 March 1929), 4; *Sovetskaia*

istoricheskaia entsiklopediia, vol. 16, p. 418; Levitsky, pp. 214–20; Wiecsynski, vol. 10, pp. 165–7.

17 Moletotov, pp. 187–8.

18 See E. H. Carr, *The Interregnum 1923–1924* (London, 1954), pp. 106, 297–8, 316–17; Schapiro, pp. 282–9.

19 Moletotov, pp. 190–202, especially p. 196.

20 *Ibid.*, pp. 206–8, 218.

21 For the 'United Opposition' see Carr, *Foundations*, vol. 2, chapter 39; Schapiro, pp. 302–5. For the Omsk group see M. Zaitsev, 'S kem i kuda idet oppozitsiia (omskie oppozitsionnye gruppy)', *NLP*, 1 (1 October 1927), 22–9.

22 I. S. Stepichev, 'Bor'ba KPSS s Trotskistsko–Zinov'evskim antipartiinym blokom v 1926–1927 gg. (po materialam irkutskoi partiinoi organizatsii)', in *Iz istorii partiinykh organizatsii vostochnoi sibiri*, 30, 3 (Irkutsk, 1962), 3–27; *NLP*, 3 (15 February 1928), 3; *Istoriia sibiri*, vol. 4, p. 240.

23 *(XV) Piatnadtsatyi s"ezd VKP(b), 2–19 dekabria 1927g., stenograficheskii otchet* (2 vols., Moscow, 1962), vol. 1, p. 599.

24 Stepichev, 'Bor'ba KPSS', 23–4.

25 A. Gendon, 'Itogi preds"ezdovskoi diskussii v sibiri', *NLP*, 6 (25 December 1927), 19; *Osnovnye itogi partiinoi-politicheskoi i khoziaistvennoi raboty. Materialy okruzhkoma k chetverti okruzhnoi partiinoi konferentsiia* (Irkutsk, 1929), p. 33.

26 For the 'Platform of the opposition' see L. D. Trotskii, *The Real Situation in Russia* (London, 1928), especially pp. 60–74, 111–33.

27 Schapiro, pp. 313, 316; Carr, *Foundations*, vol. 2, pp. 105–21; Moletotov, Table 3, p. 51; *IS*, 4 (28 February 1929), 10 (a survey of Siberian okrug and oblast party organisations on 1 January 1928 and 1929).

28 *Sibirskaia partiinaia organizatsiia v tsifrakh* (Novosibirsk, 1927), pp. 5–6; Moletotov, Table 3, p. 51, and p. 306; *IS*, 7–8 (27 April 1928), 16 (a survey of cells, candidate groups and raikoms in okruzhkom and obkom organisations in Siberia on 1 January 1928).

29 *IS*, 4 (28 February 1929), 10. For the USSR figure see Carr, *Foundations*, vol. 2, Table 52, p. 474.

30 *IS*, 1–2 (30 January 1928), 16 (a survey of the membership of plenums, bureaus and secretaryships of Siberian party committees on 1 January 1928). The following categories by occupation were used: workers, batraks and agricultural labourers, peasants, peasants working exclusively in agriculture, and others. For an analysis of the social profile of the party membership in the country as a whole under NEP, see T. H. Rigby, *Communist Party Membership in the USSR, 1917–1967* (Princeton, 1968), chapter 4.

31 *IS*, 1–2 (25 January 1929), 14 (a comparative survey of the membership of plenums, bureaus and secretaryships of Siberian party committees elected in November–December 1928 and 1927); *IS*, 13 (25 July 1928), 11; *Sib. part. org. v tsifrakh*, p. 54; Moletotov, p. 31; *Sotsial'nyi i natsional'nyi sostav VKP (b). Itogi vsesoiuznoi partiinoi perepisi 1927 g.* (Moscow, 1928), p. 41.

32 *III sib. part. konf.*, p. 32; *Sib. part. org. v tsifrakh*, p. 166; *IS*, 3 (13 February 1928), 22 (a survey of the membership of Siberian okrug party organisations in 1927); Moletotov, p. 166.

33 Rigby, *Communist Party Membership*, p. 172; *Sib. part. org. v tsifrakh*, p. 14; *IS*, 1–2 (30 January 1928), 16.

34 *(XV) Piatnadtsatyi s"ezd VKP (b)*, p. 1281 (Zimin); *Vserossiiskii TsIK XIII sozyva, II (vtoraia) sessiia (30 marta–6 aprelia 1928). Stenograficheskii otchet* (Moscow, 1928), p. 416 (Eikhe); Y. Taniuchi, *The Village Gathering in Russia in the Mid-1920s* (Birmingham, 1968), pp. 30–9; Male, pp. 110–20.

35 Moletotov, p. 37; Male, pp. 92, 97, 100–7, 144–5.

36 *Vserossiiskii TsIK . . . 1928, steno.*, pp. 240–4, 416–17 (Eikhe), 405 (Zaitsev); J. Maynard, *The Russian Peasant and Other Studies* (London, 1942), p. 176; Male, pp. 126–9; Taniuchi, *The Village Gathering*, pp. 35–6. For the high turnover of Siberian rural soviet officials see *Sibirskii krai statisticheskii spravochnik* (Novosibirsk, 1930), pp. 58–61, 76–9.

37 V. Ia. Osokina, 'Sotsial'no-ekonomicheskie otnosheniia v zapadno-sibirskoi derevne nakanune sploshnoi kollektivizatsii (1927–1929 gg.)', *Voprosy istorii sibiri*, 3 (Tomsk, 1967), 277; Kas'ian, 'Zapadnosibirskaia derevnia', p. 128; S. Sizykh, A. Strakhov and M. Brodnev, *Batrachestvo – Opora partii v derevne* (Novosibirsk, 1930), p. 17.

38 See Taniuchi, *The Village Gathering*, pp. 54–6, 65–7; Male, 108–9.

39 T. Shanin, *The Awkward Class: Political Sociology of Peasantry in a Developing Society: Russia 1910–1925* (Oxford, 1972), p. 180. See also p. 172 above.

40 Carr, *Socialism in One Country*, vol. 2, p. 349.

41 N. Ia. Gushchin, *Klassovaia bor'ba i likvidatsiia kulachestva kak klassa v sibirskoi derevne, 1926–1933 gg.* (Novosibirsk, 1972), p. 170. See also p. 22 above.

42 N. Ia. Gushchin (ed.), *Krest'ianstvo sibiri v period stroitel'stva sotsializma (1917–1937 gg.)* (Novosibirsk, 1983), pp. 165–6; *Pravda*, 12 June 1925; *Sovetskoe stroitel'stvo, sbornik II–III*, 1925, 357.

43 Il'inykh, 'Klassovaia bor'ba', pp. 111, 255; Carr, *Socialism in One Country*, vol. 2, pp. 350-1.

44 Taniuchi, *The Village Gathering*, pp. 46–7; Il'inykh, 'Klassovaia bor'ba', p. 116; I. Reshchikov, 'Predvaritel'nye itogi perevybornoi kampanii v sibkrae', *ZS*, 3–4 (1927), 44.

45 Eikhe's speech to the Kraikom plenum of December 1926 is cited in Il'inykh, 'Klassovaia bor'ba', p. 108; S. I. Syrtsov, *Rabotat' po-novomu. K predstoiashchim konferentsiiam sibirskoi partiinoi organizatsii* (Novosibirsk, 1927), p. 13; *III sib. part. konf.*, pp. 35–7 (Syrtsov).

46 Il'inykh, 'Klassovaia bor'ba', p. 116; *Itogi rabota barnaul'skogo okruzhnogo komiteta VKP (b) za 1927 g.* (Barnaul, 1927), p. 10.

47 *Sib. krai stat. sprav.*, pp. 56, 58–61, 76–7; V. N. Burkov, 'Deiatel'nost' KPSS po ukrepleniia derevenskikh partiinikh organisatsii zapadnoi sibiri v usloviiakh podgotovki i provedeniia massovoi kollektivizatsii, 1927–1932 gg.', *dissertatsiia kandidata istorii nauka* (Tomsk, 1966), p. 12; Cleinow, p. 402.

48 *III sib. part. konf.*, p. 51; S. I. Syrtsov, *Biurokratizm i biurokraty* (Novosibirsk, 1927), pp. 7, 13–16, 19, 22, and *Rabotat' po-novomu*, p. 11. For non-

communists in the cooperative apparatus at the centre see, N. Jasny, *Soviet Economists of the Twenties: Names to be Remembered* (Cambridge, 1972), p. 14.
49 *Vserossiiskii TsIK XII sozyva, II (vtoraia) sessiia (oktiabr 1925). Stenograficheskii otchet* (Moscow, 1926), p. 213.
50 *Za chetkuiu klassovuiu liniiu. Sbornik dokumentov kraikoma VKP (b) i vystuplenii rukovodiashchikh rabotnikov kraia* (Novosibirsk, 1929), pp. 69–71 (March 1928); *III sib. part. konf.*, p. 25.
51 *III sib. part. konf.*, pp. 187–8 (Eikhe).
52 *Izvestiia Ts. K. VKP (b)*, 17–18 (13 May 1927), 7–8; S. Ognetov, 'Mashinnye tovarishchestva i kollektivizatsiia sel'skogo khoziaistva', *NLP*, 2 (15 October 1927), 52–6; Vedeniapin, *NLP*, 1–2 (31 January 1928), 25; Cleinow, p. 410.
53 A. M. Pevzner, 'Organizatsionnye problemy kredita v sibiri', *ZS*, 9–10 (1927), 159–62; V. Khronin, 'Perspektivy i zadachi novogo ekonomicheskogo goda', *ZS*, 11 (1928), 9; *SSE*, vol. 1, pp. 214–20; Burkov, 'Deiatel'nost' KPSS', p. 52; S. Zagumennyi, 'S.-khoz. kredit i kollektivizatsiia sel'skogo khoziaistva', *NLP*, 1–2 (31 January 1928), 32.
54 See *Osnovnye itogi raboty (Irkutsk)*, pp. 8, 15. Other cases are discussed in A. Florenskii, 'Zadolzhennost' neobkhodimo pogasit', *SSKK*, 2 (5 February 1928), 8–10.
55 V. A. Kavraiskii and I. I. Nusinov, *Klassy i klassovye otnosheniia v sovremennoi sovetskoi derevne* (Novosibirsk, 1929), p. 94; Zagumennyi, *NLP*, 1–2 (31 January 1928), 32.
56 A. Zventsev, 'K perekhodu na novyi ustav', *SSSK*, 3–4 (1 March 1928), 10; Burkov, 'Deiatel'nost' KPSS', pp. 54–5.
57 Moletotov, pp. 161–2, 329; *IS*, 7–8 (27 April 1928), 16; *III sib. part. konf.*, pp. 47–8 (Syrtsov).
58 *IS*, 5 (15 March 1928), 15; *III sib. part. konf.*, p. 12.
59 *IS*, 1–2 (30 January 1928), 16; S. Ignat, *NAF*, 10 (1928), 82–3.
60 Syrtsov, *Rabotat' po-novomu*, p. 17.
61 P. Ia. Gurov, 'Na kraevom derevenskom soveshchanii (27 fevralia – 3 marta 1927 g.)', *ZS*, 3–4 (1927), 52.
62 *III sib. part. konf.*, p. 49.
63 *Ibid.*, pp. 125–6.
64 S. I. Syrtsov, *Tekushchii moment i zadachi sibirskoi partiinoi organizatsii* (Novosibirsk, 1927), p. 13.
65 See for examples: the editorial, 'Sposobno-li krest'ianstvo stroit' sotsializmu', *NLP*, 2 (15 October 1927) 4; S. Severnyi, 'Rubtsovskaia derevnia segodnia', *NLP*, 3 (15 February 1928), 36–8.
66 P. Parfenov, 'O "zimnikh" kulakakh i ob osennikh resul'tatakh', *NLP*, 4–5 (25 November 1927), 46–55.
67 *Ibid.*, 50.
68 *Ibid.*, 51.
69 M. Belousov, 'Zametki o derevenskikh kommunistakh', *NLP*, 11–12 (28 June 1928), 70–4.
70 Sizykh *et al.*, p. 17.

71 *(XIV) Chetyrnadtsatyi s"ezd VKP (b)*, p. 313.
72 See Carr, *Socialism in One Country*, vol. 2, pp. 466–7; Carr, *Foundations*, vol. 2, pp. 456–8. For the role of the Krestkomy during the grain crisis see pp. 166–7 above.
73 Carr, *Foundations*, vol. 2, pp. 459–63; Gurov, *ZS*, 3–4 (1927), 57; *Za chetkuiu klassovuiu liniiu*, p. 40 (Eikhe to the March 1928 Kraikom plenum); *IS*, 4 (28 February 1929), 10.
74 *Za chetkuiu klassovuiu liniiu*, pp. 83–4 (from his speech to the October 1927 plenum of the Kraikom).
75 *(XV) Piatnadtsatyi s"ezd VKP (b)*, pp. 1220–1 (Molotov), 1282 (Zimin); *Itogi rabota barnaul'skogo*, p. 17.
76 B. Tal', 'O pravo-"levom" bloke', *NAF*, 11–12 (1930), xii.
77 Cohen, p. 234.
78 See pp. 200–4 above.
79 *Pravda*, 3 December 1925, 4; 'Postanovleniia IV plenuma kraiispolkoma, 5–8 dekabria 1926 goda', *ZS*, 1 (1927), 106–7; I. Reshchikov, 'Itogi 2-go kraevogo s"ezda sovetov', *ZS*, 5 (1927), 5. The Siberian control figures are given in E. Sheftel', 'Kredit v kontrol'nykh tsifrakh na 1927–28 g.', *ZS*, 9–10 (1927), 145–52. For the Tel'bes and Turksib projects see Carr and Davies, pp. 436–7, 900–2.
80 See Sheftel', *ZS*, 9–10 (1927), 145–52.
81 Gushchin, *Sibirskaia derevnia*, p. 154.
82 *Ibid.*, p. 155.
83 See for example, N. M. Iukhnev, 'Zemleustroistvo v sibirskom krae', *ZS*, 5 (1927), 26–30.
84 Il'inykh, 'Klassovaia bor'ba', p. 144. For Mesiatsev see also pp. 71–2, 74, 77 above.
85 Extracts of Syrtsov's speech may be found in Moletotov, p. 24; Gurov, *ZS*, 3–4 (1927), 46–64. The Bukharin slogan and retraction are discussed in Carr, *Socialism in One Country*, vol. 1, pp. 259–75, 280–1, 306–7.
86 *III sib. part. konf.*, pp. 21–66, 243–58.
87 *Ibid.*, pp. 28–9.
88 *Ibid.*, pp. 30–1, 43–4.
89 *Ibid.*, p. 197.
90 *Ibid.*, pp. 123–4.
91 *Ibid.*, p. 78 (Novikov), 93–4 (Zimin). For the resolutions see *III-i sibirskoi kraevoi partiinoi konferentsii VKP (b) 25–30 marta 1927 goda, rezoliutsii* (Novosibirsk, 1927), pp. 20–30.
92 *III sib. part. konf.*, p. 49; Syrtsov, *Tekushchii moment*, p. 5.
93 A. Povolotskii, 'Direktivy po sostavleniiu perspektivnogo plana nar. khoz. i kult'urnogo stroitel'stva sibkraia. (stenogramma doklad v prezidiuma sibkraiispolkom), *ZS*, 1 (1928), 5–6. For Stalin and collectivisation see pp. 145–8 above.
94 For official attacks on the Left see the editorial in *NLP*, 2 (15 October 1927), 5–6, and Syrtsov's report on the October joint plenum of the Central

Committee and Central Control Commission in *NLP*, 3 (10 November 1927), 8–19.

3 Who was the Siberian kulak?

1 Carr, *Socialism in One Country*, vol. 1, p. 99.
2 The debate at the centre on the differentiation issue is examined in Carr and Davies, pp. 18–26, 127–32; M. Lewin, 'Who was the Soviet kulak?', *SS*, 28, 4 (October 1966), 189–212, and *Russian Peasants and Soviet Power*, chapters 2 and 3; S. G. Solomon, *The Soviet Agrarian Debate: A Controversy in Social Science, 1923–29* (Boulder, 1977). An exceptional study which considers the regional dimension to the debate (though excluding Siberia) is Shanin, *The Awkward Class*, especially pp. 122–6. For a challenging analysis of the work and influence of the leading Marxist student of differentiation in the 1920s, who drew up the methodological framework for the nationwide comparative research of V. S. Nemchinov and, in Siberia, V. A. Kavraisky and I. I. Nusinov, see T. Cox and G. Littlejohn (eds.), *Kritsman and the Agrarian Marxists* (London, 1984).
3 E. H. Carr, 'Revolution from above: some notes on the decision to collectivise Soviet agriculture' in K. H. Wolff and Barrington Moore Jr (eds.), *The Critical Spirit: Essays in Honour of Herbert Marcuse* (Boston, 1967), p. 325; Lewin, 'Who was the Soviet kulak', p. 197; R. Conquest, *The Harvest of Sorrow: Soviet Collectivisation and the Terror-Famine* (London, 1986), p. 74.
4 See Shanin, *The Awkward Class*, chapters 4–7.
5 *Ibid.*, p. 75.
6 For substantive changes in the Siberian countryside see pp. 95–6 above.
7 Carr and Davies, p. 26.
8 T. Shanin, *Russia as a 'Developing Society'*, vol. 1 (Basingstoke, 1985), pp. 156–7; Lenin, *Sochinenii*, vol. 3, pp. 378–80, 382–3.
9 For Nemchinov's studies, see Davies, *The Socialist Offensive*, pp. 24–6, and the works in note 2 above; V. A. Kavraiskii and I. I. Nusinov, *Klassovoe rassloenie v sibirskoi derevni (opyt analiza sotsial'no–ekonomicheskikh otnoshenii v sovremennoi sovetskoi derevne)* (Novosibirsk, 1927), and *Klassy i klassovye otnosheniia* (1929).
10 Kavraiskii and Nusinov, *Klassovoe rassloenie*, p. 95, and *Klassy i klassovye otnosheniia*, p. 36.
11 Lenin, *Sochinenii*, vol. 3, pp. 115–16; *SSE*, vol. 2, p. 697; Kavraiskii and Nusinov, *Klassovoe rassloenie*, pp. 16–19.
12 Lenin, *Sochinenii*, vol. 39, p. 40, and vol. 40, p. 197.
13 L. D. Trotskii, *Sochineniia*, 21 vols. (Moscow, 1925–7), vol. 17, part 2, pp. 543–4. For Preobrazhenskii's theses see E. H. Carr, *The Bolshevik Revolution, 1917–1923*, vol. 2 (London, 1952), pp. 292–3.
14 Lenin, *Sochinenii*, vol. 45, p. 98.
15 For example, in 1929 ex-tsarist officials constituted 37% of the staff of Narkomfin, 27% of that of Narkomtrud, and 26% of that of Narkomtorg; Carr, *Socialism in One Country*, vol. 1, pp. 129–30. The ultra-Nepist

'neo-populist' triumvirate of A. Chayanov, N. Makarov and A. Chelintsev, all former SRs, headed the influential Scientific Research Institute of Agricultural Economics; Carr and Davies, p. 21; Jasny, *Soviet Economists*, p. 13. For Boldyrev see *SSE*, vol. 1, pp. 363–4; Dotsenko, pp. 51–4.

16 *III sib. part. konf.*, p. 102 (Kul'guskin).

17 Burkov, 'Deiatel'nost' KPSS', p. 98, note 3.

18 See *SSE*, vol. 2, p. 714; F. A. Khorobrykh, 'Kondrat'evshchina i voprosy razvitiia sel'skogo khoziaistva sibiri', *ZS*, 11–12 (1930), 71–93; Gushchin, *Sibirskaia derevnia*, p. 8; Il'inykh, 'Klassovaia bor'ba', pp. 127–8. Kondratiev opposed any tempo of industrialisation which had detrimental impact on the growth of peasant farming; see R. W. Davies, *Soviet History in the Gorbachev Revolution* (London, 1989), p. 189. For Kondratiev's career see Jasny, *Soviet Economists*, pp. 158–78.

19 Gushchin, *Sibirskaia derevnia*, pp. 7–8; *III sib. part. konf.*, p. 247 (Syrtsov).

20 Syrtsov wrote glowing forewords to the publications by Kavraiskii and Nusinov cited in note 9 above.

21 Iarovoi's study was unavailable to the author. For details see Gushchin, *Sibirskaia derevnia*, p. 128; Brike, *NAF*, 6 (1927), 107.

22 *(XIV) Chetyrnadtsatyi s"ezd VKP(b)*, pp. 312–13.

23 Gushchin, *Sibirskaia derevnia*, p. 130.

24 For the work of the commissions see Gurov, *ZS*, 3–4 (1927), 46–8; Syrtsov, *Rabotat' po-novomu*, p. 15; Il'inykh, 'Klassovaia bor'ba', p. 155 (Mesiatsev); Gushchin, *Sibirskaia derevnia*, p. 131 (Omsk).

25 Parfenov, *NLP*, 4–5 (25 November 1927), 47.

26 V. Komarov, 'Ob obizhennikh kulakakh i ikh zashchitniki', *NLP*, 4–5 (25 November 1927), 57.

27 *Otchet biiskogo okruzhkoma VKP(b), s 1 oktiabria 1925 g. do 1 marta 1927 g.* (Biisk, 1927), pp. 6–7.

28 Gushchin, *Sibirskaia derevnia*, p. 131.

29 S. Brike, 'Zapadno-sibirskaia derevnia (Kamenskii okrug)', *NAF*, 7 (1927), 121–3.

30 *Ibid.*, 119, 124.

31 For Zinoviev's use of the data see L. I. Bozhenko, 'Sootnoshenie klassovykh sil v sibirskoi derevne nakanune kollektivizatsii', *Voprosy istorii sibiri*, 4 (Tomsk, 1969), 248. For details of D'iakov's study see Brike, *ZS*, 1 (1927), 25–6; Kavraiskii and Nusinov, *Klassovoe rassloenie*, pp. 35–6, 135.

32 Kavraiskii and Nusinov, *Klassovoe rassloenie*, pp. 36–7.

33 Brike, *ZS*, 1 (1927), 13–34; and see also the articles in *NAF*, 6 (1927), 106–22, and 7 (1927), 113–38.

34 Brike, *ZS*, 1 (1927), 23, and *NAF*, 6 (1927), 107–8. The figures of hidden sowings are in *Pravda*, 6 December 1925, 4.

35 Brike, *ZS*, 1 (1927), 18, and *NAF*, 6 (1927), 106–12, 122.

36 Brike, *ZS*, 1 (1927), 23–4, and *NAF*, 6 (1927), 119–22.

37 Brike, *ZS*, 1 (1927), 23, 25–7.

38 *Ibid.*, 29–30, and *NAF*, 7 (1927), 119, 125.

39 Brike, *NAF*, 6 (1927), 120–1; L. S. Sosnovskii, 'Chetyre pis'ma iz ssylki',

Biulleten' oppozitsii (Paris), 3–4 (September 1929), 16. The author was a close friend of Trotsky, a renowned journalist chronicler of party corruption and a member of the Left Opposition. He was exiled to Barnaul in late 1927, from where he wrote four letters to Trotsky in March–August 1928. For his career details, see Deutscher, *The Prophet Unarmed*, p. 430.

40 Brike, *ZS*, 1 (1927), 31, and *NAF*, 7 (1927), 124.

41 Brike, *NAF*, 6 (1927), 120.

42 For a report of the conference see Gurov, *ZS*, 3–4 (1927), 46–64.

43 *Ibid.*, 47–8.

44 *Ibid.*, 49.

45 Syrtsov, *Rabotat' po-novomu*, p. 14.

46 For extracts of Syrtsov's speech see Gurov, *ZS*, 3–4 (1927), 46–64; Moletotov, pp. 24–5.

47 *III sib. part. konf.*, pp. 31–2. The conference stenographic report was published in two volumes, of which only vol. 1 has been available to the author. Criticisms of Syrtsov's slogan are mentioned in Moletotov, p. 25.

48 *III sib. part. konf.*, p. 33.

49 *Ibid.*, pp. 105 (Tsvetkov), 116 (Malyshev).

50 *Ibid.*, pp. 195–7.

51 *Ibid.*, pp. 212–15 (Nusinov), 220–2 (Brike), 213–18 and 258–9 (Syrtsov).

52 *III-i sibirskoi kraev. part. konf. rez.*, pp. 24–5.

53 S. I. Syrtsov, 'Itogi kraevoi partiinoi konferentsii', *IS*, 3–4 (1927), 4–5.

54 See the articles by Brike in note 33 above.

55 Bergavinov, *Bol'shevik*, 13 (1 July 1927), 81–9. For his report on the Omsk party organisation see p. 37 above.

56 G. Safarov, 'Nastuplenie kapitala v sibirskoi derevne', *Bol'shevik*, 15–16 (31 August 1927), 90–9. For Safarov's political leanings see Deutscher, *The Prophet Unarmed*, pp. 338, 411; Carr, *Foundations*, vol. 2, p. 27 note 2.

57 Syrtsov, *Bol'shevik*, 15–16 (31 August 1927), 100–16.

58 V. Kavraiskii, 'Sostoianie i ocherednye zadachi gosudarstvennoi statistiki v sibiri', *ZS*, 7 (1927), 62–5.

59 Kavraiskii and Nusinov, *Klassovoe rassloenie*, pp. ii, 9, 25, appendix 1; Gushchin, *Sibirskaia derevnia*, p. 132.

60 Kavraiskii and Nusinov, *Klassovoe rassloenie*, pp. v, 33, 35–6, 70–7.

61 *Ibid.*, pp. 27–9, 32.

62 *Ibid.*, appendix 1, Table 15, p. 34; Table 18, p. 36; Table 20 p. 38; Table 25, p. 48; Table 33, p. 50; Gushchin, *Sibirskaia derevnia*, p. 132. For Nemchinov's figure for the number of kulaks in the country, see Davies, *The Socialist Offensive*, pp. 25–6.

63 Kavraiskii and Nusinov, *Klassovoe rassloenie*, pp. 37, 40–1.

64 *Ibid.*, pp. 44–7, 49; Cleinow, pp. 274–5; Osokina, 'Sotsial'no-ekonomicheskie otnosheniia', 276.

65 Kavraiskii and Nusinov, *Klassovoe rassloenie*, pp. 70–2.

66 *Ibid.*, p. 92.

67 Syrtsov, *NLP*, 4–5 (25 November 1927), 36–9.

68 L. Kleitman, 'Kapitalisticheskie tendentsii v sibirskoi derevne', *NLP*, 4–5 (25 November 1927), 88–103.
69 *(XV) Piatnadtsatyi s"ezd VKP (b)*, vol. 1, pp. 274–9.
70 *Ibid.*, vol. 2, pp. 1279, 1281. For the rift between Syrtsov and Zimin see chapter 7.
71 Kavraiskii and Nusinov, *Klassy i klassovye otnosheniia*, pp. 17–21, 25. Their sliding scale identified the kulaks as the following: all farms with means of production to a value exceeding 3,000 roubles; with means of production to a value of 2,000–3,000 and hiring labour or renting out equipment for any period; with a value of 1,251–2,000 roubles and with a sown area of more than 12 desiatinas and hiring labour or renting out equipment for more than 50 days, or with a sown area of up to 12 desiatinas and for more than 125 days; with a value of 501–1,250 roubles and with a sown area of more than 12 and hiring labour or renting out for more than 150 days, or with a sown area of up to 12 and for more than 225 days; with a value of 301–500 roubles and with a sown area of more than 12 and renting out for more than 225 days, or with a sown area of up to 12 and for more than 300 days. See also Gushchin, *Sibirskaia derevnia*, pp. 132–3, note 25.
72 Kavraiskii and Nusinov, *Klassy i klassovye otnosheniia*, pp. 35–9, 83. The Kraikom resolutions may be found in: *Kollektivizatsiia sel'skogo khoziaistvo zapadnoi sibiri (1927–1937 gg.), dokumenty i materialy* (Tomsk, 1972), pp. 35–9 (see clause 5).

4 The crisis of NEP

1 Dohan, 'Soviet foreign trade', pp. 405, 445.
2 Lenin, *Sochinenii*, vol. 44, pp. 206–13.
3 Dohan, 'Soviet foreign trade' pp. 439–45.
4 Carr, *Socialism in One Country*, vol. 1, pp. 192–5; Il'inykh, 'Klassovaia bor'ba', pp. 85–6.
5 Il'inykh, 'Klassovaia bor'ba', pp. 87, and Tables 12 and 13 pp. 241–2; 'Ekonomicheskaia khronika, itogi khlebozagotovki za polugodiia', *ZS*, 5 (1927), 102. The state procurement price for wheat increased from an average of 69.7 kopecks per pud in October 1924 to 112.8 kopecks in May 1925.
6 Carr, *Socialism in One Country*, vol. 1, p. 295; *Pravda*, 25 November 1925, p. 4; *Pravda*, 3 and 18 December 1925, p. 4; Il'inykh, 'Klassovaia bor'ba', Table 17, p. 246. For the grain harvest and state procurement see Table A.2, p. 214 above.
7 Il'inykh, 'Klassovaia bor'ba', pp. 95–6 (for Mesiatsev and Petukhov); R. I. Eikhe, 'Rol' khlebozagotovok v khoziaistve strany', *IS*, 1 (January 1926), 11–13.
8 'Otchet biuro kraikoma. Doklad tov. Lepa "O khlebozagotovkakh"', *IS*, 3 (March 1926), 27–8; Il'inykh, 'Klassovaia bor'ba', p. 98 and Table 11, p. 240.
9 Davies, *The Socialist Offensive*, Table 1, p. 419; Carr and Davies, p. 8.

10 See Table A.2, p. 214 above; Il'inykh, 'Klassovaia bor'ba', Table 20, p. 250 and Table 7, p. 236; B. G. Botvinik, 'Khlebozagotovki', *ZS*, 1 (1927), 35–42.

11 Botvinik, *ZS*, 1 (1927), 37; Gushchin, *Sibirskaia derevnia*, p. 176.

12 Il'inykh, 'Klassovaia bor'ba', Table 21, p. 251; Botvinik, *ZS*, 1 (1927), 39, 41–2; *III sib. part, konf.*, p. 103 (grain losses). Increased state investment in industrialisation at this time is discussed in Davies, *The Socialist Offensive*, pp. 36–8. For Siberian wheat exports see pp. 23–4 above.

13 Carr and Davies, pp. 44–6; *KPSS v rez.*, vol. 4 (1926–9), p. 318.

14 A. Gendon, 'Oshibki i nedochety khlebozagotovitel'noi kampanii', *NLP*, 1–2 (31 January 1928), 8; Gushchin, *Sibirskaia derevnia*, p. 184 gives a significantly lower revised estimate of the shortfall at just over 275,000 tons (42%).

15 Stalin, *Sochineniia*, vol. 11, pp. 4, 42–4; Bukharin, 'Zametki ekonomista', *Pravda*, 30 September 1928; *KPSS v rez.*, vol. 4 (1926–9), pp. 315–23; see also p. 181 above.

16 Conquest, pp. 87–9; Davies, *The Socialist Offensive*, pp. 37–41.

17 Jasny, *The Socialist Agriculture*, p. 727; see also R. W. Davies, 'A note on grain statistics', *SS*, 21, 3 (January 1970), 314–29; S. G. Wheatcroft, 'The reliability of pre-war grain statistics', *SS*, 26, 2 (April 1974), 157–80.

18 J. F. Karcz, 'Back on the grain front', *SS*, 22, 4 (October 1970), 278; see also his 'Thoughts on the grain problem', *SS*, 18, 2 (April 1967), 399–434.

19 Cited in Conquest, p. 88.

20 Jasny, *The Socialist Agriculture*, pp. 223–7; Davies, *The Socialist Offensive*, Table 1, p. 419; *Sel'skoe khoziaistvo SSSR*, p. 295; Carr and Davies, p. 698, and Table 38, p. 1027; Lewin, *Russian Peasants and Soviet Power*, pp. 176–7. The 'Nemchinov Table' is discussed in the articles cited in notes 17 and 18 above, and in Carr and Davies, pp. 916–19.

21 For the harvest and marketings see Tables A.1 and A.2, pp. 213–14 above; Gushchin, *Sibirskaia derevnia*, p. 108. For sowings see Vasil'ev, *ZS*, 9–10 (1927), 29; M. Lukashin, *Kratkie itogi raboty slavgorodsk okruzhkoma VKP (b)* (Slavgorod, 1928), p. 7. Harvest failures are mentioned in Gendon, *NLP*, 1–2 (31 January 1928), 9; S. G. Gendel', 'Sostoianie glavneishikh elementov sel'sko-khoziaistvennaia proizvodstva 1928 g. v sibirskom krae', *ZS*, 2–3 (1929), 98; G. A. Koniukhov, *KPSS v bor'be s khlebnymi zatrudneniiami v strane, 1928–1929 gg.* (Moscow, 1960), p. 65.

22 A. Nove, 'A debate on collectivization. Was Stalin really necessary?', *Problems of Communism*, 25, 4 (July–August 1976), 57.

23 Carr and Davies, p. 46; Davies, *The Socialist Offensive*, p. 40, note 109.

24 Gushchin, *Sibirskaia derevnia*, pp. 108, 118; see also the interview with the chairman of the Biisk Okrug Union of Agricultural and Credit Cooperatives, Sitnikov, in *SSKK*, 1 (1928), 11. For changes in the ratios of products procured see Table A.3, p. 214 above.

25 A. M. Pevzner, 'Tovarooborot dolzhen byt' ozdorovlen', *NLP*, 4 (29 February 1928), 31; A. Timpko, 'Pochemu maslozagotovki idut plokho', *NLP*, 3 (15 February 1928), 16–18; *SSE*, vol. 2, pp. 788–91. See also Gushchin, *Sibirskaia derevnia*, Table 23, p. 116.

26 *Pravda*, 29 January 1926 (from a speech of 19 January); see also Trotskii, 'O smychke', *Pravda*, 6 December 1923.

27 Carr and Davies, p. 46.

28 I. Trelin, 'Platezhesposobnyi spros sibirskoi derevni i snabzhenie ee pro-myshlennymi tovarimi', *ZS*, 1 (1928), 27; *(XV) Piatnadtsatyi s"ezd VKP (b)*, vol. 2, p. 927 (Eikhe); A. Zlobin, 'Oni tozhe za snizhenie tsen!', *NLP*, 4–5 (25 November 1927), 33–4; Koniukhov, p. 91 states that 400 wagons arrived by the end of December 1927.

29 I. Trelin, 'Itogi i perspektivy khlebnykh zagotovok', *NLP*, 1–2 (31 January 1928), 19; Koniukhov, p. 70.

30 L. P. Egorova, 'Khlebozagotovitel'naia kampaniia 1927–1928 gg. i bor'ba s kulachestvom v zapadnosibirskoi derevne', *Voprosy istorii sibiri*, 3 (Tomsk, 1967), 257; Gushchin, *Sibirskaia derevnia*, p. 171.

31 R. I. Eikhe, 'Kapital'noe stroitel'stvo i oppozitsiia', *NLP*, 3 (10 November 1927), 26.

32 Koniukhov, p. 69; Egorova, 'Khlebozagotovitel'naia kampaniia', 257.

33 V. Samsonov, 'Novyi zakon o sel'khoznaloge', *ZS*, 6 (1928), 33; M. Basov-ich, 'Novyi zakon o sel'khoznaloge i zadachi sibpartorganizatsii', *NLP*, 10 (9 June 1928), 3. For the tax reform see Carr and Davies, pp. 753–5. The Kraikombiuro decree on the tax amnesty is published in *Za chetkuiu klasso-vuiu liniiu*, p. 231. The impact of the decree on the peasantry is assessed in P. Doronin, 'O derevene mimokhodom', *NLP*, 1–2 (31 January 1928), 45–6.

34 Kavraiskii and Nusinov, *Klassy i klassovye otnosheniia*, pp. iii, 182–3; Il'inykh, 'Klassovaia bor'ba', p. 90; Egorova, 'Khlebozagotovitel'naia kampaniia', 257.

35 Stalin, *Sochineniia*, vol. 11, pp. 12–14, 44.

36 'Sibkraiispolkom o khlebozagotovkakh', *Vestnik sibirskoi sel'sko-khoziaist-vennoi kooperatsii*, 14 (1 October 1927), 19; A. Strikovskii, 'O galope v kritike potrebitel'skoi kooperatsii', *NLP*, 11–12 (28 June 1928), 27–38; *Kooperativnaia sibir'*, 3 (23 February 1928), 4.

37 Cases of price competition and other abuses by procurement agencies are discussed in S. Naumov, 'Ne oslabliat' tempa raboty', *SSKK*, 3–4 (1928), 13–14, and 'Mel'trest pukhnet, a kreditka khireet', *SSKK*, 1 (1928), 11–13; 'Vesti s mesti', *SSKK*, 2 (1928), 27; Koniukhov, p. 81; Gendon, *NLP*, 1–2 (31 January 1928), 12; *Kooperativnaia sibir'*, 3 (1928), 46. The situation in Kansk is described in M. Gusev, 'O khlebozagotovkakh derevenskikh nastroeniiakh i "tochke zreniia"', *NLP*, 3 (15 February 1928), 31–2.

38 Egorova, 'Khlebozagotovitel'naia kampaniia', 260; 'Vesti s mesti', *SSKK*, 2 (1928), 20; Naumov, *SSKK*, 3–4 (1928), 13–14.

39 Cleinow, p. 408. Cleinow was not only a writer and journalist with a special interest in the Soviet Union, but also a spy for the German Imperial secret service. He made several trips to the Soviet Union during 1922–8 and published books recounting his experiences. For his career see *Neue Deutsche Biographie*, 15 vols. (Munich, 1953–87), vol. 3, pp. 279–80.

40 S. I. Syrtsov, 'Blizhaishie zadachi sibirskoi partiinoi organizatsii (iz rezoliut-sii po dokladu t. Syrtsova na sobranii aktiva novosibirskoi organizatsii VKP

(b) 17 fevralia 1928 g.)', *NLP*, 4 (29 February 1928), 5; A. Zlobin, 'Organizatsiia khlebozagotovok 1928–29 g. (osnovnye voprosy)', *ZS*, 8 (1928), 16–17 (plan); Egorova, 'Khlebozagotovitel'naia kampaniia', 257 (Kraiispolkom cable); Khronin, *ZS*, 11 (1928), 13 (goods supplies).

41 For the problem of grain stockpiles see: *Sel'skaia kooperatsiia*, 1 (1928), 3–5. The chaos on the railway and river transport systems is described in Vl. Pinus, 'Transport i sviaz' v 1927–28 gody', *ZS*, 9–10 (1927), 120–1; Cleinow, p. 409; Koniukhov, p. 125; *III sib. part. konf.*, p. 85 (Nelidov).

42 *(XV) Piatnadtsatyi s"ezd VKP (b)*, vol. 2, p. 927.

43 *Pravda*, 24 December 1927, 4; Cleinow, p. 409; Gendon, *NLP*, 1–2 (31 January 1928), 11.

44 See J. P. Sontag, 'The Soviet war scare of 1926/27', *Russian Review*, 34, 1 (January 1975), 66–77.

45 Il'inykh, 'Klassovaia bor'ba', pp. 74, 132; Syrtsov, *Tekushchii moment*, pp. 3–4, 7.

46 R. I. Eikhe, *Likvidatsiia kulachestvom kak klassa* (Novosibirsk, 1930), p. 7; I. Liashenko, 'O voennoi propagande v derevne', *NLP*, 3 (15 February 1928), 24–5.

47 *Itogi rabota barnaul'skogo*, p. 8. See also Il'inykh, 'Klassovaia bor'ba', pp. 105–6, 128–9, 131–2.

48 Egorova, 'Khlebozagotovitel'naia kampaniia', 261.

49 Lewin, *Russian Peasants and Soviet Power*, p. 32; Koniukhov, p. 77; E. Miroshnik, 'O bor'be s samogonom', *ZS*, 3–4 (1928), 102–5; A. Loktin, 'Rasprostranenie spirtnykh napitkov v sibirskoi derevne', in *Statistika sibiri*, pp. 139–42.

50 Khronin, *ZS*, 11 (1928), 11; Gendon, *NLP*, 1–2 (31 January 1928), 10; Stalin, *Sochineniia*, vol. 11, p. 4; *Istoriia sibiri*, vol. 4, p. 234; Gushchin, *Sibirskaia derevnia*, p. 184. For Stalin's assessment of the nature of the crisis see also pp. 138, 143, 145–8 above.

51 Kavraiskii and Nusinov, *Klassy i klassovye otnosheniia*, pp. 69–79. This was a comparative study of selective spring censuses held in south-west Siberia in 1927 and 1928.

52 *Ibid.*, pp. 70–4, 81; Koniukhov, p. 47.

53 Kavraiskii and Nusinov, *Klassy i klassovye otnosheniia*, p. 75. See also *(XVI) Shestnadtsataia konferentsiia VKP(b), aprel' 1929, stenograficheskii otchet* (Moscow, 1962), p. 320 (Syrtsov); Egorova, 'Khlebozagotovitel'naia kampaniia', 260, 266.

54 Egorova, 'Khlebozagotovitel'naia kampaniia', 260–1; *Za chetkuiu klassovuiu liniiu*, p. 34 (Eikhe); Komarov, *NLP*, 4–5 (25 November 1927), 56–8.

55 *III sib. part. konf.*, p. 43.

56 Iu. S. Kukushkin, 'Kulatski terror v derevne v 1925–1928 gg.', *Istoriia SSSR*, 1 (1966), 98. See Egorova, n. 54 above.

57 Gushchin, *Sibirskaia derevnia*, p. 183; Cleinow, pp. 402–3. See also *Otchet biiskogo okruzhkoma VKP(b)*, p. 10; *Otchet kamenskogo okruzhkoma VKP(b) k chetverti okruzhnoi partiinoi konferentsii* (Kamensk, 1928), p. 4.

5 The end of NEP

1 See Carr and Davies, pp. 33–9; *(XV) Piatnadtsatyi s"ezd VKP(b)*, vol. 2, pp. 1094–5 (Mikoyan), 1164–5 (Rykov), p. 927 (Eikhe).

2 *KPSS v rez.*, vol. 4 (1926–9), p. 13.

3 R. A. Medvedev, *Let History Judge: The Origins and Consequences of Stalinism*, ed. D. Joravsky, trans. C. Taylor (London, 1976) pp. 80–1, and see also the revised and expanded edition, trans. G. Shriver (Oxford, 1989) p. 194; Cohen, pp. 278, 444 note 31.

4 W. Duranty, *Russia Reported* (London, 1934), p. 158; Nove, *An Economic History*, p. 153; Lewin, *Russian Peasants and Soviet Power*, pp. 218–20; Carr, 'Revolution from above', p. 324.

5 Stalin, *Sochineniia*, vol. 6, p. 107 (from a speech made in 1924).

6 Koniukhov, p. 117; A. A. Andreev, *Vospominaniia pis'ma* (Moscow, 1985), pp. 168–9.

7 *(XVI) Shestnadtsatyi s"ezd VKP (b), stenograficheskii otchet* (Moscow, 1930), p. 289. As the Fifteenth Congress lasted from 2–19 December this would date the Stalin–Bukharin split to 21 December.

8 *Pravda*, 24 December 1927, 5; *Pravda*, 28 December 1927, 1; Koniukhov, pp. 119, 122–3; Andreev, p. 208.

9 *Pravda*, 26 January 1928; Koniukhov, pp. 66, 95. For the problems in Smolensk see O. Narkiewicz, 'Soviet administration and the grain crisis of 1927–1928', *SS*, 20, 4 (October 1968), 237–8.

10 *Pravda*, 1 January 1928, 4; *Pravda*, 3 January 1928, 1; *The Times* (London), 3 January 1928, 11.

11 For the directive, see Stalin's letter to all party organisations of 13 February 1928, 'Pervye itogi khlebozagotovitel'noi kampanii i zadachi partii', *Sochineniia*, vol. 11, p. 11; Kas'ian, 'Zapadnosibirskaia derevnia', p. 127.

12 *Pravda*, 6, 8, 9 January 1928; Carr and Davies, pp. 49, 307–11.

13 *Sobranie zakonov i rasporiazhenii, 1928* (Moscow, 1928), part 1, no. 3 article 29, pp. 78–9; Koniukhov, pp. 90–2. For methods of 'social pressure' used by the party in the countryside during the crisis in January 1928, see Stalin, *Sochineniia*, vol. 11, p. 22.

14 The extracts from the telegrams are cited by Syrtsov in his speech to the March 1928 plenum of the Kraikom; *Za chetkuiu klassovuiu liniiu*, pp. 75–6. For the Stalin–Frumkin rift of June 1928, see Stalin, *Sochineniia*, vol. 11, pp. 127–9.

15 *Istoriia kommunisticheskoi partii sovetskogo soiuza* (Moscow, 1970), pp. 544–5; *Izvestiia Ts. K. VKP (b)*, 12–13 (17 April 1928), 1; Koniukhov, pp. 118–21.

16 L. Viola, 'Notes on the background of Soviet collectivisation. Metal worker brigades in the countryside', *SS*, 36, 2 (April, 1984), 207.

17 Koniukhov, pp. 76, 119. Syrtsov told the Kraikom plenum of March 1928 that 'nearly all' the Central Committee Secretaries toured the provinces during the grain crisis; *Za chetkuiu klassovuiu liniiu*, p. 43.

18 Koniukhov, p. 118; A. Avtorkhanov, *Stalin and the Soviet Communist Party: A Study in the Technology of Power* (New York, 1959), p. 11.

19 *Pravda*, 8, 13 January 1928; *The Times* (London), 16 January 1928, 11.

20 Koniukhov, pp. 72–3; *Pravda*, 13 January 1928. According to one source the role of the OGPU in implementing the emergency measures against the peasantry was not formally approved by Sovnarkom (Chairman: Rykov) until a decree of 2 March; P. Reiman, *The Birth of Stalinism: the USSR on the Eve of the 'Second Revolution'*, trans. G. Saunders (London, 1987), pp. 142–5 (based on documents from German diplomatic archives).

21 *The Times* (London), 21 January 1928, 9, and 27 January 1928, 14; Andreev, p. 209 (from a letter to his wife dated 27 January 1928).

22 *The Times* (London), 19 January 1928, p. 12; L. D. Trotskii, *My Life: The Rise and Fall of a Dictator* (London, 1930), pp. 460–1. A similar trip by Rykov to the Volga basin in August 1924 is reported in W. Reswick, *I Dreamt Revolution* (Chicago, 1952), pp. 84–90.

23 *Istoriia sibiri*, vol. 4, p. 235; S. Alliluyeva, *20 Letters to a Friend* (London, 1968), p. 74.

24 Stalin, *Sochineniia*, vol. 11, p. 369; Koniukhov, p. 118.

25 Avtorkhanov, p. 11; Stalin, *Sochineniia*, vol. 4, p. 118, and vol. 11, p. 11.

26 For this decree see *SSKK*, 1 (15 January 1928), 7–8.

27 M. Novikov, 'Neobkhodimo dobit'sia pereloma', *SSKK*, 2 (5 February 1928), 19; Egorova, 'Khlebozagotovitel'naia kampaniia', 263; Koniukhov, p. 122.

28 Egorova, 'Khlebozagotovitel'naia kampaniia', 262, 264–5; Zagumennyi, *NLP*, 1–2 (31 January 1928), 34; G. Doronin, *Krasnaia sibiriachka*, 1 (1928), 9; *Sobranie zak. i rasp.*, 1928, part 1, no. 3, article 25, pp. 74–5.

29 *Za chetkuiu klassovuiu liniiu*, p. 74. From his speech to the March 1928 plenum of the Kraikom.

30 See the resolutions of the March 1928 plenum of the Kraikom in *ZS*, 2 (1928), 6, and Syrtsov's speech at the plenum; *Za chetkuiu klassovuiu liniiu*, p. 78.

31 Gushchin, *Sibirskaia derevnia*, p. 185; Egorova, 'Khlebozagotovitel'naia kampaniia', 262.

32 Trelin, *NLP*, 1–2 (31 January 1928), 17; *Kollektivizatsiia s. kh. zap. sib.*, p. 32; *Pravda*, 14 January 1928, 3.

33 S. Naumov, 'K apreliu nuzhno zagotovit' ne men'she 80–85% godovogo plana', *SSKK*, 1 (15 January 1928), 9; Novikov, *SSKK*, 2 (5 February 1928), 18; Gendon, *NLP*, 1–2 (31 January 1928), 9; L. Strikovskii, 'Zadanie dolzhno byt' vypolneno', *Sel'skaia kooperatsiia*, 1 (19 January 1928), 4; *Pravda*, 14 January 1928, 3.

34 Koniukhov, p. 96; Egorova, 'Khlebozagotovitel'naia kampaniia', 262; I. Trelin, 'O tovarosnabzhenii i tovarnom golode', *NLP*, 3 (15 February 1928), 12–13; *SSKK*, 1 (15 January 1928), 8 (advertisements); S. Sergeev, 'Eshche ob iskrivleniiakh i nedochetakh nashego rukovodtsva (tovarnoe snabzhenie)', *NLP*, 4 (29 February 1928), 22–6.

35 *Za chetkuiu klassovuiu liniiu*, p. 76; Avtorkhanov, pp. 11–12.

36 *Istoriia sibiri*, vol. 4, p. 234; Stalin, *Sochineniia*, vol. 11, p. 359; Egorova, 'Khlebozagotovitel'naia kampaniia', 263; Gushchin (ed.), *Krest'ianstvo sibiri*, p. 210; *Za chetkuiu klassovuiu liniiu*, p. 43 (Syrtsov on Dogadov's

activities); Burkov, 'Deiatel'nost' KPSS', pp. 34–5, 96 reports that Siberia was also visited at various times during the crisis by Mikoyan, Kosior, Kubiak, Postyshev and others. For Stalin's pomoshchniki see N. E. Rosenfeldt; *Knowledge and Power: The Role of Stalin's Secret Chancellery in the Soviet System of Government* (Copenhagen, 1978), pp. 87–91, 182.

37 Stalin, *Sochineniia*, vol. 11, pp. 1–9; Gushchin and Il'inykh, pp. 172–3. V. V. Demidov, 'Khlebozagotovitel'naia kampaniia 1927/28g. v sibirskoi derevne' in V. I. Shishkin (ed.), *Aktual'nye problemy istorii sovetskoi sibiri, sbornik nauchnykh trudov* (Novosibirsk, 1990), pp. 123–40 at p. 125. Excerpts from the decree are published in *Kollektivizatsiia s. kh. zap. sib.*, pp. 32–3, 321 note 6. It incorporated the instructions of the Central Committee directive of 6 January 1928.

38 Stalin, *Sochineniia*, pp. 1–2; *Za chetkuiu klassovuiu liniiu*, p. 76 (from Syrtsov's report to the March plenum); *(XV) Piatnadtsatyi s"ezd VKP(b)*, p. 67.

39 Egorova, 'Khlebozagotovitel'naia kampaniia', 263.

40 Stalin, *Sochineniia*, vol. 11, pp. 3, 369; *Za chetkuiu klassovuiu liniiu*, p. 56 (from Syrtsov's speech of 17 February 1928 to the Novosibirsk party *actif*).

41 Egorova, 'Khlebozagotovitel'naia kampaniia', 263; Gushchin and Il'inykh, p. 173. See also note 37 above.

42 Avtorkhanov, p. 14; Stalin, *Sochineniia*, vol. 11 p. 4. For the Kraiispolkom decree on the distribution of 25% of the confiscated grain, see *SSKK*, 2 (5 February 1928), 62.

43 Stalin, *Sochineniia*, vol. 11, pp. 369–70; Egorova, 'Khlebozagotovitel'naia kampanii', 260–2; Sosnovskii, 'Chetyre pis'ma', 27.

44 Stalin, *Sochineniia*, vol. 11, p. 2. For Khrushchev's comment see his 'Secret Speech' of 1956 in *Khrushchev Remembers*, trans. and ed. Strobe Talbot (London, 1971), p. 610.

45 Stalin, *Sochineniia*, vol. 11, pp. 3–4, 13.

46 *Ibid.*, p. 235.

47 *Ibid.*, p. 105.

48 *Ibid.*, p. 4.

49 Avtorkhanov, p. 12.

50 Stalin, *Sochineniia*, vol. 11, p. 18.

51 For the 'Ural–Siberian Method' see Y. Taniuchi, 'A note on the Ural–Siberian method', *SS*, 33, 4 (October 1981), 519–21. For the confusion of emergency measures in early 1928 with the 'Ural–Siberian Method' of early 1929 see: Nove, *An Economic History*, p. 153; Tucker, *Stalin as Revolutionary*, p. 409.

52 Avtorkhanov, p. 12; Stalin, *Sochineniia*, vol. 12, p. 90.

53 *(XV) Piatnadtsatyi s"ezd VKP(b)*, vol. 2, pp. 1419–21.

54 Stalin, *Sochineniia*, vol. 11, pp. 5–9. Note that this version is an edited record of speeches made by Stalin in various parts of Siberia.

55 *(XV) Piatnadtsatyi s"ezd VKP (b)*, vol. 1, p. 63. According to Avtorkhanov, p. 15, Stalin returned to Moscow with a resolution endorsed by the Urals and Siberian party committees in favour of the acceleration of collectivisation. If

this report is accurate, no doubt Stalin intended to show that there was a radical upsurge 'from below' in support of his proposals.

56 R. H. McNeal, *Stalin: Man and Ruler* (Basingstoke, 1989), p. 117.
57 For the resolutions of the March 1928 plenum of the Kraikom see pp. 192–3 above. The editorial of *NLP*, 1–2 (31 January 1928), 3, published at the height of Stalin's tour, concluded with the slogan: 'Countryside – forward to large scale collective farming'.
58 Gushchin, *Sibirskaia derevnia*, p. 188; Gushchin (ed.), *Krest'ianstvo sibiri*, p. 211.
59 Stalin, *Sochineniia*, vol. 11, pp. 15–16, 46.

6 The emergency measures

1   Lenin, *Sochinenii*, vol. 31, p. 419.
2   Schapiro, p. 267; Carr, *Socialism in One Country*, vol. 1, pp. 68–73.
3   Cohen, p. 270.
4   Schapiro, p. 268; Lenin, *Sochinenii*, vol. 45, p. 200; *Sobranie uzak. i rasp.*, 1922, no. 36, article 424.
5   *Sobranie uzak. i rasp.*, 1922, no. 69, article 902; P. H. Solomon Jr, 'Local political power and Soviet criminal justice, 1922–1941', *SS*, 37, 3 (July 1985), 306–7; Fainsod, pp. 178–9.
6   V. I. Zaitseva and A. P. Ugrovatov, 'Rabota profsoiuza sel'skokhoziaist-vennik i lesnykh rabochnik i organov iustitsii po zazhite prav batrachestva sibiri (1925–1930 gg.)', in Gushchin (ed.), *Problemy istorii*, pp. 110–11; *IS*, 5 (15 March 1928), 15 (a survey of the quantity and social content of the membership of Siberian raion party organisations and institutions on 1 October 1927).
7   See Carr, *Socialism in One Country*, vol. 2, pp. 468–71.
8   *Sobranie uzak. i rasp.*, 1926, part 1, no. 80, article 600.
9   See R. Beerman, 'The grain problem and anti-speculation laws', *SS*, 19, 3 (July 1967), 127–9.
10 I. Leonidov and A. Reikhbaum, 'Revoliutsionnaia zakonnost' i khleboza-gotovki', *NLP*, 1–2 (31 January 1928), 36–40.
11 O. Barabashev, 'Pis'mo', *NLP*, 3 (15 February 1928), 43. For Barabashev see Carr, *Socialism in One Country*, vol. 2, pp. 118, 177.
12 O. Barabashev, 'Isil'kul'skie zheleznodorozhniki o khlebe', *NLP*, 1 (31 January 1928), 47–8.
13 Sosnovskii, 'Chetyre pis'ma', 18.
14 Cleinow, p. 385.
15 Syrtsov, 'V dal'neishee nastuplenie na kulaka', *Za chetkuiu klassovuiu liniiu*, pp. 62–82, especially pp. 74, 82.
16 Stalin, *Sochineniia*, vol. 11, pp. 10–19.
17 Syrtsov, 'Nekotorye uroki khlebozagotovok (iz doklada na sobranii aktiva novosibirskoi organizatsii, 17 fevralia 1928 g.)', *Za chetkuiu klassovuiu liniiu*, pp. 42–61, and see also pp. 79–81, 102.
18 See the articles by Syrtsov in *Pravda*, 14 and 29 February 1928, 3; Gushchin,

Sibirskaia derevnia, pp. 186, 190; Gushchin (ed.), *Krest'ianstvo Sibiri*, p. 211; see Table A.2, p. 214 above.

19 Miroshnik, *ZS*, 3–4 (1928), 102–3; Egorova, 'Khlebozagotovitel'naia kampaniia', 267.

20 See Table A.4, p. 215 above. For indicators of kulak status see p. 232, note 71 above.

21 *Za chetkuiu klassovuiu liniiu*, p. 57.

22 *Pravda*, 15 February 1928 (Syrtsov); Kasvraiskii and Nusinov, *Klassy i klassovye otnosheniia*, pp. 82–3; Koniukhov, pp. 75, 101.

23 Kavraiskii and Nusinov, *Klassy i klassovye otnosheniia*, pp. 115–16; *Pravda*, 15 February 1928 (Syrtsov); N. Leonidov (deputy Krai Procurator), 'Protiv dolzhnostnogo bezdeistviia v khlebozagotovkakh', *Na sovetskom postu*, 2 (1928), 2–3; Gushchin, *Sibirskaia derevnia*, p. 190; Egorova, 'Khlebozagotovitel'naia kampaniia', 267; Koniukhov, p. 125.

24 Koniukhov, p. 100.

25 *KPSS v rez.*, vol. 4 (1926–9), p. 311; *IS*, 1–2 (30 January 1928), 11; *Za chetkuiu klassovuiu liniiu*, pp. 236–8.

26 Gushchin (ed.), *Krest'ianstvo sibiri*, p. 210; Egorova, 'Khlebozagotovitel'naia kampaniia', 267; Koniukhov, pp. 101, 125; A. Gendon, 'Bednota i kulachestvo (o klassovoi bor'be v derevne i nashikh zadachakh)', *NLP*, 3 (15 February 1928), 18–23.

27 Sosnovskii, 'Chetyre pis'ma', 16, 27.

28 *Resheniia pervoi barnaul'skoi okruzhnoi konferentsii bednoty* (Barnaul, 1928), pp. 4–5.

29 Stalin, *Sochineniia*, vol. 11, p. 18; 'Iz reshenii biuro kraikoma o samooblozhenii (ot 22 fevraliia 1928 g.)', *Za chetkuiu klassovuiu liniiu*, pp. 234–5.

30 *Krasnaia sibiriachka*, 4 (1928), 4; Gendon, *NLP*, 3 (15 February 1928), 20–1 (Ukrainka); P. S., 'Prosevali', *NLP*, 3 (15 February 1928), 68–9 (Dubrovino).

31 Egorova, 'Khlebozagotovitel'naia kampaniia', 265; Koniukhov, p. 126; V. Boldyrev, 'Khoziaistvennye itogi 1 polygodiia 1927–28 g.', *ZS*, 5 (1928), 97; N. Beliaev, 'Zaem ukrepleniia krest'ianskogo khoziaistva', *Krasnaia sibiriachka*, 2 (1928), 20; Trusevich, *Krasnaia sibiriachka*, 4 (1928), 3; M. Basovich, 'Zametki o praktike samooblozhenii', *NLP*, 6 (31 March 1928), 30; P. Semenikhin, 'Itogi i novye zadachi po samooblozheniiu', *NLP*, 21 (15 November 1928), 3.

32 R. Kisis, 'Khlebozagotovki i partrabota v derevne', *NLP*, 3 (15 February 1928), 6–9.

33 *Za chetkuiu klassovuiu liniiu*, pp. 64, 148.

34 Sosnovskii, 'Chetyre pis'ma', 16–17 (from a letter dated March 1928); Koniukhov, p. 124.

35 M. Gusev, 'O khlebozagotovkakh derevenskikh nastroeniiakh i "tochke zreniia"', *NLP*, 3 (15 February 1928), 29–34.

36 'Est'-li v derevne mezhevoi kulaki', *Na sovetskom postu*, 9 (1928), 19–20 (Mezhevo); Belousov, *NLP*, 11–12 (28 June 1928), 72 (Novoselovsk); I. Nusinov, 'Khlebozagotovitel'nye piatna (ob oshibkakh rubtsovskikh tovarishchei)', *NLP*, 4 (29 February 1928), 18–20 (Berezovsk).

37 A. Gendon, 'Oshibki v regulirovanii rosta partorganizatsii', *NLP*, 10 (9 June 1928), 24 (Tat'ianovsk); M. Belousov, N Kudriatsev, 'Zametki o derevenskikh kommunistakh', *NLP*, 7–8 (25 April 1928), 70–1 (Kalichenko and Gutovsk).

38 Lukashin, p. 50

39 Bor. G., 'Istoriia s arifmetikoi', *NLP*, 5 (20 March 1928), 40–1; *Za chetkuiu klassovuiu liniiu*, p. 81 (Syrtsov to the March 1928 Kraikom plenum, citing his speech of 17 February 1928).

40 Egorova, 'Khlebozagotovitel'naia kampaniia', 266; Koniukhov, pp. 126, 146–7; Gushchin (ed.), *Kresti'anstvo sibiri*, p. 211.

41 *SSE*, vol. 2, pp. 1049–50 (Krestkomy); *Kollektivizatsiia s. kh. zap. sib.*, p. 62. One Western scholar dismissed Stalin's promise to the poor of a 25% share of confiscated grain, believing he was 'unlikely to stick to this'; A. B. Ulam, *Stalin: The Man and his Era* (London, 1973), p. 298.

42 B. Kavraiskii, 'Khleb proveriaet apparat', *NLP*, 3 (15 February 1928), 34–6.

43 Gendon, *NLP*, 1–2 (31 January 1928), 11; 'Po okruzhnym gazetam', *Kooperativnaia sibir'*, 3 (23 February 1928), 46–7.

44 P. Ligadeev, S. Ragatskin, 'Torgashi ili tsivilizovannye kooperatory', *NLP*, 7–8 (25 April 1928), 35; G. Shibailo, 'Potrebitel'skaia kooperatsiia na khlebozagotovitel'nom fronte', *NLP*, 7–8 (25 April 1928), 40.

45 'Po okruzhnym gazetam', *Kooperativnaia sibir'*, 3 (23 February 1928), 46; S. Naumov, 'Plan vypolnit' mozhno', *SSKK*, 2 (5 February 1928), 15, and 18–19 (for the decree).

46 Egorova, 'Khlebozagotovitel'naia kampaniia', 263; *Sobranie uzak. i rasp.*, 1926, part 1, no. 80, article 600, p. 975.

47 For events in Tomsk and Irkutsk, see 'Proverit' khlebozagotovitelei – privlech' vinovykh k otvetstvennosti', *Na sovetskom postu*, 2 (1928), 2–3; B. Kavraiskii, 'Problema kadrov nizovogo sovetskogo apparat', *NLP*, 10 (9 June 1928), 31; Egorova, 'Khlebozagotovitel'naia kampaniia', 263 (Biisk); 'Sel'kor znaiushchii "Pochemu zhe ran'she ne pointeresovalis?"', *SSKK*, 3–4 (1 March 1928), 68–9 (Smolianinsk scandal).

48 Burkov, 'Deiatel'nost' KPSS', p. 96; Gushchin, *Sibirskaia derevnia*, pp. 187–8. For Povolotsky's dismissal see p. 148 above. For Stalin's 'Dizzy with success' article see *Pravda*, 2 March 1930.

49 'Ne oslabliat' vnimaniia khlebozagotovkam', *NLP*, 3 (15 February 1928), 3–5; A. Pevzner, 'O nedostatakh nashego rukovodstva khoziaistvennoi rabotoi', *NLP*, 3 (15 February 1928), 45.

50 L. Iuzhnyi, 'O Nepe', *NLP*, 4 (29 February 1928), 13–14. The Dawes Plan had been adopted by the Western Allies in April 1924 to extract German war reparations and was denounced by the Soviet government as extortionist.

51 Sosnovskii, 'Chetyre pis'ma', 17; A. Kulikov, 'Proverim kachestvo raboty', *V pomoshch' zemledel'tsu*, 6 (1 May 1928), 1.

52 Nusinov, *NLP*, 4 (29 February 1928), 19–20.

53 *Za chetkuiu klassovuiu liniiu*, pp. 51, 56, 102.

54 *Ibid.*, p. 57.

55 Sosnovskii, 'Chetyre pis'ma', 18; A. Gendon, 'Posevnye zametki', *NLP*, 7–8 (25 April 1928), 53.
56 Gushchin and Il'inykh, p. 176; Demidov, p. 137.
57 Kunov, 'Zakon na strazhe interesov krest'ianstva', *V pomoshch' zemledel'tsu*, 3–4 (20 March 1928), 5–6; Leonidov, 'Za revoliutsionnuiu zakonnost'', *Na sovetskom postu*, 4 (1928), 2–3; *Sobranie uzak. i rasp.*, 1926, part 1, no. 80, article 600, p. 974.
58 *Itogi rabota barnaul'skogo*, pp. 17–18.
59 'Iz resheniia biuro kraikoma ob itogakh primeneniia 107 stat'i (ot 5 iiunia 1928 g.)', *Za chetkuiu klassovuiu liniiu*, p. 251; Demidov, pp. 134, 136.
60 *(XVI) Shestnadtsataia konferentsiia VKP (b)*, pp. 320–3; A. Agranovskii, 'O maslozagotovkakh i sibirskoi korove', *NLP*, 4 (29 February 1928), 33.
61 *Za chetkuiu klassovuiu liniiu*, p. 104 (from his speech of 17 February 1928).
62 Compare this with his speech to the Fifteenth Congress in December 1927, see pp. 93–4 above.
63 Egorova, 'Khlebozagotovitel'naia kampaniia', 264, 268; Koniukhov, p. 103; *Otchet kamenskogo*, p. 6.
64 Severnyi, *NLP*, 3 (15 February 1928), 38–9; Gendon, *NLP*, 7–8 (25 April 1928), 55–6.
65 Egorova, 'Khlebozagotovitel'naia kampaniia', 266–7; Gushchin, *Sibirskaia derevnia*, table 47, p. 198. For the peasant revolt of 1921–2, see pp. 22, 30 above.
66 G. Doronin, *Des'iat let bor'by rabotnits i krest'ianok sibiri* (Novosibirsk, 1930), p. 38; Koniukhov, p. 103; V. A. Kavraiskii and I. I. Nusinov, *Klassy i klassovaia bor'ba v sovremmenoi derevne* (Novosibirsk, 1929), pp. 143–4; *Za chetkuiu klassovuiu liniiu*, p. 152 (Syrtsov).
67 Sosnovskii, 'Chetyre pis'ma', 23.
68 *Ibid.*; *Za chetkuiu klassovuiu liniiu*, pp. 66, 151. Fear of an army revolt gripped the central party leadership also, see R. V. Daniels, *The Conscience of the Revolution: Communist Opposition in Soviet Russia* (Cambridge, Mass., 1960), p. 333.
69 A. Podchasova, 'Nekotorye uroki karasukskikh sobytii', *NLP*, 13–14 (31 July 1928), 20–5; Egorova, 'Khlebozagotovitel'naia kampaniia', 268. The phenomenon of peasant women's riots was to become a common feature of the collectivisation campaign in 1929–30, see L. Viola, 'Bab'i bunty and peasant women's protest during collectivization', *Russian Review*, 45, 1 (January, 1986), 23–42.
70 Burkov, 'Deiatel'nost' KPSS', pp. 95–6. Apparently, Rykov clashed with Stalin, immediately on his return from Siberia; *Sotsialisticheskii vestnik* (Berlin), 14 (23 July 1928), 14. At the Sixteenth Congress in July 1929 Stalin derided Rykov and Bukharin for reading letters from peasants and for the 'comical howls' with which they had greeted the emergency measures; Stalin, *Sochineniia*, vol. 12, pp. 75, 96.
71 *NLP*, 3 (15 February 1928), 3 (editorial); *Pravda*, 2 March 1928; Gushchin, *Sibirskaia derevnia*, p. 186; Stalin, *Sochineniia*, vol. 11, pp. 15–17.
72 Barabashev, *NLP*, 3 (15 February 1928), 39–40.
73 Koniukhov, p. 102.

74 See the articles by S. Naumov, 'Ne oslabliiat' tempa raboty', *SSKK*, 3–4 (1 March 1928), 13–14; 'K pervomu iiulia – na vse 100%', *SSKK*, 6 (25 April 1928), 19–20; 'Vse sily na usilenie khlebozagotovok', *SSKK*, 7 (25 May 1928), 27.
75 *KPSS v rez.*, vol. 4 (1926–9), pp. 315–33; Lewin, *Russian Peasants and Soviet Power*, pp. 237–42; Gushchin, *Sibirskaia derevnia*, pp. 105, 108, 186–7.
76 Timpko, *NLP*, 3 (15 February 1928), 16–17; Gushchin, *Sibirskaia derevnia*, pp. 108, 115–16, 121–2; *Sel'skoe khoziaistvo SSSR*, pp. 294–5, 298–9, 324–7, 330–1; *Vneshniaia torgovlia SSSR*, pp. 94, 110 (grain exports), and 94, 113 (butter exports).

7 The Irkutsk affair

1 The author had access to part one of the stenographic report of the plenum: *Plenum sibirskogo kraevogo komiteta VKP (b), 3–7 marta 1928 goda, stenograficheskii otchet*, part 1 (Novosibirsk, 1928). Long extracts of the speeches of Syrtsov and Eikhe to the plenum are published in *Za chetkuiu klassovuiu liniiu*, pp. 62–82, 145–54 (Syrtsov), and pp. 34–41 (Eikhe). The content of Zimin's speech has been construed from rebuttals made by Syrtsov and Eikhe.
2 *Plenum sib. kraev. kom.*, pp. 3, 50.
3 Eikhe, 'O nedochetakh i izvrashcheniiakh v khlebozagotovkakh', *Za chetkuiu klassovuiu liniiu*, pp. 34–41.
4 *Plenum sib. kraev. kom.*, p. 53.
5 See Stalin, *Sochineniia*, vol. 11, pp. 15–16.
6 *Za chetkuiu klassovuiu liniiu*, pp. 62–5.
7 *Ibid.*, pp. 66, 68–9, 78. See also p. 155 above.
8 *Ibid.*, pp. 74–5, 77.
9 *Ibid.*, p. 78.
10 *Ibid.*, pp. 68, 81–2. For a sample of trials held in south-west Siberia see Table A.4, p. 215 above.
11 *Ibid.*, pp. 68, 81–2; *Plenum sib. kraev. kom.*, p. 51. N. N. Zimin (1895–1938) was a Russian, the son of a schoolteacher from Porkhov, Pskov Guberniia, and had an exemplary record of party service. Like Syrtsov and Eikhe he joined the party at an early age, in 1915, while still a law student at Moscow University. He was promoted rapidly in 1917–18, serving on the Moscow Party Committee and as Chief of Staff of the Red Guards in the city. During the civil war he was appointed Deputy Secretary of the Moscow Raikom, and then Military Commissar of the Moscow railway network. He was also a member of the Collegium of the Cheka and was decorated as a 'distinguished chekist' for leading the campaign to liquidate 'anti-soviet' peasant bands in the Povolzhe. He was appointed Irkutsk Okruzhkom Secretary in late 1925, presumably as part of the series of changes made by Stalin to place loyal anti-Leftists in strategic positions in the party apparatus. His career details are in: *Soratniki, biografii aktivnykh uchastnikov*

revoliutsionnogo dvizheniia v moskve i moskovskoi oblastii (Moscow, 1985), pp. 171–2; *SSE*, vol. 1, p. 154.

12 For the resolutions, see 'Rezoliutsii IV plenuma sibraikoma VKP (b) o blizhaishikh khoziaistvenno-politicheskikh zadachakh', *IS*, 5 (15 March 1928), 7–11, or *ZS*, 2 (1928), 5–12. Selected extracts may be found in *Kollektivizatsiia s. kh. zap. sib.*, pp. 35–9.

13 'Rezoliutsii', *IS*, 5 (15 March 1928), 7–11; *Pravda*, 10 March 1928, 5.

14 For the intra-regional rivalries see p. 29 above.

15 Moletotov, pp. 43–4. Sharangovich later perished as one of the accused in the Bukharin show trial of 1938.

16 'O poloshenii v irkutskoi okrpartorganizatsii VKP (b)', *IS*, 11–12 (July 1928), 12–13. For the nomenklatura of the Central Committee see Rigby, 'Staffing USSR incorporated', 530–3.

17 Compare this with Stalin's sacrificing of Povolotsky in January 1928, see p. 148 above. The Central Committee directive on the 'Irkutsk affair' was published in *Pravda*, 2 August 1928 and *Izv. Ts. K. VKP (b)*, 24 (10 August 1928), 8–9.

18 Sosnovskii, 'Chetyre pis'ma', 24–5 (from a letter dated 28 July–22 August 1928).

19 See R. Kisis, 'O samokritike' (a speech to the Kraikombiuro session of 12 June 1928) in *Za chetkuiu klassovuiu liniiu*, pp. 130–1, and *NLP*, 11–12 (28 June 1928), 14. One Kraikom member (Kentman) expressed the hope that the wave of self-criticism against the Kuznetsk Okruzhkom 'will sweep it away'; *Za chetkuiu klassovuiu liniiu*, p. 131. Kuznetsk had already been the target of a Kraikombiuro denunciation on the 18 February over excessive use of Article 107, see p. 172 above. For the Leftist tendencies of Zimin and Novikov as regards rapid industrialisation, see *III sib. part. konf.*, pp. 78, 93–4.

20 D. R. Brower, 'The Smolensk scandal and the end of NEP', *Slavic Review*, 45, 4 (December 1986), 690; Cohen, pp. 279–80.

21 Avtorkhanov, p. 13; Sosnovskii, 'Chetyre pis'ma', 23; *Istoriia sibiri*, vol. 4, p. 241.

22 *Za chetkuiu klassovuiu liniiu*, p. 159; *Itogi rabota barnaul'skogo*, p. 7.

23 *Osnovnye itogi raboty (Irkutsk)*, pp. 32, 34, 37.

24 L. Zakovskii, 'O gosorganakh, podbore liudei i soprotivlenii apparatov provedeniiu partiinoi politiki', *NLP*, 6 (31 March 1928), 18–19; Strikovskii, *NLP*, 11–12 (28 June 1928), 27–8.

25 Zaitsev and Ugrovatov, 'Rabota profsoiuza' in Gushchin (ed.), *Problemy istorii*, pp. 116–18; *IS*, 5 (15 March 1928), 15.

26 *Za chetkuiu klassovuiu liniiu*, pp. 262–3.

27 'Pism'o iz sibkraikoma VKP (b)', *IS*, 22 (20 December 1928), 3; *IS*, 1–2 (31 January 1930), 26 (results of the purge of the Siberian party); Sizykh, 'Fakty o rabote sredi batrakov (biiskii okrug)', *NLP*, 4 (25 February 1929), 52–6; Burkov, 'Deiatel'nost' KPSS', pp. 19–21.

28 Compare the list of office-holders in *III sib. part. konf.*, pp. 293–6 and *IS*, 5–6 (25 March 1929), 4–5.

29 Stalin, *Sochineniia*, vol. 11, pp. 15–16. For Zimin's promotion, see *SSE*, vol. 1, p. 154; *Soratniki*, p. 172; Moletotov, pp. 54, 267. Stalin's use of the Orgraspred in the struggle against the Right in Moscow is discussed in C. Merridale, 'The reluctant opposition: the right "deviation" in Moscow, 1928', *SS*, 41, 3 (July 1989), 382–400.

30 See Cohen, pp. 322–9.

31 Tucker, *Stalin as Revolutionary*, p. 303.

32 Cohen, pp. 327, 458–9 notes 236, 245.

33 A Gendon, *Chto skazala IV sibirskaia kraevaia konferentsiia VKP (b)* (Novosibirsk, 1929), p. 19. For Syrtsov's speech to the Sixteenth Conference see pp. 174–5 above.

34 *BSE*, vol. 25, p. 141.

35 For Zimin's movements see note 29 above.

36 Syrtsov's speech is discussed in N. Siokawa, 'Politicheskaia situatsiia v SSSR, Osen' 1930 goda', *Acta Slavonica Iaponica*, 7 (1989), 37–8; R. W. Davies, 'The Syrtsov–Lominadze affair', *SS*, 33, 1 (January 1981), 38–42. Syrtsov's encouragement of a fast tempo of collectivisation is cited in R. W. Davies, *The Industrialisation of Soviet Russia*, vol. 2, *The Soviet Collective Farm, 1929–1930* (London, 1981), p. 82.

37 *Pravda*, 23 October 1930, 2; *Pravda*, 3 November 1930, 2.

38 For the fall of Syrtsov see Siokawa, 'Politicheskaia situatsiia', 33–45; Davies, 'The Syrtsov–Lominadze affair', 42–5. Eikhe's denunciation of Syrtsov at a Kraikom plenum in the autumn of 1930 focussed on his policy errors rather than the charge of conspiracy; *SSE*, vol. 4 (unpublished proof, Novosibirsk, 1935), pp. 351–2. Syrtsov was placed in charge of a phonograph factory and executed in 1937; *BSE*, vol. 25, p. 141; Medvedev, *Let History Judge* (1976), p. 142.

39 T. H. Rigby, 'Was Stalin a disloyal patron?', *SS*, 38, 3 (July 1986), 315.

Bibliography

Newspapers, journals and periodicals (place of publication is Novosibirsk unless otherwise stated).

Acta Slavonica Iaponica (Sapporo)
Agricultural History (Berkeley)
Bol'shevik (Moscow)
Biulleten' oppozitsii (Paris)
Istoriia SSSR (Moscow)
Iz istorii partiinykh organizatsii vostochnoi sibiri (Irkutsk)
Izvestiia sibkraikoma VKP(b)
Izvestiia tsentral'nogo komiteta VKP(b) (Moscow)
Journal of Communist Studies (London)
Kooperativnaia sibir'
Krasnaia sibiriachka
Na agrarnom fronte (Moscow)
Na Leninskom puti
Na sovetskom postu
Pravda (Moscow)
Problems of Communism (Washington D.C.)
Propagandist
Russian History (Pittsburgh)
Russian Review (Colombus)
Sel'skaia kooperatsiia
Sibirskaia sel'sko-khoziaistvennaia kooperatsiia
Slavic Review (Urbana-Champaign and Austin)
Sobranie uzakonenii i rasporiazhenii (Moscow)
Sobranie zakonov i rasporiazhenii (Moscow)
Sotsialisticheskii vestnik (Berlin)
Sovetskoe stroitel'stvo (Moscow)
Soviet Studies (Oxford and Glasgow)

The Times (London)
V pomoshch' zemledel'tsu
Vestnik sibirskoi sel'sko-khoziaistvennoi kooperatsii
Voprosy istorii sibiri (Tomsk)
Zhizn' sibiri

Books, theses and selected articles in Russian

Andreev, A. A. *Vospominaniia pis'ma*, Moscow, 1985.
Bol'shaia sovetskaia entsiklopediia, 3rd edn, 30 vols., Moscow, 1970–8.
Bozhenko, L. I. 'Sootnoshenie klassovykh sil v sibirskoi derevne naka-
    nune kollektivizatsii', *Voprosy istorii sibiri*, 4 (Tomsk, 1969), 237–52.
Burkov, V. N. 'Deiatel'nost' KPSS po ukrepleniia derevenskikh partii-
    nikh organizatsii zapadnoi sibiri v usloviiakh podgotovki i prove-
    deniia massovoi kollektivizatsii, 1927–1932 gg., *dissertatsiia
    kandidata istorii nauka*, Tomsk, 1966.
*(XIV) Chetyrnadtsatyi s"ezd VKP (b), 18–31 dekabria 1925 g., stenograf-
    icheskii otchet*, Moscow, 1926.
Danilov, V. P. 'Zemel'nye otnosheniia v sovetskoi dokolkhoznoi de-
    revne', *Istoriia SSSR*, 3 (Moscow, 1958), 90–128.
Davidenkova, V. S. *SSSR po raionam, Sibir'*, Moscow–Leningrad, 1927.
Demidov, V. V. 'Khlebozagotovitel'naia kampaniia 1927/28g. v
    sibirskoi derevne' in V. I. Shishkin (ed.), *Aktual'nye problemy istorii
    sovetskoi sibiri, sbornik nauchnykh trudov* (Novosibirsk, 1990), pp.
    123–40.
Doronin, G. *Des'iat let bor'by rabotnits i krest'ianok sibiri*, Novosibirsk,
    1930.
Egorova L. P. 'Khlebozagotovitel'naia kampaniia 1927–1928 gg. i
    bor'ba s kulachestvom v zapadnosibirskoi derevne', *Voprosy istorii
    sibiri*, 3 (Tomsk, 1967), 255–70.
Eikhe, R. I. *Likvidatsiia kulachestvom kak klassa*, Novosibirsk, 1930.
Frumkin, M. I. *Prodovol'stvennaia politika v svete obshchego khoziaist-
    vennogo stroitel'stva sovetskoi vlasti, sbornik materialov*, Moscow,
    1920.
Gendon, A. *Chto skazala IV sibirskaia kraevaia konferentsiia VKP (b)*,
    Novosibirsk, 1929.
Gushchin, N. Ia. *Klassovaia bor'ba i likvidatsiia kulachestva kak klassa v
    sibirskoi derevne, 1926–1933 gg.*, Novosibirsk, 1972.
Sibirskaia derevnia na puti k sotsializmu, Novosibirsk, 1973.
*Soiuz rabochego klassa i krest'ianstva sibiri v period postanovleniia sot-
    sializma 1917–1927 gg.*, Novosibirsk, 1978.

(ed.) *Problemy istorii sovetskoi sibirskoi derevni*, Novosibirsk, 1977.

(ed.) *Krest'ianstvo sibiri v period stroitel'stvo sotsializma (1917–1937 gg.)*, Novosibirsk, 1983.

Gushchin, N. Ia. and Il'inykh, V. A. *Klassovaia bor'ba v sibirskoi derevne, 1920-e – seredina 1930-x gg.*, Novosibirsk, 1987.

Gushchin, N. Ia. and Zhdanov, V. A. *Kritika burzhuaznykh kontseptsii istorii sovetskoi sibirskoi derevni*, Novosibirsk, 1987.

Il'inykh, V. A. 'Klassovaia bor'ba v sibirskoi derevne v usloviiakh Nep'a (1924–1927 gg.)', *dissertatsiia kandidata istorii nauka*, Novosibirsk, 1985.

Istoriia kommunisticheskoi partii sovetskogo soiuza, Moscow, 1979.

Istoriia sibiri, vol. 4, Leningrad, 1968.

Itogi rabota barnaul'skogo okruzhnogo komiteta VKP(b) za 1927g., Barnaul, 1927.

Kas'ian, A. K. 'Zapadnosibirskaia derevnia v 1926–1929 gg.' in *Istoriia sovetskogo i kolkhoznogo stroitel'stva v SSSR*, Moscow, 1963, pp. 120–9.

Kavraiskii, V. A. and Nusinov, I. I. *Klassovoe rassloenie v sibirskoi derevne (opyt analiza sotsial'no–ekonomicheskikh otnoshenii v sovremennoi sovetskoi derevne)*, Novosibirsk, 1927.

Klassy i klassovaia bor'ba v sovremmenoi derevne, Novosibirsk, 1929.

Klassy i klassovye otnosheniia v sovremennoi sovetskoi derevne, Novosibirsk, 1929.

Kollektivizatsiia sel'skogo khoziaistvo zapadnoi sibiri (1927–1937 gg.), Tomsk, 1972.

Koniukhov, G. A. *KPSS v bor'be s khlebnymi zatrudneniiami v strane, 1928–1929 gg.*, Moscow, 1960.

KPSS v rezoliutsiiakh i resheniiakh s"ezdov, konferentsii i plenumov Ts. K. (1898–1986), 9th edn, 12 vols., Moscow, 1983–6.

Kukushkin, Iu. S. 'Kulatskii terror v derevne v 1925–1928 gg.', *Istoriia SSSR*, 1 (Moscow, 1966), 94–104.

Lenin, V. I. *Polnoe sobranie sochinenii*, 5th edn, 55 vols., Moscow, 1958–65.

Lukashin, M. *Kratkie itogi raboty slavgorodsk okruzhkoma VKP(b)*, Slavgorod, 1928.

Moletotov, I. A. *Sibkraikom*, Novosibirsk, 1978.

(XI) Odinnadtsatyi s"ezd RKP (b), 27 marta–2 aprelia 1922 g., stenograficheskii otchet, Moscow, 1961.

Osnovnye itogi partiinoi-politicheskoi i khoziaistvennoi raboty. Materialy okruzhkoma k chetverti okruzhnoi partiinoi konferentsiia, Irkutsk, 1929.

Osokina, V. Ia. 'Sotsial'no-ekonomicheskie otnosheniia v zapadno-sibirskoi derevne nakanune sploshnoi kollektivizatsii (1927–1929 gg.)', *Voprosy istorii sibiri*, 3 (Tomsk 1967), 271–82.

Otchet biiskogo okruzhkoma VKP(b), s 1 oktiabria 1925 g. do 1 marta 1927 g., Biisk, 1927.

Otchet kamenskogo okruzhkoma VKP(b) k chetverti okruzhnoi partiinoi konferentsii, Kamensk, 1928.

(XV) Piatnadtsatyi s"ezd VKP(b), 2–19 dekabria 1927 g., stenograficheskii otchet, 2 vols, Moscow, 1962.

Plenum sibirskogo kraevogo komiteta VKP(b), 3–7 marta 1928 goda. stenograficheskii otchet, part 1, Novosibirsk, 1927.

Resheniia pervoi barnaul'skoi okruzhnoi konferentsii bednoty, Barnaul, 1928.

Sel'skoe khoziaistvo SSSR 1925–1928, Moscow, 1929.

(XVI) Shestnadtsataia konferentsiia VKP(b), aprel' 1929 goda, stenograficheskii otchet, Moscow, 1962.

(XVI) Shestnadtsatyi s"ezd VKP (b), stenograficheskii otchet, Moscow, 1930.

Shishkin, V. I. *Revoliutsionnye komitety sibiri v gody grazdianskoi voiny (1919–1921 gg.)*, Novosibirsk, 1978.

Sibirskaia partiinaia organizatsiia v tsifrakh, Novosibirsk, 1927.

Sibirskaia sovetskaia entsiklopediia, 3 vols., Novosibirsk, 1929–32, vol. 4 (unpublished proof), Novosibirsk, 1935.

Sibirskii krai statisticheskii spravochnik, Novosibirsk, 1930.

Siokawa, N. 'Politicheskaia situatsiia v SSSR. Osen' 1930 goda', *Acta Slavonica Iaponica*, 7 (1989), 33–45.

Sizykh S., Strakhov, A. and Brodnev, M. *Batrachestvo – opora partii v derevne*, Novosibirsk, 1930.

Soratniki, biografii aktivnykh uchastnikov revoliutsionnogo dvizheniia v moskve i moskovskoi oblastii, Moscow, 1985.

Sosnovskii, L. S. 'Chetyre pis'ma iz ssylki', *Biulleten' oppozitsii* (Paris), 3–4 (September 1929), 15–29.

Sotsial'nyi i natsional'nyi sostav VKP(b). Itogi vsesoiuznoi partiinoi perepisi 1927 g., Moscow, 1928.

Sovetskaia istoricheskaia entsiklopediia, 16 vols., Moscow, 1961–76.

Stalin, I. V. *Sochineniia*, 13 vols., Moscow, 1946–51.

Statistika sibiri, sbornik statei i materialov, vol. 1, Novosibirsk, 1930.

Stepichev, I. S. 'Bor'ba KPSS s Trotskistsko–Zinov'evskim antipartiinym blokom v 1926–1927 gg.' in *Iz istorii partiinykh organizatsii vostochnoi sibiri*, 30, 3 (Irkutsk, 1962), 3–27.

Syrtsov, S. I. *Biurokratizm i biurokraty (iz rechei i statei otnosiashchiksia k period sentiabr' – oktiabr' 1926 goda)*, Novosibirsk, 1927.

Rabotat' po-novomu. K. predstoiashchim konferentsiiam sibirskoi partiinoi organizatsii, Novosibirsk, 1927.

Tekushchii moment i zadachi sibirskoi partiinoi organizatsii, Novosibirsk, 1927.

III sibirskaia kraevaia partiinaia konferentsiia VKP(b)., *stenograficheskii otchet*, vol. 1, Novosibirsk, 1927.

III-i sibirskoi kraevoi partiinoi konferentsii VKP(b) 25–30 marta 1927 goda, *rezoliutsii*, Novosibirsk, 1927.

Trotskii, L. D. *Sochineniia*, 21 vols., Moscow, 1925–7.

Vaganov, F. M. *Pravyi uklon v VKP(b) i ego razgrom (1928–1930 gg.)*, Moscow, 1970.

Vneshniaia torgovlia SSSR za 1918–1940 gg., *statisticheskii obzor*, Moscow, 1960.

Vserossiiskii TsIK XII sozyva, II (vtoraia) sessiia (oktiabr 1925). Stenograficheskii otchet, Moscow, 1926.

Vserossiiskii TsIK XII sozyva, II (vtoraia) sessiia (oktiabr 1925), postanovleniia, Moscow, 1926.

Vserossiiskii TsIK XIII sozyva, II (vtoraia) sessiia, (30 marta–6 aprelia 1928). Stenograficheskii otchet, Moscow, 1928.

Za chetkuiu klassovuiu liniiu. Sbornik dokumentov kraikoma VKP(b) i vystuplenii rukovodiashchikh rabotnikov kraia, Novosibirsk, 1929.

Books, theses and selected articles in other languages

Adelman, J. R. 'The development of the Soviet party apparat in the civil war; center, localities and nationality areas', *Russian History*, 9, 1 (January 1982), 86–110.

Alliluyeva, S. *20 Letters to A Friend*, London, World Books, 1968.

Avtorkhanov, A. *Stalin and the Soviet Communist Party; A Study in the Technology of Power*, New York, Atlantic Books, 1959.

Baranskii, N. *An Economic Geography of the USSR*, trans. S. Belskii, Moscow, Foreign Languages Publishing House, 1956.

Beerman, R. 'The grain problem and anti-speculation laws', *SS*, 19, 3 (July 1967), 127–9.

Brower, D. R. 'The Smolensk scandal and the end of NEP', *Slavic Review*, 45, 4 (December 1986), 689–706.

Carr, E. H. *The Bolshevik Revolution, 1917–1923*, vol 2, London, Macmillan, 1952.

The Interregnum, 1923–1924, London, Macmillan, 1954.

Socialism in One Country, 1924–1926, 2 vols, London, Macmillan, 1958–9.

'Revolution from above: some notes on the decision to collectivise Soviet agriculture' in K. H. Wolff and Barrington Moore Jr (eds.),

The Critical Spirit: Essays in Honour of Herbert Marcuse, Boston, Beacon Press, 1967.

Foundations of a Planned Economy, 1926–1929, vol. 2, London, Macmillan, 1971.

Carr E. H. and Davies, R. W., *Foundations of a Planned Economy, 1926–1929*, vol. 1, London, Macmillan, 1969.

Cleinow, G. *Neu-Siberien*, Berlin, Hobbing, 1928.

Cohen, S. *Bukharin and the Bolshevik Revolution; A Political Biography 1888–1938*, London, Wildwood House, 1974.

Conquest, R. *The Harvest of Sorrow; Soviet Collectivisation and the Terror-Famine*, London, Hutchinson, 1986.

Cox T. and Littlejohn G. (eds.), *Kritsman and the Agrarian Marxists*, London, Frank Cass, 1984.

Daniels, R. V. *The Conscience of the Revolution: Communist Opposition in Soviet Russia*, Cambridge, Mass., Harvard University Press, 1960.

Davies, R. W. *The Industrialisation of Soviet Russia*, vol. 1, *the Socialist Offensive, The Collectivisation of Soviet Agriculture, 1929–1930*, London, Macmillan, 1980; vol. 2, *The Soviet Collective Farm 1929–1930*, 1981.

Soviet History in the Gorbachev Revolution, London, Macmillan, 1989.

'A note on grain statistics', *SS*, 21, 1 (January, 1970), 314–29.

'The Syrtsov-Lominadze affair', *SS*, 33, 1 (January, 1981), 29–50.

Deutscher, I. *Stalin: A Political Biography*, London, Oxford University Press, 1949.

The Prophet Unarmed, Trotsky, 1921–1929, London, Oxford University Press, 1959.

Dohan, M. R. 'Soviet foreign trade in the NEP economy and Soviet industrialization strategy', unpublished Ph.D. thesis, Massachusetts Institute of Technology, 1969.

Dominique, P. *Secrets of Siberia*, trans. Warre B. Wells, London, Hutchinson, 1934.

Dotsenko, P. *The Struggle for a Democracy in Siberia, 1917–1920*, Stanford, Hoover Institution Press, 1983.

Duranty, W. *Russia Reported*, London, Victor Gollancz, 1934.

Ellison, H. J. 'Peasant colonisation of Siberia. A study on the growth of Russian rural society in Siberia, with particular emphasis on the years 1890 to 1918', unpublished Ph.D. thesis, University of London, 1955.

Erlich, A. *The Soviet Industrialisation Debate, 1924–1928*, 2nd edn, Cambridge, Mass., Harvard University Press, 1967.

Fainsod, M. *Smolensk Under Soviet Rule*, Cambridge, Mass., Harvard University Press, 1958.

Getty, J. Arch. *The Origins of the Great Purges: the Soviet Communist Party Reconsidered*, Cambridge, Cambridge University Press, 1987.

Gleason, A., Kenez, P. and Stites, R. (eds.) *Bolshevik Culture: Experiment and Order in the Russian Revolution*, Bloomington and Indianapolis, Indiana University Press, 1989.

Karcz, J. F. 'Back on the grain front', *SS*, 22, 4 (October 1970), 262–94.

Jasny, N. *The Socialist Agriculture of the USSR: Plans and Performance*, Stanford, Stanford University Press, 1949.

Soviet Economists of the Twenties: Names to be Remembered, Cambridge, Cambridge University Press, 1972.

Khrushchev Remembers, trans. and ed. Strobe Talbot, London, Andre Deutsch, 1971.

Kuromiya, H. *Stalin's Industrial Revolution: Politics and Workers*, Cambridge, Cambridge University Press, 1988.

Levitsky, B. *The Stalinist Terror in the Thirties. ·Documentation from the Soviet Press*, Stanford, Hoover Institution Press, 1974.

Lewin, M. 'Who was the Soviet kulak', *SS*, 28, 4 (October 1966), 189–212.

Russian Peasants and Soviet Power: A Study of Collectivisation, London, G. Allen & Unwin, 1968.

Male, D. J. *Russian Peasant Organisation Before Collectivisation; A Study of Commune and Gathering, 1925–30*, Cambridge, Cambridge University Press, 1971.

Matthews, W. K. *The Structure and Development of Russian*, Cambridge, Cambridge University Press, 1953.

Maynard, J. *The Russian Peasant and Other Studies*, London, Victor Gollancz, 1942.

McNeal, R. *Stalin: Man and Ruler*, Basingstoke, Papermac, 1989.

Medvedev, R. A. *Let History Judge: The Origins and Consequences of Stalinism*, ed. D. Joravsky, trans. C. Taylor, London, Spokesman, 1976; revised and expanded edn, ed. and trans. G. Shriver, Oxford, Oxford University Press, 1989.

On Stalin and Stalinism, Oxford, Oxford University Press, 1979.

Mote, V. L. 'The Cheliabinsk grain tariff, and the rise of the Siberian butter industry', *Slavic Review*, 35, 2 (June 1976), 304–17.

Narkiewicz, O. *The Making of the Soviet State Apparatus*, Manchester, Manchester University Press, 1970.

'Soviet administration and the grain crisis of 1927–1928', *SS*, 20, 4 (October 1968), 235–45.

Neue Deutsche Biographie, c. 25 vols., vols. 1–15, Munich, Duncker and Humboldt, 1953–87.

Nove, A. *An Economic History of the USSR*, London, Allen Lane, 1969.

Novomeiiskii, M. A. *My Siberian Life*, trans. A. Brown, London, Max Parrish, 1956.

Phillips Price, M. *Siberia*, London, Methuen, 1912.

Radkey, O. H. *The Election to the Russian Constituent Assembly of 1917*, Cambridge, Mass., Harvard University Press, 1950.

Reiman, P. *The Birth of Stalinism: the USSR on the Eve of the 'Second Revolution'*, trans. G. Saunders, London, I. B. Tauris, 1987.

Reswick, W. *I Dreamt Revolution*, Chicago, Saunders, 1952.

Rigby, T. H. *Communist Party Membership in the USSR, 1917–1967*, Princeton, Princeton University Press, 1968.

'Was Stalin a disloyal patron?', *SS*, 38, 3 (July 1986) 311–24.

'Staffing USSR incorporated: the origins of the nomenklatura system', *SS*, 40, 4 (October 1988), 523–37.

Robinson, G. T. *Rural Russia Under the Old Regime*, London, G. Allen and Unwin, 1932.

Rosenfeldt, N. E. *Knowledge and Power: The Role of Stalin's Secret Chancellery in the Soviet System of Government*, Copenhagen, Rosenkilde and Bagger, 1978.

Schapiro, L. *The Communist Party of the Soviet Union*, 2nd edn, London, Methuen, 1970.

Service, R. *The Bolshevik Party in Revolution: A Study in Organisational Change 1917–1923*, London, Macmillan, 1979.

Seton-Watson, H. *The Russian Empire, 1801–1917*, Oxford, Oxford University Press, 1967.

Shanin, T. *The Awkward Class: Political Sociology of Peasantry in a Developing Society; Russia, 1910–1925*, Oxford, Clarendon Press, 1972.

Russia as a 'Developing Society', vol. 1, Basingstoke, Macmillan, 1985.

Snow, R. E. *The Bolsheviks in Siberia, 1917–1918*, London, Fairleigh Dickinson University Presses, 1977.

Solomon, S. G. *The Soviet Agrarian Debate: A Controversy in Social Science, 1923–1929*, Boulder, Westview Press, 1977.

Souvarine, B. *Stalin: A Critical Survey of Bolshevism*, London, Secker and Warburg, n.d. [1938].

Soviet Union Yearbook 1928, London, G. Allen and Unwin, 1928.

Strong, J. W. (ed.) *The Soviet Union under Brezhnev and Kosygin: The Transition Years*, New York, Van Nostrand, 1971.

Taniuchi, Y. *The Village Gathering in Russia in the Mid-1920s*, Birmingham, Birmingham University Press, 1968.

'A note on the Ural–Siberian method', *SS*, 4 (October 1981), 518–47.

Timoshenko, V. P. *Agricultural Russia and the Wheat Problem*, Stanford, Stanford Jr University–Food Research Institute, 1932.

Treadgold, D. W. *The Great Siberian Migration: Government and Peasant in Resettlement From Emancipation to the First World War*, Princeton, Princeton University Press, 1957.

'Russian expansionism and Turner's American frontier', *Agricultural History*, 26, 4 (October 1952).

Trotskii, L. D. *The Real Situation in Russia*, trans. M. Eastman, London, G. Allen and Unwin, 1928.

My Life. The Rise and Fall of a Dictator, London, Thornton Butterworth, 1930.

Tucker, R. C. *Stalin as Revolutionary 1879–1929: A Study in History and Personality*, London, Chatto and Windus, 1974.

(ed.) *Stalinism: Essays in Historical Interpretation*, London, W. W. Norton, 1977.

Ulam, A. B. *Stalin: the Man and his Era*, London, Allen Lane, 1973.

Urban, G. R. (ed.) *Stalinism. Its Impact on Russia and the World*, London, Temple Smith, 1982.

Viola, L. *The Best Sons of the Fatherland: Workers in the Vanguard of Soviet Collectivisation*, Oxford, Oxford University Press, 1987.

Vucinich, W. S. *Russia and Asia. Essays on the Influence of Russia on the Asian Peoples*, Stanford, Hoover Institution Press, 1972.

Wiecsynski, J. L. (ed.), *The Modern Encyclopedia of Russian and Soviet History*, 51 vols., Gulf Breeze, Florida, Academic International Press, 1976–85.

Index

Achinsk Okrug, 22, 134, 168
administration, 28–9
agriculture, use of machines in, 5–6, 10, 13, 17, 76, 80–1, 205–6; butter procurements, 19–21, 109, 182; dairy industry, 10, 12–13, 16–17, 19–21, 59–60, 98, 101, 207; industrial crops, 23; growth under NEP, 5, 18, 205–6, 208; and land consolidation, 60–1; land tenure, 7–9, 11–13; meat procurements, 16, 108–9, 182, 214 Table A. 3; and 'Temporary Rules', 57, 81; Tsar's personal demesne, 8–9; technical infrastructure of, 17–18, 103. *See also* agricultural taxation, collective farms, grain, grain crisis of 1927/8, kulaks, peasantry, Siberian Party Organisation
agricultural taxation, 11, 67, 111, 129, 160, 162, 165, 206
All Russian Agricultural Bank, 49
All Union Migration Committee, 10
Altai region, 5–6, 8–9, 11–13, 22, 45, 47, 78, 93, 101, 103, 107, 121, 160
Andreev, A. A., 125, 131
Arcos, the raid on, 117
Article 107, cases under, 130–1, 151–9, 164, 174, 176–7, 180, 190, 215 Table A. 4; decision to use, 127, 141–2, 181–2, 184–93, 195; opposition to, 140, 143, 164–5, 169, 171–4, 210; and grain bounty, 142, 166–7, 177, 211, 241 n. 41
Avtorkhanov, A. A., 138, 144, 145

Barabashev, O., 153–4, 180
Barabinsk Okrug, 16, 40, 81, 117
Baranov, F. N., 168
Barnaul, 54, 114, 118, 142, 162, 230–1 n. 39

Barnaul Okrug, 6, 47–8, 50, 69, 81, 92, 110, 121, 160, 215 Table A. 4
Barnaul Party Organisation, 50, 57, 134, 138, 165–6, 171, 173, 198
Belenky, G. Ia., 37
Benckendorff, Count A. K., 153
Bergavinov, S. A., 37, 49, 86–7
Bialyi, I. A., 37
Biisk Okrug, 6, 75–6, 93, 107, 118, 166, 174, 178, 214–15 Tables A. 3 and A. 4
Biisk Party Organisation, 40, 50, 116–17, 134, 142, 169, 171
Boldyrev, V. G., 70–1
Brest-Litovsk, Treaty of, 32
Brike, S. K., 72, 78–82, 84–6, 89, 92, 208
Brower, D. R.,. 211
Bubnov, A. S., 33
Bukharin, N. I., 15, 61, 65, 105, 128–9, 132, 201; on emergency measures, 124, 179, 242 n. 70; pro-peasant policy of, 3, 61, 98, 151, 200, 208–9; relations with Stalin, 31, 36, 65, 125, 129, 173, 201

Carr, E. H., 45, 64–5, 124
Census of 1926, 10, 88
Central Asia, 59, 126–7
Central Statistical Administration [TsSU], 66, 73–4, 88–9, 107
Central Trade Union Council, 138
Chayanov, A. V., 65, 229–30 n. 15
Cheka (OGPU), 196, 243 n. 11; and emergency measures, 130–1, 139–41, 148, 187, 190; powers of, 149–50; Stalin on use of, 138, 140
Cheliabinsk grain tariff, 19, 21, 206
Chelintsev, A., 230 n. 15
Chernov, V. M., 27

255

38 DAVID A. DYKER
The process of investment in the Soviet Union

36 JEAN WOODALL
The socialist corporation and technocratic power
The Polish United Workers Party, industrial organisation and workforce control 1958–1980

35 WILLIAM J. CONYNGHAM
The modernization of Soviet industrial management

34 ANGELA STENT
From embargo to Ostpolitik
The political economy of West German–Soviet relations 1955–1980

32 BLAIR A. RUBLE
Soviet trade unions
Their development in the 1970s

31 R. F. LESLIE (ED.)
The history of Poland since 1863

30 JOZEF M. VAN BRABANT
Socialist economic integration
Aspects of contemporary economic problems in Eastern Europe

28 STELLA ALEXANDER
Church and state in Yugoslavia since 1945

27 SHEILA FITZPATRICK
Education and social mobility in the Soviet Union 1921–1934

23 PAUL VYSNÝ
Neo-Slavism and the Czechs 1898–1914

22 JAMES RIORDAN
Sport in Soviet society
Development of sport and physical education in Russia and the USSR

14 RUDOLF BIĆANIĆ
Economic policy in socialist Yugoslavia

The following series titles are now out of print:

1 ANDREA BOLTHO
Foreign trade criteria in socialist economies

2 SHEILA FITZPATRICK
The commissariat of enlightenment
Soviet organization of education and the arts under Lunacharsky, October 1917–1921

3 DONALD J. MALE
Russian peasant organisation before collectivisation
A study of commune and gathering 1925–1930

4 P. WILES (ED.)
The prediction of communist economic performance

5 VLADIMIR V. KUSIN
The intellectual origins of the Prague Spring
The development of reformist ideas in Czechoslovakia 1956–1967

6 GALIA GOLAN
The Czechoslovak reform movement

7 NAUN JASNY
Soviet economists of the twenties
Names to be remembered

8 ASHA L. DATAR
India's economic relations with the USSR and Eastern Europe, 1953–1969

9 T. M. PODOLSKI
Socialist banking and monetary control
The experience of Poland

10 SHMUEL GALAI
The liberation movement in Russia 1900–1905

11 GALIA GOLAN
Reform rule in Czechoslovakia
The Dubcek era 1968–1969

12 GEOFFREY A. HOSKING
The Russian constitutional experiment
Government and Duma 1907–1914

13 RICHARD B. DAY
Leon Trotsky and the politics of economic isolation

15 JAN M. CIECHANOWSKI
The Warsaw rising of 1944

16 EDWARD A. HEWITT
Foreign trade prices in the Council for Mutual Economic Assistance

17 ALICE TEICHOVA
An economic background to Munich
International business and Czechoslovakia 1918–1938

18 DANIEL F. CALHOUN
The united front: the TUC and the Russians 1923–1928